Foucault's Critical Project

PHILOSOPHY   POLITICAL THEORY   AESTHETICS

Judith Butler and Frederick M. Dolan

EDITORS

Foucault's Critical Project

BETWEEN THE TRANSCENDENTAL
AND THE HISTORICAL

BÉATRICE HAN

Translated by Edward Pile

STANFORD UNIVERSITY PRESS
STANFORD, CALIFORNIA 2002

Foucault's Critical Project: Between the Transcendental and the Historical was originally published in French in 1998 under the title *L'Ontologie manquée de Michel Foucault*, © 1998, Editions Jérôme Millon.

Stanford University Press
Stanford, California

Assistance for this translation was provided by the French Ministry of Culture.

Printed in the United States of America on acid-free, archival-quality paper

Library of Congress Cataloging-in-Publication Data
Han, Béatrice.
    [Ontologie manquée de Michel Foucault. English]
    Foucault's critical project: between the
transcendental and the historical / Béatrice Han ; translated
by Edward Pile.
        p. cm.—(Atopia)
    Includes bibliographical references and index.
    ISBN 0-8047-3708-8 (alk. paper)—
    ISBN 0-8047-3709-6 (pbk.: alk. paper)
        1. Foucault, Michel—Contributions in concept of truth.
2. Truth—History—20th century. I. Title. II. Atopia
(Stanford, Calif.)
    B2430.F724 H3613 2002
    194—dc21   2002003858

Original Printing 2002
Last figure below indicates year of this printing:
11 10 09 08 07 06 05 04 03 02

Typeset by BookMatters in 10.5/13 Adobe Garamond.

Contents

viii   Contents

Foreword

As this book was written in 1995 and came out in French for the first time in the spring of 1998, I have had a few years to reflect more on the issues covered in the original, and to explore them further, or differently, in various papers. Living in Britain and teaching in the friendly and stimulating environment of the philosophy department at Essex for the past four years has also broadened my horizon and introduced me to new ways of thinking. Consequently, I have made minor modifications in the text to incorporate the changes in perspective brought by the passing of time. A few pages have been rewritten, and examples and some references to more recent work of mine have been added—all of which, I hope, will clarify the original text without changing its overall dynamics or claims.

During the six years of research that led to the book's elaboration, I worked mostly alone. I am deeply indebted, however, to a few people whose care and influence were essential to me. Although they rarely expressed it, my parents never doubted me or my ability to write a thesis, and knowing this helped me to overcome the doubts that seem to accompany any long-term research project. From a more scholarly point of view, I benefited considerably from attending Francis Wolff's seminars on ancient philosophy at the Ecole Normale Supérieure d'Ulm, in Paris. I also was very lucky to be supervised by both Hubert L. Dreyfus and Michel Haar, who during all these years never failed to give me attention, constructive criticism, and encouragement. Without the care and knowledge of these two mentors, who became (with Francis) my closest friends, I would not have been able to carry out this project. As Michel Haar has, very sadly, prematurely suffered from a stroke and is now retired from the philosophical scene, I would like to dedicate this book to him with affection and gratitude.

Finally, I am very grateful to Edward Pile for translating this book and giving it new life.

Abbreviations

Certain works by or about Foucault are cited with the abbreviations listed below.
All sources are by Foucault unless otherwise noted.

AK *The Archaeology of Knowledge*, trans. A. M. Sheridan Smith (London:
    Routledge, 1997).

BC *The Birth of the Clinic: An Archaeology of Medical Perception*, trans. A. M.
    Sheridan Smith (London: Routledge, 1986).

 C *Commentary*. When he defended his doctoral dissertation, *Histoire de la
    folie à l'âge classique* (partially translated as *Madness and Civilization*),
    Foucault also submitted a translation of Kant's *Anthropology from a
    Pragmatic Point of View*, accompanied by a commentary 128 pages long.
    The translation was later published by Vrin but the commentary remained
    unknown. To my knowledge, there are only two places where it can be
    accessed: the Bibliothèque de la Sorbonne (Paris-IV) and the Centre
    Michel Foucault, rue du Saulchoir, in Paris. Because of the text's relative
    inaccessibility, all of the longer passages quoted in this book are also given
    in French in the notes.

DE *Dits et écrits: 1954–1988*, vols. 1–4 (Paris: Gallimard, 1994). Collected
    shorter writings and interviews.

DP *Discipline and Punish: The Birth of the Prison*, trans. Alan Sheridan
    (London: Penguin, 1991).

 F *The Foucault Reader*, ed. Paul Rabinow (New York: Pantheon, 1984).

FF *The Final Foucault*, ed. James Bernauer and David Rasmussen
    (Cambridge, Mass.: MIT Press, 1988).

FL *Foucault Live: Interviews, 1966–84*, trans. John Johnston, ed. Sylvère
    Lotringer (New York: Semiotext[e], 1989).

HS *The History of Sexuality*, vol. 1, trans. Robert Hurley (New York: Vintage,
    1990).

LCP   *Language, Counter-Memory, Practice: Selected Essays and Interviews*, ed. Donald F. Bouchard (Ithaca: N.Y.: Cornell University Press, 1986).

MF   Hubert L. Dreyfus and Paul Rabinow, *Michel Foucault, Beyond Structuralism and Hermeneutics*, 2nd ed. (Chicago: University of Chicago Press, 1983).

OD   *The Order of Discourse* (Paris: Gallimard, 1970). This has been published in English as an appendix to *The Archaeology of Knowledge.*

OT   *The Order of Things: An Archaeology of the Human Sciences*, trans. from the French (New York: Vintage, 1994).

PK   *Power/Knowledge: Selected Interviews and Other Writings*, ed. and trans. Colin Gordon (New York: Pantheon, 1980).

PPC   *Politics Philosophy Culture: Interviews and Other Writings, 1977–84*, trans. Alan Sheridan et al., ed. Lawrence D. Kritzman (New York: Routledge, 1990).

UP   *The Use of Pleasure*, vol. 2 of *The History of Sexuality*, trans. Robert Hurley (London: Penguin, 1992).

Periodization of Foucault's Books

The dates given refer to the French publication. This periodization is only indicative and is discussed and criticized in the book itself.

"Archaeological" Period

1963   *The Birth of the Clinic*

1966   *The Order of Things*

1969   *The Archaeology of Knowledge*

"Genealogical" Period

1970   *The Order of Discourse*

1975   *Discipline and Punish*

1976   Volume 1 of *The History of Sexuality*

The "History of Subjectivity"

1984   *The Use of Pleasure*, volume 2 of *The History of Sexuality*

1984   *The Care of the Self*, volume 3 of *The History of Sexuality*

Introduction

The chronology of Foucault's major works is interrupted by two silences of five and eight years, at the end of each of which Foucault seems to have abandoned, or reexamined and reformed, his previous methods. Thus, archaeology is followed by genealogy, and that in its turn by the study of the "techniques of the self." To each of these investigative methods corresponds an apparently different object— *épistémès*, "regimes of truth," or "problematizations." Moreover, while the first two inquiries study similar periods (approximately from the Middle Ages to the nineteenth century), the last one opens onto a time so remote (Greek and Roman antiquity and the beginnings of Christianity) that it appears to have little connection with the previous two. Given these apparent discontinuities, is it possible to restore to Foucault's corpus the coherence of a single project? Many of his texts, starting with ones published after each of the silences, attempt to establish this unity; thus the lecture series given at the Collège de France in January 1976 explicitly joins archaeology and genealogy by an indissoluble complementarity (*PK*, 78–108). Similarly, the introduction of *The Use of Pleasure* reestablishes a continuity between the five studies (that were planned at the end of the first volume of *The History of Sexuality* but were never carried out) of the different forms taken by subjectivation in the nineteenth century and the examination of "the care of the self" in Greek antiquity (*UP*, 7). Foucault himself summed up his explorations as follows: "One might have changed point of view, one has gone round and round the problem, *which is still the same, namely, the relations between the subject, truth and the constitution of experience*" (*PPC*, 48; modified, my italics).

But how can Foucault say that he was always concerned with "the same problem"? Especially since he employed himself with such energy in the 1960s in chasing all figures of subjectivity from the philosophical stage, starting with that of the "author."[1] What justifies Foucault's redefinition of his project as having always been the study of "the relations between the subject, truth and the constitution of experience"? Given these conditions, is it possible to attribute to his enterprise any unity other than purely formal, a continuity that wouldn't appear to be merely a fiction arising from retrospective illusions and a belated concern for coherence?

If the Foucauldian project is coherent, then it should be possible to organize it around a central theme to which the others could be subordinated. The present book's hypothesis will be that this central theme is situated at the convergence of an initial question with an object that appears later, a convergence that occurs only retrospectively to Foucault himself, by means of a reflection on his own course and strategies. The question itself appears quite early in the Foucauldian corpus, in *The Birth of the Clinic*, where it is prevalent:

> The research that I am undertaking here therefore involves a project that is deliberately both historical and critical, in that it is concerned . . . with determining the *conditions of possibility* of medical experience in Modern times. . . . Here as well as elsewhere, it is a study that sets out to uncover, from within the density of discourse, the *conditions of its history*. (*BC*, xix; modified, my italics)

In the same spirit, three years later, *The Order of Things* defines the "archaeological level" as that which "makes knowledge [*savoir*] possible" (*OT*, 31)[2] and assigns to the Foucauldian enterprise the project of "reconstituting the general system of thought whose network, in its positivity, *renders* an interplay of simultaneous and apparently contradictory opinions *possible*. It is this network that defines the *conditions of possibility* of a controversy or of a problem, and that bears the historicity of knowledge" (*OT*, 75; my italics).[3] Similarly, *The Archaeology of Knowledge* indicates that it is "not a question of rediscovering what can legitimize an assertion, but of freeing the *conditions of emergence* of statements" (*AK*, 127). Another text from the same period focuses on the "general theme of the *conditions of possibility* of a science," identifying "two heteromorphic systems," one of which concerns "the *conditions* of science as science," while the other has to do with "the *possibility* of a science in its historical existence" (*DE*, 1: 724).

Thus, during the archaeological period Foucault's guiding concern is the question of the conditions of the possibility of knowledge. By doing this, he inscribes his enterprise within the lineage of Kant,[4] who was the first to question the conditions of possibility of representation and consequently of all knowledge, thereby opening the space of modern thought:

> Kant seems to me to have founded the two great critical traditions between which Modern philosophy is divided. Let us say that in his great critical work Kant posed and laid the foundations for that tradition of philosophy that poses the question of the conditions in which true knowledge is possible and, on that basis, it may be said that a whole stretch of Modern philosophy from the nineteenth century has been presented, developed as the analytics of truth. (*PPC*, 95)

Insofar as he constitutes the cornerstone and horizon of modern philosophy, Kant thus established the space in which Foucault's work is inscribed and must be situated: "We are all Neo-Kantians," he added in 1966, evoking "the ceaselessly repeated injunction to return to the break established by Kant—both to rediscover its necessity and to understand its consequences more fully" (*DE*, 1: 546).

However, the critical question of the possibility of true knowledge was, for Kant, intrinsically connected to the introduction of the distinction between the empirical and the transcendental—a distinction which allowed him to provide the famous answer given in *The Critique of Pure Reason*. But Foucault denies the relevance of this answer, for two reasons. Firstly, by retracing in his commentary the genesis of the transcendental theme in the *Anthropology from a Pragmatic Point of View*, he shows that there are within Kant's own work two ambivalently related versions of this theme. The initial critical formulation, which distinguished carefully between the empirical field and its *a priori* conditions, undergoes in the *Anthropology* an inflection symbolized by the recentering of Kant's triple interrogation onto the question "What is man?" and philosophically materialized by the transposition of the *a priori* into the "originary." But such a displacement is highly problematic, as it tends to make the contents of empirical experience work as their own conditions of possibility; moreover, it seeks within human finitude the elements of a transcendental determination henceforth made impossible in principle by the anthropological confusion between the empirical and the *a priori*. Foucault's second rejection of the Kantian solution comes out of his critique of post-Kantian theories, denounced in *The Order of Things* as being imprisoned by the "Analytic of finitude," itself a result of the monopolization of the field of possible knowledge by "man" and his doubles.

Because of this fundamental ambivalence, it appears that Kant, although he certainly was the "initiator"[5] of the discursive space in which modernity deployed itself, was also its insurmountable limit. Consequently, Foucault's relation to the critical project reveals itself to be much less clear than it initially appeared. Indeed, Foucault signals a fidelity to Kant by taking up the critical question himself; but in the same movement, he shows the impossibility of answering it on Kantian grounds and with Kantian concepts. His thought at this time seems animated by two contradictory demands: to repeat Kant's critical questioning, while attempting to escape the anthropological configuration to which the latter involuntarily gave birth. But how should we understand this reopening of the critical question? What are its proper objects of inquiry? How can it be analyzed?

It is probably in order to address these issues that Foucault introduces the "startling" (*AK*, 127) and somewhat paradoxical concept of the "historical *a priori*," as well as a new method, archaeology, an innovation that results in doubly distinguishing his position from its Kantian background. The first displacement is Foucault's adoption of a resolutely antihumanist problematic in his systematic refusal to take the subject, be it empirical or transcendental, as a starting point for his analyses: although he still deems it appropriate to define an *a priori* for knowledge, this won't be done anymore through an analysis of human faculties. The second reversal is connected to the specifically *historical* character claimed by Foucault for his *a priori*. The notion of an "historical *a priori*" was first articulated in *The Origin of Geometry*; however, the underlying debate with Husserl established by *The Archaeology of Knowledge* is concerned precisely with the way in which this historicality should be defined. For Husserl, the historical *a priori* turns out to be "suprahistorical," in the sense that it exists essentially to guarantee the possibility of recovering, beyond the sedimentations of history and tradition, the primary evidences originally thematized by the "protofounder" of geometry. But against the ahistorical character of the Kantian *a priori* and the transhistoricality of its Husserlian equivalent, Foucault proposes the paradoxical hypothesis of an *a priori* fully given in history, which transforms itself with it, and which nevertheless somehow lies beyond it in defining the conditions of possibility, themselves variable, from which the knowledge of an epoch can and must form itself.

In this sense, archaeology appears as a gamble, the interest of which lies precisely in the paradoxical form of the venture: to find a historical transposition of the transcendental, or again to define in concrete terms the "historical transcendental" studied long ago by Foucault in reference to Hegel and distantly echoed by his own historical *a priori*.[6] Perhaps even more than his debates with structuralism or the indirect homage that he paid to French epistemology and the Ecole des Annales,[7] the identification of the Kantian aporia provided Foucault with a guideline with which he was able to build *a contrario* an original method and conceptual apparatus and which allowed him to reopen the critical question of the conditions of possibility of knowledge while attempting "to throw off the last anthropological constraints" (*AK*, 15).[8] It also permits us to identify the specifically *philosophical* ambition of Foucault's project, which is all too commonly masked by the reception and use of his writings by the social sciences. Foucault's main question is not only that of the genesis of the human sciences and of contemporary forms of subjectivity, but above all of the possibility of defining a new way of connecting history to philosophy, a middle path between an idealism he judged excessive—that of Kant and the post-Kantians—and the too reductive materialism of the thinkers lumped together by Foucault under the rubric "Marxists."[9]

Thus the critique of the transcendental in Foucault's early writings reveals itself to be essential, since it governs both the denunciation of the "anthropological illusions," which according to Foucault have ensnared modernity, and the project of finding a valid response to the question of the conditions of the possibility of knowledge in the renewal of the transcendental theme through the historical *a priori*. Correspondingly, this critique serves to highlight the very ambivalent relationship between archaeology and phenomenology, which as Foucault subsequently affirmed was "the horizon of departure" from which he "would try once again to detach himself."[10] Indeed, if phenomenology can appear to be for him both interlocutor and favored target, it is precisely because it also attempts—like Husserl in the *Cartesian Meditations*—to overcome the obstacle of pure transcendentalism. Such is the function of such notions as the *a priori* of existence and above all the "originary": to express within the paradoxical form of retrospection the movement by which the transcendental can appear within the empirical as an "already there," always present but perpetually elusive in its foundation. Despite appearances, archaeology is profoundly connected to phenomenology in that it attempts to find a solution to the same problem (providing a new version of the transcendental) and adopts a method that is often similar—in its descriptive rather than explicative outlook, for example.[11] Nonetheless archaeology distinguishes itself from phenomenology by exposing the impossibility of the phenomenological "solution," that is, by criticizing the notions of the "originary" and the "origin" as further instances of the confusion between the empirical and the transcendental. Consequently, Foucault deems contemporary thought to be enclosed within a vicious circle (the "Analytic of finitude"), in which the conditions of possibility are assimilated within that which they were meant to found—an unfortunate move that destroys the very possibility of any foundation. The violence of Foucault's attacks against the idea of the subject can be understood in terms of his renunciation of the Husserlian starting point (the transcendental ego) in order to cast a nonoriginary version of the historical *a priori*—that is, to look for a transcendental without a subject. It is on archaeology, sister and rival of phenomenology, that Foucault will henceforth confer the task of finding this nonanthropological version of the fundamental.

From this perspective we shall see that it is possible to distinguish three phases[12] within the archaeological period in which the historical *a priori* implicitly receives different definitions. But correspondingly, new questions appear. How can the various concepts progressively introduced by the author be differentiated? How can the succession of texts in which they appear be understood? If the concept of the historical *a priori*[13] does not have the same content in *The Birth of the Clinic* as in *The Order of Things*—to say nothing of *The Archaeology of Knowledge*—how can we distinguish and connect these different meanings, and what philosophical presuppositions do they assume? If one agrees with Foucault that *The Archaeology of Knowledge* was the result of the desire to establish the legality of the method and concepts he had previously employed, is this attempt successful? How can we understand the new definitions of the historical *a priori* and of the *épistémè* given there?[14] Are they consistent with their precedents and between themselves? And why does Foucault feel it necessary to introduce two supplementary terms: "discursive formations"[15] and the "archive" (*AK*, 128–31)? Is there complementarity, redundancy, or contradiction between these four concepts? Finally can one really grant to the discursive and its "laws" the autonomy that archaeology postulates? In other words, is the positivism that turns the historical *a priori* into a "purely empirical figure" (*AK*, 128) as "happy" as its author suggests? Although it was conceived as a sort of "counterphenomenology"—sharing phenomenology's project but following the opposite path—doesn't archaeology itself risk falling into the "anthropological sleep"?

Notwithstanding reasons that we will come to later, Foucault's own abandonment of the concept of the historical *a priori* seems to constitute an answer to this question. To Julio Preti, who interviewed him in 1972, Foucault declared, that the "*épistémè* has nothing to do with Kantian categories" (*DE*, 2: 371),[16] before more generally reproaching his interlocutor for being "Kantian or Husserlian." He himself was struggling to "escape any reference to this transcendental, which would be a condition of possibility of any knowledge [*connaissance*]. . . . I try to historicise as much as possible in order to leave the least possible space for the transcendental."[17] Against his first excess of transcendentalism, Foucault now steers his course toward the historical and the dialogue with phenomenology takes second place. But while he renounces the type of *answer* previously constituted by his archaeological transposition of the transcendental, Foucault clearly stays with what he calls the "critical question,"[18] as can be seen from the manner in which the idea of "discipline" is introduced in *The Order of Discourse* of 1970: "A discipline is not the sum of all that can be truthfully said about something. . . . a proposition must fulfil complex and heavy requirements to be able to belong to the grouping of a discipline; before it can be called true or false, it must be 'in the true,' as Canguilhem would say" (*OD*, 60). Thus *The Order of Discourse* gives a new expression to the critical question by reinterpreting it through the distinction (borrowed from Georges Canguilhem) between the actual predication of truth and the possibility for a statement to be "in the truth"—its "acceptability."[19] As we shall see, rather than responding to the same criteria as predication, acceptability is the backdrop from which these criteria can be derived. By showing that acceptability logically and chronologically precedes the predication of truth, Foucault will thus open the way to a fourth interpretation of the historical *a priori*, one that therefore could be defined, through a retrospective reading of previous texts, as the set of conditions that determine, independently of its truth-value, the "acceptability" of a discourse. Like archaeology itself, genealogy will henceforth seek to "grasp [discourse] in its power . . . to *constitute domains of objects* [acceptability], in relation to which one can *affirm or deny true or false propositions* [*predication*]" (*OD*, 73; my italics).

But while giving the keys to such a rereading, *The Order of Discourse* lays the ground for the new impossibility of thinking these conditions of acceptability from the neutral and purely epistemological perspective of archaeology. Thus, the questioning of the acceptability of discourse opens directly onto an interrogation of truth itself, its status and the "effects of power" that are specific to it. Foucault's central hypothesis is that these arise from a "will to truth," specific to the West, which first appeared with Platonism; the archaeological inquiry will henceforth be doubled with a genealogical one. As it does not examine a purely discursive level but rather the collection of practices in which truth is produced, genealogy is the only approach that can make this will to truth appear, complete with all its history and ramifications. *Discipline and Punish* and the first volume of *The History of Sexuality*, therefore, through their analyses of disciplinary practices continue to explore the theme of the formation of the human sciences, and to demonstrate the impossibility of dissociating their apparition from that of modernity's own form of power, "power-knowledge" [*pouvoir-savoir*]. Correspondingly, Foucault gives the old historical *a priori* a new identity in the form of the "regime" that "governs statements, and the way in which they govern each other so as to *constitute a set of propositions which are scientifically acceptable, and hence capable of being verified or falsified by scientific procedures*. In short, there is a problem of the regime, the politics of the scientific statement" (*PK*,

112). Inasmuch as it "governs" the field of acceptability of propositions, the regime establishes a second transposition of the transcendental, more "political" than the first, which understood the critical question in a purely epistemological register. While responding once more to the question of the apparition and transformation of truth, the regime constitutes a new interpretation of the nature of the veridictional field, one that subordinates the discursive and its laws to the play of forces and processes of subjectivation.

Several questions arise: firstly, if truth is the central object of Foucault's inquiry, how should it be defined? It is clear that Nietzsche's influence prevents Foucault from adopting the traditional response, which understood truth as a purely intellectual object by identifying it with an *adequatio rei et intellectus*; Foucauldian nominalism would anyway refuse any relevance. Like Nietzsche himself, Foucault shows himself to be antimetaphysical in the sense that truth is not for him *a*temporal, lacking any historicity or a birth within history. On the contrary, he attempts to refer truth to the practices, discursive or not, from which it originates, and reconnects its genesis and effects to the networks of power from which it is indissociable. But does this understanding of truth belong to Nietzschean perspectivalism only? To what extent does it integrate the consequences of the new distinction between the acceptability and the predication of truth? If it is clear that " 'truth' is linked in a circular relation with systems of power which produce and sustain it, and to effects of power which it induces and which extend it" (*PK*, 133), how can the relationship between truth and power itself be understood? What contents can be given to this "circularity"? Finally, Foucault—unlike Nietzsche—only rarely evokes the most "incontestable" truths, the truths of mathematics or physics given by the fundamental sciences. Why is this?

Secondly, what form should be given to the questioning of truth? If truth must be reconnected with the networks of institutions and practices where it is formed, this questioning clearly should not be understood as a purely logical or formal study of what constitutes a proposition's truth. But it should be equally distinguished from a purely materialist approach, which, far from questioning the field of acceptability itself, would only attempt to give an account of the historical forms taken by truth and falsehood, thereby disregarding the critical question of the conditions of the possibility of knowledge. Foucault attempts to escape from this dilemma between formalism and materialism by opting for a "genealogy"; but how exactly is this "genealogy of the modern subject" indebted to its Nietzschean model, and how can it be related to that older form of inquiry, archaeology?

Finally, what are the consequences for the critical question of this refocusing on the problem of truth? What content can be given to the new "answers," the "regime of truth" or the "discursive regime"? Foucault presents the regime as a genealogical avatar of the *épistémè* by attributing to it the function of identifying "what effects of power circulate among scientific statements, what constitutes, as it were, their *internal regime of power*, and how and why at certain moments that regime undergoes a global modification. It was these different regimes that I tried to identify and describe in *The Order of Things*" (*PK*, 112; my italics). But precisely insofar as it inherits the archaeological problematization, will the regime be able to escape the obstacles that archaeology itself stumbled on? If the problem is to preserve the critical question, while renouncing the transposition of the transcendental given by the historical *a priori*, doesn't genealogy risk a recurrence (perhaps generated by the question itself) of a "wild" transcendentalism? More specifically, how can the status of the power-knowledge "nexus" be thought about, since the conditions of the possibility of veridiction must ultimately be referred to it? The problem is that the idea of a "perpetual articulation of power on knowledge [*savoir*] and of knowledge on power" (*DE*, 2: 753),[20] mentioned several times in *Discipline and Punish*, might turn the power-knowledge network into an independent quasi-metaphysical reality, which would successively transform itself through history. "I cannot rule out the possibility that one day I will find myself faced with a not negligible residue which will be the transcendental" (*DE*, 3: 373), declared Foucault to Julio Preti, even while repudiating the transcendental theme. Could it be that, despite Foucault's lively denials, there is a "metaphysics of power" secretly at work here?[21]

As we shall see, in the progression from archaeology to genealogy the tension swings between the transcendental and the historical and back again. The initial insistence on the transcendental, after having given way to a historicism of Nietzschean inspiration, reappears as an unrecognized shadow at the end of the genealogical research. It is perhaps the search for a solution to these difficulties that drives the later Foucault to once again shift the question of the conditions of the possibility of truth by reformulating it in the following fashion: "After first studying the games of truth [*jeux de verité*] in their interplay with one another . . . then studying their interaction with power relations . . . , I felt obliged to study the games of truth in the relationship of self with self and the forming of oneself as a subject" (*UP*, 6). This reelaboration of the critical question as the "study of games of truth" leads Foucault to "reintroduc[e] the problem of the subject" (*FL*, 329)[22] by recentering his approach on the essential notion of "subjectivation." The strategical move that had led *The Order of Discourse* to question the effects of truth rather than its conditions of possibility reaches its culmination in the analysis of the constitutive role played by truth in subjectivation. The introduction, in *The Use of Pleasure*, of the theme of the "history of truth" therefore aims at synthesizing the Foucauldian itinerary by drawing together the previously studied themes around the problem of the constitution of the self. Thus, Foucault's interest in the human sciences receives a retrospective illumination by the idea that the truths they generate are precisely those which, transmitted by the power-knowledge nexus, preside over the contemporary forms of the constitution of the self. Correspondingly, it appears that the common genesis of these forms of knowledge, as well as of institutional forms of bio-power, is the underlying reason for the transformation of the processes of subjectivation into techniques of subjection. The Greek model, therefore, plays the role of a simpler first matrix from which to evaluate *a contrario* modernity. Following this retrospective logic, the Foucauldian journey as a whole could therefore be described as the passage from an archaeological interrogation of the *conditions* under which a subject can speak the truth, to the genealogical claim that truth is *per se* the major condition of possibility for the construction of the self as subject.

This last displacement immediately demands a particularly close questioning. Firstly, how can the "return to the subject" be reconciled with the archaeological/genealogical enterprise as a whole? Foucault innocently notes that "it was a matter therefore of reintroducing the problem of the subject that I had more or less left aside in my first studies" (*FL*, 329). This is a curious understatement, considering that archaeology's exact aim was the elimination of any avatars of the subject, whether transcendental or empirical, and that genealogy was always most careful to guard itself against taking as point of departure the consciousness— the "soul" (*DP*, 23)—of the individual, privileging instead the study of disciplinary practices directed at the body. "If there is one approach that I do reject," declared Foucault in 1970, "it is that (one might call it, broadly speaking, the phenomenological approach) which gives absolute priority to the observing subject, which attributes a constituent role to an act, which places its own point of view at the origin of all historicity" (*OT*, xiv).[23] In such a context, how could this "reintroduction" not transform itself into a regression, be it toward the transcendental humanism formerly rejected by archaeology or toward the intellectualizing idealism criticized by genealogy?

Clearly, everything hangs on what Foucault understands by the "subject," which, he declares, "is not a substance, it is a form and this form is not above all or always identical to itself" (*FF*, 10). Therefore, it is not an immutable and inert given (a "substance" definable ahistorically and *a priori*), but must understand itself, rather, within the dynamic perspective of a nonidentity with itself ("is not above all or always identical to itself") and therefore of a self-becoming—hence the possibility and necessity of a genealogy. Corresponding to this idea, for Foucault, is the establishment of the essential theme of "subjectivation," understood as a "recognition" (*UP*, 4)[24] through which the individual "constitutes itself as subject." Thus it is "the process through which results the constitution of a subject, or more exactly, of a subjectivity which is obviously only one of the given possibilities of organizing a consciousness of the self" (*FL*, 330). Subjectivation thus appears as the reflective operation (hence the theme of "self-consciousness") by which the subject "constitutes" itself by recognizing itself in "such and such a determined form" (*FF*, 10). But the problem is that this definition of the subject and of subjectivation seems to implicitly revive the transcendental understanding that archaeology had always sought to banish, which sees subjectivation through the model of a reflective appropriation of the self doubled by the simultaneous positioning of a collection of exterior objects. How is it possible to return to the idea of a constitutive subjectivity without reopening the aporiae of transcendentalism?

Correspondingly, how can this intellectualist theme of a consciousness, lord and master of the forms of subjectivity that it imposes on itself, be reconciled with the genealogical perspective that focused on the body and the disciplines of which it is the object and that understood self-consciousness as merely derived? This problem crystallizes itself around the question of the status that should be accorded to subjectivizing practices: for the later Foucault, the role of such practices would only be to give to the constitution of the self a concrete dimension by offering the subject the possibility of modifying itself conforming to the model provided by the knowledge that it has of itself—hence, the recurrent theme in *The Use of Pleasure* of "intentional and voluntary actions" through which men "seek to transform themselves" by reference to "certain stylistic criteria" (*UP*, 10–11). But isn't the idea of subjectivation as a reflective constitution of the self—in which practices would play only an instrumental role—antigenealogical? Don't the Foucauldian analyses of subjection clearly show the impossibility of understanding subjectivation exclusively by reference to the activity of a subject, and don't they render moribund the idea of a "constitution of the self as an autonomous subject" (*F*, 42), by virtue of the genealogical thesis that "the subject is constitut*ed* . . . in real practices—historically analyzable practices" (*MF*, 250)?

Thirdly, how can these last interpretations of the historical *a priori*, the "problematizations" or the "games of truth," be understood? Indeed, the manner in which Foucault defines them clearly indicates that these two notions are meant to be a final answer to the critical question. Thus the games of truth are characterized as the "rules according to which what a subject can say about certain things *involves the question of truth or falsehood*" (*DE*, 4: 632; my italics), while problematizations are identified with the set of conditions that "*makes something enter into the play of the true and false, and constitutes it as an object for thought*" (*FL*, 296; my italics). Games of truth and problematizations are both therefore characterized by the fact that they govern the field of acceptability of each epoch. According to the genealogical method they are to be found at the confluence of "a certain institutional practice and a certain apparatus of knowledge" (*FL*, 295), and should thus be analyzed through the practices, discursive or nondiscursive, that are at work in any given epoch. But the problem is that other passages give a totally different version of these concepts; how can we correlate the games of truth simultaneously with the "practices" and "institutions of power" (*FF*, 10) that are exercised on the individual, on the one hand, and the "relationship of self with self and the *constitution* of the self as a subject" (*UP*, 6; modified) on the other? Similarly, Foucault invokes the notion of an "effective problematisation by thought" (*F*, 388), thought itself being understood as "the act which posits, in their different possible relations, a subject and an object" (*DE*, 4: 632). But how can this problematization be understood at the same time as the epistemic "field" (*UP*, 37) that "makes possible" the knowledge of an epoch, and as the individual operation by which the subject, by "constituting itself as an object," forms a reflective interpretation of its own nature? In other words, how can these last avatars of the historical *a priori* simultaneously define the voluntary, constituent activity of the subject, while supposedly conditioning from the outside the forms taken by subjectivation by governing the impersonal models of knowledge used in the constitution of the self?

Notwithstanding this, one of the most important points remains the complex relationship maintained by Foucault's work with phenomenology. As suggested above, this relationship was from the beginning susceptible to two readings: the first, superficial, insists on the antihumanism of archaeology, while the second, more profound, shows the continuity of the two projects as well as their common Kantian roots. At the end of this analysis, the common parentage of archaeology and phenomenology paradoxically seems even more thoroughly affirmed, since there is good evidence that Foucault ends up repeating the same error that he initially attributed to Husserl, namely, seeking to "to give empirical contents transcendental value" by "displacing them in the direction of a constituent subjectivity" (*OT*, 248). However, the Husserlian research is not the only possible model for thinking phenomenology, and certain clues indicate that Foucault was perfectly conscious of this. Among these is the well-known text where he affirms that all his "philosophical development was determined by (his) reading of Heidegger," who had always been for him "the essential philosopher" (*FL*, 326),[25] even though he never dedicated any specific study to him. By Foucault's own admission the reason for this absence is not contingent but structural, being tied to the breadth of the subterranean "work" effected on him by Heideggerian ideas. Given this admission, perhaps the Heideggerian ontology could be read as the *unthought* of Foucault's oeuvre—not that which it did not think, or had forgotten, but that which worked within it without being able to be clearly formulated, thereby needing external elaboration.

Is it possible, on the evidence of these elements and the several texts in which Foucault reasserts his admiration for Heidegger, to look within hermeneutic ontology for a more coherent foundation for the analysis of problematization and subjectivation, and more generally, for the "historical ontology of ourselves" (*MF*, 237)[26] planned by Foucault? Indeed, if the relation to truth is effectively the "structural, instrumental, and ontological condition for establishing the individual as a subject" (*UP*, 89), and if it is truly an "ontology" of the "ethical subject" (*UP*, 37) that is at stake in the later writings of Foucault, *what would this ontology be*? Could it avoid the obstacles that the preceding attempts of Foucault encountered, and outmaneuver the recurrent forms of the transcendental?

PART I

The Archaeological Transposition of the Critical Question and the Aporiae of the Transcendental Theme

The *Critique* and the *Anthropology*: The Two Versions of the Transcendental Theme According to Foucault

The Ambivalence of Kant's Position in *The Order of Things*

In chapters 7 and 8 of *The Order of Things*, Foucault traces back to Kant the caesura that marks the end of the age of representation. According to him, criticism marked a shift from the horizontal interrogation of representation to the vertical questioning of its conditions of possibility, which were henceforth situated outside of representation and consequently escaped the epistemic horizon that the latter had previously assigned to thought.

> The Kantian critique . . . marks the threshold of our Modernity; it questions representation . . . on the basis of its rightful limits. Thus it sanctions for the first time that event in European culture which coincides with the end of the XVIIIth century: the withdrawal of knowledge [*savoir*] and thought outside the space of representation. That space is brought into question in its foundation, its origin, and its limits: and by this very fact, the unlimited field of representation, which Classical thought had established . . . now appears as metaphysics. (*OT*, 242–43)

The importance of the critical caesura lies in its paradoxical movement, which makes the creation of the new epistemic space the very solution of the questions that can be asked within it. Kant's introduction of the "transcendental theme" (*OT*, 244) thus was meant to renew and solve an older question, that of the conditions of possibility of knowledge. This question had already been addressed, but in a metaphysical way (*OT*, 160 ff., 236 ff.) by natural history, and, for example, by Etienne Bonnot de Condillac's ideology. According to Foucault, Kant renews this question by looking beyond the space of representation for what thereafter could no longer be found within it—the "conditions of the constitution and legitimacy of all possible knowledge."[1] He resolves it, following the now well-known movement of the "Copernican" revolution, by referring these conditions to the transcendental subject in its capacity as "the foundation of a possible synthesis of all representations" (*OT*, 244; modified)—a prodigious tour de force, in which the questioning subject ends up *defining by its very interrogation* the field in which its answer will be given, thus revealing itself to be the "condition of possibility of experience itself" (*OT*, 244; modified).

In chapter 7 of *The Order of Things*, the specificity of criticism is, therefore, that by the simple fact of its apparition it determines the general configuration in which all possible reflection must take place. But chapter 9 disturbs this picture, for two main reasons. Firstly, it is now the "Analytic of finitude," and no longer the transcendental theme, which defines the "threshold of our Modernity": "Our culture crossed the threshold beyond which we recognise our Modernity when finitude was conceived in an interminable cross-reference with itself" (*OT*, 318; modified). So now, far from being architectonic, the transcendental theme constitutes the first of the "doubles" produced by the specific structure of finitude and therefore seems to become identified with the contents of knowledge rather than with the space that determines it. Secondly, the status of Kantianism itself becomes very ambiguous. Kant, Foucault tells us, is the first to have emphasized human finitude and dethroned the sovereignty of "I think": "When to his traditional trilogy of questions he added an ultimate one: the three critical questions (What can I know? What must I do? What am I permitted to hope for?)[2] then found themselves referred to a fourth, and inscribed, as it were, 'to its account': *Was is der Mensch?*" (*OT*, 341). Foucault continues, without transition, in the following way: "This question, as we have seen, runs through thought from the early nineteenth century: this is because it produces, surreptitiously and in advance, the confusion between the empirical and the transcendental, even though Kant had demonstrated the divide between them" (*OT*, 341; modified). But these two statements hardly complement each other. It would mean that the same Kant had, on the one hand, "demonstrated the divide" of the empirical and the transcendental, and on the other, blurred the frontiers of this same division by recentering the three critical questions around that of man! Is it therefore the "divide," as analyzed by chapter 7, or is it indeed the focusing on man in which this division found itself undone—the thesis of chapter 9— that actually marks the break with the classical age? Does this mean that there would be in Kant a "good" and a "bad" version of the transcendental theme? A "critical" version that would initially separate the constituting from the consti- tuted, and an "anthropological" version that would then superimpose the two elements? Should we see the recentering of Kantian thought on the question of man as a decentering of the transcendental theme and therefore of the critical project itself? And if it should appear necessary to pluralize the transcendental theme, how could we articulate its different formulations with the Analytic of finitude, an articulation that is veiled by the linear succession of chapters 7 to 9 as well as by the passage quoted above? Is the transcendental theme, therefore, just one of the many forms of this Analytic, or is it really the primary element from which the Analytic itself must be diachronically understood as a deviation resulting from the recentering of Kantian thought on man?

The "threshold of our Modernity," declares Foucault, attempting to synthe- size his two preceding statements, "is situated . . . by the constitution of an empirico-transcendental doublet that was called *man*" (*OT*, 19). It is therefore in the latter that the transcendental theme—clearly presupposed by the definition of man as a "double"—merges with the Analytic of finitude. But where and how was the conjunction of the transcendental theme and "man" effected? For the Foucault of chapter 7, the point of emergence of this theme is *The Critique of Pure Reason*. But if man is really a "strange *empirico*-transcendental double," then he cannot be the object of Kant's argument there, since the *Critique*

> questions the conditions of a relation between representations from the point of view of what in general makes them possible: it thus uncovers a transcen- dental field in which the subject, *which is never given to experience (since it is not empirical)* but which is finite (since there is no intellectual intuition) determines in its relation to an object = *X* all the formal conditions of experi- ence in general. (*OT*, 243)

Neither can it be "man" that the *Critique of Practical Reason* is concerned with, since, a few years after the first *Critique*, it extended the project of the *a priori* study of the subject, this time by examining the latter from the perspective of its practical powers and its status as a noumenally free will. Whether envisaged in its power of knowing or of acting, the subject is studied from the point of view of an *a priori* determination, either of the conditions of possibility of knowledge or of free action, from which it always appears in its constitutive power and never as a constituted subject. But if the critical perspective is not grounded in "man," then why tie the transcendental theme to anthropology?

The stakes of these questions are doubly important. Firstly, the coherence and pertinence of the theses put forward by Foucault in the last chapters of *The Order of Things*, which refer to the transcendental theme in a global and, as we saw, quite indecisive manner, depend on the possibility of answering them. Secondly, and most importantly, it is essential for the continuation of Foucault's project that he should be able to determine the exact point where the connection between the transcendental theme and anthropology was made. Indeed, the fact that this theme was negatively interpreted by the post-Kantians does not necessarily mean that it was already irredeemable at its Kantian origin. If the possibility remained of isolating a nonanthropological form of the transcendental theme, while analyzing in detail the way in which this theme has been perverted, then nothing would prevent Foucault from searching elsewhere, notably in what he called the "historical *a priori*," a revised and nonsubjective version of the transcendental. It is therefore crucial for him to know whether the anthropological usurpation of the transcendental theme was already effective within Kant's work, in which the later confusions would then originate, or whether the critical question was untainted at its origin by the anthropological tendency, although it opened the way for it in the post-Kantian thinkers.

At this point, the reading of one particular text becomes essential to answering these questions: Foucault's complementary doctoral thesis,[3] which pursues the examination begun by the translation of the *Anthropology from a Pragmatic Point of View* of the role played by "man" in Kant's oeuvre. Foucault emphasizes from the first pages of his *Commentary* that the anthropological "self-observation" has the specific characteristic of reaching "neither the subject in itself, nor the pure I of synthesis, but a self which is object and present only its phenomenal truth. Yet this object I, which is given to the sense in the form of time, is nevertheless not alien to the determining subject, since in the end it is nothing but the subject as it is affected by itself" (*C*, 23).[4] The object of the *Anthropology* would therefore be neither the "subject in itself" of the Second *Critique*, nor the "pure I" as studied in the first,[5] but an "object-I"—also "subject"—in other words, man in his paradoxical identity as determined and determining subject. Thus the great interest of the *Anthropology* is that, contrary to the two *Critiques*, which are only concerned with the transcendental, it takes account of man in his ambivalence as an *empirico*-transcendental double. For this reason, it constitutes a privileged site—indeed the only possible one—from which to reply to the questions discussed above, which are naturally reformulated into the interrogation that marks the *Commentary* like a Leit-motiv: what has the transcendental theme become in the Kantian corpus, and what is the relationship between the *Critique* and the *Anthropology*?

But Foucault's response is itself ambivalent. On one hand, he seems to read the *Anthropology* as a simple "repetition" of the *Critique*, in which case there would be only one version of the transcendental theme. It would therefore be possible, through an "archaeology of the text," to reveal the constitutive role of the *Critique* in "the birth and the evolution of human forms" (*C*, 14):[6] the explicit foundation of the *Anthropology* would then be the transcendental conditions of possibility defined by the *Critique* some twenty-five years earlier. There would be "a certain critical truth of man, born from the critique of the conditions of truth" (*C*, 14).[7] As we shall see, Foucault gives a privileged expression to this first interpretation through the concept of the "fundamental," which allows us to think the relation of the empirical and the *a priori* from a perspective that, although symmetrical to that of the *Critique*, nonetheless remains in conformity with it.

But this hypothesis of the subordination of the *Anthropology* to the *Critique*, which would preserve the univocity of the transcendental theme, is not the only possibility, as Foucault indicates from the beginning of his *Commentary*: "Was there, as early as 1773, a certain *concrete* image of man that no philosophical elaboration has essentially altered, which perhaps subsists in the very heart of the *Critique* and is formulated, without any major modifications, in the last of Kant's published texts?" (*C*, 14).[8] The same logic that would cause Kant to move from the question of the limits of knowledge to that of the nature of man, would therefore have shaped the critical enterprise from the beginning,[9] assigning to this "concrete image of man" the task, if not of "organizing and ordering," at least of secretly "guiding" and "orientating" Kantian thought (*C*, 4). Far from being founded by the *Critique*, the *Anthropology* would be its mute presupposition. There would therefore be an "inner fault [*faille*] affecting the transcendental revolution of criticism" (*C*, 67), a fault that generated a new version—anthropological, this time—of a theme originally believed to be pure.

These two interpretations—the repetition or the decentering of criticism—appear incompatible, and it is therefore curious that they should be featured without further justification in the same text. However, for Foucault it is not merely a exegetic problem: thinking the relation of the *Critique* to the *Anthropology* is in reality to understand the development of the transcendental theme, its articulation with the birth of man, and the apparition of the Analytic of finitude. Should the *Commentary* establish that the internal evolution of the Kantian corpus prefigures in miniature that of modernity, it would be possible to isolate even *within the Kantian oeuvre itself* the paradigm of the first empirico-transcendental "divide," as well as what Roland Barthes might have called the "degree zero" of the "confusions" (*OT*, 341) that enmeshed the post-Kantians. Thus the *Commentary* is crucial as it alone allows us to identify the most simple—since the most original—forms of the various stages of this development, and thus to uncover the foundational configuration of the three events, however dissimilar, that Foucault indifferently identifies as modernity's moment of birth, namely: the transcendental theme, the appearance of man, and the Analytic of finitude.

The Critical Version of the Transcendental Theme: The "Fundamental"

The theme of anthropological repetition recurs very frequently in the *Commentary*.[10] The following passage is one of its clearest expressions: "The anthropological question *asks*, by *taking them up*, the questions that pertain to them. We are at the level of the structural fact of the *anthropologico-critical repetition*: the *Anthropology* does not say anything else than the *Critique*" (*C*, 76).[11] It is possible to give four meanings to this "anthropologico-critical repetition." Firstly, the *Anthropology* could be the merely formal repetition of the arguments of the *Critique*—an obvious mirroring form of repetition. Secondly, it could repeat the *Critique* by presupposing it in its totality, that is, by grounding itself implicitly in it, in a massive, silent, but structurally necessary repetition. Thirdly, it could from this base shed a new light on some major critical concepts, a more modest kind of repetition whose explicit task would be to bring the critical project to completion without transforming it too greatly. Finally, repetition itself, or retelling, could move the *Critique* toward a more finished form, of which anthropology itself was the hidden presupposition, provided that repetition is given its greatest range and the dialectical and dynamic sense of an *Aufhebung*. To these four forms of repetition correspond four possible relations between the *Anthropology* and the *Critique*: mirroring, foundation, complementarity, or mediation, all of which are entertained by the *Commentary*.

From a formal point of view, Foucault declares, one can interpret the table of contents of the *Anthropology* as the retracing of that of the *Critique*: to the "Transcendental Theory of Elements" would correspond the "Anthropological Didactic," while the "Anthropological Methodology" would double the "Transcendental Theory of Method." Beyond this formal likeness, the totality of the text follows in the wake of criticism, in the sense that it directly pursues its questioning: "The internal structure of the *Anthropology* and the question that animates it have the same form as the critical interrogation itself" (*C*, 119).¹² So the *Anthropology* renews the question of the conditions of the possibility of knowledge by embedding itself within the general economy of a repetition of the critical problems: for example, paragraphs 7 to 11 redefine the question of the relation between sensibility and understanding, seen in accordance with the *Critique* as "passivity" or "receptivity," on the one hand,¹³ and as the "faculty to represent something through concepts" or the "power of rules," on the other.¹⁴ This examination operates through the reactivation of some fundamental themes of criticism—notably the analysis of time and space, or the distinction between passivity and spontaneity. Similarly, paragraphs 41 onward take up the critical definition of reason as "the ability to represent to itself what is general according to principles and inasmuch as it is necessary,"¹⁵ again, while reformulating the study of its speculative power and limits. There is, therefore, in the *Anthropology* "a claim to know the possibilities and the limits of knowledge: it mimics, from the outside and with the gestures of empiricity, the movement of a *Critique*" (*C*, 119).¹⁶

However, the reason why the relation between the two texts can only be one of "mimicry" is that the anthropological project is not autonomous; it requires as its hidden foundation the critical edifice in its entirety. In fact, the relation between the *Anthropology* and the *Critique* is not merely mimetic—in which case there would be a simple parallelism between the two texts—but foundational: "The empiricity of the *Anthropology* cannot ground itself in itself. It cannot encompass the *Critique*, but must refer to it: and the reason it looks like its empirical and external *analogon* is because it rests upon some already named and uncovered structures of the *a priori*" (*C*, 120).¹⁷ These "structures of the *a priori*," described notably in the preface of the second edition of *The Critique of Pure Reason*,¹⁸ can be understood by means of a passage from the "Analytic of Principles" that establishes a distinction between two sorts of determinations. There, Kant describes the two ways in which a representation and its object can agree. In the first, the existence of the object makes representation possible by generating the various impressions collected by our sensibility, in which case the determination is causal. But the second type of determination given by Kant "in itself does not produce its object inasfar as *existence* is concerned, . . . [but] nonetheless the representation is *a priori* determinant of the object, if it be the case that only through the representation is it possible to *know* anything *as an object*."¹⁹

This determination is not relative to the material reality of an object (the concrete characteristics of which can only be given *a posteriori* to intuition), but to the formal possibility of knowing it. To the extent to which it is *a priori*, that is, that it "must in . . . [itself], independently of experience, be clear and certain,"[20] transcendental determination is "universal" and "necessary,"[21] and therefore constitutes the foundation of a knowledge that is certainly limited, but absolutely certain, thereby giving an apparently definitive solution to the Kantian project of "knowing knowledge."[22] The *Anthropology* cannot therefore "fail to refer" to the *Critique*, to the extent that it is only from the transcendental perspective, and not from the agreement or contradiction of empirical evidence, that the field of experience (and the anthropological domain itself) can be understood in its entirety. While reproducing the subordination of "applied" philosophy to pure philosophy (*C*, 45 ff.), this relation of the *Anthropology* to the *Critique* repeats the Copernican inversion that some fifteen years earlier had made experience revolve around conditions of possibility *a priori* defined by reason. The formal repetition noted above, therefore, only has significance insofar as the *Critique* implicitly constitutes the place from which to think an *Anthropology* that henceforth refers constitutively, in its nature even more than in its object, to the achievements of transcendental idealism.

The third form of repetition elaborates on the second to establish a relation of complementarity between *The Critique of Pure Reason* and an *Anthropology*, which therefore appears, within the terms of a "particular reversed analogy," as its "negative" (*C*, 56). If the first was the "investigation of the conditioning in its foundational activity," the second is only the "inventory of what is unfounded in the conditioned" (*C*, 61).[23] This in itself attests to the *Anthropology*'s dependence on criticism—indeed, one passes from an "investigation," that is, a reflexive analysis, which justifies its conclusions by its methodical progression, to an "inventory," that is, to a catalogue, which finds its principle of organization by arbitrary means and outside of itself. However, if the theme of the "conditioning" does not require supplementary clarification, that of the "unfounded" is more obscure, as it can hardly refer to the empirical itself, since as we just saw this finds its foundation precisely in transcendental determination. Thus, the "unfounded" for Foucault designates a certain use of our faculties, which is neither *a priori* nor constitutive, but which is empirically submitted to the risk of illusion and error. The third figure of the anthropologico-critical repetition is therefore tied to an inversion of the perspective from which human faculties are analyzed: "The *Anthropology* follows the division of faculties of the *Critique*: but its privileged domain is not that of their positive power, but that where they risk losing themselves" (*C*, 60).[24]

Therefore the text of 1797 does continue the study of the faculties analyzed by the *Critique*, but by enumerating the eventual "abuses" (*C*, 63) revealed by their empirical use. Thus, "self-consciousness" is no longer defined as the "form of experience and condition of a knowledge, that is, limited but founded," but as the "temptation of a polymorphic egoism" (*C*, 60).[25] Henceforth, "possible experience defines, in its limited circle, the field of truth just as well as the field of the loss of truth" (*C*, 61).[26] So the *Anthropology* completes the *Critique* by revealing the ambivalence of experience. It is the "field of truth" in the sense that truth itself refers to the "constitution of the necessary within the field of experience" (*C*, 103),[27] and because experience is transcendentally determined by the demands of the *a priori*—necessity and universality. But the *Anthropology* also indicates the site of a possible disorientation for the empirical, rather than transcendental, use of the faculties—hence the Foucauldian thematic of perdition or of "adventure" (*C*, 63). The *Anthropology* thus repeats the opposition between *Schein* and *Erscheinung* by insisting on the seduction of appearances, rather than on the founded character of phenomena; where the *Critique* only gave the "possibilities in the order of conditions" (*C*, 63),[28] the *Anthropology* examines the risks inherent in the empirical engagement of the human faculties.

Finally, the last form of repetition is the most essential: arguing from the fact that, paradoxically, the question of man is not posed in the *Anthropology* itself but in later works,[29] Foucault insists on the necessity of interpreting the text of 1797 in the light of all the later writings of Kant, gathered in the *Opus posthumum*. Anthropological repetition is then defined as the mediation through which "transcendental philosophy," as a yet unrealizable project introduced by *The Critique of Pure Reason*, would be realized. The *Anthropology* is therefore doubly tied to the critical perspective: firstly, and retrospectively, in that it presupposes it; secondly, and prospectively, as it precipitates its achievement. It is thus, paradoxically, "marginal for the *Critique*, and decisive for the forms of reflection that would claim as their task its achievement" (*C*, 83).[30] Its mediating character can, at a first level, be interpreted from the character of its object. In the sections of the *Opus posthumum* that concern transcendental philosophy,[31] Kant returns to the question of the relationship between God, the world, and man; but whereas the first two were given identical status in the "Transcendental Dialectic" as "ideas" of pure reason, the third now reveals itself as the mediation through which the two ideas can be united. Man is the "*medium terminus*" (*C*, 65) between the world and God, the "concrete and active unity by which God and the world find their unity" (*C*, 69).[32] However, if man can achieve this synthesis between the world and God, it is only in his double nature as empirically limited being and transcendentally determining subject, in other words in his properly *anthropological* dimension. He is indeed the "*real* unity in which God's personality and the objectivity of the world are joined," but also that only from which "the absolute can be *thought*" (*C*, 71).[33]

For Foucault, this constitutive ambivalence of man is developed by the *Opus posthumum* in the following way. On the one hand, man's synthetic ability stems from his status as thinking subject,[34] and therefore from the faculties defined in the *Critique*. Thus, man "affects himself in the movement by which he becomes an object for himself. . . . The world is uncovered . . . as the figure of the movement by means of which the ego, becoming an object, inscribes itself within the field of experience and finds a concrete system of belonging" (*C*, 72).[35] But on the other hand, and conversely, man should equally be understood "from the start" as a "denizen of the world" (*C*, 72):[36] "As for man, he is their synthesis—that in which God and the world are actually unified—and yet in regard to the world he is merely one of its inhabitants, and in regard to God merely a limited being" (*C*, 104).[37]

At this point, the anthropological repetition reveals its most profound significance as the attempt to avoid two disturbing dangers. Firstly, the analysis could appear enclosed within a vicious circle, which, via human ambivalence, would refer "any reflection on man to a reflection on the world" (*C*, 72),[38] and vice versa. Secondly, and most importantly, this circularity itself could generate the possibility that man, far from being a constituting entity, would now appear only as a being totally determined by his belonging to the world. The transcendental perspective would therefore be forgotten to the benefit of a sort of return to a precritical empiricism, which would only allow between man and the world "empirical and circular relationships of immanence, at the level of a necessary natural knowledge" (*C*, 81).[39] But the anthropological repetition prevents such an error by reminding us each time, and in accordance with the second of the forms of repetition studied above, of the need for a foundation for empirical contents, thus distinguishing carefully between transcendental determination and positive limitations. Taking up again the tripartite structure that according to him characterizes the *Opus posthumum*, Foucault reminds us that although the world is the "source" of knowledge (which therefore is denied any pretension to the absolute), it can only be so on the basis of a "transcendental correlation between passivity and spontaneity," that is, for the transcendental subject, in that it *a priori* unites sensibility and understanding. Equally, the world can be only the "domain" of an action (the possible range of which it therefore limits from the start) "against the background of a transcendental correlation between necessity and freedom," that is, in reference to a noumenally free subject. Finally, the world can only be the "limit" of possible experience (which excludes any constitutive use of the idea) because reason has "anticipated the totality and has prethought it precisely as a limit" (*C*, 79).[40] In other words, the empirical limitation effected by the world can only appear *as such* because it has already been thought, at the transcendental level, by a reason that has nonetheless been shown its finite character by its lack of intellectual intuition.

The fourth form of anthropological repetition, therefore, has the function of helping critical thought to reach "through its very repetition, the level of the fundamental, and to substitute for systematic divisions the organization of transcendental correlates" (*C*, 80).[41] Thus anthropology is essential because it "carries the *a priori* toward the fundamental" (*C*, 108),[42] a concept that will remain quite vague in *The Order of Things* (where it nonetheless appears several times), but which can be clarified with the help of the *Commentary*.[43] Its etymology clearly refers to the theme of the transcendental foundation; but while it presupposes the critical perspective, the fundamental differs from it, in the sense that rather than allowing us to think the empirical from the transcendental standpoint, according to the top-down logic of foundation described in the *Critique*, it opens up the opposite direction by showing that empirical limitations can only make sense in reference to the transcendental determination that they unknowingly presuppose. While the transcendental allows the *a priori* determination of the form that experience must take, the fundamental, on the contrary, takes empirical contents as its point of departure and shows that they are marked by "irreducible transcendences" (*C*, 81),[44] which should not be understood dogmatically but which reveal the impossibility of the empirical being its own foundation. Thus the theme of the fundamental is structurally tied to the retrospection through which empirical finitude always appears as already transcendentally founded.

If the *Anthropology* is important, therefore, it is so because it defines the place from which it is simultaneously possible to think the empirical under its concrete forms and to return to that which founds them. By doing so, it follows a circle which, far from being vicious, turns out to be quasi-dialectical, in that it achieves the "passage from the *a priori* to the fundamental, from critical thought to transcendental philosophy," described by the *Commentary* (*C*, 123).[45] Its mediating character does not only come from its object, but from the terrain that it defines: insofar as it opens onto the thinking of the "fundamental," the *Anthropology* offers the only version of the transcendental theme that, far from perverting criticism, completes it by reversing its first perspective, while insisting on the necessity of referring the limitations brought by empirical contents (the general model of which is the "world," as understood in the *Opus posthumum*) to their transcendental conditions of possibility. By contrast, the mistake of "philosophical anthropologies," according to Foucault, will be to believe that there could be a "natural access" (*C*, 123)[46] to the fundamental, that is, that the empirical could "free itself from a preliminary critique of knowledge and from a primary question about the relationship to the object" (C, 123).[47] Consequently, these anthropologies will attempt to make the empirical work as its own foundation by constituting it as the "field of a positivity from which all the human sciences would derive their foundation and their possibility" (C, 123).[48] But the most refined form of the anthropological repetition reinscribes the *Anthropology* "within the wake of the *Critique*" (C, 123),[49] reaffirms the primacy of the *a priori* over the empirical, and thus produces, by means of the concept of the "fundamental," the model of the only relation that can be established legitimately from the empirical toward the transcendental—and the paradigm from which Foucault will find it easiest to think through the post-Kantian deviations.

The Anthropological Decentering of the Transcendental Theme: The "Originary"

We have just seen how the definition of the "fundamental" at once conserves and confirms the "divide" formerly established in the *Critique*. However, the fundamental is not the only type of relation that the *Anthropology* establishes between the transcendental and the empirical. Another model, much more polemical, is given by Foucault's study of *Geist* and its relation to reason. It is probably not by chance that *Geist* should serve as the pivot of the analysis, since its function in the *Commentary* was to secure the binding of the *Anthropology* to the *Critique*. Thus it is in what should be both the thesis of repetition's peak and most stable foundation that it gives way to that of decentering. Indeed, if *Geist* can serve, like freedom in the second *Critique*, as the "keystone" of the *Anthropology*, it is because, contrary to *Gemüt*, which is identified with an "empirical and passive nature," the study of which would belong to psychology, it permits the legitimization—not merely the acknowledgement—of the nonidentity of the subject with its empiricity. According to Foucault's reading, *Geist* effectively provides a ground for the possibility of spontaneous action through which *Gemüt* is "not only what it is, but also what it does with itself" (C, 52).[50] Because it includes a reference to noumenal causality, it accounts for the "pragmatic" (C, 33 ff.)[51] dimension of the 1797 text, and therefore for the specificity of the anthropological terrain. Thus, "because it opens to a dimension of freedom and totality, in which each fact is taken up within the complex network of *sollen* and *können*, the *Anthropology* can be nothing but pragmatic" (C, 54).[52] *Geist* is more precisely defined by a passage of the *Commentary* which is, in fact, a free translation of an extract of the *Anthropology*:[53] "the principle that animates the spirit by means of the ideas, this is called the *Geist* [*Man nennt das durch Ideen behbende Prinzip des Gemüts Geist*]" (C, 50).[54]

To clarify this "animating" function of the *Geist*, the *Commentary* refers obliquely to the "Appendix to the Transcendental Dialectics," a passage from which is paraphrased in the following way: "[The idea] anticipates a schema that is not constituting but that opens up the possibility of objects. It does not reveal the nature of things through an 'ostensive' move, but indicates how this nature can be sought" (*C*, 51).[55] The idea is therefore initially described as a "regulative,"[56] rather than constitutive principle that does not determine any object within the order of knowledge. However, Foucault minimizes this first aspect by stating twice that *Geist* is "not regulative" (*C*, 49, 50), stressing instead the dynamic character of ideas, which allow reason to satisfy its natural desire for the absolute by outlining for it the horizon of a totality, and therefore by giving its sense, as orientation and meaning, to the movement of the spirit. The *Commentary* thus establishes a functional parallelism between the dynamic that pushes reason to exceed the limits of experience at the theoretical level, and the concrete movement through which *Geist* "causes the empirical and concrete life of *Gemüt* to continue on" (*C*, 52).[57] Because it accounts for the constitutive separation of the subject from all nature, including its own, the dynamic of ideas should therefore permit the *Commentary* to give the anthropological repetition its real center.

And yet, just having concluded, in agreement with his preceding analyses, that *Geist* "tears the *Gemüt* away from its determinations" (*C*, 53),[58] Foucault claims without transition that there is a mysterious connection between *Geist* as defined and the "enigmatic *nature* of our reason" (*C*, 54),[59] which was described in the "Methodology" in the following way: "Reason is impelled by a *natural drive* to go out beyond the field of its empirical employment, and to venture in a pure enjoyment, by means of ideas alone, to the utmost limits of all knowledge, and not to be satisfied save through the completion of its course in [the apprehension of] a self-subsistent systematic whole."[60] Thus, Foucault is enabled by the lack of precision regarding this "natural drive" to operate the qualitative and daring leap that permits the *Commentary* to identify this "enigmatic nature" of reason with *Geist* itself, henceforth defined as "something that would be the kernel of pure reason, the un-uprootable origin of its transcendental illusions . . . , the principle of its movement within the empirical field where the faces of truth ceaselessly appear" (*C*, 55).[61] *Geist* does not, therefore, "animate" only *Gemüt*, but reason itself, which finds itself suddenly deposed from its sovereign position and returned to that which, from the shadows, would have already determined its speculative movement, and which, as its "nature," would be constitutively destined to escape it.

Thus occurs an inversion of the previously studied relationship of subordination of the *Anthropology* to the *Critique*, which "seems to refer the *Critique*, from its apex, to an *empirical* region, to a *domain of facts* where man would be condemned to a most originary passivity" (*C*, 54; my italics).[62] Playing on the ambiguity of the concept of "nature," which can refer both to the essence of a thing and to the synthetic connection of "natural" (and therefore empirical) phenomena, Foucault assimilates *Geist* to an "originary fact," in which reason would find both its truth and the source of the empirical determinations that bear upon it. Henceforth, it is within this secret nature of *Geist* that the impossibility of reason mastering or escaping its own essence will be determined, along with the empirical limitations that it is bound to encounter under various forms—for example, in its constitutive aspiration to the unconditioned, in the impossibility of intellectual intuition, or in the absence of the necessary obedience to the moral law that would define sanctity. If the *Critique* is "referred to an empirical reason," it is because this definition of *Geist* reveals a previously excluded possibility: that the transcendental power of reason should be dependent on empirical determinations. The consequence of this for "man" is the uncovering of a "most originary passivity," which precedes any constitutive activity, a passivity that *The Order of Things* will refer to the exterior empiricities of life, labor, and language, the primary form of which can be internally identified through the redefinition of *Geist* in the *Commentary*.

Foucault expresses this major inflection of the transcendental theme through the concept of the "originary":

> Therefore, the relationship between the given and the *a priori* takes in the *Anthropology* a structure that is the reverse of that which was uncovered by the *Critique*. What was *a priori* in the order of knowledge becomes in the order of concrete existence an *originary* that is not chronologically first, but which, as soon as it has appeared . . . reveals itself as *already there*. (*C*, 60)[63]

The originary thus marks the impossibility, as soon as the level of transcendental determination ("the order of knowledge") has been abandoned for that of real and empirical determinations ("the order of concrete existence"), of accepting the foundational logic originally established by the *Critique* and later reaffirmed by the fundamental through anthropological repetition. To this impossibility corresponds the movement of retrospection that characterizes the originary: "What is, from the point of view of the *Critique*, an *a priori of knowledge*, does not transpose itself immediately, through anthropological reflection, as an *a priori of existence*, but appears within the density of a becoming where a sudden apparition necessarily takes in retrospection the meaning of an already-there" (*C*, 57).[64] This "transposition" has as its consequence the paradoxical inscription of the transcendental within experience. For the *a priori* of knowledge to always appear as "already there," it must in some way preexist its own empirical "emergence"; but conversely, if it is only "retrospection" that allows us to make sense of it, then it can no longer have the radical independence it enjoyed in the *Critique*. The thematic of the "already there" specific to the originary consequently establishes a new relationship between the two terms, a relationship of retrospective presupposition. In accordance with the dual nature of man, both empirical *and* transcendental, the *a priori* must appear within experience; but it can only do so insofar as it is presupposed by experience as that of which it is the condition of constitution, the fact that it can never be simultaneous with itself and must remain inscribed within a logic of recurrence signaling its heterogeneity from the empirical.

Thus appears the impossibility of establishing the relation of foundation between the empirical and the *a priori* previously expressed by the "fundamental," a relation that underlined the absolute necessity of referring empirical contents to their *a priori* conditions and therefore gave the transcendental the logical priority that separated the constitutive from the constituted. On the contrary, the mutation of the transcendental theme into the "originary" has the consequence of ruining the critical project by devoting the *Anthropology* to the search for a foundation that is by definition denied to it by its theoretical presuppositions and the ambivalence of its object. Thus the *Anthropology* is finally defined as a "knowledge of man, by a movement that objectifies the latter at the level and in the content of its animal determinations; but it is also the knowledge of the knowledge of man, in a movement that questions the subject itself about its own limits and what it makes possible in the knowledge that it takes of itself" (*C*, 118).[65] Insofar as it is concerned with a content that is objectified "at the level of its animal determinations," the "knowledge of man" first mentioned above is clearly empirical, and should be subordinated to the transcendental perspective. Indeed, the *Critique* gave in the "Transcendental Analytic"[66] the model of such a subordination by carefully distinguishing between two forms of intuition of the self (pure apperception and empirical apperception), precisely so as to avoid any confusion between the "pure I" of synthesis and the empirical self,[67] the first being the transcendental condition of possibility for the second. But the *Anthropology* emblematically introduces a third term between these two elements, in the form of a "spoken I" claimed to be the "empirical and manifest form in which the synthetic activity of the I appears as an *already synthetized form*, as an *indissociably primary and secondary structure*" (*C*, 57).[68] Following the retrospective movement specific to the originary, the empirical nature of man becomes the "*a priori* limit of his knowledge" (*C*, 118),[69] so that the empirical understanding that the subject forms of itself now supposedly generates a knowledge of what the subject is in its constitutive power. Thus transcendental determination is reversed, while the "[empirical] knowledge of man" becomes "a [pseudo-transcendental] knowledge of the knowledge of man."

Thus Foucault denounces the apparition of a level of reflection that he categorizes in the *Commentary* as "mixed" and "impure," and which is described in an interview with Paul Ricoeur in the following way: "As soon as one tries to define an essence of man which could articulate itself from itself and which at the same time would be the foundation of all possible knowledge and of any possible limit to knowledge, one swims in total parallogism" (*DE*, 1: 452).[70] Following the pernicious logic that seeks to "make the man of nature, exchange, or discourse [i.e., man as empirically finite] serve as the [transcendental] foundation of his own [empirical] finitude" (*OT*, 341), the *Anthropology* superimposes the transcendental and empirical dimensions of man as a "double," by introducing the new necessity of referring the *a priori* back to the positivities that determine man in his empirical being.[71] "The insidious values of the question 'Was is der Mensch?' are responsible for this homogeneous, destructured, and indefinitely reversible field in which man presents his truth as the soul of truth" (*C*, 126),[72] adds the *Commentary* in the same spirit. *The Order of Things* echoes this description, defining anthropology as "the fundamental disposition which has governed and controlled the path of philosophical thought from Kant until our own day" (*OT*, 342; modified), insofar as there man reveals himself as "such a being that knowledge will be attained in him of what renders all knowledge possible" (*OT*, 318).[73] So the "Analytic of finitude" unknowingly anchors its truth in this "Analytic of man" (*OT*, 341), which the *Commentary* reveals as logically and chronologically coextensive with the anthropological version of the transcendental theme.

The Strategic Importance of the *Commentary* for Archaeology

It seems clear that the main interest of this Foucauldian reading of the *Anthropology* does not lie in its potential contribution to Kantian studies—which is probably why it has not been published along with Foucault's translation of Kant's text. Indeed, one could object that it considerably distorts the theses developed in *The Critique of Pure Reason*, and that the anthropological slippage, if that is what it is, needs not necessarily have the unfortunate significance it is given here. For example, the idea of an "*a priori* of existence," although familiar to the author of the *Cartesian Meditations*,[74] does not, as such, make much sense for Kant himself. The very question of the *Critique*—how there could be an

"agreement" between experience and the conditions defined *a priori* by the transcendental subject—excluded from the start the hypothesis of an inscription of
the transcendental within the empirical. Equally, the theme of a "density of
becoming" seems foreign to the definitions of time given in the *Critique* (either
as the *a priori* form of sensibility through which experience is constituted, or as
the constituted and objective time that one can measure from the observation
of the regular course of phenomena).[75] The idea of an "emergence" of the transcendental within becoming requires a different conception of temporality. This
is indirectly confirmed by the rest of the *Commentary*, which indicates that in
the *Anthropology* time is revealed as that which "undermines synthetic activity
itself" (*C*, 85),[76] and that to which the subject is linked by "already effected syntheses" (*C*, 43)[77] which, in a certain sense, always precede the active transcendental
syntheses. But these assertions, although they could easily have figured in
Experience and Judgment as they look like barely veiled allusions to the Husserlian
theme of "passive syntheses," hardly seem to belong in *The Critique of Pure
Reason*.

But perhaps this debate is not essential; the overall importance of Foucault's
interpretation of Kant is *strategic* rather than theoretical, and is played out *within*
the Foucauldian corpus. Indeed, the *Commentary* can be read as a tentative
attempt to show that as soon as Kant left the terrain of the *Critique* for that of
the *Anthropology*, the "Fold" (*OT*, 341)[78] of the transcendental onto the empirical and the "network of radical misunderstandings and illusions" (*C*, 123)[79] that
it engendered were irrevocably generated by man's duality as the empirico-transcendental double. From this perspective, the chronology of the Kantian itinerary gives, despite itself, in the relationship of the *Critique* to the *Anthropology*, a
miniature image of the divisions that will fracture modernity, while allowing us
to identify the successive stages of the evolution of the transcendental theme
implicitly presupposed by *The Order of Things*.

This idea is corroborated by the fact—itself highly symbolical—that the
Commentary permits us to pinpoint, within the *Anthropology* itself (and therefore in a manner *internal* to Kant's thought), the prefiguration of each of the three
"doubles"[80] through which Foucault will study the details of the anthropological confusions in *The Order of Things*. Thus, because of the description of *Geist*
as the "nature" of reason, reason encounters in the very exercise of its constitutive power its first experience of a limit that it cannot reduce through thought.
In this confrontation with the ineluctability of its empirical determinations,
which teaches it that it is neither unconditioned nor divine, reason painfully
comes for the first time to understand its own finitude: "*Geist* would be this originary fact, which, in its transcendental version, implies that the infinite is never

there" (*C*, 55).[81] The relationship of *Geist* to reason thus anticipates the circularity between the empirical and the transcendental specific to the *Anthropology*. Although it is transcendentally determining, reason reveals itself as empirically determined by this "nature," which appears as a sort of ungraspable anteriority. Conditioned in the order of being, reason seeks to release itself from this original passivity by taking it up in the order of knowledge, where, on the contrary, it can appear as conditioning. But the *Anthropology*, by uncovering that which the *Critique* had hidden—the presence and nature of *Geist*—invalidates this emancipating attempt exactly in the way described by section 9 of *The Order of Things*, that is, by folding back "the specific dimension of the critique on the contents of an empirical knowledge" (*OT*, 319; modified), thus anticipating the "empirico-transcendental redoubling" later described by Foucault.

Secondly, because of its definition as limit—that is, as that which is necessary, not from external and contingent requirements, but from the internal configuration of the limited object—*Geist* entails a paradoxical decentering of thought to itself. It is that part of itself which reason attempts to recover by the movement of reflection, but which, as it is presupposed in the attempt itself, is destined to escape from reason. Thus, "*Geist* is the root of the possibility of knowledge. And because of this, it is indissociably present to and absent from the figures of knowledge" (*C*, 55).[82] Although not heterogeneous to it, *Geist* never gives itself to reason as the reassuring object whose possession would comfort it with the knowledge that it could form both of itself and of experience, thus allowing reason its liberation from the constraints of its own nature. On the contrary, *Geist* appears as that which leads reason always to lose itself in the opacity of a nature that from the beginning functions as a given, "present" indeed because it determines the originary rational impulse, but "absent" from the field of knowledge because of its constitutive indeterminacy. Henceforth, the relation of reason to *Geist* anticipates the movement that defines in *The Order of Things* the relation of the cogito to the unthought, by which man is ineluctably referred "from a part of himself not reflected in a *cogito* to the act of thought by which he apprehends that part" (*OT*, 322), and which "exposes his thought to the risk of being swamped by his own being, and also enables him to gather himself on the basis of what eludes him" (*OT*, 323; modified).

Finally, the *Commentary* clearly indicates that *Geist* is never given to reason as actual and present, as it is: "This withdrawal, this invisible and visible reserve in the inaccessibility of which knowledge takes place and acquires its positivity. Its being is not being there, sketching by this the locus of freedom" (*C*, 56).[83] Being there without being there, *Geist* is therefore a "never-there": like the originary, whose paradoxes it takes up, *Geist* is never simultaneous with reason because it cannot inscribe itself homogeneously in the temporality that it defines, and as "nature," preexists all constitution. Being at once "invisible" and "visible," it can only appear retrospectively as this "primitivity"[84] which precedes the critical foundation and yet can only be thought through it. But the way in which *The Order of Things* exposes the "withdrawal" of the origin—a thematic which is not without connection to that of the "retreat" specific to *Geist*—seems exactly to take up this paradoxical structure again, by transposing it to the exteriority that unites man no longer with his own nature, but with things: as Foucault indicates, although, in the empirical order, things are always withdrawn from him, so that they are inapprehendable at their zero point, nevertheless man finds himself fundamentally withdrawn in relation to that withdrawal of things, and it is by this means that they are able to weigh down upon the immediacy of original experience with their solid anteriority" (*OT*, 332; modified).

Given this triple relationship of prefiguration, the *Commentary* functions as a matrix from which to interpret the Foucauldian critique of anthropology, in a way constituting the philosophical "prehistory" of the archaeological texts. In the light of this understanding, it becomes possible to redefine the relationship between the transcendental theme, man and the Analytic of finitude, and by doing this, to resolve the tension, identified above, between chapters 7 and 9 of *The Order of Things*. As we have seen, the *Commentary* permits us to establish that it is not the "Kantian critique" in its totality that marks the "threshold of our modernity," but that the line of division passes within Kant's work itself, separating the original formulation of the transcendental theme from its later versions. In chapter 7, this latter appears in its critical version; however, it is not this that truly marks the break with the classical age; the *Commentary* shows that it is only from the *Anthropology* onward that the dual structure that defines man becomes clearly visible. It is this inflection of the transcendental theme that chapter 9 takes into account, defining it as the real epistemic revolution that gave birth to the "anthropological sleep" (*OT*, 340) characteristic of modernity.

One could certainly object that the constitution of the empirico-transcendental doublet was presupposed by the *Critique* itself, since the inversion that gave finitude the power of self-foundation rested on the doubling of the subject itself. But for Foucault, the specificity of finitude in its critical version is that it could only become the *ratio cognoscendi* of experience on condition that *man was erased, as the founding transcendental subject, from a field in which he can henceforth only appear as an empirical subject*. Thus the subject, in the *Critique*, is "never given to experience" (*OT*, 243), declares Foucault: a curious statement, which only makes sense if one adds "as transcendental subject." But this partial erasure is very close to that of man from the space of representation, which Foucault ana-

lyzed in chapter 1 of *The Order of Things* through the painting by Velázquez !
Because he withdraws in his transcendental dimension from the empirical field,
which this retreat itself permits him to constitute, man as the empirico-transcendental *doublet* is by definition just as absent from Kantian criticism as he is
from *Las Meninas*, being in both cases a "blind spot"—a paradoxical point, structurally incapable of inscribing itself in the visible field, but which, however, guar-
antees the very possibility of vision.

So the ambivalent status of Kant in *The Order of Things* derives from this
impossibility of man appearing in the *Critique* in his full ambiguity "as an object
of knowledge and as a subject that knows" (*OT*, 312), even though he is presupposed by this same text in his empirico-transcendental duality—whereby he constitutes, *stricto sensu*, the *unthought* of criticism. In this sense, the deepest stake
of the *Commentary* is precisely to bring this unthought to light through an explicit
reflection on the relation between the *Critique* and the *Anthropology*, and to out-
line the resulting consequences. The conclusion that Foucault comes to, therefore, is that the inflection of the transcendental theme could only drive contemporary thought into a series of impasses, themselves thrice prefigured in the
relation of reason to *Geist*. These aporiae concern the ambition of the *Anthropology*
to "count as a *Critique* that would be freed from the assumptions and the inert
weight of the *a priori*" (*C*, 123),[85] the problem thus being that the end sought
and the means used are contradictory. How could the *a priori* conserve any sort
of founding power if empirical knowledge is sufficient to determine it in its turn?
The *Anthropology* is misled in searching within the empirical for a knowledge
that could have transcendental value, as the "turn towards the empirical"
attempted is sufficient in itself to empty of all meaning the concept of a transcendental foundation.

Henceforth, Foucault's question will be whether it is possible to give the question of the conditions of possibility of knowledge a nonanthropological transposition. The evidence and instruments of this attempt to "deanthropologize"
the *a priori* while keeping open the need for a foundation are the concepts of the
"historical *a priori*," then the *épistémè*, and finally the "archive." However, one
can immediately underline a serious problem: given the extreme ambivalence of
the Kantian heritage and the shadow that it throws over modernity, why borrow
from Kant the problematization as well as the necessary concepts to formulate
the archaeological analyses? The conceptual framework provided by Kantian terminology is clearly the grounding for passages in which the "anthropological
sleep" (*OT*, 340) echoes the "dogmatic sleep" from which Hume, the good "geog-
rapher of human reason,"[86] rescued Kant, or indeed the extracts in which
Foucault interprets the modern configuration of knowledge as a dialogue of a

"quasi-Aesthetics" and a "quasi-Dialectics," whose foundation would be given by an "Analytic" (*OT*, 320). Foucault himself recognized having borrowed the term "archaeology" from Kant, who according to him "used it to refer to the history of what *makes* a certain form of thought *necessary*" (*DE*, 2: 221).[87]

One might suggest that by virtue of Foucault's very inscription within the modernity that he historically criticizes, he must be defined as a post-Kantian, and that it is therefore coherent that he should use the vocabulary of the epistemic configuration to which he belongs, so revealing himself against his wishes— and as prophesied by Hegel long before him in the *Lessons on the History of Philosophy*—as the "son of his time." Nonetheless, the hypothesis of the historical necessity of the Kantian inheritance seems insufficient to explain the fact that Foucault recasts the critical question in the very terms that according to him doomed it to fail. It is well known that he claimed to be the herald of a new *épistémè*, in which language, previously relegated to the margins of literary production by the eruption of man onto the scene of knowledge, would once again reign. But one may wonder whether in this attempt to push the Kantian heritage to its limits by reformulating it, archaeology has not from the start ruined its very foundation, condemning itself to repeat the same contradictions for which its author criticized the *Anthropology*. If at the very heart of the archaeological project, a final redoubling of the empirico-transcendental circle specific to modernity should be uncovered, then perhaps one will have to conclude, in ironic and anticipatory reference to Nietzsche, that the early Foucault, by reactivating the Kantian theme . . . has defeated himself from the very beginning?

TWO

The Different Meanings of the Historical
a Priori and the Transcendental Theme:
The Methodological Failure of Archaeology

Strange though it may appear, Foucault hardly ever troubles himself to give the historical *a priori* clear theoretical definition.[1] Only a few texts—the preface to *The Order of Things*; chapter 3, section 5, of *The Archaeology of Knowledge*; and a few scant articles—provide more precise descriptions, to which, however, the rest of the texts concerned barely refer.[2] There is a strong contrast between the detailed character of Foucault's empirical analyses and the general imprecision of the theoretical armature on which these are supposed to rest. It is almost as if the author were actually maintaining two parallel discourses: a background interrogation of the nature of history as *historia*, to which he responds implicitly by introducing the notion of an historical *a priori*, and a collection of sharp analyses of the *rerum gestarum*, which presupposes the first questioning and its answer without articulating them precisely. Focusing mainly on this last aspect, numerous commentators have reproached Foucault for the vagueness, even the falsehood, of his conclusions.[3] Rather than entering into this debate, I shall attempt a vertical critique of these empirical arguments by interrogating the philosophical presuppositions on which Foucault's examination of the historical *a priori* rests.

Such an attempt immediately encounters a major difficulty: although the concept figures in all the works from the so-called archaeological period, it does not seem to have a univocal meaning for Foucault. The historical *a priori* first appears in *The Birth of the Clinic*, where it is defined as the "originary distribution of the visible and the invisible insofar as it is linked with the division between what can be stated and what remains unsaid" (*BC*, xi), that is as a kind of preconceptual articulation between seeing and saying. *The Order of Things* proposes a much more general definition, as "the experience of order" by which "knowledge [*savoir*] was constituted" (*OT*, xxii). Finally, *The Archaeology of Knowledge* sees it more formally as "that which must account for statements in their dispersion" (*AK*, 127; modified). But how can these definitions, which one feels intuitively are not identical and cannot rely on the same philosophical underpinnings, be articulated and related? And why does Foucault feel the need to vary the concept? Should we see in these different approaches three isolated attempts to define the object of archaeological research? Or should we see in their succession an indication of a continuous reformulation by Foucault, each new understanding being aimed at answering the problems linked to the preceding one? Does the concept of the historical *a priori* maintain a specific unity in the course of these successive reworkings? Above all, does archaeology really succeed in providing the historical *a priori* with a coherent definition, freed from the anthropological version of the transcendental theme?

The Foucauldian Transposition of the Critical Question

When he places the preface of *The Order of Things* under the patronage of Borges, Foucault seems far from Kant, separated from the seriousness of criticism by the distance of irony and the apparent incongruity of the themes evoked—the revolting animals teaming under Eusthenes' tongue or the dislocated rubrics of the lost "Chinese encyclopedia." From this text, which gives the greater share to literature and metaphor, philosophical questioning in general and Kantian questions in particular appear singularly absent. What relation can there be, at first sight, between the exquisite corpses, the surrealists' encounter of the umbrella and the sewing machine, and the critical interrogation of the conditions of the possibility of knowledge? But as one leaves the exoticism of form to one side and approaches the underlying content, the possibility of a rapprochement appears. After all, the sewing machine and the umbrella could never have met, as Foucault says, if it wasn't for the "table" on which the juxtaposition took place, and which is the real object of the inquiry: "On what 'table,' according to what grid of identities, similarities, analogies, have we become accustomed to sort out so many different and similar things?" (*OT*, xix). Indeed, what is this "table," this "certain mute order" (*OT*, xxi; modified) in which beings are juxtaposed, this "site" where things can "neighbor" or not, if not the historical *a priori* that allows them to be ordered and thought? What is described by means of these spatial metaphors is in reality "that from which forms of knowledge [*connaissances*] and theories became possible" (*OT*, xx; modified); and the "history" that *The Order of Things* intends to construct is that of the "*conditions of possibility*," the "*configurations* which have given rise to the diverse forms of empirical knowledge [*connaissance*]" (*OT*, xxi; modified), or the "network which defines the *conditions of possibility* of a debate or a problem" (*OT*, xxi; modified, my italics).

However, an attentive reading of the rest of the preface shows that Foucault is not content with a general reactivation of the question of the conditions of the possibility of knowledge. Indeed, he implicitly takes as his point of departure the Aristotelian claim that empirical knowledge rests on the establishment of specific and hierarchical relations between its objects, that is, on their ordering. The presupposition of *The Order of Things* is, therefore, that to define the conditions of possibility of knowledge is to understand the nature of that order. Foucault immediately excludes two hypotheses. Order is neither "determined by an *a priori* and necessary concatenation" nor "imposed on us by immediately perceptible contents" (*OT*, xix). The first definition would leave aside the domain of empirical knowledge for that of mathematics or logic. It would be concerned with the hypothetical-deductive order that permits us to "link consequences together," whose objects and laws are certainly definable *a priori* but purely formal. The second hypothesis does concern itself with experience, but understands order from the perspective of an immanence which turns knowledge into the simple deciphering of a state of affairs, whether organized by the prescience of a great Architect (as in Leibniz), or more realistically by a set of natural determinations. For idealism or realism, order would be, respectively, "that which only exists through the grid generated by our gaze," or "what gives itself through things as their internal law" (*OT*, xx; modified). One might note in passing that the ambivalence of the "table"—at once "operating-table," "nickel-plated" and "rubbery," therefore the *objective* place of the encounter—and "table, *tabula*, that enables thought to order the entities of the world" (*OT*, xvii; modified), that is, the subjective principle of organization from which the meeting itself can be conceived, prefigures the ambivalence of that of which it is the metaphor: order itself.

But don't the very terms of this alternative echo an older, and indeed very Kantian, problem? One knows that *The Critique of Pure Reason* opposed, to better refute them, "transcendental realism," which "considers time and space as something that is given in itself (independently of our sensibility)," to "material" idealism, which "states that the existence of things in space and outside of ourselves is simply dubious . . . or false."[4] If one agrees that the establishment of the differences necessary to any order relies on the possibility of defining relations of spatial coexistence and temporal succession between objects, as Foucault himself invites his reader to do two pages later (by affirming that the "modalities of order" are always "tied to space and time" [*OT*, xix; modified]), then one can identify here the same givens as in the problem of the preface. "There is nothing more empirical (*superficially, at least*) than the process of establishing an order among things" (*OT*, xix; modified), declares the author, thus rejecting the hypothesis of a natural order, without, however, subscribing to the idea that this structure could be purely arbitrary, as it requires "the application of a preliminary criterion." This problem was resolved for Kant by denouncing the paralogism that consists in attributing to "exterior objects" the quality of "things in themselves," a solution which allowed him to assert the knowability of exterior objects but only as phenomena, that is, as "mere kinds of representation."[5] Foucault distinguishes himself from Kant by stating that order is "simultaneously" the "secret network" of things *and* the "grid" imposed by the gaze that is turned upon them—Kant's thesis, rather, would be that order is only "in things" *because* it is in the gaze, or, more exactly, because "things" themselves are constituted as objects of knowledge by the gaze. Neither really objective nor truly subjective, order is present in the preface as a mixed reality that cannot be analyzed by reusing the terms of the Kantian solution. Therefore, probably to hold himself equidistant from a precritical realism and an excessively idealistic transcendentalism, Foucault introduces, in the form of the concept of the "historical *a priori*," his own solution for accounting for the temporal variations in the "experience of order."

This has the effect of situating him both close to and far from Kantianism. Close, because the manner in which the historical *a priori* is defined largely takes up *The Critique of Pure Reason*'s demands for necessity and systematicity. This is a controversial point, as it is well known that Foucault vigorously denied, notably in *The Archaeology of Knowledge*, having used the concept to operate "totalitarian periodisations" (*AK*, 150; modified). It remains true nonetheless that one can find in both *The Birth of the Clinic* and *The Order of Things* passages which are unequivocal. In the first, the historical *a priori* is defined as "that which *systematizes* [men's thoughts] *from the outset*" (*BC*, xix), and in the second as the "fundamental network which defines the *implicit but unavoidable unity* of knowledge [*savoir*]" (*OT*, 74; modified). The systematic and necessary character of the Kantian *a priori* is taken up further by the Foucauldian definition of the historical *a priori* as a "single, *necessary* arrangement" (*OT*, 74),[6] a "rigorous and general epistemological arrangement" (*OT*, 168) to be interrogated, or "the archaeological network that provides . . . thought its laws" (*OT*, 71). In another passage, Foucault goes so far as to assert that it is the historical *a priori* that "provides a foundation for, and makes possible, all the empirical sciences of order" (*OT*, 71), and even that "in any given culture and at any given moment, there is always only one *épistémè* that defines the conditions of possibility of all knowledge [*savoir*], whether expressed in a theory or silently invested in a practice" (*OT*, 168).

Correspondingly, Foucault rejects, as did Kant, the idea that the question of the conditions of possibility of knowledge could find a purely empirical answer. This is one of the principal reasons why he distinguishes archaeology from the history of sciences or ideas. As he indicates, although archaeology is really concerned with "that on the basis of which various forms of knowledge [*connaissances*] and theories became possible," it "does not belong to the history of ideas or of science" (*OT*, xxi). Despite their differences,[7] these disciplines share a horizontal perspective for understanding the conditions of possibility of the "forms of knowledge and theories" by studying them through "the persons involved and their history" (*OT*, 200) seeking to discover influences and establish relationships between authors, concepts, or currents of thought.[8] By contrast, the specificity of archaeology is that it revives the critical question through a vertical displacement that "questions thought at the level of what *made it archeologically possible*," the opposition between the "surface," where continuities and discontinuities are inscribed, and the "depth" analogically taking up the distinction set up by the *Critique* between the founded and the founding. However, this "depth" should not be taken in a Marxist sense, as the set of the relations of production that determine the organization of the social body. "I have never been a Marxist" (*PPC*, 22), declared Foucault, describing in another passage "the empirical and soft-bellied Marxists which [he is] very willing to have a go at" (*DE*, 2: 408). In a less polemical manner, *The Archaeology of Knowledge* explicitly rejects the pertinence of "causal"[9] analyses for the understanding of the conditions of possibility of knowledge. By affirming that the historical *a priori* is not identical to "determinations which, formed at the level of institutions, of social or economic relations, would transcribe themselves by force on the surface of discourses" (*AK*, 74; modified). Foucault clearly rejects any materialist explanation that would make economics the dominant authority and the historical *a priori* a mere superstructure.[10]

However, it is immediately necessary to nuance this analogy between Foucault and Kant, for two reasons. The first is that the object of the archaeological inquiry is specifically "that on the basis of which various form*s* of knowledge [*connais-sance*s] and theorie*s* were made possible" (*OT*, xxi; my italics). Note the use of the plural and the past perfect—not knowledge, but the "various forms of knowl-edge": against the universalism of the Kantian project, Foucault plays on the spa-tially and temporally localized character of the objects of archaeology.[11] The his-torical *a priori*, he adds slightly further on, insisting on the local character of his analyses, is that which "at a given period, delimits in our experience a field of possible knowledge [*savoir*]" (*OT*, 158; modified). However, the idea that expe-rience can be "delimited" into different "fields of knowledge" would have no meaning for Kant, as for him experience is itself *a form of knowledge*, not a merely empirical content. According to his well-known phrase, the "conditions of the possibility of experience in general" are the "conditions of the possibility of the *objects* of experience,"[12] and thus the latter is not a medium in which empirical objects could be isolated; on the contrary, it is only through experience that they are constituted. On these points, Foucault thus reverses both the direction of the critical process and the significance of experience: where Kant sought to *antici-pate* the possibility of all knowledge by prescribing to it in advance its own laws, Foucault instead intends to begin from already constituted forms of knowledge to define *retrospectively* that which rendered them possible. Thus experience is, for Foucault, who here intends it in a precritical sense, a given whose conditions of possibility must be searched for elsewhere—in the historical *a priori*.

The second limit of the analogy is concerned with the invalidation of any nor-mative perspective. Although the historical *a priori* does determine the field of knowledge, it cannot, unlike its purely transcendental counterpart, legitimate *a priori* the possibility of certain knowledge. What Foucault takes from criticism, therefore, is not the demand for an absolute foundation for knowledge, but the idealist thesis that the conditions of possibility of knowledge are not homoge-neous with the objects that they determine. In this regard, it is significant that the reproach of excessive normativity directed by Foucault at the history of ideas and that of the sciences could easily be applied to Kant himself.[13] What could be more normative, by definition, than the critical enterprise, as it attempts to determine not merely the truth of this or that theory, but the very possibility of truth as an "agreement"[14] of knowledge with its object? However, although Foucault takes the question of truth itself, its nature and the way in which it is produced, very seriously from *The Order of Things* on, he is not concerned with the truth-value of individual statements. On the contrary, one of the functions of archaeology is to bracket the legitimacy of normative judgments by referring each formation of knowledge to the *épistémè* from which it arises, and from which alone it can be judged.[15]

Notwithstanding these important restrictions, it remains the case that the Foucauldian historical *a priori* has the function, like its Kantian counterpart, of accounting for the possibility of the constitution of knowledge. Thus, in the only elaborated definition that he gives, Foucault distinguishes his *a priori* from "a certain state of acquired forms of knowledge [*connaissances*] laid down in the course of the preceding ages," as well as from the "mentality or 'framework of thought' of any given period" (*OT*, 158), as these would merely be empirical contents seen alternatively from an objective or subjective perspective. On the contrary, the historical *a priori* is the condition of the possibility of knowledge, being "what makes it possible and necessary" (*OT*, 168)—the problem being to know how it does so. The preface of *The Order of Things* formulates the question in the following manner:

> On what conditions was Classical thought able to reflect relations of similarity or equivalence between things, relations that would provide a foundation and a justification for their words, their classifications, their systems of exchange? What historical *a priori* provided the starting point from which it was possible to define the great checkerboard of distinct identities established against the . . . indifferent background of differences? (*OT*, xxiv)

By means of the parallel between the two phrases, the historical *a priori* can be identified here with the "conditions" of classical thought. In the same manner, *The Birth of the Clinic* identified the most recent *épistémè* as "what *made possible* contemporary thought" (*BC*, 199; my italics). But how can such "conditions" be understood?

As shown by Foucault's critique of the history of ideas, these conditions cannot be a collection of psychological characteristics, which would be susceptible to variation from one individual to another, and which thus could not determine necessarily the way in which the knowledge of a given epoch must be formed. Correspondingly, it is clear that, contrary to Kant, Foucault cannot refer these conditions to an immutable organization of the subject's faculties, definable *a priori*. Beyond the fact that this would not allow him to account for the relativity of truth, this "solution" would have the major disadvantage of giving the historical *a priori* an openly anthropological nature, very likely to condemn archaeology in advance to the anthropological aporia identified by the *Commentary*. But, as we have seen, these conditions are not of a material nature either, and should be understood as neither infra- nor super-structural. Moreover, and in spite of the spatializing metaphors used by Foucault (he occasionally talks of the "space" or the "arrangement" of knowledge [*savoir*] that would be the "ground" or "soil" of the positivities), these conditions cannot be identified with "knowledge" (*savoir*) itself, as the historical *a priori* is by contrast "what defines the conditions of possibility of all knowledge [*savoir*]" (*OT*, 168), which clearly indicates that the above mentioned "configurations" of knowledge are only derivative.

Taking into account these multiple restrictions, the most reasonable hypothesis is probably that before *The Archaeology of Knowledge* the historical *a priori* should be understood as a structure endowed with a limited range and with historically variable forms—Foucault's two successive versions of which will be analyzed a little further on. To the extent that it conditions the "forms of visibility" (*BC*, 196) or the "experience of order" specific to a given epoch, this structure determines a field of possible objects of knowledge, following modalities that change according to the domain and that are examined in detail by *The Order of Things*. In this sense, the concept of the historical *a priori* has the function of introducing into the field of knowledge a principle of nonsubjective determination, which defines for a given period and geographical area the historical form taken by the constitution of various forms of knowledge. For example, although men could always see and say things, the medical doctor of the classical age could only see and identify as a symptom that which appeared to him as immediately sayable. However, two centuries later the anatomo-pathologist will no longer establish a diagnosis from such a presumption of transparency between language and reality, but from the opposite assumption, that the body has a fundamental opacity that resists immediate linguistic representation and must be opened by the knife of the surgeon in order to become knowable.

One might immediately object that this definition of the historical *a priori* seems to assimilate Foucault to structuralism, a claim that he always denied (see chapters 1 and 5 of *The Archaeology of Knowledge* and numerous other texts),[16] mainly by pointing out that, far from examining the virtual sets of possibilities offered by formal systems, he was only preoccupied by the real and its conditions of possibility. But this objection does not really seem to apply here. Firstly, Foucault himself uses the term in defining the historical *a priori* as the "the common *structure* that delineates and articulates what is *seen* and what is *said*" (*BC*, xix; modified). Secondly, the fact that the historical *a priori* is defined as a structure does not prevent it from being solely identifiable from the study of actual phenomena and not from the possibilities of a "virtual system" such as a "language." Finally, as we shall see shortly, the Foucauldian understanding is distinguished from the structuralist model in that the historical *a priori* is understood neither as universal nor as invariant; rather, it undergoes the historical transformations that archaeology is intended to identify.

In fact, the historical and therefore relative aspect of the *a priori* should be understood in a strong sense: although it is a structure, it is not a *universal* structure. Despite occasionally haphazard statements concerning the extension of the concept (which, as seen above, can alternatively refer to this or that positivity, or to the thought of an epoch in general), it is likely that Foucault never understands the *a priori* as a principle of the constitution of objects in general, but sees it as a variable historical structure that only intervenes in the production of local knowledge, when it is a matter of articulating truth in a particular domain. Hence the historical *a priori* can be understood as that which "provides man's everyday gaze with theoretical powers and defines the conditions in which one can sustain a discourse on things that is recognised as true" (*OT*, 158).[17] According to the different historical modalities of this structure (understood as the connection of seeing and saying or of words and things) and what they do or do not allow in each case, certain elements of knowledge (*savoir*) can be constituted as objects of possible knowledge (*connaissance*) and regrouped in more or less formalized theoretical works. From this perspective, the historical *a priori* indicates the (historically variable) conditions through which "the mode of being of the objects which appear in the field [of experience]" (*OT*, 158) can be defined. So, for example, it is only through the functioning of the historical *a priori* of the nineteenth century that, while previously there were only "living beings," now life could be constituted as a possible object for a biology itself in the process of its elaboration (cf. *OT*, 161).

Thus it is only through returning to the historical *a priori* that the common constitution of different epistemic figures can be understood, and the isomorphic relations between them within given epochs (such as the links between natural history, general grammar, and the theory of wealth during the classical age) accounted for, as archaeology was intended to do for each of the "ages" that it identified. Henceforth, the problem becomes whether or not, in this renewal of the critical question and in this historicizing reformulation of the transcendental theme, Foucault really succeeds in escaping the "anthropological illusions" denounced by the *Commentary*. To answer this we must look more closely at the definitions of the historical *a priori* proposed in the archaeological texts.

The First Two Understandings of the Historical *a Priori*: The Birth of the Clinic and The Order of Things

Although *The Birth of the Clinic* focuses on a more limited topic (the development of modern medicine from the previous "medicine of types") and on a much less expansive period than *The Order of Things*,[18] the two texts have in common a concept, the historical *a priori*,[19] as well as a method employed for the first time, "archaeology."[20] The preface to *The Birth of the Clinic* postulates that to grasp the "mutation of medical discourse" it is necessary to question, not its "thematic contents" or its "logical modalities"—anticipating the formulation of the problem of order in *The Order of Things*—but the "common structure that delineates and articulates what is *seen* and what is *said*" (*BC*, xix; modified). Insomuch as it is "*necessary* to all concrete knowledge [*savoir*]" (*BC*, xii), which it "makes *possible*," this "relationship between the visible and the invisible" possesses the three characteristics specific to the *a priori* examined above. The "concrete and historical *a priori*" sought by Foucault is therefore defined in *The Birth of the Clinic* as a specific distribution of the visible and the sayable, a "new alliance between words and things, enabling one to *see* and to *say*" (*BC*, xii), which determines the different stages of the constitution of medical knowledge. The fate of the clinic is thus referred not to a "reorganization of medical knowledge," which could be studied horizontally by the history of the sciences, but vertically, to the fundamental "spatialization" and "verbalisation" of pathology that are the "conditions of possibility of a discourse on disease" (*BC*, xi).

On these premises, *The Birth of the Clinic* proposes to write a history of this configuration, in which three principal stages can be very schematically identified, each creating a different relationship between the sayable and the visible. Firstly, the "medicine of types," defined by a prevalence of the sayable over the visible: in this mode, it is possible to define diseases as *a priori* as types, that the order of the visible masks as much as it reveals, since within the Aristotelian tradition no science of the individual is possible and so no ideal type could be incarnated as such in a sick body. The task of the "medical gaze" is to rediscover in the visible the already-said of the disease, despite the double blurring performed by the corporeality of the patient and the potential failures of the doctor himself (*BC*, 9–9). The second mode of articulation of seeing and saying is given at the end of the classical age by the clinic, through which

> medical perception is freed from the play of essence and symptoms, and from the no less ambiguous play of species and individuals: the figure disappears by which the visible and the invisible were pivoted in accordance with the principle that the patient both conceals and reveals the specificity of his disease.
> A domain of clear visibility was opened up to the gaze. (*BC*, 105)

The historical *a priori* of clinical experience is, therefore, the "formidable postulate" that "all that is visible is *expressible* and that it is *wholly visible* because it is *wholly expressible*" (*BC*, 115).[21] For Foucault, this "residueless transferability of the visible into the sayable" is shown by the ambivalent status of the symptom as the natural and immediate manifestation of the disease in the order of the visible, and the sign that allows it to be identified and thus spoken of. Finally, the third form of the historical *a priori*, which enabled the formation of anatomical pathology as a discipline at the beginning of the nineteenth century,[22] is characterized by the dissolution of the alliance of seeing and saying: the latter is replaced by the primacy of the invisible over the sayable, which reflects the discovery of the opacity of the sick body—this "tangible space" and "opaque mass" (*BC*, 121) rebellious to the gaze. It is henceforth necessary to "bend back language entirely towards that region in which the perceived, in its singularity, runs the risk of eluding the form of the word and of becoming finally imperceptible because no longer capable of being said . . . , to introduce language into that penumbra where the gaze is bereft of words" (*BC*, 169).

These different figures of the historical *a priori* are what give archaeology its specificity, by allowing it to write the history, not of "the accumulated forms of knowledge [*connaissances*]," but of that which "determines the reciprocal positions and the mutual play of the knowing subject and that which is to be known" (*BC*, 121). Certain clues could suggest that Foucault is here implicitly referring to the analyses of Merleau-Ponty: for example, the problematic of "seeing" and "saying" is exactly that which opens *The Visible and the Invisible*. Having defined "perceptive faith" as the belief according to which "we see the things themselves, the world is what we see," the first chapter questions "what is this *we*, what *seeing* is, and what *thing* or *world* is,"[23] which is exactly the thematic of the preface of *The Birth of the Clinic*. Furthermore, the Foucauldian idea that the articulation of seeing and saying, inasmuch as it preexists all formulated knowledge, is preconceptual and refers to the "spoken structure of the perceived" as the "full space in the hollow of which language assumes volume and size" (*BC*, xi), seems to echo the well-known statements of Merleau-Ponty that the lived experience (*vécu*) is a "spoken lived experience" and that vision itself is "structured as a language."[24] Thus, the articulated discourse is only second as it presupposes the "speaking word" (*parole parlante*) in which is played out the "the folding over . . . of the visible and the lived experience upon language, and of language upon the visible and the lived experience."[25] Equally, the articulation of seeing and saying is no more conscious or intellectual for Foucault than it is for Merleau-Ponty, since, on the contrary, it constitutes for both the condition of possibility of any theoretical discourse.

However, if the "distribution of the visible and the invisible" is, for Foucault, "originary" (*BC*, xi; modified), and refers to a "region where, at the most fundamental level of language, 'things' and 'words,' ways of seeing and of saying still belong to each other," then perhaps this "belonging" should be understood through the concept of "perception."[26] In *The Birth of the Clinic*,[27] the notion is strongly connoted by all the recurrent metaphors of the "gaze" and repeatedly recurs as such in the text. Foucault evokes the "world of perception" involved in the "gaze that a doctor turns to a patient" (*BC*, 154) his "perceptive attention" (*BC*, 4), the "concrete perceptions" of the "medical gaze" (*BC*, 16), its "fundamental perceptual codes" (*BC*, 54) and, again, its "perceptual field" (*BC*, 102).[28] Archaeology could therefore be interpreted, from the foundations laid out by *The Phenomenology of Perception*, as an attempt to identify historical variations of the structures of perception in a given domain. In this sense, Foucault's definition of the articulation of seeing and saying as "a general organization of knowledge [*savoir*]" would be a specific case of Merleau-Ponty's statement that "all knowledge takes its place within the horizons opened up by perception,"[29] turning *The Birth of the Clinic* into a sort of applied phenomenology of perception.

Unfortunately, this comparison is immediately limited by the fact that Foucault does not suggest any analysis of what Merleau-Ponty called *le corps propre*, and which was the starting point for his own study of perception. However, the manner in which *The Birth of the Clinic* is described in *The Archaeology of Knowledge* would leave open the possibility of such an analysis.[30] Indeed, Foucault affirms that he "did not wish to reduce to a single founding act, or to a founding consciousness, the general horizon of rationality against which the progress of medicine gradually emerged," nor did he try to "describe the empirical genesis, nor the various component elements of the medical mentality" (*AK*, 54). Similarly, the Merleau-Pontian understanding of perception requires neither of these approaches, since it refers neither to a *founding consciousness* (as the critique of Husserlian idealism by Merleau-Ponty shows), nor to an *empirical subjectivity*, but to one's own body (*le corps propre*) and the corporeal schemas through which the synthesis of the sensorial given is effected. In this sense, Foucault's retrospective reconstruction of his work would allow archaeology the possibility of such a phenomenological rooting of the medical gaze. The only reproach that one could make to this development would be that it neither defined nor even identified its own theoretical foundation.

But in reality, this possibility is ruled out by *The Birth of the Clinic* itself, which defines the historical *a priori* as a "deep space, *anterior to all perceptions and governing them from afar*" (*BC*, 5). Such an anteriority would be inconceivable for Merleau-Ponty, either logically or chronologically. Moreover, the very idea of an "*a priori*" is contrary to his thinking and is explicitly refuted, most notably in *The Phenomenology of Perception* and in *The Visible and the Invisible*.[31] If Foucault were to take up Merleau-Ponty's conceptual framework, he would therefore find himself confronted by an uncomfortable choice. He could maintain his own conception of the historical *a priori*, in which case he would expose himself to a contradiction between the form and the content of his analyses, since the very principle of his explanation (the historical *a priori*) would be refuted in advance by the presuppositions of the content. Alternatively, he could take the concept of the historical *a priori* in a Merleau-Pontian direction by referring it to the structure of perception, and therefore to one's own body, which would immediately inscribe archaeology within the contradictory space of the "originary," identified by the *Commentary* as being caused by the anthropological confusions between the empirical and the transcendental.

Due to this impasse, *The Birth of the Clinic* finds itself without any real theoretical support, as it implicitly refers to a phenomenological theory of perception that it does not possess and to which it could not subscribe anyway. Henceforth, the idea that the historical *a priori* could be defined as an articulation of the "seeable and the sayable" (*BC*, xix) appears as difficult to understand as it is to demonstrate, and remains very abstract. Most paradoxically, although it rejects any thought of "man,"[32] for the reasons established in the *Commentary*, the archaeology of the medical gaze seems, after all, to require a phenomenology that it is incapable of formulating. In this sense, the early Foucault seems caught within a contradiction that opposes his antihumanism to the presuppositions of his own approach—an implicit conception, if not of subjectivity[33] at least of the opening of the world and the constitution of meaning. Foucault later will admit as much, by reproaching himself for having accorded "far too great a share, and a very enigmatic too, to what I call an 'experience,' thus showing how close one still was to admitting an anonymous and general subject of history" (*AK*, 16; modified). But the problem is perhaps not so much that of having given too "great" a share to this "experience," but that of not having known how to think it—a lacuna that Foucault will try to remedy later, not by renouncing every reference to the subject, as in *The Archaeology of Knowledge*, but by rethinking the constitution of subjectivity itself.

In *The Order of Things*, by contrast, any reference to perception is abandoned. Although Foucault does not explicitly define it, the historical *a priori* can be textually reconstructed as an implicit relationship between "words" and "things,"[34] or, as Foucault says, between "language" and "being" (*OT*, 207). What now defines the conditions of possibility of knowledge and serves as point of departure for the archaeology of the human sciences is the relation between the being of signs and being in general. The breaks in the history of the successive *a priori* identified by *The Order of Things* are well known: the Renaissance is characterized by the fact that words "inhere in things" (*OT*, 129; modified), and that language is not an arbitrary system, being "set down in the world" equally with natural objects (*OT*, 35). The reason why the mode of being of words is thought of as "raw," or "primitive," is probably that since words themselves are things, they somehow remain prior to all the significations that they can serve to elaborate,[35] and therefore only give themselves to reflection paradoxically, both as commentary and as the text to be commented on.[36] The passage to the classical age is characterized by a double movement. Firstly, the mode of being of language is distinguished from that of things; secondly and conversely, the new understanding of the sign as a "doubled representation" immediately allows this distance to be overcome (*OT*, 63 ff.; modified). If the Renaissance is characterized by the "opacity" of both words and things, the classical age is one of "transparence," representation having the function of "interweaving words and things" (*OT*, 160), and of restoring, through the quasi-immediate mediation of language, their original immanence. Thus the "ordering of empiricities"[37] has as its condition of possibility an "ontology," the postulate of which is that "being is given to representation without any breaks" (*OT*, 206; modified).[38] Finally, the passage to the modern age is marked by the establishment of the empirico-transcendental redoubling—with Kant occupying, as we saw, an ambiguous position—and therefore by the new impossibility of understanding being within the space of representation. Thus, "representation is in the process of losing its power to define the mode of being common to things and to knowledge [*connaissance*]. The very being of what is represented is now going to fall outside representation itself" (*OT*, 240).[39]

It should be noted that the chronology of the different forms of the historical *a priori* given in *The Birth of the Clinic* can entirely be inscribed within that of *The Order of Things*. Indeed, it is likely that the reversibility of the visible in the expressible as a "generalised form of transparence" (*BC*, 117) rests precisely on the reversibility of representation, and, conversely, that the discovery at the beginning of the nineteenth century of "obscure masses," "impenetrable shapes," and "the black stone of the body" (*BC*, 117) corresponds as much to the impossibility of representing "being" as to the emergence of the new empiricity, "life."[40] This hypothesis is confirmed by the fact that both texts refer to Condillac's "Ideology." In *The Order of Things*, the latter constitutes the apex of the classical *épistémè* as it forms the project, at once critical and precritical, of defining the conditions of possibility of representation by analyzing, within the epistemic space that it defines, all the forms that it can take. But the reason why clinical experience is "isomorphic with Ideology," is that "in the clinic, as in Analysis, the armature of the real is designed on the model of language" (*BC*, 96).[41] Even more explicitly, Foucault affirms that the clinician's gaze and the philosopher's reflection have similar powers because they both presuppose a structure of identical objectivity in which the totality of being is exhausted in manifestations that are its signifier-signified, in which the visible and the manifest come together in a least a virtual identity, in which the perceived and the perceptible may be wholly restored in a language. (*BC*, 96)

However, in this chiasmatic identity of the "visible" and the "manifest," of the "perceived" and the "perceptible," and in the idea that the visible is, so to speak, structured by the language of representation, it is not difficult to identify a clear anticipation of the definition of the classical *épistémè*.[42] One might add that the preface of *The Birth of the Clinic* from the beginning provided the means of a rapprochement between the two understandings of the historical *a priori* (as the interweaving of the visible and the expressible, or as a variable relation between words and things), by explicitly referring the "visible" to things, and the "expressible" to words: moreover, its project was to interrogate this "region where 'things' and 'words' have not yet separated and where, at the most fundamental level of language, seeing and saying are still one" (*BC*, xi), and refer the "alliance" between "seeing and saying" to a relationship established between "words and things" (*BC*, xi). Similarly, *The Order of Things* attempts to comprehend the end of the Renaissance *épistémè* through a description of how this "uniform layer, in which the *seen* and the *read*, the visible and the expressible, were endlessly interwoven, vanished too" (*OT*, 43).[43]

One should note, however, that this possible connection between the two definitions of the historical *a priori* is immediately limited by the quasi-total absence from *The Order of Things* of the concept of perception (which, as we have seen was extensively used in *The Birth of the Clinic*) and by the disappearance of the twinned themes of the "visible" and the "expressible" (with the exception of the passage quoted above). Notwithstanding this change of perspective, the principal problem of the "archaeology of the human sciences" is that it too rests upon a theoretical foundation that, however different it may be from that of *The Birth of the Clinic*, is hardly ever made explicit and is difficult to support. Indeed, and even though Foucault denied it soon afterward, the analysis of the different forms of the historical *a priori* reveals that he still presupposes an ontology in which "words" and "things" would be separate entities, endowed with autonomous modes of existence and capable of engaging in the relations described by the succession of different *épistémès* (identity, then separation and immediate superposition through the power of representation, and finally dispersion). One can find confirmation of this hypothesis in a text contemporary with *The Birth of the Clinic* and *The Order of Things*, where the author analyzes the "void" from which language speaks. This void, explains Foucault in *Raymond Roussel*, is not the "psychological condition" of the work: it is not subjective, and "must not be understood metaphorically" (*OT*, 43; modified). On the contrary, it possesses an *ontological* dimension through which it refers to "the deficiency of words which are less numerous than the things they describe, and owe to this economy the desire to say something. If language was as rich as being, it would be the useless and mute double of things; it would not exist. And yet, without names with which to name them, things would remain in darkness."[44] Words and things, therefore, do possess independent existences (as the first are "less numerous" than the second), language having the role of establishing between these two orders of reality correspondences that can only be partial or fallible (the idea of a fundamental "deficiency"). As *The Order of Things* shows, the condition of possibility of this paradoxical relation is tied to the passage from the classical age to the contemporary historical *a priori*, defined by the new impossibility of representation giving being to thought without residue. This "darkness" in which innumerable things would remain unnamed is not therefore that of nonbeing, but simply that of the unspoken. But even without names, things remain, and the infinite effort of contemporary language is precisely to give them names that the new epistemic configuration condemns in advance to be inadequate.

In *The Archaeology of Knowledge*, Foucault will deny these claims by affirming that the title given to his preceding work was "ironical" (*AK*, 48) and by assigning himself the task of henceforth "not—*or no longer*—treating discourses as groups of signs (signifying elements referring to contents or representations)" (*AK*, 49). The notion of the "object" (insofar as it is constituted by discourse) thus comes to supplant that of the "thing" (as already possessing existence and natural qualities that language would seek to capture). Archaeology should therefore

> substitute for the enigmatic treasure of "things" anterior to discourse the regular formation of objects that emerge only in discourse. To define these *objects* without reference to the *ground, the foundation of things*, but by relating them to the body of rules that enable to form them as objects of a discourse and thus constitute the conditions of their historical appearance. (*AK*, 47–48; modified)

Such a refutation seems to have the implicit role of avoiding the difficulties encountered in *The Order of Things*, through the use of a newly introduced "nominalism"[45] that Foucault will henceforth never cease to claim for his own. Thus, *The Archaeology of Knowledge* proposes to study discourse at the level of the purely discursive, without any referent, to analyze the "discursive practices from which one can define what things are and identify the use of words" (*DE*, 1: 776).[46] The archaeological reduction of the traditional metaphysics formerly presupposed by *The Order of Things* therefore rests on a double postulate. Firstly, the nominalist thesis that it is not through reference to "things" that one defines "words," but through "words" that one can conceive of "objects" produced by discourse. Secondly, the quasi-structuralist claim that since the identification of these "objects" can no longer be achieved through their hypothetical "correspondence" with "things," the only way of understanding their identity is to start from the "set of rules" that allows their formation—that is, by adopting a holistic perspective. These theses will be confirmed in subsequent passages of *The Archaeology of Knowledge*, notably by the idea that the enunciative function puts into play not even "objects," but "a 'referential' that is not made up of 'things,' 'facts,' 'realities' or 'beings,' but laws of possibility, rules of existence for the objects that are named, designated or described within it" (*AK*, 91).

The Preface to *The Order of Things*: An Impossible Third Way

It is therefore probable that this twofold revision of the archaeological method (firstly, to erase "things," then to refer the "objects" themselves to the systems of dispersion to which they belong) is implicitly designed to neutralize the overbearing ontological presuppositions of *The Order of Things*.[47] We shall see later whether *The Archaeology of Knowledge* successfully suggests a more satisfactory version of the historical *a priori*. Before that, I would like to show that the preface to *The Order of Things* itself might have held the possibility of a solution to this problem. Indeed, having stated the problem of order in the Kantian terms examined above, the preface continues without transition with a quite different theme: it is necessary to distinguish, declares Foucault, between the "fundamental codes" of a culture—those which, by governing "its language, its schemas of perception, its exchanges, its techniques, its values, the hierarchy of its practices," establish "from the start" the "empirical orders with which any man will be dealing and within which he will be at home"—and the "scientific theories" or the "philosophical interpretations," which explain "why there is order in general" (*OT*, xx; modified). It is very difficult to know what these "fundamental codes" are, since they are not further clarified. Although the fact that they are given "from the start" suggest that they should be assimilated to the historical *a priori*, the text later clearly indicates that they should be distinguished from it, as the historical *a priori* reappears as a third element in the general configuration they belong to. One could be tempted to read the opposition between these "fundamental codes" and the "scientific theories" as a reactivation of the Husserlian problematic of the *Krisis*, which sought to show how the alleged "objectivity" of the sciences is rooted in the *Lebenswelt*. But the very concept of "code," with its suggested formalism, already seems to reject such an interpretation. It would seem more reasonable to understand these "fundamental codes," these "linguistic, perceptual, practical grids" (*OT*, xx; modified), through the model used by Lévi-Strauss in *The Structural Anthropology*. This model was an attempt to unify the "different features of social life" by reaching "a deep enough level to make it possible to cross from one to the other; or to express the specific structure of each in terms of a sort of universal code [*code universel*], valid for each system separately and for all of them taken together."[48] According to this hypothesis—which cannot be further supported due to a lack of sufficient information in the preface—the difference between the different historical *a priori* and these "fundamental codes" would be due to the historicity of the first as opposed to the unvarying character of the second.

However, what really matters here is that Foucault is postulating the existence of an "intermediary" but "fundamental" domain that, by allowing a "discrepancy" with the "primary" codes, allows a culture to extricate itself from them, that is, not only to discover that other (empirical) orders are possible, but above all to "find itself faced with the stark fact that there are, below the level of its spontaneous orders, things that are in themselves capable of being ordered, that belong to a certain mute order: the fact, in short, that *there is* order" (*OT*, xx; modified). Bearing in mind the homage rendered to Heidegger in Foucault's last interview,[49] it is not absurd to see in these italics, the author's own, an implicit reference to Heidegger's famous *es gibt* (explored notably in the paper *On Time and Being*),[50] through which Being lets itself be thought, beyond any metaphysics, as "presence" and "giving."[51] This allusion is reinforced by the Foucauldian idea of a return to the "mute order" of things, beneath all conscious organizing activity, a return that could analogically evoke the "letting be" through which alone Being can deploy itself within presence.

The following text appears to confirm this interpretation by asserting that this "middle region" is "the most fundamental of all: anterior to words, perceptions and gestures which are taken to express it in more or less happy ways. . . . Thus, in any culture, between the use of what might be called the ordering codes and reflections upon order itself, *there is the naked experience of order and of its modes of being*" (*OT*, xxi; modified, my italics). It appears possible to identify within this dual conception of order an analogue to the ontological difference. For Heidegger, indeed, if one must say that "there is" Being, it is because Being "is" not in the same way as beings. The use of the "there is" shows the nonmetaphysical character of the Heideggerian project,[52] and his refusal to understand Being as "only grounded and interpreted in terms of beings and for beings as their ground."[53] Equally, for Foucault, the possibility of returning to the "brute fact" that "there is" order prior to any empirical experience of it clearly indicates that order should not be confounded with its various modalities, but is in fact presupposed by them. To say that "there is" order is, therefore, to evoke an original ordering from which "empirical"—or "ontic," as Heidegger would say—orders become thinkable.

Moreover, the preface adds that this "experience of order" is "more solid, more archaic, less dubious, *always 'truer'* than the theories that attempt to give those expressions explicit form, exhaustive application or philosophical foundation" (*OT*, xxi; modified, my italics). This "truth" of order can hardly be understood as adequation (for which the conditions would surely be given by the "modes of being" of order). On the contrary, the idea that it is more "archaic" reminds one of what Heidegger calls in his paper "that ancient something which conceals itself in *a-letheia*,"[54] the ontological definition of truth as the unveiling from which alone the ontic conceptions of truth can appear.[55] This interpretation finds further confirmation in a later passage of *The Order of Things*, where Foucault states that "what we must grasp and attempt to reconstitute are the modifications that affected knowledge [*savoir*] itself, at that archaic level which *makes possible both knowledges* [connaissances] *and the mode of being of what there is to know*" (*OT*, 54; modified). To distinguish order from its "modes of beings," and to say that the "naked experience" of order is "always truer" than all others, could therefore be interpreted as an oblique reference to the theme of the ontological difference, itself expressed both by the distinction between being and beings and by that of truth as *aletheia* and *homoiosis*.

Finally, Foucault's project of retracing the history of "the ways our culture has manifested that there is order" (*OT*, xx; modified), of the "modalities of order," seems close enough to what was previously formulated by Heidegger in "The Age of the World Picture."[56] Some clear parallels can be found between the two texts: the initiatory role accorded to Descartes; the equal importance and critique of the theme of representation;[57] the idea that the characteristic trait of modernity is connected to the fact that "man becomes that being upon which all that is, is grounded as regards the manner of its Being and its truth"[58] (and so the primacy of anthropology, as a "theory of man,"[59] over all other forms of reflection); or the insistence on the theme of finitude itself. This latter point was developed by Heidegger at the end of *Kant and the Problem of Metaphysics*, where he declares, apropos the four Kantian questions, that "human reason does not disclose finitude, in these questions; rather its innermost interest is with finitude itself. . . . it is precisely a question of becoming certain of this finitude in order to hold oneself in it."[60] One also notes, which is perhaps not so anodyne, that this understanding is singularly close to those developed in *The Order of Things*; for example:

> At the foundation of all . . . that can indicate itself as a concrete limitation of man's existence, we discover a finitude . . . : the limitation is expressed not as a determination imposed upon man from outside (because he has a nature or history), but as a fundamental finitude which rests on nothing but it's own existence as fact, and opens upon the possibility of all concrete limitation. (*OT*, 315)

But, most important, neither Heidegger nor Foucault is concerned to propose a history of representations of the world simply as chronologically variable contents, a point that *The Archaeology of Knowledge* will indirectly confirm by its forceful rejection of the Hegelian *Weltanschauung*.[61] For Heidegger, the age of representation is only one of the "epochs" in the history of the West, that which began with the Cartesian understanding of truth as certitude and of man as *subjectum*.[62] What must be questioned is the "basis [that] holds complete domination over all the phenomena that distinguish that age,"[63] that is, the implicit comprehension of Being and truth through which each historical epoch opens up the possibility of beings appearing as this or that, or in Foucault's own words, that from which their "mode of being" is determined. From this perspective, the very notion of a "conception" or an "image" (*Bild*), to the extent that it presupposes the possibility of holding the world in front of oneself and making it the object of a representation, shows its historical character and reveals itself as characteristic of modern times. Similarly, although Foucault begins by stating that he is above all seeking that which, within the epistemological order, "makes possible" representations and forms of knowledge (*connaissances*), the preface clearly suggests that this perspective should in fact be subordinated to a more "archaic" research, which alone would make it possible to discover what determines the "mode of being" of the knowable (*OT*, 54). In this sense, the epistemic question of the conditions of possibility of knowledge is subordinated by Foucault to the ontological problem of the way in which things are given, the "there is" of order.

Taking up these Heideggerian themes could have offered Foucault a third path to resolve the dilemma discussed above, according to which order should reside either "in the gaze" of the beholder or "in things." Foucault could have escaped the dilemma of opposing the precritical perspective to a transcendentalism acceptable to Kant but not to him, by displacing the terms of the problem. He could have defined the different orders established by the "gaze" as the *ontic* forms of order, which would then only make sense on the basis of the *ontological* understanding of order as the "there is." Using the ontological difference in this way would thus have allowed him to understand the status of the historical *a priori* more coherently, as an "epoch" of Being, that is, not as a "span of time in occurrence,"[64] but as the historically variable conditions of possibility of a particular understanding of Being. In this way, Heidegger's fundamental ontology could have provided Foucault with the theoretical foundation that was lacking as much from *The Birth of the Clinic* as from *The Order of Things*, without the risk of falling back into the anthropological versions of the transcendental denounced by the *Commentary*. Indeed, Foucault's antihumanism being close to Heidegger's,[65] the latter's claim[66] that the question of Being must be asked from Being itself, bypassing even the existential analytic of *Dasein* established by *Being and Time*, could perhaps have served as a nonsubjective ground for the Foucauldian notion of a "history of order and its modes of being" (in the sense that the question of the "there is" of order clearly is not asked from the subjective point of view of the knowers—this would be dealt with by the history of ideas—but by trying to identify the *épistémè* underlying the empirical configurations of knowledge themselves).

Unfortunately, this attempt at identifying Heideggerian strands in the preface—which would provide Foucault with the ontology he is both presupposing and lacking—falls short for two reasons. The first is that the possibility of identifying order with Being, even analogically, is doubtful: order has a more restricted extension and seems to already presuppose *per se* a certain understanding of Being—that nothing can be unless it is ordered, that is, that "being" means "being ordered." According to Heidegger, this would probably be true from the Roman period on, and especially true at the age of representation; however, it would not pertain to the Greek understanding of being as *physis*, and perhaps not to ours either—since everything for us tends to become standing resource (*Bestand*), entities do not retain enough singularity in the technological age to be orderable qua entities. Therefore, the assimilation of Being to order would at worst be ontic (order would be identified with its various empirical forms, the charting of similarities and analogies specific to the Renaissance, the classifications and tables of the classical age, etc.). At best, it would work at the ontological level, but with the experience of things as orderable only pertaining to certain epochs of the history of Being—therefore, it could not possess the "naked," *a priori* status that Foucault claims for it in the preface.

The second failure of the parallel is that the preface itself presents numerous contradictions. To begin with, it hesitates between two incompatible conceptions of order: the first, objective and spatializing, sees order as a "middle region," a "domain," a "ground," while the second, more subjective, understands it in reference to a hypothetical "experience." But how can order be defined *simultane-ously* as a nonsubjective, self-subsistent configuration and as the experience of a subject whose status is left dubious? Thus we encounter again the problems of *The Birth of the Clinic*. Notwithstanding this internal tension, each of these two conceptions (objective and subjective) is itself irreducible to the Heideggerian perspective. On the one hand, the idea of a "*middle* region," beyond the fact that it seems to give order a substantiality impossible to understand within the frame of fundamental ontology, suffices to prevent any eventual identification of order with Heideggerian Being. For the ontological difference to be respected, such a region could not be intermediary: on the contrary, it would have to be *prior* even to the "fundamental codes" mentioned above, whose ontological condition of possibility it would be. On the other hand, the hypothesis of a subjective order leads Foucault to detect in the coming to light of this problematic "middle region" the result of a "liberation" by which culture "breaks away from the immediate and invisible powers of codes." However, this movement would hinge on a sud-den coming to consciousness the logic of which revives precisely the humanist tradition (notably Hegelian), refuted equally by archaeology and by Heidegger, which would then suggest a contradiction between Foucault's claims and his methodological principles.

Secondly, the preface affirms that this "brute" order is the "*positive* ground" of the "general theories of the ordering of things" (*OT*, xxi; modified), which would once more amount to denying the very possibility of the ontological difference. Following the same logic (or the same absence of it), Foucault assim-ilates the "naked experience of order" to the historical *a priori* itself. Having announced that his study would be devoted to the first (*OT*, xxi), he continues a few lines later, declaring that it concerns "that on the basis of which various forms of knowledge [*connaissances*] and theories were made possible . . . , the his-torical *a priori* on the background of which ideas could appear," which consti-tutes a supplementary negation of the ontological difference (as the different his-torical *a priori* would have to correspond to the "modes of being" of order and not to the "naked" experience that one can have of them). Finally, the rest of *The Order of Things* contradicts the idea, central to the preface, that archaeology should have order as its sole object: indeed the beginning of chapter 7, "The Age of History," describes a "mutation from Order into History" (*OT*, 220) through which it is *History*, and no longer Order, which becomes the "fundamental mode of being of empiricities." This in itself suffices to equally invalidate as a global principle of interpretation the idea of a "history of order" and any general assim-ilation of order to Heideggerian Being:

Just as Order in Classical thought was not the visible harmony of things, or their observed arrangement, regularity or symmetry, but the particular space of their being, that which, prior to all effective knowledge, established them in the field of knowledge [*savoir*], so History, from the XIXth century, defines the birthplace of the empirical, that from which, prior to all established chronology, it derives its own being. (*OT*, 219)

Unfortunately, all these internal tensions rule out the possible solution that the "Heideggerian path" could have offered Foucault. It remains to be seen if he succeeds on his own terms, and whether *The Archaeology of Knowledge*, by referring the historical *a priori* to the level of discourse alone, succeeds in giving it coherence, while avoiding the aporiae specific to the anthropological version of the transcendental theme, now symbolized by man's doubles.

Épistémès and the Historical *a Priori* in *The Archaeology of Knowledge*: A "Happy Positivism"?

By Foucault's own admittance, *The Archaeology of Knowledge* is the only text in which he forces himself to formulate and give a foundation to the method used "blindly" in the preceding works.[67] One might, therefore, justifiably expect this archaeological "discourse of method" to coherently define the concepts of the *épistémè* and the historical *a priori*. But curiously, these themes, which lay at the very center of *The Birth of the Clinic* and *The Order of Things*, are introduced very late in the 1969 text,[68] which begins with a new term, the "discursive formation." Moreover, while Foucault employed them in an interchangeable manner in *The Order of Things*, the historical *a priori* and the *épistémès* are defined separately in *The Archaeology of Knowledge*, but without the relationship between the two being clearly articulated. Equally, although the notion of the "statement" (*énoncé*), Foucault's principal innovation in this text, intervenes in the redefinition of the historical *a priori*, it is totally absent from the description of the *épistémè*. Finally, the author adds a new one to his two old concepts—the "archive," which he does connect to the historical *a priori*, but not to the *épistémè*. Should we still understand these last two notions as being identical? If not, what are their meanings, are they complementary or redundant? And what is the benefit of the introduction of the two new terms—the "discursive formation" and the "archive"?

The well-known definition of the *épistémè* given by *The Archaeology of Knowledge* barely seems to relate to the versions previously given in *The Birth of the Clinic* and *The Order of Things*, since it introduces new concepts (discursive "practices" and "formations," "thresholds") and appears to be much more technical:

By *épistémè* we mean, in fact, the *total set of relations* that can unite, at a given period, the discursive practices that give rise to epistemological figures, sciences and possibly to formalized systems: the *mode* in which, in each of these discursive formations, the transitions to epistemologization, scientificity, and formalization are situated and operate; the *distributions of these thresholds* . . . in time; the *lateral relations* that may exist between epistemological figures or sciences in so far as they belong to neighbouring but distinct discursive practices. (*AK*, 191; modified, my italics)

This definition is both more precise and more restrictive than those of *The Order of Things*. The *épistémè* no longer has the function of accounting for the "thought" of an epoch in general, but is inscribed within a rigid network of concepts that aim at distinguishing archaeology from the history of the sciences. To the extent that it unites "practices" which themselves "give rise" to "epistemological figures," the *épistémè* seems to occupy the superior position in a two-tiered system having the function of thinking the status and transformations of "knowledge" (*savoir*).[69] The inferior level of this system is constituted by the analyses of "discursive formations," the empirical units that can be isolated by identifying the systems by which their "objects"—"enunciative modalities," "concepts," and "strategies"—are formed.[70]

The aim of such a mapping is to establish the unity of archaeological objects without having to take as points of departure the "wild" units analyzed in the preceding works,[71] while maintaining the project of vertically referring empirical positivities to their conditions of possibility. Indeed, the movement of analysis is the same in each of the four cases considered: Foucault begins by wondering whether the constituted contents (the "invariants" allegedly identified by discourse, the "author," specific "concepts," or "themes") are what one could use to ground the unity of a discipline; and he concludes by emphasizing the necessity of returning to the "interplay of the rules that make possible the appearance of objects during a given period of time" (*AK*, 33).[72] He thus defines the discursive formation as that which one "deals with" each time that one can identify "rules of formation," which are the "conditions to which the elements of this distribution (objects, modes of statement, concepts, thematic choices) are subjected" (*AK*, 38). It is logical, therefore, to conclude that the *épistémè* is meant to allow us to understand, at a higher level, the relations between the different "discursive practices" themselves, since they are the starting point from which the "epistemological figures, sciences and possibly formalized systems" (*AK*, 191) are formed—all of the latter being (of same order as the "thresholds")[73] the different forms taken by discursive formations in the course of their transformations.

But the second characteristic of the *épistémè* disturbs this picture by presenting the *épistémè*, in reference to the theory of thresholds, as the "mode in which, *in each of these discursive formations*, the transitions to epistemologization . . . operate" (*AK*, 191; modified, my italics). But this contradicts the previous definition in two ways. Firstly, the *épistémè* no longer appears as the space whose relative exteriority allowed discursive practices to be discretely interconnected.[74] It is now understood "in each of the discursive formations" as a "mode of trans-formation" (*AK*, 191; modified). But how can the *épistémè* be at once *exterior* to several discursive formations (as the "field" in which they can be articulated), and *interior* to only one of these formations? Moreover, how can it be both a (syn-chronic) *space* of relations and a (diachronic) *mode* of transformation? In the first case, it appears as a principle of order that would allow us to understand the dis-tribution of different discursive formations, and therefore to somehow organize the epistemological profile of a given period (as Foucault did for the classical age in *The Order of Things* by connecting the analysis of wealth, natural history, and general grammar). In the second, the *épistémè* is incompatibly presented as a prin-ciple of evolution that would account, by means of the theory of thresholds, for the internal future specific to each of these discursive formations. The third of the characteristics of the *épistémè* does not clarify much, as it defines it as the "distribution of these thresholds . . . in time," alluding to the possibility that a discursive formation may reach the four thresholds, either successively or simul-taneously (as was the case, for example, in mathematics). The *épistémè* now receives the task of accounting for the fate of discursive formations, which is con-sistent with the idea that it is a "mode of transformation" but not with its definition as a "space." Far from moving beyond the structuralist perspective, therefore, Foucault seems to have internalized the tensions specific to the oppo-sition between structure and history without resolving them successfully.

Moreover, the second characteristic of the *épistémè* no longer refers to the *prac-tices* (see *AK*, 191; modified) but to the discursive *formations* themselves, which blurs the distinction between the two levels mentioned above (the discursive prac-tices from which the "epistemological figures" stem, and the relationships between them that defined the *épistémè*), as we just saw that discursive forma-tions are not themselves rules, but, rather, the units that can be defined from the rules as "systems of formation." This confusion is repeated in relation to the fourth characteristic of the *épistémè*, now seen as the "lateral relations" that can exist between "epistemological figures or sciences," which refer to "distinct dis-cursive practices"; that is, as relations between elements formed by the practices and no longer in play between the practices themselves. This unhappy ambiva-lence can be found again in a more generalized form in the global definition of the discursive formation as "what one deals with" when one can isolate "a system of formation."[75] But in other places the discursive formation is itself assimilated to this system; for example, when Foucault states that "systems of formations are no strangers to time" and analyzes the diverse "systems of rules"[76] of which they are composed, concluding without transition that a "discursive formation, then, does not play the role of a figure that arrests time . . . but determines a regularity proper to temporal processes" (*AK*, 74). So the discursive formation is identified both with the system and the empirical figures that are supposedly "ruled" by it, while the *épistémè* is defined as the bringing together of either the rules of formation or the contents formed from these rules. Because the different Foucauldian definitions of the *épistémè* repeatedly confuse the different levels of the archaeological system in the very attempt to distinguish between them, they appear to analogically reproduce the structure of confusion between the conditioning and the conditioned that was identified by the *Commentary* as lying within the empirico-transcendental double.

Given these first aporiae, we must turn to the new version of the historical *a priori* in order to understand the conditions of the possibility of knowledge. Foucault proposes the following definition:

> What I mean by the term is an *a priori* that is not a condition of validity for judgments,[77] but a condition of reality for statements. It is not a question of rediscovering what might legitimize an assertion, but of identifying the conditions of emergence of statements, the *law of their coexistence with others*, the *specific form of their mode of being*, the principles according to which they survive, are transformed, and disappear. (*AK*, 127; modified, my italics)[78]

To know the nature of the historical *a priori*, it is therefore necessary to begin with a new concept—the statement (*énoncé*). This, declares Foucault, can be understood from the "enunciative function," which defines the general conditions that a group of signs must satisfy in order to be considered as a statement. There are four of these conditions. Firstly, the group of signs should involve a "correlate," which is neither a "referent" nor an "object" constituted by the discourse, but the law that allows the thinking of the distribution of possible objects. Secondly, it should define a certain number of possible positions for the subject in which the statement originates. Thirdly, it should refer to an "associated field" constituted by other statements that coexist with, and are taken up by or made possible by, the statement under consideration. Finally, the statement should be endowed with a certain "materiality" that permits it to be inserted within an institutional framework and to be made the object of strategies of appropriation.[79] Thus only a group of signs that puts into play a "correlate," an "author function," an "associated field," and a "materiality" can be a statement.

One could object that Foucault alternatively defines the statement either as the function itself[80] or as the element that it allows us to identify,[81] succumbing again to the confusion specific to the empirico-transcendental double. But even if we were to accept his claim at face value, Foucault would still remain confronted with a major difficulty, in that the concept of the enunciative function, taken *per se*, does not permit him to differentiate between statements or to say which will be recognized historically as candidates to truthfulness. Although, as an instrument of analysis, it allows Foucault to define the structure common to all statements, the enunciative function is not in itself the criterion by which the selection that presides over the production, and therefore the "rarity" (*AK*, 118) of statements could be explained. This is why Foucault needs the historical *a priori* and introduces it, very coherently, not as the enunciative function itself, but as its "*conditions of exercise,*" or as the "*condition of reality* of statements" (both *AK*, 127; my italics)—which amounts to the same thing. Among the vast collection of possibilities offered by logic and grammar, the historical *a priori* has the function of circumscribing a more restricted domain by defining the conditions of possibility of statements in their character as "things *actually said*" (*AK*, 127; my italics).[82] It is defined, therefore, as a principle of selection at work in the discursive field (a first hint of the theme of exclusion that will be developed a slightly later in *The Order of Discourse*), a principle which, "[by grasping] discourses in the law of their effective realisation, must be able to account for the fact that a discourse, at a given moment, may accept . . . or on the contrary exclude . . . this or that formal structure" (*AK*, 128; modified).

Although this programmatic reference to the function of the *a priori* is hardly explicit, one can nonetheless define *a contrario* its nature from the way in which Foucault contrasts it with another *a priori*, the "formal *a priori* whose jurisdiction extends without contingence" (*AK*, 128), and in which we can recognize, although it is not explicitly mentioned,[83] the "universal historical *a priori* of history" established by Husserl in *The Origin of Geometry*.[84] This text attempts to demonstrate how it is possible, despite the sedimentations of language's historicity and tradition, to recover, by means of an "activity of free variation,"[85] the "primal self-evidences" intuited by the "proto-founder" of geometry. The concept of the historical *a priori* allows Husserl to thematize both the suprahistorical permanence of these "self-evidences" and the possibility of their recovery. However, in his thinking the idea has a meaning radically opposed to that which Foucault gives it.

Firstly, the Husserlian *a priori* has the status of a "strictly unconditioned and truly apodictic self-evidence extending beyond all historical facticities,"[86] and is therefore defined in the Kantian tradition as "universal." Secondly, being "universal and also fixed," it is "always originally genuine,"[87] and therefore presupposes for its recovery exactly the "sort of historical phenomenology" that "treats archaeology as a search for the origin [*archē*], for formal *a priori*, for founding acts" (*AK*, 203), which Foucault vigorously rejects. Further, for the reasons which have just been mentioned, the Husserlian *a priori* is not truly historical: on the contrary, Husserl's idea is that it is universal historicity itself which possesses an "essential structure"[88] that the phenomenological method will bring to light.[89] Finally, the most profound justification for the Foucauldian critique stems from the fact that the Husserlian *a priori* is, as its name indicates, "formal," and for Foucault, the real historical *a priori* should not be understood as an "*a*temporal structure," on the contrary, it is a "purely empirical figure" (*AK*, 128), not "imposed from the outside" on the elements that it relates together, but "caught up in the very things it connects," as a "transformable group [of rules]" (*AK*, 127). In the preceding passage, Foucault referred it to the "positivities" that "play the role of a historical *a priori*" (*AK*, 128; modified). Since one of the essential postulates of *The Archaeology of Knowledge* is that it is possible to analyze statements at their own level, without involving any other relations than the "discursive,"[90] it is most probable that, contrary to Husserl, Foucault is not committing himself to any transcendentalist claims and simply intends his "historical *a priori*" to indicate and underline the possibility of studying discourses in an autonomous way, through their "own type of historicity" (*AK*, 165).

One might think, therefore, that as a reaction against the confused phenomenology of *The Birth of the Clinic* and the hidden metaphysics of *The Order of Things*, Foucault has deliberately taken the side of the "happy positivism" of which he twice boasted, and now understands the historical *a priori* as a purely empirical figure. However, a more profound examination makes one wonder whether this positivism is really as "happy" as its author hoped. Indeed, although it is now understood as "positive" and its "*a priori*" aspect only serves to mark the autonomy of the discursive, the historical *a priori*, as the "rule" and "principle" that allows us to account for the "reality" of statements, must nonetheless involve a specific kind of determination, which must be distinct from causal determination—as otherwise the very possibility of archaeology as the study of statements at their own level would vanish. But what could be the nature of such a determination? This problem has already been broached by Hubert Dreyfus and Paul Rabinow in relation to the status of the "rules" specific to the discursive. As they clearly showed, the question is whether the rules analyzed by Foucault are "descriptive, so that we should say merely that people act *according to* them, or [whether] they are meant to be efficacious, so that we can say that people actually *follow* them" (*MF*, 81). In order to be coherent, the archaeological perspective should only require the rules to be descriptive, as they are never directly accessible to the consciousness of the subjects who supposedly model their discourse on them.[91] However, the analysis reveals that they are prescriptive, and "operate on the phenomena" (*MF*, 81). In seeking to give the rules a causal power, Foucault widely exceeds the limits of the "modest empiricism" (*MF*, 84), which he claims for himself. Because archaeology "identifies the rules at the same time with *discursive regularities* and *prescriptive working principles*" (*MF*, 84; modified, italics), it once again repeats the empirico-transcendental confusion that assimilated empirical contents to their own conditions of possibility. This circularity is clearly identified in Dreyfus and Rabinow's conclusion, which shows that Foucault "must locate the productive power revealed by discursive practices in the regularity of the same practices. The result is the strange notion of regularities which regulate themselves" (*MF*, 84).

One finds another version of the anthropological doubles in the Foucauldian definition of the historical *a priori* as the "set of rules that characterise a discursive formation." Indeed, the only definition of the "discursive practice" which is given in *The Archaeology of Knowledge* is the following: "the set of anonymous, historical rules, always determined in the time and space, that define at a given period, and for a given social, economic, geographical, or linguistic area, the conditions of operation of the enunciative function" (*AK*, 117; modified). However, if one recalls that Foucault has equally defined the historical *a priori* as the "conditions of reality for statements," one obtains, by a simple game of substitution, the thesis according to which the "conditions of reality for statements" are "a set of anonymous, historical rules that define . . . the conditions of operation of the enunciative function." But this is a no-win situation: either the definition is tautological, and takes a rather convoluted path only to end up by characterizing— if not, as Molière said, opium by its dormitive virtues—at least the conditions for the exercise of the enunciative function by themselves (since they are precisely, as the historical *a priori*, the conditions for the reality of statements); or the definition is not tautological, but then generates a regression in the order of conditions of possibility, since one could only account for the conditions for the exercise of the enunciative function by means of an "set of rules" which itself would require another "set of rules" identical to the first,[92] in which case archaeology would never have the possibility of ever encountering its object. From this perspective, and although—despite its etymology—it absolutely denies being a quest for origins, archaeology seems well set on the path that consists in trying to account for the conditions of possibility of knowledge by means of other conditions of possibility—which would analogically repeat the movement of the "retreat" of the origin identified in *The Order of Things* in relation to the third of man's doubles.

One might have hoped to find a solution to these difficulties in the Foucauldian definition of the archive. Unfortunately, a quick analysis shows that it only amplifies them. Indeed, the archive is neither a particular set of contents nor an institution, but "the law of what can be said, the system that governs the appearance of statements as singular events. . . . It reveals the rules of a practice that enables statements both to survive and to undergo regular modifications. It is *the general system of the formation and transformation of statements*" (*AK*, 129–30; modified). This definition strikingly resembles that of the historical *a priori*: the archive is described in the same terms[93] and seems to serve the same function (to define the conditions for the exercise of the enunciative function, i.e., the "general system of the formation and the transformation of statements"). One might therefore think that it would have been more coherent for Foucault to assimilate the historical *a priori* and the archive. But this is not the solution that he chooses, stating that the archive refers to the "domain of statements thus articulated in accordance with historical *a priori*" (*AK*, 128). But nothing in the definition of the historical *a priori* suggested that there could be, for the same epoch and for the same domain, *several a priori!* On the contrary, Foucault always mentioned it in the singular and gave it an architectonic function. Moreover, even if one were to grant this revision (although it is not argued for) by accepting the archive as a sort of historical meta–*a priori*, one would have to conclude that *The Archaeology of Knowledge* operates a system of *three* (no longer two) levels: at the lowest, the discursive formations and the *épistémès* (which, as we saw, are impossible to articulate coherently), defining the conditions of the possibility of knowledge; then, the historical *a priori*, which would allow the more general understanding of the conditions of the enunciative function; and at the highest level, the archive, which would articulate the historical *a priori* within a still more general "system." But it is clear that beyond the internal contradictions analyzed above, this progression complicates the archaeological structure even more by making the conditions of possibility of knowledge retreat another step, and therefore seems to repeat in an even stronger form the "retreat of the origin" that was just mentioned.[94]

Although the so-called archaeological period is generally governed by the question of the conditions of the possibility of knowledge, it is thus possible to distinguish two distinct moments within it. In *The Birth of the Clinic* and *The Order of Things*, Foucault offers a first answer to the critical question by means of the concept of the historical *a priori*, which he assimilates in the second of these texts to that of the *épistémè*. He then gives the notion a strong definition, conceiving it as a variable structure from which the objects of knowledge are epistemologically determined and organized into more or less formal theoretical bodies. As this approach reveals itself to be incapable of justifying the various philosophical presuppositions on which it rests, *The Archaeology of Knowledge* attempts to give archaeology a new and autonomous theoretical foundation by understanding it as a pure description of statements. Foucault is thus led to considerably weaken the meaning of a historical *a priori*, which is thereafter distinguished from the *épistémès* and assimilated to a purely empirical figure. However, despite Foucault's methodological efforts, neither does *The Archaeology of Knowledge* succeed in giving a coherent response to the question of the conditions of the possibility of knowledge. The new concepts that it introduces (the "discursive formation" and the "archive"), besides being often incoherently defined, shed no light on their predecessors. In fact, one occasionally feels that archaeology would have gained in coherence if Foucault had been able to dispense with any reference to the historical *a priori* and the *épistémè*[95]—thus avoiding the regression of the conditions of possibility mentioned above—and wonders if he only took up his former concepts because he was concerned to give his work an internal coherence, which, bearing in mind the variations in definition studied above, still remains largely formal.

It is plausible that these are the reasons that implicitly motivated Foucault's abandon of the historical *a priori*.[96] Significantly, one of the few mentions of the *épistémè*[97] that can be found during 1970–76 has the explicit aim of rejecting any obedience to Kant, and clearly describes the *épistémè* as an empirical figure:

> When I speak of an *épistémè*, I mean all the relationships that have existed at a given time between the different domains of science. . . . It is all these phenomena of relations between the sciences or the different discourses within the different scientific discourses which constitute what I call the *épistémè* of an age. Therefore, for me the *épistémè* has nothing to do with the Kantian categories. (*DE*, 2: 371)

Foucault will henceforth give himself the clear task of disentangling his thought from the transcendental theme, with an insistence in which one might read the implicit denial of his preceding positions:

> In all my work, on the contrary, I have been fighting to avoid any reference to this transcendental as a condition of possibility of whatever knowledge [*savoir*] there is. . . . My way of proceeding now is more regressive: I try to assume a growing detachment so that I can *define the historical conditions and the transformations of our knowledge* [savoir]. (*DE*, 2: 371)

The initial question of the conditions of the possibility of knowledge is therefore at once reaffirmed and reformulated in empirical terms ("historical conditions and transformations"). Similarly, the writing of *Discipline and Punish*, the first "postarchaeological" work,[98] seems animated by an identical desire to ground the study of prisons on a purely empirical base, and thus to give a "happier" version of the impossible positivism of *The Archaeology of Knowledge*. It is this new response to the critical question, as well as the genealogical turn on which it rests, that I shall examine next.

PART II

The Reopening of the Critical Question: Genealogical Solutions and Difficulties

THREE

The Reformulation of the Archaeological Problem and the Genealogical Turn

Although it produces—through horror—an effect of estrangement similar to that of the Chinese encyclopedia of Borges which *The Order of Things* opened with, the description of the execution of Damiens in the Place de Grève in chapter 1 of *Discipline and Punish* hardly seems to respond to the same theoretical preoccupations. Where previously the focus was on knowledge and its conditions of possibility, now the body and the material transformations of which it has historically been the object is the issue. The concept of the historical *a priori* is totally eclipsed, that of the *épistémè* is only mentioned once (*DP*, 305), while a whole set of new ideas comes to the front—those of "discipline," "strategy," "technology," not to mention "power"—the most obvious of Foucault's additions to his previous work. The only "archaeological" concept that remains central is that of "knowledge" (*savoir*), but without the clear certainty that it keeps its previous meaning, as it is not further defined in *Discipline and Punish*. As for archaeology itself, whose procedures and aims Foucault had taken such care to define, it is mentioned neither in *Discipline and Punish* nor even in *The Order of Discourse*, a text published only one year after *The Archaeology of Knowledge*, in which Foucault prefers to speak of a "'critical' set" (*OD*, 70; modified) (this Kantian formulation clearly not being accidental) to define the previously employed method.

These substitutions within the conceptual order correspond to a global modification of the theoretical horizon within which Foucault's analyses are inscribed. The epistemological configuration formed by the history of the sciences, the history of ideas, and the structural or linguistic studies in relation to which *The Archaeology of Knowledge* had sought to locate itself, tends to disappear. Foucault's new interlocutors are legal theorists,[1] Marxists in general (and in particular Althusser),[2] and even "para-Marxists" (*PK*, 58) like Marcuse and Reich,[3] all of whom, although they make an eclectic collection, share a questioning of politics rather than of the nature or the conditions of the possibility of knowledge. Although archaeology was overtly placed under the auspices of Kant, it is toward Nietzsche that Foucault now polemically turns, by asking how one can "take Nietzsche seriously," and again, "what serious use" (*PPC*, 31) one can make of him—not to mention that "genealogy of Modern morality,"[4] *Discipline and Punish*. Foucault does not forget Kant, but, symbolically enough, after 1970 it is no longer the author of *The Critique of Pure Reason* that interests him, but that of "What Is Enlightenment?"[5] If the latter appears worthy of interest, it is because he was the first philosopher to "problematise his own discursive contemporaneity [*actualité*]" (*PPC*, 88)[6] by asking the question of the meaning and the political implications of the then present *Aufklärung*. The first critical question, that of the conditions of possibility of knowledge, is therefore doubled by "another critical question," which polemically displaces the epistemological interrogation of the conditions of possibility of true knowledge toward a reflection on the coextensive relationship between truth and power:

> Criticism is the movement by which the subject gives itself the right to question truth about its effects of power and power about its discourses of truth. . . . Criticism essentially has the function of freeing the subject in the context of what one could call, in a word, the politics of truth. This definition, . . . I have the presumption to think, is not very different from that which Kant gave: not of criticism but of the *Aufklärung*.[7]

Foucault still agrees that the "prolegomenon of any *Aufklärung* present or future" is to "know knowledge,"[8] and therefore reasserts the Kantian primacy of the first critical question over this "critical attitude" that allegedly marked the threshold of modernity by inaugurating the philosophical questioning of actuality, which Foucault's famous "history of the present" echoes (*DP*, 31).[9] However, the direction of this shift is clear: an authentically critical thought cannot be satisfied with the interrogation of truth's *a priori* conditions of possibility. It can only grasp the real nature of truth through a historical questioning of the relations between truth and power, as well as of the real effects that it produces on those that say it or are forced to say it. A questioning which, to the extent to which it has a "de-sub-jugating" direction, reveals a new ethical and political dimension.

Such a revision raises many questions. To begin with, how can we justify the central place newly attributed to the concept of truth in his work by Foucault himself, as he affirms that his "problem has always been the question of truth, of telling the truth, the *wahr-sagen*—what it is to tell the truth" (*PPC*, 33)? He adds in another passage, "I would say that this has always been my problem: the effects of power and the production of 'truth'" (*PPC*, 118). But beyond the fact that there is little concern with power in archaeology, the notion of truth hardly plays a notable role in it, being only rarely mentioned and never defined. The first text to give the concept a place of importance is *The Order of Discourse*, where the new theme of the "will to truth" nonetheless only figures as one of the "pro-cedures of exclusion" at work in discourse (the third). Given this, is it possible to confer anything other than a "lightly fictitious" (*PPC*, 118) coherence on the Foucauldian project? Unless truth can be shown to be effectively central from the texts of the archaeological period onward, the later idea of a "history of truth" (*UP*, 6) will be threatened, and with it the thematic unity of Foucault's work. Such a demonstration, if it is possible, must answer the following questions: If truth really was, implicitly, a fundamental concept of archaeology, what, given Foucault's bracketing of any normative perspective, was its meaning and func-tion? What is its connection to the openly central notions of the historical *a pri-ori* and the *épistémè*? And what was Foucault's understanding of truth at that time, since he never clearly defined it?

From being the focus of these questions, the idea of an "archaeological" pres-ence of truth also leads to others. From the 1970s onward Foucauldian thought experiences considerable modifications that affect its operative concepts as much as its theoretical horizon. If our uncovering of the underlying theme of truth suggests that there is no real break within it, it also makes it more imperative for us to identify the precise points on which the transformations are carried out, and to wonder whether the initial project—the questioning of the condi-tions of possibility of knowledge—is really maintained. Two answers could immediately appear plausible: either Foucault had implicitly admitted the methodological impasse of *The Archaeology of Knowledge*, and consequently turned his attention away from the discursive and its autonomous rules to inter-rogate nondiscursive practices; or the reference to Nietzsche is sufficient in itself to mark the difference between archaeology and genealogy. But these two expla-nations, for all their simplicity, are controversial. Firstly, the concept of "practice" was meant, as early as *The Birth of the Clinic*,[10] precisely to overcome the opposition between the discursive and the nondiscursive. Rather than strictly distinguishing between the two levels, it is more important for Foucault to define the manner in which the practices, discursive or not, crystallize the relations of power, and involve truth effects. As the following text explains—in which the "institutional" refers to "all the non discursive social," that is, precisely, to a set of practices:

> It doesn't much matter for my notion of the apparatus to be able to say that this is discursive and that isn't. If you take Gabriel's architectural plan for the Military School together with the actual construction of the school, how is one to say what is discursive and what institutional? That would only interest me if the building didn't conform with the plan. But I don't think it's very important to be able to make that distinction, given that my problem isn't a linguistic one. (*PK*, 198)

Secondly, it is in no way evident that the reference to Nietzschean thought alone accounts for the transformations of the Foucauldian project. Indeed, Nietzsche plays a privileged role and enjoys a double status in the *whole* of Foucault's work: as a model or emblem, he was present from the *Commentary*, which ended with a reflection on the overman. Equally, *The Order of Things* gave him an important position, notably by seeing in the announcement by the madman of the death of God the anticipation of that of "man." But Nietzsche is more than a privileged example, and the archaeology is not content merely to pay him homage. It is worked through with Nietzschean themes: "My archaeology owes more to Nietzschean genealogy than to structuralism,"[11] Foucault laconically declared to Raymond Bellour in 1967. The archaeological "debt" is essentially concentrated in two points: firstly, as he stated repeatedly (*DE*, 1: 675),[12] it is under Nietzsche's aegis that Foucault placed the critique of founding subjectivity and the themes affiliated to it (such as that of the author or of the phenomenological subject). Secondly, archaeology sometimes adopted a strategy which is analogically reminiscent of the Nietzschean critique of logical categories,[13] notably when it sought to "remove the privilege indefinitely reconnected to the cause" (*DE*, 1: 684), while replacing it with a multiple and variable "play of dependencies," or again when it proposed to "replace the great mythology of change and evolution with a serious description of types of events . . . and of the establishment of series."[14] Foucault's critique is certainly less radical and perhaps less profound than that of Nietzsche, in the sense that it is more restricted: but if it contests these "grand categories," it is in a similar way, notably by rejecting the idea of an explicative synthetic principle, unifying and totalizing through its very indetermination.

Other traces could doubtless be found—for example by comparing the nominalism of *The Archaeology of Knowledge* with the Nietzschean critique of language.[15] However, this already suffices to show that the reference to Nietzsche alone cannot work as a differentiating principle between the early and the later periods of Foucault's work.

How, then, can the transition from archaeology to genealogy be understood? *The Order of Discourse* shows that this Foucauldian "turn" is due to the importation of a specific Nietzschean concept, the "will to truth," which forms the background to *Discipline and Punish* and reveals itself as central to *The History of Sexuality*. This import is essential for two reasons. Firstly, it gives the critical question a new dimension by showing the impossibility of defining the conditions of possibility of knowledge on a purely epistemological level. If all knowledge arises constitutively from a will to truth, which therefore shapes it from the beginning, it becomes impossible to account for it by means of the historical *a priori* or by *épistémès*, since all these previously examined concepts presupposed the possibility of studying knowledge in relative autonomy, and at its own level. On the contrary, the only legitimate option will now be to genealogically question the type of will to truth that animates it. Secondly, the idea of a will to truth leads Foucault to develop the question of the conditions of possibility of truth from the viewpoint of a new reflection on the relationship between knowledge and power. Far from putting them in a relationship of exteriority (the search for knowledge being independent of power, and therefore able to exercise a critical function),[16] or of instrumentality (following the adage of Bacon, for whom "human knowledge and human power meet in one"),[17] Foucault seeks to show that knowledge and power have a common genesis, which ties one to the other structurally and co-originally determines the forms that knowledge can take: "In short, it is not the activity of the subject of knowledge that produces a corpus of knowledge, useful or resistant to power, but power-knowledge, the processes and struggles that traverse it and of which it is made up, that determines the forms and possible domains of knowledge" (*DP*, 28).

Henceforth, to respond to the question of the conditions of possibility of knowledge will involve, not only an archaeology of knowledge, but also the genealogy of this "power-knowledge nexus,"[18] which remains to be defined. But what will the consequences for the critical question be? Is it necessary to totally renounce the archaeological perspective and affirm that the conditions of possibility of knowledge are identical with those of its empirical genesis? Or should one take up the idea that the *épistémès* define a set of relatively autonomous rules for knowledge, while bearing in mind, however, the necessity (born of genealogy's discoveries) of questioning the relationship of these rules to power-knowledge? Or should we, more radically, reexamine the concept of the *épistémè* itself, in order to *structurally* account for the mutual engendering of knowledge and power? But if this last hypothesis is right, how can the contradiction be avoided that would make power-knowledge the condition of possibility of knowledge, so providing, by superimposing the conditioning and the conditioned, a new version of the anthropological form of the transcendental theme?

More generally, the extent and nature of Foucault's borrowing from Nietzsche needs to be questioned. What is meant by this "will to truth"? Should the concept be understood in a strictly Nietzschean sense—an approach that would appear disqualified from the start by the absence of any reference to the will to power in *The Order of Discourse*? And if not, in what way(s) does Foucault make the "serious use" of Nietzsche that he recommends? Correlatively, what understandings of knowledge and truth does the hypothesis of the will to truth involve? And how does it differ from that previously given or presupposed by archaeology? Indeed, if Foucault now and then analyzes the *function* of truth, he defines it *per se* only very rarely.[19] The fact that he has a hermeneutic conception of it is implied by the very concept of genealogy, but if truth is an interpretation, should we understand it, in a Nietzschean sense, as a vital error? And, if not, how? Finally, how precisely should the articulation of knowledge and power be defined? Should we give it a purely local and empirical extension? Or should we see it as an archetypal model—in which the "return of the transcendental" so feared by Foucault would loom dangerously?

However, before trying to respond to these questions, it is necessary to raise a preliminary objection. Is it so certain that the critical question conserves the preeminence during the genealogical period that it is granted here? Wouldn't it be more correct to say that Foucault leaves it aside in order to develop an autonomous reflection on power, its "technologies," the manner in which it subjugates "souls" (*DP*, 23) by controlling bodies? This is a hypothesis that could find partial confirmation in the central place given by *Discipline and Punish* to the notion of "discipline," as well as in the multiplicity of texts devoted by Foucault to defining his notion of power by opposing it to the so-called "juridico-repressive"[20] conceptions. Foucault himself said,

> Thus, I am far from being a theoretician of power. That the limit, I would say that power, as an autonomous question, does not interest me. In many instances, I have been led to address the question of power only to the extent that the political analyses of power which was offered did not seem to me to account for the finer, more detailed phenomena I wish to evoke when I pose the question of telling the truth about oneself. (*PPC*, 39)[21]

In other words, it is only because he discovered that the question of truth led *per se* to a reflection on power that Foucault sought to give this concept an adequate definition. This assertion finds confirmation elsewhere in the way in which Foucault presents his affiliation to Nietzsche, whom he declares he read from the perspective of an "inquiry into the history of knowledge—the history of reason."[22] If Nietzsche is important, it is because he is the first to have posed "the problem" of "*the value given to truth*, which placed us under its absolute control" (*PPC*, 106–7; modified, my italics). More generally and finally, a reference to truth is what allows the author to justify the philosophical character of his project: "If someone wanted to be a philosopher but didn't ask himself the question, 'what is knowledge?', or, 'what is truth?', in what sense could one say he was a philosopher? *And for all that I may like to say I'm not a philosopher, nonetheless if my concern is with truth then I am still a philosopher*" (*PK*, 66; my italics).

"Being in the Truth" and "Speaking the Truth": "Acceptability"[23] and Predication of Truth in *The Order of Discourse*

The first text written by Foucault after *The Archaeology of Knowledge*, *The Order of Discourse*, marks both a rupture and a transition in relation to the preceding works. A rupture, because symbolically the very word *archaeology* does not appear in it, and because Foucault's angle of approach becomes more incisive and polemical—the neutral analysis of the "rules" supposed to govern the discursive gives way to an interrogation of the forms of "control" to which discourses are submitted. A transition, because among the "internal procedures" through which "discourses themselves exercise their own control" (*OD*, 56), the new notion of "discipline," in reference to which Foucault introduces the theme of truth, implicitly returns to the old archaeological definition of the discursive formation:[24] "A discipline is defined by a domain of objects, a set of methods, a corpus of propositions *considered to be true*, a set of rules and definitions, of techniques and of instruments: all this constitutes a sort of *anonymous system*" (*OD*, 59; modified, my italics). Whatever the understanding of truth proposed by Foucault is, its extension will therefore be limited to a certain type of proposition: those which obey the criteria by which disciplines are defined. It does not follow, however, that belonging to a discipline will itself be a sufficient guarantee of truth: Foucault's presupposition here is that one can only predicate truth from inside a discipline. For the time being, Foucault does not propose a general reflection on truth, but only a restricted paradigm applying to propositions that aim at scientificity and can be defined and ordered using the theory of "thresholds" laid out in *The Archaeology of Knowledge*.

It is in relation to the "discipline" that Foucault, in a well-known passage, exposes his conception of truth for the first time:

> A discipline is not the sum of all that can be truthfully said about something; it is not even the sum of all that can be accepted about the same data in virtue of some principle of coherence or systematicity. . . . For a proposition to belong to botany or pathology, it has to fulfil certain conditions, *in a sense stricter and more complex than pure and simple truth; but in any case, other conditions.*
> (*OD*, 59; my italics)

A discipline, therefore, is not an accumulation of contents, a "sum"—a now familiar theme. One should note immediately, however, that Foucault implicitly invokes an "objective" conception of truth ("that which can be said truthfully," "simple truth"), which supposes the possibility of an absolutely normative judgment that would establish the scientific validity of the proposition considered. This conception is also presupposed by the following interrogation: "People have often wondered how the botanists or biologists of the nineteenth century managed not to see that what Mendel was saying was true. . . . Mendel spoke the truth" (*OD*, 60). Foucault does not ask *if* Mendel was right or if he will *always* be right. He begins with the principle that Mendel said the truth (objectively), and then inquires about the historical conditions that meant that this truth could not be "seen." Moreover, by suggesting a little further on that one can always "speak the truth in the space of a wild exteriority" (*OD*, 61)—that is, whatever the conditions in which one speaks it and whatever the identity or status of the speaker—Foucault himself implicitly acknowledges that one can define truth objectively, at least in the scientific domain. This possibility will be indirectly confirmed two years later by means of the distinction between "two histories of the truth," of which the first is "a sort of internal history of the truth, of a truth which corrects itself through its own regulative principles: this is the history of truth such as it makes itself through the history of the sciences" (*DE*, 1: 541).[25] Even if the nature of this truth is not defined, one can infer some of its characteristics from *The Order of Discourse*. It does not change (Foucault never doubts that what Mendel said still is and will always be true), and it can become the object of a sufficiently large consensus within the scientific community so that it can be said that Mendel objectively "spoke the truth."

Unexpectedly, one reencounters here the essential characteristics of the metaphysical conception of truth: permanence, objectivity, universality. Foucault nowhere clarifies the nature of the criteria that would allow one to judge such a truth: chapter 3 of *The Archaeology of Knowledge* suggests that, for him, simple logical coherence is not enough, except perhaps in the case of a discipline as formalized as mathematics. As for the traditional conception of truth, as *adequatio rei et intellectus*, Foucault does not discuss it and appears to consider it undecidable. Even while stating that a discourse constitutes its objects, he nonetheless leaves open the possibility of a "history of the referent" (*AK*, 47), and therefore of the existence of a referent to which propositions could refer. It is rather surprising to find in an apparent relativist like Foucault the underlying idea that such an "objective" truth exists; but in fact, this conception was already partially presupposed by the archaeological method. Indeed, Foucault never denied that the claims he examined had different truth-values; his point was that these truth-values were not relevant to archaeological analysis. The bracketing of all normative judgments, which is the initiatory act of archaeology, is not in itself a *denial* of the possibility of a norm. On the contrary, it only makes sense as a *bracketing* by assuming that that there is indeed a norm, but that, methodologically speaking, it should not be taken into account.

Nonetheless, it is not this idea of truth, which appears here rather as an implicit counterpoint, that the above text stresses. If the discipline does not refer to "all that can truthfully be said about something" (objectively) or to "the sum of all that can be accepted about the same data in virtue of some principle of coherence or systematicity," it is because it refers to some specific "conditions," defined more precisely in one of the most famous passages from *The Order of Discourse*: "Before it can be called true or false, [a proposition] must be 'in the truth' [*dans le vrai*], as Canguilhem would say" (*OD*, 60; modified). The thrust of this passage is that the effective predication of truth depends at least partially on specific conditions that precede it both logically and chronologically. The Foucauldian answer is thus particularly interesting, because, instead of thinking the conditions of possibility of truth univocally, it creates a dissociation between the *criteria of the active predication* of truth, by virtue of which a proposition can be judged true or false, and what Foucault calls its "*acceptability*,"[26]—the conditions of possibility of predication itself. To take an example from the *Archaeology of Knowledge*, the truth-value of a statement such as "Green thoughts sleep furiously" cannot be predicated within the scientific community because the sentence, although grammatically correct, is not acceptable. If the conditions of acceptability were to shift—for example, if the statement were a coded message and one knew the code—then predication could occur. So for a statement to be "in the truth" means that it is "acceptable," prior to its truth-value being established or negated (thus, a new scientific hypothesis can be acceptable and yet temporarily undecided for lack of proper experimentation); to be said "true," the statement must have been the object of an actual predication that constitutes a superior stage in the determination of its truth-value. Thus, the theses of the German botanist Schleiden, even though objectively false (according to the first conception of truth analyzed above), were deemed acceptable and therefore could be (although wrongly) judged true in their time. Conversely, those of Mendel—however (objectively) true—could not be judged as such because they were unacceptable.

On the basis of this distinction, we can understand better why Foucault, paradoxically, gives the possibility of being "in the truth" exactly the opposite meaning to Canguilhem's.[27] The latter introduced the expression apropos the opposition between Galileo and the ecclesiastical hierarchy of his own time in the following way: "And yet . . . it is Galileo who is in the truth. To be in the truth does not mean to always say the truth."[28] But when Canguilhem says that Galileo is "in the truth," he does not mean that his discourse belonged homogeneously to the discursive space of his epoch, thereby satisfying the conditions of acceptability currently valid. On the contrary, he means that Galileo was *per se* right to sustain the Copernican thesis, even if he was wrong on other points—for example, in refusing to admit Kepler's explanation of the orbit of planets using ellipses rather than circles. "To be in the truth," for Canguilhem, is therefore to discover a universal and objective truth,[29] whose proofs will only become acceptable later: one is "in the truth" in an absolute fashion.[30] The difference between "being in the truth" and "saying the truth" is justified, therefore, not by the opposition between the acceptability and predication of truth, but only by the necessarily nebulous character of anticipation, due to which one can neither exhaust nor exactly set in advance all that could be truthfully said on a given subject. For Canguilhem, if one is in the truth, one necessarily speaks truly about that which one talks (the Copernican hypothesis), even if one does not "always" and in everything say the truth (Galileo's refusal of Kepler's explanation). Correspondingly, one can only speak the truth if one is in the truth. For Foucault, however, one can be "in the truth" without speaking the truth, and one can speak the truth without "being in the truth"—paradoxes that I shall examine shortly. Foucault opposes Canguilhem precisely insofar as he uses the expression "being in the truth" to establish the distinction between the acceptability and predication of truth, and to affirm their mutual independence. This fundamental disagreement between the two authors is symbolized by the fact that Mendel, who speaks the truth *without* "being in the truth," clearly occupies a position in *The Order of Discourse* similar to that occupied in the *Etudes d'histoire et de philosophie des sciences* by Galileo, who could speak the truth only *because* he was "in the truth."

After having distinguished the acceptability from the prediction of truth, it is essential for Foucault to demonstrate that, contrary to appearances, these two elements do not determine each other in a reciprocal relationship. This is the aim of his well-known analysis of Mendel and Schleiden:

Mendel spoke the truth, but he was not "within the truth" of the biological discourse of the time: it was not according to such rules that biological objects and concepts were formed. . . . Mendel was a true monster, which meant that science could not speak of him; whereas thirty years earlier, at the height of the nineteenth century, Schleiden, for example, who denied plant sexuality, but in accordance with the rules of biological discourse, was merely formulating a disciplined error. (*OD*, 61; modified)

Schleiden's case is the easiest, and allows Foucault to establish two complementary points. Firstly, a thesis can be "in the truth" ("following the rules of biological discourse") and recognized in the same epoch as false ("a disciplined error"), which proves that its being "in the truth" does not itself indicate that a proposition is "true," and therefore that the criteria for the predication of truth are different from those of acceptability. Secondly and inversely, although the first criteria are not conditioned in a relation of cause and effect by the second, neither are they separated: indeed, it is only *because* a proposition is "in the truth" that it can be judged false, which is confirmed by the idea that "error can only arise and be decided inside a definite practice" (*OD*, 60).

So the predication of truth or falsehood, although not *determined* by the acceptability of the corresponding statement, is nonetheless *dependent* on it. In any given epoch and domain, acceptability partially conditions the predication of truth, in the sense that it predetermines (in accordance with the modalities that the historical *a priori* and the archaeological *épistémès* were intended to describe) the objects and the form of the propositions considered. Although acceptability is not the *criterion* for predication, it is nonetheless its *historically variable condition*, as it opens a space for predication that predefines its exercise and outside of which truth is unidentifiable. This space is characteristically distinguished from the predication of truth or falsehood, which it conditions, by the fact that *it itself escapes the criteria whose application it makes possible*. Indeed, while one can say something false (predication) while being in the truth (acceptability), it is impossible to be "in the false"—except metaphorically and in a secondary sense, that is, by being the victim of an error that one cannot precisely identify. To take up, while inverting it, one of Foucault's favorite themes, the space in which one is in the truth has no "outside," which shows its heterogeneity from its eventual contents. "Outside of the truth" there is neither truth nor falsity: there is only a "teratology of knowledge," where "there are monsters on the prowl whose form changes with the history of knowledge [*savoir*]" (*OD*, 60). This is where Mendel's status is located.

Contrary to Schleiden, Mendel does not say something false while being in the truth. He says the truth without being in the truth, which would seem to radically contradict the thesis developed above. Corresponding to this apparent contradiction is the theme of monstrosity: Mendel is a "true monster," that is, by analogy, a being that according to natural rules should not exist, a being outside of norms, a "living being of negative value."[31] Not that Mendel is a freak of nature, obviously; his monstrosity is that he attempts to speak the truth without his discourse conforming itself to the demands of his epoch's standards of acceptability. The monstrosity of a proposition thus has nothing to do with its apparent strangeness: the idea of a time machine, as bizarre as it could seem in the nineteenth century, had nothing "monstrous" about it, since the text of H. G. Wells had no scientific pretensions and obeyed other norms—those of literary practice. But the monstrous proposition is that which pretends to truth, should never have been identified as true or false (not being acceptable), and is true all the same. It is in this sense that it is "wild" (*OD*, 61), falls into the ineffable and is only capable of being made to the object of a "monstration"[32]—the etymological root of "monster." Monstrosity is therefore the symbolic translation of the logical paradox by which truth is actually predicated of a proposition while never having been legitimately predicable.

But, in reality, this monstrosity rests on an effect of retrospection that allows one to explain its paradoxical character while avoiding the above contradiction, as the following passage suggests: "It needed a complete change of scale, the deployment of a whole range of objects in biology for Mendel to *enter into the truth* and for his propositions to *appear* (in large measure) *correct*" (*OD*, 61; my italics). Mendel did not voluntarily "enter into the truth": rather it is the space of truth itself that eventually caught up with him, making acceptable after the fact his previously unacceptable theses. Mendel's theses can "appear correct" only *retrospectively*, by virtue of the archaeologist belonging to a different epistemic configuration. The "monstrosity" of Mendel is thus relative, and only apparently contradicts the principle that acceptability is a necessary condition for predication in any given epoch. Foucault's statement that the science of Mendel's time "could not speak" about him reinforces *a contrario* the idea that, by definition, each epoch can only give a truth-value to that which appears to it as acceptable. It is only from another space of truth, from another manner of being "in the truth," that archaeology can show that truth is not necessarily acceptable (the theses of Mendel), and that what was predicated as true at a given epoch may not be true (those of Schleiden). In this sense, the paradoxical possibility of speaking the truth without being "in the truth" is revealed as a retrospective illusion induced by archaeology itself for the sake of its own demonstrations.

It is on this fundamental distinction between the acceptability and the predication of truth that the meaning of the archaeological *épochē* is founded and becomes clear. Far from being an arbitrary decision, it finds its profound justification in the priority of the first over the second. In this context, indeed, it is of little importance to the archaeologist whether the criteria of truth should be objective or relative, as the object of his study, acceptability, is anterior to and independent of them. Correspondingly, he can legitimately state that he is concerned with truth—in the sense that he studies its conditions of possibility—even though he does not question the truth-value of the propositions examined.[33] This is confirmed in a later text, which retrospectively defines the archaeological enterprise as a study that starts from the empirical observation of the *de facto* acceptance of a set of propositions and then refers them vertically to the analysis of their conditions of acceptability. This mirrors the process that chapter 2 of *The Archaeology of Knowledge* described as the necessity of searching, starting from the empirically constituted unities (the "disciplines"), for the discursive formations on which the propositions depend.

> In short, it seems to me, that from the empirical observability for us of a set [of propositions] to its historical acceptability, at the very epoch where it is clearly identifiable, the road passes through an analysis of the power-knowledge nexus that underlies it,[34] takes this set up from the fact that it is accepted, in the direction of what makes it acceptable, certainly not in general, but only where it is accepted: this is what one could characterize as re-seizing it in its positivity. . . . Let us say that that is the level, approximately, of *archaeology*.[35]

One may well wonder whether this "redefinition" isn't rather a new definition, as there is no notion of the "power-knowledge nexus" in the texts of the archaeological period—a problem that will be discussed later. But regardless of whether the conditions by which a system can be "in the truth" should be referred to a historical *a priori* or to power-knowledge itself, the essential idea for the moment is that archaeology is concerned with acceptability itself, some of the characteristics of which can be perceived from this passage: it is relative—a system is acceptable "certainly not in general," but "only where it is accepted," historically constituted—the system is "observable" only at a precise "epoch" and is therefore changing. Relativity, historicity, mutability: the attributes of acceptability are exactly contrary to those of objective truth, a problem to which I shall return.

However, if the interrogation of the conditions of acceptability really is what has guided Foucault's whole development—as he himself said—it should be possible to rediscover its trace throughout the works of the archaeological period. By rereading these texts in the order reverse to their production, I would like to show that such really is the case and that the main concepts established by archaeology are each, in their different ways, various attempts to solve this problem.

The Retrospective Identification of the Historical *a Priori* with the Conditions of the Acceptability of Truth

In *The Order of Discourse* itself, this theme is evident; indeed, this is the text in which the problem is stated. There Foucault shows, as we just saw, that the acceptability of a proposition is tied neither to the demands of logic for noncontradiction nor to its belonging to a formal system—ideas that echo one of the favorite themes of *The Archaeology of Knowledge*, that is, the impossibility of the archaeologist identifying his approach with that of the logician or the linguist. On the contrary, acceptability is defined by its conformity to the norms that are established by a discipline. In order to be able to be "recognized as true" a statement must, therefore, involve "a determinate plane of objects" (*OD*, 60), using "conceptual instruments or techniques of a well-defined type," and belong to a particular "theoretical horizon"—in short, it must satisfy the "rules of a discursive 'policing'" (*OD*, 61) that governs (organizes and commands) the production of discourse of any given epoch and domain. Once more, Foucault opposes common sense by stating that it is not the intrinsic truth of a proposition that allows its scientificity to be determined, but, on the contrary, its disciplined character that enables it to be predicated as true or false.

However, the very terms of this response singularly remind one of the way in which Foucault had defined "knowledge" two years earlier:

> Knowledge [*savoir*] is not a *collection of knowledges* [*connaissances*]—as one should always be able to *say if these are true or false*, exact or not, approximate or definite, contradictory or coherent; *none of these distinctions is pertinent to describe knowledge* [*savoir*]. . . . It is *within the element of knowledge* [*savoir*] that the conditions for the apparition of a science are determined, or at least of a collection of discourses which welcome or reject scientific models. (*DE*, 1: 723; my italics)

This passage exhibits again the move that distinguished empirical contents from their conditions of possibility—the distinction through which Foucault introduced the idea of discipline. But the interesting point here is that knowledge (*savoir*) is metaphorically defined as a space, a field ("in the element of knowledge"), in which alone a discourse with scientific pretensions could find its "conditions of appearance." From the analyses of the preceding chapters, neither the conditions nor the field can be understood through economic or social determinations: it appears more reasonable to compare the "element of knowledge" to this other field, which in *The Order of Discourse* defined the possibility of "being in the truth"; this approach is confirmed by the idea that knowledge (*savoir*) forms the "precondition of what is later revealed and which later functions as an item of knowledge [*connaissance*] or an illusion, an accepted truth or an exposed error" (*AK*, 182). To the extent that knowledge (*savoir*) is not a "pre-knowledge" (*AK*, 182) (a still unformed content), its anteriority (as a "precondition") cannot be understood as homogeneous with the development of science, and suggests, rather, the "before" of the subordination of the predication of truth to "being in the truth"—the logical anteriority of the condition of possibility to that which it allows. Correspondingly, the idea of an *a posteriori* "revelation" of truth echoes the theme of "apparition" already encountered in *The Order of Discourse* (where the thesis of Mendel "appeared" as "correct").

The difference between knowledge (*savoir*) and knowledges (*connaissances*) is therefore not quantitative but qualitative. Foucault declared above that none of the "distinctions" that opposed true to false, correct to incorrect, contradictory to coherent, were "pertinent to describe knowledge [*savoir*]." However, it seems that this curious thesis, running counter to common sense, for which knowledge is precisely defined by the possibility of being true or false, can only be explained if one admits that knowledge (*savoir*) itself defines, in an ante-predicative manner, the conditions of the acceptability of truth in a given domain. Thus, knowledge withdraws from the very criteria that it puts in place, just as the space to which the possibility of being "in the truth" referred was *per se* neither true nor false, being that from which one can judge truth or falsehood. Another passage confirms this hypothesis by describing the conditions of acceptability in a manner closely similar to *The Order of Discourse*: "Knowledge [*savoir*] is profoundly different from the knowledges [*connaissances*] which one can find in scientific books, philosophical theories, religious justifications: it is that which makes possible, at a given movement, the apparition of a theory, of an opinion, of a practice" (*DE*, 1: 498).[36] Knowledge (*savoir*) is therefore the condition of possibility of knowledge (*connaissance*), not in the sense that it provides a reservoir of contents and preformed statements, but because it presides over the formation of particular objects or statements about which truth or falsehood will consequently be predicated. *The Archaeology of Knowledge* specifies the nature of these conditions of acceptability similarly to *The Order of Discourse*, and with the same insistence on spatial metaphors, by referring them to the rules by which knowledge (*savoir*) defines a "domain" constituted by "different objects," a "space" of possible positions for the subject, a "field of co-ordination and subordination of statements" and of "possibilities of use" (*AK*, 182–83).

Explicit references to truth are rare in *The Order of Things*, and so it is even more significant that the only elaborated definition of the historical *a priori* that it gives says that this *a priori* . . . [is not] made up of a certain *state of acquired knowledges* [connaissances] *laid down in the course of the preceding ages* and providing a ground for the more or less irregular, more or less rapid, progress of rationality. . . . This *a priori* is what, in a given period, delimits in the totality of experience a field of knowledge [*savoir*], defines the mode of being of the objects that appear in that field, provides man's everyday gaze with theoretical powers, and *defines the conditions in which he can sustain a discourse about things that is recognized to be true.* (*OT*, 157–58; modified, my italics)

Like knowledge (*savoir*) itself, the historical *a priori* is distinguished qualitatively and not quantitatively from cognitive contents and their future development (as it is not a "state of sedimented knowledge"). Correspondingly, the theme of the conditions of possibility of the predication of truth is explicitly enough drawn out: the historical *a priori* is not a criterion that allows a discourse to be "recognized as true," but "defines the conditions" under which a discourse so recognized can take place. The historical *a priori* is, therefore, a condition of possibility in the sense that it determines the "field of knowledge" (*savoir* should be understood here in its usual sense of a more or less well established form of knowledge), the "objects" that appear there, as well as the "theoretical powers" of the gaze. These themes can likewise retrospectively compare with the "planes of objects" and the "theoretical horizon" mentioned above (*OD*, 61), the idea of the "horizon" echoing the theme of the "gaze." This hypothesis finds confirmation in a later text, where Foucault redefines the *épistémè* precisely in reference to the opposition between conditions of acceptability and predication of truth:

The *épistémè* I would define, in return, as the stategic apparatus [*dispositif*] which allows to discriminate, among all possible statements, those which will be *acceptable within, I would not say a scientific theory, but a field of scientificity, and which it is possible to say are true or false.* The *épistémè* is the "apparatus" which makes possible the separation, not of the true from the false, but of what is from what is not scientifically determinable. (*PK*, 197; modified, my italics)

Finally, at first sight the theme of truth is hardly more present in *The Birth of the Clinic* than in *The Order of Things*. But, significantly, it is similarly in (indirect) reference to the historical *a priori* that it is mentioned in the preface: "The breadth of experience seems to be identified with the domain of the careful gaze. . . . The eye becomes the depository and source of clarity; it has the power to bring to light a truth that it receives only to the extent that it has bought it to light; as it opens itself, the eye *opens up a first opening for truth*" (*BC*, xii; modified, my italics). Since the historical *a priori* is defined in *The Birth of the Clinic* as the articulation of the visible and the sayable, it does not appear exaggerated to think that the theme of the "gaze" could and should be referred to it. This extract seems analogous to that of *The Order of Things*, to the extent that it does make the historical *a priori* the ante-predicative condition of possibility of truth, as it is only the opening of the eye that "opens up a first opening for truth." For each epoch and in any given domain, the possibility of truth thus depends on the modality of the articulation of the visible and the sayable that determines the "space of experience" in which the objects of a possible knowledge can appear, and in reference to which propositions can be formulated. For example, for the practitioner of the medicine of types, to be "in the truth" meant to be able to see and identify in the teeming of symptoms the obscuration of an ideal type of illness, and to seek to distinguish this latter from the confusion of the visible. But in the classical age, to be in the truth involved an attempt to directly decipher within these visible symptoms the disease that reveals itself in them to those who both know how to see and how to say what they see. It should be noted, however, that the apparent circularity of the process—the eye "receives" a truth that it has "brought to light" and so appears as both passive and active, while truth seems to preexist itself—revives the logic of the originary of the anthropological version of the transcendental theme. Thus, truth "received" or "brought to light" in the time of experience does actually preexist itself, but only "primitively" and not empirically, as the opening that experience, by constituting itself as such, retrospectively reveals as an already present origin.

So Foucault appears able to state legitimately that his "problem has always been the question of truth." The introduction in *The Order of Discourse* of the distinction between "being in the truth" (acceptability) and "saying the truth" (predication) allows the meaning of the critical question to be sharpened and the task of archaeology to be specified: to uncover the conditions of the acceptability, not the predication, of truth. But a new problem arises, connected to the difficulty of reconciling the objective and universalizing understanding of truth both presupposed and bracketed by *The Order of Discourse*, with the idea that truth has variable conditions of acceptability to which the predication of truth is relative. If a proposition must be "in the truth" to be judged true, and if the conditions that permit it to be there change with the epoch, how could it ever be said to be "objectively" true? The double system of acceptability and predication of truth itself appears to render meaningless the possibility of an objective truth, which, however, is suggested, as we have seen, by the idea of a "simple truth" and the absolute categorical manner in which *The Order of Discourse* twice states that Mendel "spoke the truth." It is also clear that in Foucault's eyes it would have been better (notwithstanding the irrefutable chronological impossibility) to be treated by Bichat than by Dr. Pomme, the unfortunate consequences of whose methods are described in the first pages of *The Birth of the Clinic* (*BC*, ix ff.). Although he hardly concerns himself with it, Foucault does not deny the idea of scientific progress—what he does question is the idea that only "true" theories are worthy of analysis.

To the extent that the conditions of acceptability do not determine the criteria of truth (being a necessary but insufficient precondition for its attribution), as the example of Schleiden has shown, one might be tempted to give this tension a Hegelian resolution by seeing the different historical predications of truth as the various forms taken by truth during the dialectical movement leading to its ultimate recognition. We would have to distinguish, as in *The Phenomenology of Spirit*, between the perspective of the "for us" that would reveal truth in its objective and universal progression, and each epochal point of view for which truth would only be relative and could not appear in its dependence on successive *Aufhebungen* until each stage was completed. Thus, no theoretical discourse was acceptable during the Renaissance unless it obeyed its epistemic requirements for acceptability—identifying the resemblances between things (according to its four cardinal forms, *aemulatio, convenientia, analogy* and *sympathy*) and providing a hierarchical description whose infinite and repetitive nature was commanded by the background assumption that things and words, being signs, were homogeneous. Provided that they conformed to this implicit model, the claims put forward by the various scholars could be predicated as true or false (depending on whether there could be agreement on the actual existence of these resemblances in the prose of the world).

From the Hegelian perspective suggested above, during the seventeenth century the identification and ordering of *differences* would have superseded the Renaissance form of acceptability and generated a new type of discourse, intended this time to discriminate between objects by analyzing their differences in terms of elementary elements (as described by Descartes in the *Regulae*, for example), rather than link things together in their holistic belonging to the cosmos. Correlatively, the underlying principle of the methodic decomposition into simple elements was the implicit belief in the transparency of being to representation, which laid the ground for the new possibility of finite and exhaustive descriptions. Although from the medieval scholars' perspective, their understanding of acceptability was just as valid as that of the classical age was to the grammaticians, natural historians, or economists of that time, for us this second form of acceptability would be a higher one, in the sense that it paved the way toward our current model—scientificity. However, it is clear that such an interpretation has to be rejected because it would *per se* contradict many of Foucault's statements, as he was in principle opposed to any totalization of this sort.[37]

It might be preferable, therefore, to focus on the analysis of Mendel's case and ask whether the idea of a universal truth is not also an effect of retrospection produced by archaeology. From this perspective, Foucault's actual position would be that it is only because we are no longer "in the truth" of the nineteenth century sciences that we can affirm that Mendel spoke the truth, and that the truth of what Mendel said only appears universal because our own space of truth makes it acceptable to us. The advantage of such a hypothesis is that it escapes the tension described above by establishing that, in fact, Foucault has only a relativist understanding of the criteria of truth. It appears to be reinforced by other texts from the archaeological period, for example, the following extract that concerns the sixteenth-century naturalist Belon's comparison of the human skeleton to that of birds: "In fact, Belon's description has no connection with anything but the positivity in which, in his day, made it possible. It is neither more rational nor more scientific than an observation such as Aldrovandi's comparison of man's baser parts to the fouler parts of the world" (*OT*, 22). Foucault expresses the same relativism when he describes the eighteenth-century naturalist Buffon's reading of his Renaissance predecessor Aldrovandi:

> Later, Buffon was to express astonishment at finding in the work of a naturalist like Aldrovandi such an inextricable mixture of exact descriptions, reported quotations, fables without commentary. . . . Whereupon Buffon comments: "Let it be judged after that what proportion of natural history is to be found in such a hotch-potch of writing. There is no description here, only legend." And indeed, for Aldrovandi and his contemporaries, it was all *legenda*—things to be read. . . . *Aldrovandi was neither a better nor a worse observer than Buffon*; he was neither more credulous than he, nor less attached to the faithfulness of the observing eye or to the rationality of things. *His observation was simply not linked to things in accordance with the same system or by the same arrangement of the "épistémè."* For Aldrovandi was meticulously contemplating a nature that was, from top to bottom, written. (*OT*, 39)

However, these texts do not refer to *truth* itself, but only to the *scientific character* of the observations of Belon or Aldrovandi ("neither more rational nor more *scientific* than such an observation as Aldrovandi . . ."). According to the terms of *The Order of Discourse*, what gives a proposition its scientific character is precisely *not* its truth content but the fact that it is or is not "in the truth." The relativism suggested by these passages, therefore, does not apply to truth, but to the conditions of acceptability themselves—which is implicitly confirmed by the reference to the "same system" and the "same disposition of the *épistémè*," which, as we saw, concerns the acceptability rather than the predication of truth.

Consequently, it is difficult to say, from the archaeological period alone, what the real extent of Foucault's relativism is, whether it bears on the conditions of acceptability of truth alone or on truth itself.[38]

Foucault's Reappropriation of the "Will to Truth"

The Order of Discourse follows in the wake of archaeology by taking up and refining the analysis of the "internal procedures of exclusion"—the rules that statements must conform with to be "in the truth." However, this text is distinguished from its predecessors in that it asserts the existence of "*external* procedures of exclusion" that also govern discourses, with which he begins his analysis. Thus Foucault implicitly renounces *The Archaeology of Knowledge*'s postulation of the possibility of studying the discursive in an autonomous manner. This renunciation could have been accompanied by a return to the previous form of archaeology modeled in *The Birth of the Clinic*, which was already preoccupied by the relationship of discursive practices to their nondiscursive counterparts. But this is not the case, and Foucault gives his approach a new inflection by formulating the following hypothesis: "In every society the production of discourse is at once controlled, selected, organised and redistributed by a certain number of procedures whose role is to ward off its powers and dangers" (*OD*, 52). This passage introduces two new themes; firstly, that a "control" is exercised on discourses from the outside, of which exclusion is the necessary complement; secondly, the corresponding, but still very vague idea, that certain discourses possess particular "powers," and therefore also "dangers," which motivate the need for control. But who, or what, exercises this control and exclusion, and to what ends? Over what or whom are these powers exercised? More problematically, why do certain discourses possess "powers"? Are these powers connected to the identity of the speaker, or to his function? Or should we attribute a specific form of power to the discursive, different from the performative element revealed by Austin's and Searle's analyses of language acts?

Archaeology cannot reply to these questions. Insofar as it treats the discursive from the epistemic point of view alone, and limits itself to asking the question of the conditions of possibility and the rules of formation of discourses that attempt to attain scientific status, it can only establish that which concerns the possibility of a statement being "in the truth." Thus, the denunciation of the human sciences in chapter 10 of *The Order of Things* profoundly differs from that of *Discipline and Punish*, as it is not concerned with their social role, nor the consequences of their appearance on individual lives, but only with their lack of real scientificity and their corresponding attempts to mime fundamental science. But while genealogy begins, as did archaeology, from the empirical observation of existing discourses, it does not attempt to return from the post hoc to the *a priori* by questioning their conditions of possibility at a merely epistemic level, but sets them in a wider sociopolitical context and links them to their source(s), function(s), and aim(s). Thus to the hypothesis of exclusion and control corresponds a change of perspective that no longer gives Foucault's project a solely epistemological dimension, but a polemical one—literally, as he is concerned to show how discourses are the products and vectors of more or less identifiable struggles (*polemoi*). Thus Foucault places his interrogations within Nietzsche's direct lineage:[39]

> Why, in fact, are we attached to the truth? Why the truth rather than lies? Why the truth rather than myth? Why the truth rather than illusion? And I think that, instead of trying to find out what truth, as opposed to error, is, it might be more interesting to take up the problem posed by Nietzsche: how is it that, in our societies, "the truth" has been given this value, thus placing us absolutely under its thrall? (*PPC*, 107)

This is the position from which Foucault defines the three principles of external exclusion (*OD*, 52), which are "prohibition," the "opposition between reason and madness," and the "will to truth," itself explicitly referred to Nietzsche. Of these three "great systems of exclusion," the importance of the last is such that the two others become negligible—in fact, the theme of prohibition will be explicitly refuted by Foucault through the later critique of the "repressive hypothesis," while the division of reason and madness will only appear as an example. From the beginning of *The Order of Discourse*, Foucault clearly establishes the predominance of the will to truth over the other systems of exclusion, justifying it, in a very Nietzschean manner, through an allusion to its ever growing influence of human destiny: "The first two [systems] are constantly becoming more fragile and more uncertain, to the extent that they are now invaded by the will to truth, which for its part constantly grows stronger, deeper, and more implacable" (*OD*, 56). Similarly, the survey of the principles of exclusion made by Foucault in the *Annuaire du Collège de France*, in 1971, gives preeminence to the idea of a "will to knowledge" that appears as a historical avatar of the will to truth: "These principles of exclusion and choice . . . do not refer to a knowing subject (historical or transcendental) who would successively invent or found them at an originary level; rather they indicate a will to knowledge, anonymous and polymorphous, capable of regular transformation and held within a play of identifiable dependencies."[40] Just as for Nietzsche himself,[41] the concept of will now allows Foucault to criticize the idea of a unified subjectivity, foundational and a historical[42]—characteristics to which those of the will to knowledge present an exact counterpoint, being "anonymous and polymorphous" and "susceptible to regular transformations." But how can we understand this "will" of Foucault's? What will be the consequences of the introduction of this new theme for the relationship between archaeology and genealogy, and for the critical question itself?

Two essential characteristics of the will to truth stand out from *The Order of Discourse*. Firstly, it is historical (it has "crossed so many centuries of our history" [*OD*, 54]); secondly, and correspondingly, it exerts a "power of constraint" over discourses (*OD*, 55). Faithful to the Nietzschean project of a "morphology," Foucault analyzes this history and constraining power through the notion of a "historical division" that would originally have given this will its "general form" and then experienced two "variations" (*OD*, 54). These are mentioned twice, but only schematically: the first describes the apparition, "particularly in England," of "schemas of possible, observable, measurable, classifiable objects" (*OD*, 55), or of a "science of the gaze, of observation, of the established fact" (*OD*, 70), probably an allusion to the changes of which Bacon's *Novum organum* was the foremost expression. The second refers to the "great foundational acts of Modern science"; it takes place at the beginning of the nineteenth century, obviously being the industrial revolution and its consequences. Although Foucault speaks no more about it, the common ground of these two variations is clearly that they both share an obsession with scientificity that never ceases to grow: the first identifies the birth of the experimental sciences and the second marks both a major leap in their theoretical development and the growth of their socioeconomic influence due to the diffusion of new techniques.

It is with reference to this first division that the apparition and nature of this obsession with scientificity can be understood. Although Foucault does not date it exactly, an allusion to the expulsion of the Sophist from the city ("the Sophist is banished") suggests that it is simultaneous with the apparition of Platonism. *The Birth of Tragedy* had already identified with Socrates' invention of reason that "countertyrant" against the unruliness of his instincts, the birth of the theoretical man, and thus the appearance of the nihilistic form of the will to power, the will to truth—a point to which I shall return shortly. But beyond Nietzsche, Foucault is very likely thinking of Marcel Détienne's *The Masters of Truth in Archaic Greece*, when, in order to understand the division on which the Western will to truth depends, he contrasts the discourse of the "Greek poet of the 6th century"[43] to that of the philosopher. Indeed, the three characteristics he assigns to the poet's use of language (to be "poetic," "to dispense justice," "to prophesy the future" [*OD*, 54]) exactly correspond to the three "social functions" of archaic discourse identified by Détienne ("poetry, prophecy and justice").[44] Equally, the Foucauldian thesis according to which the "true" discourse was "the one pronounced by men who spoke as of right and according to the required ritual" (*OD*, 54) faithfully echoes Détienne's conclusion that in ancient Greece "'truth' was established by the correct application of a procedure duly carried out according to ritual."[45] The idea that "the highest truth . . . resided in what discourse was or did" (*OD*, 54) clearly takes up the statement that "speech charged with efficacy is not separated from its realisation; it is immediately a reality, a realisation, an action."[46] Finally, Foucault's thesis that "a day came when truth was displaced from the ritualised, efficacious and just act of enunciation, towards the utterance itself, its meaning, its form, its object" (*OD*, 54) reflects the statement of Détienne, for whom this event was connected with the thought of Parmenides, in which the "first version of objective truth" was formed.[47]

Following in Détienne's wake, Foucault rests the "division" on which the Western will to truth depends on two main innovations. The first of these is the appearance of a new understanding of truth, in which the latter is no longer derived from the identity or status of the speaker, but from the content of a statement. Spoken truth ceases to need the sanction of the "Masters of truth"—poets, judges, or prophets—to be true. It can be so objectively, according to codifiable criteria. Thus appears the idea of a rational truth, preexisting discourse and achievable only by submitting to certain rules. Henceforth, that which will determine truth is the adequation of the discourse to that which it names, not the authority of the speaker—an idea of which the Aristotelean *logos apophanticos* will become the ultimate expression.[48] Secondly, true discourse changes its status: the judge, poet, and prophet were effectively gifted with a power that one could describe as "veridictional," as their discourse was the very realization of the truth that it pronounced. By "prophesying the future," discourse "not only announced what was going to happen but helped to make it happen" (*OD*, 54),[49] declares Foucault. The true discourse was "performative," in the sense that truth was indissociable from the spoken word that expressed it. On the contrary, the new objective nature of truth corresponds with the apparition of a different type of discourse, meant to describe states of affairs: "A day came when truth was displaced from the ritualised, efficacious and just act of enunciation, towards the utterance itself, its meaning, its form, its object, its relation to its reference" (*OD*, 54). Discourse itself does not effect the truth of what it says, but must limit itself to expressing a truth that is independent of it and can be discovered simply by following some specific rules and methods (such as Socratic dialectics). Correspondingly, far from being reserved to a few initiates, this truth becomes by nature accessible to all and capable of being taught and diffused on a greater scale.

To these two modifications, which mirror the ones identified by Détienne, a third, of more Nietzschean inspiration, is added. For Foucault, the annexation of any conception of truth to the supposedly neutral and objective model of scienticity should also be referred to the Platonic division. The significance of this triple displacement becomes clearer. The "general form" received by the will to truth from this "historical division" is a rationalizing and logical inflection that will find in the two stages that follow the Platonic division mentioned above (i.e., the birth of empirical sciences and the industrial revolution) the possibility of a more technical development than that of the Greeks. Similarly, Foucault will affirm several years later, in terms very close to those of *The Order of Things*, that the will to truth has "sustained the establishment of scientific discourse in the West" (*HS*, 55). Thus, one will find in Foucault a Nietzschean theme much commented on by Heidegger, the idea that the destiny of the Western world is governed by "this great power-knowledge which traverses humanity" (*LCP*, 163; modified) and reveals a growing, ever more dangerous and more nihilist obsession for rationalization. This theme is explicitly expressed from 1971 onward.

> Even in the greatly expanded form it assumes today, the will to knowledge does not come close to a universal truth; man is not given an exact and serene mastery of nature. On the contrary, it ceaselessly multiplies the risks, everywhere it creates dangers. . . . Knowledge does not slowly detach itself from its empirical roots, the initial needs from which it arose, to become pure speculation subject only to the demands of reason; its development is not tied to the constitution and affirmation of a free subject; rather, it brings with itself an ever-growing obsession: its instinctive violence accelerates and grows. (*LCP*, 163; modified)

Thus *The Order of Discourse* gives a central importance to the theme of the will to truth, an importance that will be ultimately confirmed by the "rather extravagant homage" (*PPC*, 31) of the French title of the first volume of *The History of Sexuality*, as well as by the very project of writing "a history of the will to truth" (*HS*, 79). Foucault analyzes this latter theme principally in two places (in an article entitled "Nietzsche, Genealogy, History" and in his 1971 course at the Collège de France). But while these texts express a reflection on the nature of the will to truth *for Nietzsche*, Foucault remains singularly mute on the meaning that he *himself* gives the concept in the context of his own analyses. Although, in compliance with his own indications, *The History of Sexuality* can be conceived as the analysis of one of the various *forms* of the will to truth programmatically described in 1970, the text contains no indication about the *nature* of this will. Some of Foucault's claims certainly refer to famous Nietzschean themes, beginning with the above examined idea that knowledge, far from being neutral, rests on a division between truth and falsity the criteria for which have nothing scientific about them.[50] Equally, the hypothesis according to which it is from this will and its forms that we must interpret our history evokes the Nietzschean analyses of the different stages of nihilism.[51] Or again, the central statement—which I shall examine in the next chapter—that "truth" has no particular essence and is only the "effect"[52] of this division evidently recalls Nietzsche's thesis that truth is the product of an original falsification by a reactive will to power, which, incapable of bearing the mobile and contradictory reality of becoming, invented logical categories (identity, noncontradiction, causality, finality, and the principle of sufficient reason) to stabilize and fix itself—and so acquire the mastery of what it henceforth sees as "real."[53] The fact that, for Foucault, the will does not require intentionality or a subject as it involves a multiplicity of local strategies is reminiscent of the Nietzschean critique of the psychologizing conceptions that saw the will as a unifying principle and the decision-making power of a sovereign consciousness.

But despite these parallels, it is impossible, for two reasons, to understand the will to truth in Foucault's work from this Nietzschean perspective. Firstly, the theme is introduced by Foucault in an autonomous fashion, without reference to what was for Nietzsche its necessary correlate, the will to power. Indeed, for the latter, the will to truth is a weak will, which, because it lacks the power to affirm life and to will it despite the contradictions and suffering that it entails, prefers to deny them by creating the "true world" described in *Twilight of the Idols*. Ascetic ideals and the secret tendency to self-destruction that moves the search for knowledge are the symptoms of this negation, which can only be revealed by a genealogy. For Nietzsche, the will to truth is not, therefore, *per se* the most fundamental concept: it is a derived notion that describes the negative inflection of the will to power and does not take up all the options open to this latter. On the contrary, Foucault presents the will to truth as a self-referring absolute, therefore implicitly giving it the place held by the will to power for Nietzsche.[54]

Consequently, the second divergence between Foucault and Nietzsche is due to the total absence of any Foucauldian equivalent to the Dionysian. As is well known, for Nietzsche the latter offers a counterpoint to the nihilism specific to the will to truth, because it opens up for the will to power the possibility of an ecstatic transformation (in the literal sense of a leaving of the self) through art. The logical schematization/ossification of the real performed by sciences can be counterbalanced by the artistic schematization of the self, from which a renewed understanding of reality (as in flux) and truth (as originating in the transformed subject) can be generated.[55] It is only by virtue of this opposition that the appreciation and ordering of values becomes possible, as the Dionysian offers a counterperspective to the negativity of the rationalist will to truth and therefore discloses the possibility of a different evaluation: values can be reassessed according to the fundamental orientation of the will that they express (assertive for art, negative for logical schematicism). Thus Nietzsche's genealogical reinterpretation of values rests on this opposition between the two forms of the will to power, logical and artistic, which allows the quality of the forces present in the will to power to be seen and judged accordingly. On the contrary, the "monism" with which Foucault envisions the will to truth has the paradoxical consequence of destroying the possibility of this reassessment by depriving him of any criterion on which to ground value. This theoretical problem finds a more concrete expression in the reproach often addressed to Foucault by his commentators, namely, that he can justify neither his critique nor the necessity of resisting the ever growing influence of the will to truth (the "normalization" and "disciplinarization" of Western societies described at the end of *Discipline and Punish*, for example), a point to which I shall return at the conclusion of Chapter 4.

Foucault's position thus seems very ambiguous, insofar as his notion of the will to truth derives its meaning and importance from an implicit Nietzschean foundation, from which he takes up certain themes but to which he is unfaithful on fundamental points. Moreover, his use of the concept in his own work is changeable: sometimes the expression clearly has an ontological dimension, for example, when Foucault speaks generally of the "specific history" of the will to truth and describes the imperious necessity with which it "grows stronger, deeper and more implacable" (*OD*, 56). But at other moments, it can be understood in a psychologizing sense, as a simple desire to know, which would be one of the structural characteristics of the Western mentality, the "never-ending demand for truth" (*HS*, 77)[56] or this "petition to know" (*HS*, 78) mentioned in *The History of Sexuality*, which, however, also reinforces the ambiguity by describing in a single stroke the "*will* that sustains them [the discourses] and the strategic *intention* that supports them" (*HS*, 8; my italics). But these two definitions, ontological and psychologizing, are clearly incompatible (the first having precisely the function of combating the second) and, moreover, are never discussed by Foucault.

Given these multiple uncertainties and the impossibility of using as such the Nietzschean model to which Foucault refers, it seems clear that the interest of the notion of will to truth does not reside in its possible definition. Its existence

remains a postulate that no element of the archaeological period gave us to antic-
ipate, and it is neither justified nor explained. There therefore remains the
hypothesis—theoretically lighter and doubtless more productive—that its importance is *strategic* rather than theoretical, and is due to the *role* played by the idea
at a crucial moment of the evolution of Foucault's work. The introduction of
the will to truth has a double benefit for Foucault. Firstly, adopting the notion
allows him to also import the method elaborated for its study, that is, genealogy,
and therefore to escape the impasses of archaeology by shifting from the study
of the discursive to a contextual analysis of *all* practices. Secondly, the concept
provides him with a new angle of approach from which to analyze truth and
answer the question mentioned above: why certain discourses have specific "powers" while others do not. In order to test the fecundity of this hypothesis, I shall
now explore these two points.

Foucauldian Genealogy and Its Aims

Foucault's characterization of Nietzschean genealogy is well known and has been
studied many times.[57] Rather than proposing yet another general description, in
order to clarify its differences as a method from archaeology I shall analyze the
concrete manner in which Foucault puts it into practice in *The Order of Discourse*.
From this perspective, the way in which the theme of the will to truth is introduced is emblematic:

> Certainly, when viewed *at the level of a proposition*, on the inside of a discourse,
> the division of true and false is neither arbitrary nor modifiable nor institu-
> tional nor violent. But when we view things *on a different scale*, when we ask
> the question of what this will to truth has been and constantly is, across our
> discourses, this will to truth which has crossed so many centuries of our
> history; what it is, in its general form, the type of division which governs our
> will to know [*notre volonté de savoir*], then what we see taking shape is perhaps
> something like a system of exclusion, a historical, modifiable, and institution-
> ally constraining system. (*OD*, 54; my italics)

The distinction between the two levels ("at the level of a proposition" and "at
another scale") reveals Foucault's methodological turn: the first of the two levels, "on the inside" of discourse, clearly refers to archaeology itself, and describes
an internal "division" whose nature remains imprecise, but which is clearly connected to the predication of truth seen as a procedure of exclusion (of "false" discourses). Significantly, this division is spelled out in the above passage by means
of a series of negations that evoke the metaphysical conception of truth analyzed

above, defining it as immutable ("neither modifiable"), nonconventional ("neither arbitrary . . . nor institutional") and neutral, or objective ("nor violent"). But the possibility of placing oneself "at another level" and of using a historicizing lens immediately throws doubt on the status and pertinence of such an understanding. Indeed, despite the notion of scale connoting quantity rather than quality, the change in question is not of a quantitative order. It does not try to enlarge the perspective, to study more discourses and practices, but rather, to bring to the fore the perspectival nature of the object under consideration: the division of the true and the false that archaeology describes is neither primary nor immutable nor objective, but must be referred to a center of interpretation (the "will to truth"), which, not being of a discursive order, cannot be examined by archaeology. Thus the stake of such an analysis is to show that the division of true and false, previously seen as the principle of an "internal" and supposedly atemporal exclusion, in reality responds to the "external" demands of the "historical division" studied above, and to its requirements for truth understood as objective and rational.

This approach clearly displays some of the characteristics of Nietzschean genealogy: it places itself at the level of practices (the internal division of the true and the false), interrogating not only the forms of their realization but also the values (truth) and the interests (those of the "will") that they put into play. It therefore adopts the principle that each practice must be historically analyzed[58] and referred back to the type of interpretation that it secretly expresses (here, the Platonic division), while insisting, however, that this historical analysis does not take the metaphysical form of a teleology or, conversely, the search for a founding origin (the division is "historical" and "modifiable," as already suggested by the variations studied above [LCP, 154]).[59] Thus Foucault's genealogy questions the allegedly neutral and disinterested character of the practices under study (the division is not "arbitrary"), by showing that they obey imperatives that have nothing to do with theory (LCP, 154),[60] as the following passage indicates:

> "True" discourse, freed from desire and power by the necessity of its form, cannot recognise the will to truth which pervades it; and the will to truth, having imposed itself on us for a very long time, is such that the truth it wants cannot fail to mask it. Thus all that appears to our eyes is a truth conceived as a richness, a fecundity, a gentle and insidiously universal force, and in contrast we are unaware of the will to truth, that prodigious machinery designed to exclude. (OD, 56)

Therefore, genealogical analysis radically questions the notion of truth itself,[61] which appears as the "mask" secreted by the will to truth to disguise its natural voracity with an apparent impassibility. Directly echoing Nietzsche's analyses,[62] Foucault suggests that all truth arises from a first appropriation and violence (carried out by the philosopher at the expense of the Sophist) hidden by the apparently positive character of the object that it produces (the "richness," "fecundity," and "gentleness" of truth).[63] Against the "insidious universality" of truth, genealogy reveals its constituted character—and that it is only, as Foucault says elsewhere, an "invention of the ruling classes" (*LCP*, 142).

The consequence of this, as one might have expected, is the bringing to the fore of the concept of interpretation, central both to the analyzed object and to the genealogical method itself. The object, because there is no more for Foucault than for Nietzsche an "original signified," "nothing absolutely primary to interpret, because at bottom everything is already interpretation" (*DE*, 1: 572). The method, as the only possibility remaining open to the genealogist, is to combat the carefully sedimented interpretations with a new interpretation, whose only merit is that it knows and does not try to disguise its own interpretative nature:

> If interpretation were the slow exposure of the meaning hidden in an origin,
> then only Metaphysics could interpret the development of humanity. But if
> interpretation is the violence or surreptitious appropriation of a system of rules,
> which in itself has no essential meaning, in order to impose a direction . . .
> then the development of humanity is a series of interpretations. The role of
> genealogy is to record its history: the history of morals, ideals, and metaphysi-
> cal concepts, the history of the concept of liberty or of the aesthetic life; as they
> stand for the emergence of different interpretations. (*LCP*, 151–52)[64]

The point of interpretation, therefore, is not to reveal an original given, but to retrace the appearance and absorption of previous interpretations (in *The Order of Discourse*, the different forms taken by the division of the true and the false), that is, to reveal the perspectival characteristic of all truth by returning it to the interpretation from which it springs and to those that it has the function of masking. Thus it is "destined to interpret itself, and cannot escape returning on itself" (*DE*, 1: 573).

As shown by Hubert Dreyfus and Paul Rabinow, this understanding of interpretation returns neither to traditional exegesis (the "commentary" that the archaeologist despised so much) nor to a hermeneutics of suspicion such as Ricoeur's, which presupposes the existence of a profound meaning deformed by everyday comprehension and practices of subjects, recoverable through an analysis of these distortions. Instead, it leads Foucault to the elaboration of an "interpretative analytic" (*MF*, 120 ff.) with which to "interrogate the sources and uses of [anterior] concepts," without, however, giving them a "universal grounding in either thought or Being" (*MF*, 122). Because it adopts a concrete and empirical approach, the Foucauldian hermeneutic is distinguished, at least in appearance, from that of Heidegger and places itself resolutely under the aegis of Nietzsche, as the following passage says explicitly:

> Husserl and Heidegger bring up for discussion again all our knowledge and its foundations, but they do this by beginning from that which is original. This analysis takes place, however, at the expense of any articulated historical content. Instead, what I liked in Nietzsche is the attempt to bring up for discussion again the fundamental concepts of knowledge, of morals, and of metaphysics by appealing to a historical analysis of the positivistic type, without going back to origins. (*FL*, 77)

One also notes that this revival of the theme of interpretation presents Foucault with a supplementary advantage, in that it allows him to "justify" archaeology by genealogy: "Empirical studies . . . allowed the identification of the level of discursive practices. The general character of these practices and the correct methods for their analysis were catalogued under the name of archaeology. The research undertaken in relation to the will to knowledge must now give this collection a theoretical justification."[65] What could this "justification" be? It is probably connected to the honesty with which genealogy reflexively interrogates the perspective presupposed by its own questioning, following the paradox according to which the only possibility for an interpretation to be authentic lies in the explicit illumination of its own interpretative character. It is probably from this standpoint that this curious statement of Foucault's can be understood: "I am very well aware that I have only ever written fictions. However I do not wish to say by that that they are outside of truth. It seems to me that there is a possibility of making fiction work in truth, of generating effects of truth with a fictional discourse."[66] Genealogically speaking, it is indeed strictly impossible to contrast fiction and truth, as both are interpretations (and the very idea of such an opposition would be metaphysical, if only because of the strict dualism it presupposes). Therefore, the only possible truth for the genealogist consists in not disguising the "fictive" or "fictionalizing" nature of his enterprise, as the text goes on to say, and in struggling against the dominant interpretation (which valorizes scientific "truth") by seeking to produce precisely the effects of truth that this interpretation values in order to turn them against it. In short, it consists in apparently playing the game of scientificity in order to better put it in question, without, however, pretending to articulate an absolutely "true" interpretation—which would amount to taking up, despite himself, the ideal he is fighting against.

In fact, what I want to do, . . . consists in elaborating an interpretation, a reading of a particular reality which would be such that, on one the hand, this interpretation could produce effects of truth, and that, on the other, these effects of truth could become the instruments at the heart of possible struggles. To say the truth to make it attackable. (*DE*, 3: 633)

More generally, for Foucault the use of genealogy results in the need to redefine the relationship between archaeology and genealogy, both of which respond to the same need: to delineate the possibility for discourses of being "in the truth":

The genealogical portion, on the other hand, applies to the series where discourse is effectively formed: it tries to grasp it in its power of affirmation, by which I mean not so much a power which would be opposed to that of denying, but rather *the power to constitute domains of objects, in respect of which one can affirm or deny true or false propositions.* (*OD*, 73; my italics)[67]

Like archaeology, genealogy therefore seeks to determine the conditions of acceptability of truth, as Foucault will later confirm:

By speaking of archaeology, strategy and genealogy, I don't think that it is a matter of distinguishing three successive levels which would have developed one from the other, but rather of characterizing three necessarily simultaneous dimensions of the same analysis, three dimensions which should allow in their very simultaneity the recovery . . . *of the conditions which make a singularity acceptable.*[68]

Yet although it could never have been a question for Foucault of abandoning the archaeological problem of the conditions of possibility of knowledge,[69] it now becomes necessary to place these conditions within a larger context by polemically referring them to the will to truth that works through them: "The great mutations in scientific thought can perhaps be read as the consequences of a discovery, but they can also be read as the appearance of new forms in the will to truth" (*OD*, 54). This passage revives the archaeological theme par excellence of the mutations of knowledge, as well as the opposition between surface (the "discoveries") and depth. However, these mutations do not refer to an epistemic change anymore, but to a break in the history of the will to truth. The same shift is expressed in another text, which implicitly takes up the theme of the historical *a priori* by describing the apparition of a "will to know which imposed on the knowing subject, and *in some sense prior to all experience*, a certain position, a certain gaze and a certain function (to see rather than to read, to verify rather than make commentaries on)" (*OD*, 55).

Thus the introduction of the concept of the will to truth grounds the difference of "point of entry" and "perspective" between the two methods described by *The Order of Discourse*. As we have seen, the idea was introduced by Foucault to discover why certain discourses have specific "powers" that necessitate the "constraint" exercised on them by the will to truth, a problem that could only plunge the archaeologist into perplexity because it was incapable of resolution at the discursive level alone. Now the genealogist is able to reply that these powers are explained by the value given since the Platonic division to truth is conceived as "objective," which prefigures the "scientific" type developed by the two later divisions. These "powers" are therefore connected to the fact that truth is fundamentally *willed* in the West, and show themselves as proportional to the coefficient of truth/scientificity attributed to each discourse. This is the reason for the powerlessness of discourses that have no pretension to this sort of truth (children's tales for example, although they have specific structures and obey precise rules,[70] or more simply, the non-"serious" everyday statements with which archaeology was not concerned).[71]

Through this analysis of the power of true discourses and, more generally, of the relationship between truth and power, the genealogist is led to redefine the conditions of acceptability of truth. As the following chapter will establish, the major contribution of genealogy is the idea that truth, when actually predicated, influences in return the conditions of its own acceptability. In other words, it is not only as a function of epistemic rules, but also in reference to what is *effectively* recognized as true, that the field of acceptability of propositions is constituted and transformed. Thus the analyses of the relationship of power and knowledge in the case of the human sciences will show that the rules of acceptability themselves are shaped *internally* by the *nonepistemic* demands that control the effective predication of the truth—for Foucault, for example, the "truth" of psychoanalytic discourses is shaped by the social and political requirement that psychoanalysis should "heal" (i.e., normalize) its patients. If it is still necessary to be "in the truth" in order to say the truth, the demands to which one must conform to be there can no longer be considered as purely theoretical: in fact, they depend on the power relations specific to each epoch; the problem then becomes to determine whether the field defined by the acceptability and predication of truth should be considered as transcendental or not.

Genealogy thus profoundly transforms the critical question by taking the opposite path to the old archaeological *épochē*, whose principle was the possibility of dissociating the conditions of acceptability from the criteria for the predication of truth, and therefore to treat acceptability neutrally. To be interrogated now is the way in which the effective predication of truth rebounds on its conditions of acceptability: Foucault now has to focus his analysis on the "effects of power" of discourses considered as "true," and therefore, given the history of the will to truth sketched by *The Order Of Discourse*, as "scientific." Such a refocusing is for the most part the aim of the following passage, where the displacement described above can easily be observed:

> It is really *against the effects of the power of a discourse that is considered to be*
> *scientific that the genealogy must wage its struggle.* . . . It is surely necessary to
> question ourselves about our aspirations to the kind of power that is presumed
> to accompany such a science. It is surely the following kinds of question that
> would need to be posed: what types of knowledge do you want to disqualify in
> the very instance of your demand: "Is it a science?" Which speaking subject . . .
> do you then want to "diminish" when you say: "I who conduct this discourse
> am conducting a scientific discourse, and I am a scientist"? (*PK*, 84; my italics)

One can recognize a theme dear to archaeology (to study the discourses aiming at scientificity) and some of the characteristics of the genealogical interrogation (its polemical character, the establishment of "types," the suspicion cast over the secret interests and motivations of the speaker). But rather than analyzing the conditions under which a proposition can be said to be scientific, Foucault now questions the status of science itself and the effects that are attached to it, assigning himself the task of reexamining the "inscription of knowledges [*savoirs*] in the hierarchy of power belonging to science" (*PK*, 85; modified). In all likelihood, this new type of interrogation motivates his growing interest in the human sciences, as they are the discourses in which the effects of the power of truth are most material and most clearly identifiable. Consequently, *Discipline and Punish* and the first volume of *The History of Sexuality*, which analyze respectively the births of criminology and psychoanalysis, respond to the project of "making a free use," through a "series of examples,"[72] of the Nietzschean model put in place by *The Order of Discourse*.

However, if the aim of genealogy is indeed, as the passage indicates, to question the model of scienticity itself, Foucault could logically be expected to choose as his targets the discourses that present the highest truth-values, for example the fundamental sciences such as mathematics or physics.[73] But, strangely enough, these are almost absent from his analyses.[74] Is this due to Foucault's implicit belief in objective truth whose traces can be found in *The Order of Discourse*, as analyzed above? Or should one conclude that the truth-value accorded to the discourses studied is not the only criterion of interest for Foucault? I shall show that this paradox can only be explained by the more refined model of truth established by the later Foucault, which allows the distinction between the "subjectivizing" truths and those that are less directly so (a category to which mathematics and physics belong) to be established and historically founded. But at the present stage the question can only remain unanswered.[75]

Notwithstanding this particular point, this interrogation of the power of discourses of truth leads Foucault to examine the relationship between power and truth itself:

> Science, the constraint of truth, the obligation to truth and the ritualized procedures for its production have traversed absolutely the whole of Western society for millennia and are now so universalized as to become the general law for all civilizations. What is the history of this "will to truth"? What are its effects? How is all this interwoven with relations of power? (*PK*, 66; modified)

Such a shift was predictable from *The Order of Discourse*'s insistence that the will to truth, far from being an abstraction or a fiction, is historically invested in the practices and material institutions through which knowledge is constituted and defined:

> This will to truth, like the other systems of exclusion, rests on an institutional support: it is both reinforced and renewed by a whole strata of practices, such as pedagogy, of course; and the system of books, publishing, libraries; learned societies in the past and laboratories now. But it is also renewed, no doubt more profoundly, by the way in which knowledge is put to work, valorised, distributed, and in a sense attributed, in a society. Let us recall at this point, and only symbolically, the old Greek principle: though arithmetic may well be the concern of democratic cities, because it teaches about the relations of equality, geometry alone must be taught in oligarchies, since it demonstrates the proportions within inequality. (*OD*, 55)

This allusion to the "old Greek principle" beautifully illustrates the claims studied above, as it suggests by implicit reference to Plato and Aristotle that to each political regime corresponds a specific knowledge (arithmetical equality for democracy, geometrical "equality" for oligarchy), and that each regime tends to propagate only that particular one. "Another power, another knowledge" (*DP*, 226), as Foucault will say later about prisons. Equally, this passage demonstrates in advance the impossibility of separating the study of the will to truth from that of the institutions (the "systems of publishing," "libraries," *sociétés savantes*) and from the practices ("pedagogy") that convey it. What is immediately apparent here is the fundamental impossibility of thinking power in an asymmetrical perspective, as the source or the cause of truth; correspondingly, truth cannot be considered as the prerogative of a single person or structure (for example, the king or the state) that would unilaterally determine the appearance of truth discourses. Truth can no longer be explained by reference to a power that would have precedence over it as the principle of its genesis. On the contrary, the task of the genealogist is to show how the functioning of power generates effects of truth that reinforce it in a circular dynamic. Between truth and power there is no simple relationship of determination, but a structural enmeshing: "There can be no possible exercise of power without a certain economy of discourses of truth which operates through and on the basis of this association. We are subjected to the production of truth through power and we cannot exercise power except through the production of truth" (*PK*, 93).

Two paths are therefore opened to enquiry, which will be successively explored in the following chapter: firstly, the study of the concrete developments of the "initial model of analysis"[76] established by *The Order of Discourse*, and the identification of the understanding of truth that they presuppose; secondly, the examination in turn of the consequences of this new orientation for the original critical question. The general horizon for such a questioning is to determine if this transformation of the problem of the conditions of the possibility of truth escapes the return of the transcendental to which archaeology fell prey.

FOUR

The Genealogical Analysis of the Human Sciences and Its Consequences for the Revising of the Critical Question

An examination of Foucault's texts that appeared between 1975 and 1978 reveals at first sight a considerable contrast between the empirical approach of *Discipline and Punish* and volume 1 of *The History of Sexuality*—both focus on a specific problem (the birth of the modern penal system and the nineteenth-century formation of a *scientia sexualis*), and the articles and interviews where the claims expressed are more general and often more ambitious. More subtly, this methodological dichotomy is displayed by the very fabric of both these works, which alternate the examination of precise examples (this house of correction, that use of time, such and such a disciplinary procedure) with passages that are concerned with the nature of power and the appropriate means to analyze it.[1] This peculiar structure presents two difficulties. Firstly, it makes the reader wonder about the possibility of reconciling the detailed analyses of concrete techniques where a specific power and a specific knowledge are articulated,[2] with Foucault's general declarations about "power," "knowledge," and "truth."[3] While bearing in mind his rejection of any "metaphysics of power with a capital *P*" (*DE*, 3: 630), we shall have to see whether these two approaches, empirical and theoretical, give their objects identical definitions, and whether the generalizations proposed are legitimate or not. Secondly, this dual approach suggests two divergent paths for reading Foucault: either to follow his progress step by step and to repeat the enmeshing of the general and the particular, at the risk of losing the distance necessary to assess Foucault's wider theoretical claims; or to start with the relationship of power and knowledge itself, and analyze it in a precise example, thus giving a detailed illustration of the results of the genealogical approach before considering the extension of the model—a solution that has the disadvantage of presupposing the knowledge of the more general definitions with which Foucault dots his empirical analyses. As it appears to be clearer and more fertile, and because it reflects the movement of generalization that animates Foucault's own progress, I have chosen the second approach and taken as point of departure the genealogical analyses of the human sciences.

Three Countermodels to Understand the Relationship of Power and Knowledge

Although the domains concerned are different, *Discipline and Punish* and volume 1 of *The History of Sexuality* have almost the same angle of approach, as is shown by the similarity of the two following passages:

> Thus by an analysis of penal leniency as a technique of power, one might understand . . . in what way a specific mode of subjection was able to give birth to man as an object of knowledge for a discourse with a "scientific" status. (*DP*, 24)

> [It is necessary] to locate the procedures by which that will to knowledge regarding sex, which characterizes the Modern Occident, caused the rituals of confession to function within the norms of scientific regularity: how did this immense and traditional extortion of the sexual confession come to be constituted in scientific terms? (*HS*, 65)

In both cases, Foucault attempts to apply to the human sciences the program established by *The Order of Discourse*, that is, to examine genealogically the empirical conditions of their birth ("a specific mode of subjection," the new "scientific regularity" of the "rituals of confession"); and, on the basis of this examination, to resume the archaeological interrogation of the conditions of possibility of knowledge that are formulated in them ("to give birth to man as an object of knowledge," which, as we recall, was exactly the problematic of archaeology in the last two chapters of *The Order of Things*).

From this perspective, one of the major contributions of *Discipline and Punish* is the discovery of the impossibility of understanding the birth of the human sciences without taking into account the development of new forms of power:[4] "What struck me, in observing the human sciences, was that the development of all these branches of knowledge can be in no way be dissociated from the exercise of power. . . . The birth of the human sciences goes hand in hand with the installation of new mechanisms of power" (*PPC*, 106; my italics). It is in order to ground this claim and define these "new mechanisms of power" that Foucault is progressively led to formulate a conception of power distinct from that which he labels "juridico-repressive,"[5] as well as to thinking about the articulation of knowledge and power according to a model focused around the notion of "discipline."[6] The importance of this model is considerable, as beyond its inherent interest it constitutes the theoretical foundation for the revision of the critical question, giving this its specifically genealogical dimension through the analyses of subjection and objectification, and of their implied understanding of truth. The examination of the model of "power-knowledge" is, therefore, the necessary prelude to any analysis of the critical question itself. In order to analyze it and demonstrate *a contrario* its originality, I shall contrast it with three other paradigms that constitute its more or less explicit counterpoints in Foucault's thought.

The idea that there is, or should be, an articulation between knowledge and power at the political level is not new *per se*. In the *Republic*, Plato had already developed the thesis that only those should govern who are made worthy by nature, education, and the superior knowledge that they command (the Guardians).[7] Conversely, the denunciation of the abusive exercise of power expressed in the *Gorgias* rests on the idea that the tyrant, not being enlightened by knowledge, is incapable of identifying and obtaining the real object of his striving (i.e., what is truly good for him) and therefore, contrary to appearances, cannot attain happiness: he has most of what he desires but nothing he really wants.[8] According to this model, knowledge is capable of exercising two inverse and complementary functions in relation to power: firstly, a regulative and foundational role, symbolized in Plato's work by the figure of the philosopher-king who is illuminated by a knowledge that legitimates the power that he exercises, guiding its application and keeping it within the limits of right; secondly and conversely, a critical function, whose most illustrious paradigm is given by the death of Socrates, the ambiguous symbol of knowledge questioning the abuse of a blindly exercised power through its very submission to it.[9]

Clearly, Foucault does not understand the relationship between power and knowledge in this perspective, for two reasons. The first is that both of the above hypotheses presuppose an anteriority and exteriority of knowledge in relation to power. Whether its role is normative or critical, knowledge is held to enjoy an independence from power that would serve as a guarantee at a moral level. It is precisely this independence that Foucault seeks to question: "Perhaps, too, we should abandon a whole tradition that allows us to imagine that knowledge can exist only where the power relations are suspended and that knowledge can develop only outside its injunctions, its demands and its interests" (*DP*, 27). Foucault's position is thus the opposite to Plato's, as he sees an interdependence of power and knowledge, even a subordination of knowledge to power, which would *per se* deprive the former of its critical vocation.[10] This is why Foucault will question the neutrality of the various sciences of man (such as criminology, psychiatry, etc.), by showing that they are the correlates of new power practices, that they respond to social, political, and economic aims (which have no hint of disinterestedness in them), and therefore that they obey necessities other than the purely epistemic requirements formerly described by the archaeology.

In this sense, he comes close to some of the analyses of the Frankfurt School, even while differing on essential questions.[11] For example, he shares the suspicion cast by Theodor Adorno and Max Horkheimer on objectivity and scientific neutrality, the uncovering of the instrumental character of Western rationality and its forms of domination, the denunciation of the encroaching standardization of individuals, even the chronological divisions that identify the end of the eighteenth century as the beginning of modernity. This comparison should be strongly qualified, however, as Foucault felt it necessary to distinguish his project from that of the Frankfurt School, for example by clearly stating that he was "not a Weberian"[12] and by criticizing the (Habermasian) idea of a single rationality and historical division.[13] More generally, his opposition to these thinkers is centered around three essential points: firstly, his insistence on the multiplicity of the rationalities and strategies of power, as opposed to the model of a single rationality; secondly, his emphasis on the productive, not repressive, character of power; and finally, the fact that Foucault never believed in the possibility of escaping the dominant instrumental logic through a different, liberated, use of reason—this fundamental distrust of the Enlightenment project setting him in explicit opposition to Jürgen Habermas.[14]

The second shortcoming of the Platonic model is due to the representation of power involved, which strongly resembles that which Foucault criticizes in denouncing the "theory of sovereignty" (*PK*, 105). Whether partisans of the divine right or contractual models, these theories share the idea that power is the prerogative of a monarch, entitled, within rightful limits, to use it as he sees fit.[15] But whether this use should be enlightened or not by knowledge (following the Platonic opposition) is not the real problem for Foucault, as the understanding of power on which this hypothesis rests does not correspond to the reality of its functioning. Power, he indicates, must not be referred to the single source of the person of the sovereign, nor even thought in an "economic" manner, that is, as a good capable of being gained or lost. Moreover, if power does involve knowledge, it is neither in the form of a reflective and conscious decision taken by an elite in (or against) the interests of those whom it governs,[16] nor, conversely, in the form of a resistance whose voice would be independent of that which it denounces (*HS*, 95 ff.). Foucault explicitly and totally opposes the tradition of the philosophy of rights that understands the connection of knowledge and power either as a relationship of tutelage or as a critical relation, and which seeks in both cases to normalize power through knowledge. For Foucault, knowledge is neither the guide nor the conscience of power, and contrary to what Pascal thought, ideal power, if it exists, is not that which is accompanied by science.

It may therefore be more tempting to compare the position taken by Foucault to that of Francis Bacon, which is apparently closer since it renounces any normative perspective in order to subordinate knowledge to power. When he states, following the now famous adage (Foucaldian *avant la lettre*) that "human knowledge and human power meet in one,"[17] Bacon implicitly contradicts the Platonic paradigm by defining the power-knowledge relationship as doubly instrumental. On the one hand, he is clearly musing over the uses that could be made of knowledge to better the human condition through technical innovation. Thus, by providing the knowledge of the "secret movements of things," natural philosophy could produce inventions useful to the State and the people.[18] This is not merely an additional consideration, but the motor of the search for knowledge itself: "It is not the pleasure of curiosity, nor the quiet of resolution, nor the raising of the spirit . . . that are the true ends of knowledge. . . . It is a restitution and reinvesting (in great part) of man to the sovereignty and power . . . which he had in his first state of creation."[19] Consequently, the foundation of the "House of Solomon" in the *New Atlantis* has two main aims: the "knowledge of causes" and the "enlargement of the frontiers of the human empire," the first being destined to make the second possible. On the other hand, Bacon explicitly places knowledge under the tutelage of power, as he judges it preferable that in Solomon's court only a few devoted servants of the state, "apt and chosen," should be authorized to practice natural philosophy. Equally, only those discoveries judged "profitable" for society and the state should be made public. The "Brothers" of the House of Solomon are tasked with elaborating, by means of a highly complex and institutionalized organization, a knowledge that a special council alone then decides whether it is desirable to render public.[20] It is therefore clear that, for the author of the *New Atlantis*, the perfecting of the exercise of power and the interests of the state depend on the development and mastery of an adequate knowledge.

Foucault seems to borrow two major points from Bacon: the idea of the functional usefulness of knowledge for power, and the necessity of establishing institutions and a procedure of control for its production and diffusion. However, the following statement implicitly contests this comparison: "We should rather admit that power produces knowledge (*and not by simply encouraging it because it serves power or by applying it because it is useful*)" (*DP*, 27; my italics). For Foucault, the problem is not that Bacon (whose position is summarized under its two aspects within the parentheses) was wrong, but that he didn't go far enough. He understood the relationship of knowledge and power as unilateral, making the first dependent on the second, but without considering that the exercise of power could be constitutively modified by the discoveries of natural philosophy. Knowledge remains an auxiliary whose presence is certainly desirable but which does not fundamentally transform the functioning of the power that controls it. Conversely, Bacon does not doubt the possibility of objective knowledge; on the contrary, it is the objectivity of natural philosophy that gives it its value in the eyes of the statesman. Although Bacon admits the possibility and even the necessity of the use of knowledge by power, he does not consider that the norms of knowledge could be modified, even created, by the control that is exercised on its production. Hence the relation between the two terms remains, despite appearances, a relation of exteriority and relative contingence.

Finally, there is a third model which can be compared with the Foucaldian approach: the Marxist analysis of ideology, to which Foucault seems to come close on at least two points. Exactly as Marx did before him, he takes the opposite direction to the tradition of philosophical idealism—that of the meditation in the study, the "retreat" dear to Descartes or Malebranche, and desacralizes knowledge by affirming that it is not "the child of protracted solitude" (*PK*, 131), insisting on the contrary that it is embedded in circuits of production where it is elaborated and diffused just as economic commodities are. Correspondingly, the discourses of the human sciences could be interpreted as "ideological," as they reinforce in the ideal order of representations the material domination guaranteed for the bourgeoisie by the development of disciplinary processes, by hiding it beneath the mask of universality and objectivity. Thus one could say that the pretension to scientificity that characterizes the human sciences in reality disguises the "corpus of methods and knowledge," the "trifles" where the "man of Modern Humanism" was born (*DP*, 141). Foucault would thus echo Marx, for whom ideology is characterized by its effects of legitimization, which seek to establish the ascendancy of the dominant class by giving the point of view of that part as that of the whole:

"Each new class which takes the place of that which dominated before is obliged, if only to arrive at its ends, . . . to give its thoughts the form of universality, to represent them as the only reasonable ones, the only universally valid."[21]

However, three factors prevent the adoption of the Marxist paradigm. Firstly, Foucault rejects the idea that the deformed knowledge of the human sciences could be opposed with a truer knowledge, freed from ideological distortions. Further still, the very pretension to scientific status displayed by certain Marxists[22] appears eminently suspect to him: "I shall seem reactionary: why should Marxist practice be called scientific?" (*DE*, 2: 168).[23] He thus turns the Marxist denunciation of ideology against itself by showing that it is haunted precisely by the ideal of the free knowledge whose existence it denies:

> I have always felt uncomfortable with this notion of ideology which has been used in recent years. It has been used to explain errors or illusions, or to analyze presentations—in short, everything that impedes the formation of true discourse. It has also being used to show the relation between what goes on in people's heads and their place in the conditions of production. (*PPC*, 118)

On the contrary, the critique of the "repressive hypothesis" established in chapter 1 of *The History of Sexuality*, volume 1, is meant to refute the idea that power would have the function of "preventing" the formation of such a "true" knowledge.

Secondly, Foucault rejects the hypothesis that only an increase in awareness could liberate the oppressed class from ideological fictions. He does not deem it relevant to analyze the relationship of power and knowledge by reference to representations that would be more or less falsified by power, as the following passage indicates: "What is said about sex must not be analyzed as the simple *surface of projection* of these power mechanisms. Indeed, it is *really in discourse* that power and knowledge are joined together" (*HS*, 100; modified). Foucault thus rejects the idea that knowledge could be merely an ideological "projection" of relations of material domination, an idea that Marx himself illustrated by the famous metaphor of the *camera obscura*. Foucault does not believe that one could analyze "power-knowledge" by distinguishing two levels, that of representations, which would have the task of hiding the second, that of brute reality. Neither does he believe that it would be profitable to focus the analysis on the opposition, as developed by Lukács for example, between consciousness and false consciousness, as expressed by the following passage: "The more I go, the more it seems to me that the formation of discourses and the genealogy of knowledge need to be analyzed, not in terms of types of consciousness, modes of perception and forms of ideology, but in terms of tactics and strategies of power" (*PK*, 77).[24]

The final reason for rejecting the Marxist model, beyond that it presupposes the possibility of an intrinsically true but repressed discourse and gives too much importance to representations, is that it rests on a dualistic opposition between infra- and super-structures, which causes it to miss the specificity of disciplinary mechanisms.[25] Foucault rejects both the reductionism of the functionalist thesis, which defines power through an analysis of the economic processes at work in the social body,[26] and the idea that knowledge could be explained by a unilateral determination by them. According to him, the Marxist representation of ideology makes the mistake of always placing knowledge "in second position in relation to something which, at the end of the day, must function for it as an infra-structure or as economic, material, etc., determinant" (*DE*, 2: 148). However, as the study of the Platonic and Baconian models has shown, so long as one understands the relationship between knowledge and power through a logic of linear anteriority, one cannot but miss the circular dynamic of their common genesis, whichever the direction chosen.

The Power-Knowledge "Nexus" as the Matrix of Truth: Subjection and Objectification

"Between techniques of knowledge and strategies of power, there is no exteriority" (*HS*, 98), declares the first volume of *The History of Sexuality*, while in the same spirit *Discipline and Punish* describes "the machinery by which the power relations give rise to a possible corpus of knowledge, and knowledge extends and reinforces the effects of this power" (*DP*, 29). The central idea of these two works, therefore, is that the various types of knowledge of man and the historical forms of power entertain a necessary connection in which the two terms are indissociable, neither of them having precedence over the other—whence the metaphor of the "enmeshing" or the "circularity" dear to Foucault. The particularity of this relationship is that it is neither normative nor instrumental, but makes each the condition of possibility for the development of its counterpart. Thus Foucault adopts the genetic perspective that alone will allow him to establish the coextensive nature of knowledge and power within the human sciences by genealogically returning them to their common birth: "A corpus of knowledge [*savoir*], techniques, 'scientific' discourses is formed and becomes entangled with the practice of the power to punish. This book is intended as a . . . genealogy of the present scientifico-legal complex from which the power to punish derives its basis" (*DP*, 23).

But given the impossibility of having recourse to the preceding models, how can this "scientifico-judicial complex" be understood? Which "knowledge" and which "power" does it involve? An answer to these questions can be found in Foucault's concept of "discipline," which is given a double function. Firstly, following the terminology established in "Nietzsche, Genealogy, History," the disciplines are both the *Entstehung* (provenance) and the *Herkunft* (emergence) of modern power and knowledge. Thus Foucault identifies the "provenance" of the reform of the prisons by showing how it takes up and amplifies the disciplinary techniques established more than a century before in specialized establishments.[27] Correspondingly, he identifies its conditions of "emergence" by connecting them to the modifications in the balance of political forces introduced in response to the growing need for the large-scale control and management of populations (*HS*, 139 ff.).[28] The analysis of disciplines thus plays an essential role for genealogy, as it allows the identification of the type of power that still rules us, bio-power (*HS*, 142), and of its historical conditions of birth. Secondly, this study permits Foucault to kill two birds with one stone, by defining both the nature of the "new mechanisms of power," mentioned above, and these "ignoble archives" (*DP*, 191)—an implicit reference to the *pudenda origo* described by Nietzsche—which were constituted simultaneously with the mechanisms of power and gave birth to the human sciences.[29] The disciplines therefore constitute for Foucault an original theoretical paradigm from which to understand, within a genetic and genealogical perspective, the imbrication of power and knowledge, a paradigm I shall now analyze in itself before examining its consequences for Foucault's understanding of truth and the critical question.

Disciplines, declares Foucault, are techniques that were developed in well-circumscribed loci (prisons, barracks, hospitals, schools, regiments, etc.), and which sought to increase the productivity of the individual while reducing his potential for insubordination—in other words, to place in an inversely proportional relationship the individual's economic profitability and his political autonomy. Thus they mark the birth of a new form of power,[30] a capillary and individualizing form, on all accounts opposed to the old monarchical version described in relation to the Platonic paradigm. Their principal theoretical interest is that they establish the conceptual armature needed to understand power-knowledge by introducing the two essential notions of "subjection" (*assujettissement*) and "objectification" (*objectivation*). The first of these notions is involved in Foucault's very definition of the disciplines: "These methods, which made possible the meticulous control of the operations of the body, which assured the constant *subjection* of its forces and imposed upon them a relation of docility-usefulness, might be called 'disciplines'" (*DP*, 137). In *Discipline and Punish*, objectification is the almost obligatory correlate of subjection: the first pages of chapter 1 immediately emphasize this complementarity by describing the "relations that invest human bodies and subjugate them by turning them into objects of knowledge" (*DP*, 28; my italics).[31] In the rest of the book the two terms are generally mentioned together, as in the following phrase: "the subjection of those who are perceived as objects and the objectification of those who are subjected" (*DP*, 185).

Nevertheless, despite their initial reciprocity the two terms increasingly gain an unequal importance for Foucault, who will progressively stress subjection to the detriment of objectification, and give it a more accomplished theoretical elaboration. Thus, volume 1 of *The History of Sexuality* complicates the notion of subjection by understanding it as "men's subjection: their constitution as subjects in both senses of the word" (*HS*, 60), "senses" that are clarified in a later text as follows: "There are two meanings of the word 'subject': subject to someone else by control and dependence, and subject tied to his own identity by a conscience or self-knowledge. Both meanings suggest a form of power which subjugates and makes subject to [*assujettit*]" (*MF*, 212). To these two meanings correspond, respectively, the approaches of *Discipline and Punish* and *The History of Sexuality*, volume 1. For the moment I shall only examine the first, keeping the examination of the second for Part III of this book.

In *Discipline and Punish*, subjection is presented as one of the two operations specific to disciplines. It is defined both by its object (the human body, and not the "soul" [*DP*, 138, 155]),[32] its scale (far from being exercised massively, from top down, it controls the smallest "details" [*DP*, 139]), its methods (an ever finer "partition" [*DP*, 137] of time, space, and the movements of the subject concerned), and its ends (the increase of productivity by a continual encouragement [*DP*, 219]). It describes the material investment of the body, through which—by exercising themselves on the apparently insignificant aspects of everyday life, by "governing our gestures" and "dictating our behaviour"—disciplines assure the mass production of docile individuals. If there is indeed a production of "subjects," it is therefore not in the traditional sense, such as used by a legal theoretician like Hobbes to describe the subjects of Leviathan. Subjection does not aim at generating subjects of law, but "obedient subjects"[33] whose principal characteristic is their malleability and permeability for disciplinary mechanisms—an idea that will be taken up in volume 1 of *The History of Sexuality*.[34] Once again, it is an idea that opposes any juridico-political conception of the exercise of power. On the contrary, the definition of subjection appears to have as its theoretical foundation the second dissertation of *The Genealogy of Morals*, which Foucault does not quote but to which he alludes transparently enough: "Rather than worry about the problem of the central soul, I believe that we must try—as I have tried—

to study the peripheral and multiple bodies, these bodies constituted as subjects by effects of power" (*PK*, 98; modified). Beyond the unifying role it plays by linking the texts of the mid-1970s to the *Order of Discourse*, where the notion of genealogy was originally put into practice, this Nietzschean affiliation is important as it allows Foucault to reverse the direction of analyses centered on consciousness and representation by showing that the modern "soul" is nothing but an effect of the training of bodies—just as the capacity to promise, particular to civilized man, was for Nietzsche (*DP*, 24).[35] This anticipates the second dimension of subjection, the internalization of specific types of subjectivity by individuals, an idea to which I shall soon return.

For the moment, the essential point is that this material and corporeal investment of individuals by power is accompanied in the theoretical order by a specific process, objectification, following a movement that Foucault describes, apropos prisons, as follows:

> The power relation that underlies the exercise of punishment begins to be duplicated by an object relation in which are caught up not only the crime as a fact to be established according to common norms, but the criminal as an individual to be known according to specific criteria. . . . *The processes of objectification originate in the very tactics of power and of the arrangement of its exercise.* (*DP*, 101; my italics)

Foucault's central idea is thus that any technique of subjection simultaneously gives rise to procedures of objectification through which the newly born human sciences can develop—which is why, a little later, he refers the birth of the *homo criminalis* and of criminology itself to the modifications of punitive techniques (*DP*, 101–2). Objectification describes the process by which new objects are constituted within the ideal order of knowledge, the specific nature of this constitution being that it operates from techniques of subjection (for example, examination or surveillance) that turn each subjected individual into an object of observation for the human sciences. Thus, the "criminal" mentioned above appears as an "individual to be known according to specific criteria." As this process of constitution by definition excludes the possibility that its objects might be natural phenomena to which the human sciences could refer objectively, objectification has as double theoretical foundation the initial nominalism deployed by Foucault in *The Archaeology of Knowledge*,[36] and the Nietzschean principle evoked in the previous chapter that things only have the essence that the dominant interpretation gives them. Disciplinary power is an

> *epistemological power*, the power to extract from the individuals a knowledge [*savoir*] and to extract a knowledge from these individuals submitted to the

gaze and already controlled by different powers. . . . One can see . . . a knowledge of observation being born, a knowledge of a clinical kind, like that of psychiatry, of psychology, of psycho-sociology, of criminology. (*DE*, 2: 619–20; my italics)

Conceptual objects are therefore the discursive correlates of the material points of application of disciplinary power: contrary to common sense, "man" is not a "real man, object of knowledge, of philosophical reflection, or of technical intervention," but an invention of the human sciences, or more exactly "the effect of a subjection much more profound than himself" (*DP*, 30). Equally, "sex" is not an "anchorage point" (*HS*, 152) existing "in reality" for *scientia sexualis* (i.e., in the terminology of *The Archaeology of Knowledge*, a "referent"), but on the contrary "an *ideal* point made necessary by the deployment of the apparatus of sexuality and its operation" (*HS*, 155; modified, my italics). Without a doubt, the most paradigmatic example of this connection between material subjection and ideal objectification is that of the body. According to Foucault, only the investment of the body by disciplines (notably military) enabled the constitution of a new object on a theoretical level, the "exercising body," which is different from the machine-body analyzed by Descartes and which became the object, not of a medicine, nor even of a physiology, but of the procedural knowledge of military manuals:[37]

> Through this technique of subjection a new body was being formed; slowly, it superseded the mechanical body—the body composed of solids and assigned movements. . . . *In becoming the target for new mechanisms of power, the body is offered up to new forms of knowledge.* It is the body of exercise, rather than that of speculative physics; a body manipulated by authority, rather than imbued with animal spirits; a body of useful training and not of traditional mechanics. (*DP*, 155; modified, my italics)

So it is not surprising that Foucault should insist on the mutual dependence of subjection and objectification, and show that they are actually conditions of possibility for each other, following the expansive circular dynamic that characterizes "power-knowledge" (*DP*, 27) and that gives the proposed paradigm its originality. On the one hand, only the controlled gathering of men in a single place (prison, hospital, etc.), and the controlled management of their behavior allowed the observation and comparison of cases, their recording through the creation of archives, the communication of the results obtained, and therefore the gradual constitution of a scientific community.[38] In this sense, the disciplines as "specific forms of subjection" constitute the empirical condition of possibility of the processes of objectification:

> The modelling of the body produces a knowledge of the individual, the apprenticeship of the techniques induces modes of behaviour and the acquisition of skills is inextricably linked with the establishment of power relations. . . . Submissive subjects are produced and a dependable body of knowledge built up around them. This disciplinary technique has a double effect: a "soul" to be known and a subjection to be maintained. (*DP*, 294)

But this relationship of dependence is not unilateral, since, on the other hand, objectification tends to reinforce subjection itself. If the human sciences truly find their "conditions of emergence" in the great nineteenth-century effort to discipline and normalize, the perfecting of disciplinary power depends in turn on the sciences' own development, as the latter enable the steadily increasing rationalization and profitability of techniques that aim at a subjection that "has never reached its limit" (*DP*, 162).

One can identify several examples within Foucault's work of the circular dynamic through which the subjection and objectification of individuals mutually reinforce themselves. I shall only survey these rapidly, as they have already been often discussed. The most well-known are doubtless those of the panopticon (*DP*, 206),[39] that "Columbus's egg of the political domain,"[40] and the examination, "this tiny operational schema" (*DP*, 185) that can be deemed paradigmatic to the extent that it is common to all the human sciences (whether in the form of the hospital "visit," military inspection, or the educational evaluation of knowledge). Moreover, far from being restricted to the "sciences," it is diffused throughout the institutions of the social body (from the health examination to the job interview). In all cases the examination has a double function: to discipline the individual by normalizing his behavior—to subject him—and to extract from him a knowledge that allows this control to be strengthened, to objectivize him:

> The formation of knowledge and the increase in power regularly reinforce one another in a circular process. . . . It was this link, proper to the technological systems, that made possible within the disciplinary element the formation of clinical medicine, psychiatry, child psychology, educational psychology, the rationalisation of labour. It is a double, then: an epistemological "thaw" through a refinement of power relations; a multiplication of the effects of power through the formation and accumulation of new forms of knowledge. (*DP*, 224)

Thus the characteristic of objectification is that it gives rise to a specific knowledge of the individual through which a paradoxical relationship between the universal and the particular is instituted, following a dynamic that reinforces subjection itself. Indeed, objectification allows the human being to be turned into the concrete starting point for the material investment and increase of knowledge, the ideal being that "any mechanism of objectification could be used in them as an instrument of subjection, and any growth of power could give rise in them to possible branches of knowledge" (*DP*, 224). Objectification turns each individual into a particular case; but a "case" describes an individual only to the extent that he can be referred to the general, whether interpreted from it or, inversely, used as an example to aid the development of the theoretical model. The individual can therefore become a "case" on sole condition that he retains only the qualities that remain pertinent at the greater scale of a theory—in other words, if his particularity is measured from the depersonalizing standard of the general.[41] Thus the connection between political subjection and theoretical observation is very deep. While the first paradoxically deprives the individual of his identity as legal subject by constituting him as "subject of obedience," the second, by extracting knowledge from him, strips him of his dignity as a moral subject. The two terms are connected by a subtle dialectic that attempts to induce in the individuals concerned a physical and mental passivity as well as the belief in the impossibility of resistance. Nothing, therefore, remains of the individual but a malleable material (the "docile body"), the result of a double process: the political reduction of subjects as entities with rights (subjection) and their transformation on an epistemic level into individualized but identity-less cases, entirely available to the examining knowledge of the human sciences (objectification). Thus, "the individuals on which power is exercised are either *that from which will be extracted the knowledge* that they have formed themselves and which will be re-transcribed and translated according to new norms, or *the objects of a knowledge* [savoir] *which will also make possible new forms of control*" (*DE*, 2: 62; my italics).[42]

The Foucauldian analyses of the relationship between subjection and objectification have a double interest. On the one hand, they give substance to the idea of a constitutive imbrication of power and knowledge by showing, in a series of precise examples, the inseparability of the births of disciplinary power and the human sciences. On the other hand, these analyses make possible the establishment of a theme, that of *normalization*, whose importance will be emphasized by the analysis of truth and which identifies the disciplines' real aim: "In short, the art of punishing, in the regime of disciplinary power, is aimed neither at expiation, nor even precisely at repression. . . . The perpetual penalty that traverses all points and supervises every instant in the disciplinary institutions compares, differentiates, hierarchises, excludes. In short, it *normalizes*" (*DP*, 182). Indeed, the concept of the norm grounds the reciprocity of subjection and objectification while allowing us to understand the convergence of their effects. The norm, declares Foucault, is opposed to the law because it tends to displace it in both the evaluation and the punishment of crimes. Under the cover of assuring the application of the law, disciplinary mechanisms have engendered a "penality of the norm," which is "irreducible in its principles and functioning to the traditional penality of the law" (*DP*, 183),[43] and whose figures (the psychiatric doctor or criminologist) progressively displace that of the judge as a deciding authority. Correlatively, the depersonalization that results from objectification is doubly coextensive with the norm, since it is both the very process through which the norm is constituted, following the above-examined transformation of individuals into "cases," and the aim of any norm as principle of coercion, as Foucault explains by declaring that "the power of normalisation imposes homogeneity" (*DP*, 184). The paradox of the norm, therefore, is that it plays individuation against individuality, as the measurement of the individual that it presupposes is effected to the detriment of the respect for the individuals themselves.

From this, the substitution by subjection of "subjects of law" by subjects of obedience appears as the reflection of a more general process, in which the norm grows parasitically from the law, a process of which modern society is the direct product: "Today, control is less severe and more refined, but it is no less terrifying for that. For the whole course of our life, we are totally held within different authoritarian systems; first at school, then in our work and even in our pastimes. *Each individual, considered separately, is normalized and transformed in a file controlled by an IBM*" (*DE*, 3: 670; my italics). Normalization is thus revealed as the general horizon of Foucault's analysis of subjection and objectification.[44] The last pages of *Discipline and Punish* draw the conclusions of this dynamic of mutual reinforcement by showing the way in which the "carceral archipelago" had transported "this technique from the penal institution to the entire social body" (*DP*, 299), while vigorously denouncing "the steep rise in the use of these mechanisms of normalisation and the wide-ranging powers which, through the proliferation of new disciplines, they bring with them" (*DP*, 306).

The "Regime of Truth" and Foucault's Definition of Truth

It therefore remains for Foucault to draw the consequences of this genealogy of the human sciences by casting suspicion on the nature of the truths involved. From the imbrication of knowledge and power studied above, it is clear that, by definition, these will not be independent of relations of power, as the following extract shows, in which Foucault proposes to "revive the will to know the source

of the power exerted upon sex. My aim is not to write the social history of a prohibition but the *political history of the production of 'truth'*" (*PPC*, 112; my italics).

Equally, one can infer *a contrario* from the analyses of objectification and subjection that truth will be defined neither by logical coherence, as the human sciences are not formalized sciences,[45] nor by adequation, as their objects are constituted simultaneously to them. But how can a positive determination of truth
be made? The following passage, in its very generality, gives some clues as to its
nature:

> Each society has its regime of truth . . . i.e., types of discourse which it accepts
> and *makes function as true*; the mechanisms and instances which enable one to
> distinguish true and false statements, the means by which each is sanctioned;
> the techniques and procedures which are valorised in the acquisition of truth;
> the status of those who are charged with saying *what functions as true*. (*PK*, 131;
> modified, my italics)

To conform with the teaching of genealogy, truth should therefore be understood
in the sense of a "general politics" (*PK*, 131) whose specificity is that it rests on a
functional definition of truth, as emblematically demonstrated by the recurrence
of the notion of "functioning" in Foucault's work at the time (twice in the extract
quoted). Foucault carefully refrains from any assertion about the possibility of a
statement being truthful due to its own properties; on the contrary, he exclusively refers the truth of discourses to the regime that "welcomes" them by governing their formation and distribution. Thus, rather than an essentialist determination of truth, he prefers to establish an analogy ("function *as* true") that
annuls or at least suspends the possibility of an objective characterization of truth.
In a very polemical manner, everything looks at first sight "as if" the only truth
imaginable related, not to the nature of the discourse considered, but to the function that it plays in it.

Significantly, one of the few passages of *Discipline and Punish* that deals with
the problem of truth introduces it again through its function, which it clarifies
in the following way: "In fabricating delinquency, it gave to criminal justice a
unitary field of objects, authenticated by the 'sciences', and thus enabled it to
function on a general horizon of 'truth'" (*DP*, 256; my italics). The repeated use
of quotation marks (which as for Nietzsche signal both distancing from and distrust of the concept considered) suggests a highly controversial hypothesis: it may
be the case that truth can be understood as "true," not by virtue of its possible
intrinsic characteristics (such as correspondence with reality), but rather *because*
it forms the "general horizon" of reference from which criminology or psychiatry "authenticates" the functioning of justice, that is, gives it a guarantee which,

however dubious on a theoretical level, is very effective on a practical one. Similarly, the idea expressed a little further on, according to which the controls used in prisons were "firmly encased in a medicine or psychiatry that provided them with *a form of 'scientificity'*" (*DP*, 296; modified, my italics), strongly emphasizes the subjecting function of these sciences and thus of the truth they formulate, since, as another passage explains, "in societies like ours . . . 'truth' is centred on the form of scientific discourse and the institutions which produce it" (*PK*, 131).

So Foucault seems to measure the truth of discourses not by their objective content, but by their function. Moreover, he brings this already polemical thesis to its full stature by suggesting that the human sciences, far from owing their "scientific nature" to the quality of their methods and experimental protocols, have on the contrary derived their scientific status from the disciplinary framework that they supported. This inversion is marked by the very form of Foucault's questioning, which genealogically refers truth not to metaphysical characteristics, but to the actual locus of its production: "How did the power exerted on insanity *produce the 'true' discourse* of psychiatry?" (*PPC*, 111; modified). The answer is found in the first volume of *The History of Sexuality*: "Spoken in time, to the proper party, and by the person who is both the bearer of it and the one responsible for it, truth heals" (*HS*, 67; modified). In fact, this apparently objective statement (truth heals) covers over a very different mechanism. If truth heals, it may not be because it is true, and it is certainly not due to any essential qualities: the multiplication of conditional propositions ("if it could be said," etc.) clearly indicates that the action of truth requires a particular *kairos*. On the contrary, Foucault seems to think that the discourse of medicine owes its "truth" at least as much to its therapeutic properties as to its inscription within the theoretical forms of scientificity that were recognized at the time, and therefore, that its acceptability depends in fact on practical rather than theoretical imperatives. If medical discourse is true, it is mainly *because* it cures and, more generally, because the "cure" is desirable as part of a general process that allows individuals to be controlled by encouraging them to talk about their sex and their pleasures, and would ultimately make possible the mastery and treatment of any "deviancies." Another passage is clearer still: "It was indeed through a certain mode of domination exercised by certain people upon certain other people, that the subject could undertake *to tell the truth about its madness*" (*PPC*, 38; my italics).[46] Equally, the prison is defined in reference to its function, as the place where "punishment will be able to *function* openly *as* treatment and the sentence *will be inscribed among the discourses of knowledge*" (*DP*, 256; my italics). This statement clearly implies that if the sentence is able to take the place of knowledge, this is so precisely relative to the "therapeutic" virtues—the subjecting effects, that is—of the punishment that it displays. Contrary to any metaphysical conception, the "essence" of truth lies in its *normalizing* character: "If I tell the truth about myself, as I am now doing, it is in part that I constitute myself as a subject across a number of power relations which are exerted over me and which I exert over others" (*PPC*, 39; modified).

This idea finds additional confirmation in a course given by Foucault in 1974 at the Collège de France, which analyzes the effects of truth specific to medical discourse:

> The great doctor is he who can both *speak the truth of the illness* by using the knowledge [*savoir*] that he has of it, and *produce the illness in its truth and master it in its reality* through the power that his will exercises over the sick person herself. . . . The doctor's power allows him to produce the reality of a mental illness whose characteristic is to reproduce phenomena entirely accessible to knowledge [*connaissance*]. The hysteric was the perfect patient, as she generated knowledge: she herself transcribed the effects of medical power in forms which the doctor could describe in accordance with a scientifically acceptable discourse.[47]

Thus medical discourse elaborates a theoretical object (by "speaking the truth of the illness"), following a process made possible by the hospital structure and therefore by the techniques of subjection practiced on the patient. But by the same token, this discourse generates a real object corresponding to its knowledge (it "produces the illness in its truth"). The conceptual objectification of the illness therefore is doubled by a second material form of objectification, in which the hysterical woman "reproduces" in her very person the "entirely accessible to knowledge" phenomena. The objectification process is thus transposed from the theoretical level to that of reality, where in turn it produces concrete effects, since real "forms" of illness end up corresponding to the newly constituted concept of the patient's sickness. In an ironical inversion of the problematic of *The Order of Things*, language, far from "corresponding" with the real, thus creates its own "referent."

This radicalization of archaeological nominalism is accompanied by a radical critique of the truth of medical discourse. According to Foucault, "to speak the truth of the illness" has the single and unique aim of "mastering it in its reality," an operation made possible via objectification in its material sense, that is, through the bodily "transcription" by the hysteric of the symptoms described. This perfect reversibility of the discursive object and the real object can certainly give the illusion of compliance with the traditional conception of truth as *ade-*

quatio by guaranteeing that the scientific description will leave no unexplained residue. But in reality, it polemically inverses the traditional definition, as it is not the discourse that is adequate to reality but "reality" that is adequate to the discourse—the "scientifically acceptable discourse" being in fact the mere description of the symptoms that it itself has induced. By revealing in such a shocking manner the perverse effects of objectification and the absence of any objective referent for medical truth, Foucault attacks any metaphysical conception of truth by showing that, at least in this specific example, it is only defined by its therapeutic and subjecting function.[48] This claim is taken up and widened by volume I of *The History of Sexuality*, in relation to the *scientia sexualis*:

It was by the same token a science mainly subordinated to the imperatives of a morality whose divisions it reiterated under the guise of the medical norm. *Under the pretext of speaking the truth, it stirred up people's fears.* . . . It assumed other powers; it set itself up as the supreme authority in matters of hygienic necessity . . . ; it claimed to ensure the physical vigour and the moral cleanliness of the social body; it promised to eliminate defective individuals, degenerate and bastardised populations. In the name of a biological and historical urgency, it justified the impending racism of the State. *It grounded it in "truth."* (*HS*, 53, 54; my italics)

Such a reinterpretation of the nature and function of truth has major consequences for the critical question, as it affirms that the conditions of the acceptability of truth cannot be understood on a purely epistemic level. Indeed, what the genealogy of the human sciences shows is that these conditions do not simply depend on epistemic parameters (scientific criteria, for example). On the contrary, the discourse accepted as true is the one that doubly responds to the demands of the disciplines; on a practical level by allowing them to perform better, and on a political level by giving them an apparent legitimacy. This point is emphasized by the very way in which Foucault formulates his problematic:

In a specific sort of discourse on sex, in a specific form of extortion of truth, appearing historically and in specific places . . . , what were the most immediate, the most local power arrangements at work? *How did they make possible these kinds of discourses, and conversely, how were these discourses used to support power relations?* How was the action of these power relations modified by their exercise . . . so that there has never existed one type of stable subjugation once and for all? (*HS*, 97; modified, my italics)

The "forms of the extortion of truth" and "types of subjection" are thus connected by a circular logic and relationship of mutual creation. In this sense, the fact that relationships of power "make possible" discourses of truth, and that these "serve to support" the former, is ultimately founded in the empirical imbrication of knowledge and power, which makes the truth thus produced directly dependent on the mechanisms of subjection and objectification.

Thus Foucault draws the general conclusions to his analysis of the genesis of the human sciences in the following way. As their objects are only the transposition into theory of the points of application of power, and as objectification itself rests on and seeks the subjection of the individuals concerned, it is logical to define the truths stemming from the various forms of the knowledge of man as the *norms* by which disciplinary power can support and extend its action. It is from this highly critical perspective that Foucault's introduction of the famous notion of the "regime of truth" can be understood: " *'Truth' is linked in a circular relation with systems of power which produce and sustain it, and to effects of power which it induces and which extend it.* A 'regime' of truth. This regime is not merely ideological or superstructural" (*PK*, 133; my italics).[49] Thus understood, the "regime" describes the circular dynamic through which the subjection of individuals and the production of subjecting truths mutually reinforce each other. The semantic ambivalence of the term, which evokes both the establishment of norms (as in a dietary regime) and a particular type of political system (democracy, oligarchy, etc.), allows Foucault implicitly to take up again—at a more conceptual level this time—the theme of the inseparability of knowledge and power. These two aspects of the regime, economic and political, are the reasons why Foucault can speak interchangeably of a "political economy" or a "general politics" of truth, whose principal characteristics he describes as follows:

> [Truth] is subject *to constant economic and political incitement* (the demand for truth, as much as for economic production as for political power); it is the object, under the diverse forms, of *immense diffusion and consumption* (circulating through apparatuses of education and information whose extent is relatively broad in the social body, notwithstanding certain strict limitations); it is *produced and transmitted* under the control, dominant if not exclusive, of a few great political and economic apparatuses (university, army, writing, media). (*PK*, 131; my italics)

Once again, Foucault takes the opposing position to metaphysics by defining truth in a materialist way,[50] as an empirical content (which can both be "produced" and "transmitted" as a good), submitted to economic and political rules dictated by the regime ("stimulation," "consumption," "diffusion"), and whose production is controlled by specific authorities that are themselves endowed with an economico-political role. The regime can therefore be understood as the collection of empirical and historically variable conditions where truth is produced and diffused—after the first extract quoted, the text continues to say that the regime has been a "condition of the formation and development of capitalism" (*PK*, 133). If the West really needs truth, such a "need"[51] has nothing metaphysical about it: it simply signals that, far from being independent, truth obeys the same imperatives of profitability and control as subjection itself.

Hence the idea of a "regime of truth" has the principal function of generalizing Foucault's theses about the birth of the human sciences by showing in a critical way that, in any society, the production of truth responds to a certain number of imperatives that are not purely theoretical, but practical, even utilitarian. One might consider that the instrumental character of this definition, notably in its opposition to the metaphysical idea of an objective truth and because it makes truth subordinate to interest, is of Nietzschean inspiration. However, although this seems broadly true, Foucault differs from Nietzsche on two points: firstly, the Nietzschean critique of metaphysics does not operate from the political point of view, which is so strongly presented in *Discipline and Punish* and the first volume of *The History of Sexuality*. Secondly, although he does have an interpretative understanding of truth, Nietzsche is not a relativist, in that he maintains a criterion that allows him to create a hierarchy of perspectives (the affirmative or negative character of the form of will to power they stem from). Thus, the very fact that scientific truth can be described as a "vital error" presupposes the possibility of adopting another, supposedly superior, point of view—that of an affirmative will to power, for which "truth" is identified with the "appearances" denounced by metaphysics. The problem is that Foucault does not appear to have at his disposal a similar means of ordering the different conceptions of truth.[52] He is no more an absolute relativist than Nietzsche—remember that *The Order of Discourse* suggested, at least in the domain of the fundamental sciences, the existence of an objective truth that he implicitly endorsed. But because he did not take up or reformulate the theoretical foundation of Nietzsche's thought (as we saw, he particularly lacks a deeper analysis of the concept of the "will to truth" or an equivalent of the Dionysian), Foucault finds it impossible to identify criteria that would allow him to ground his critique of the political forms of truth, a point to which I shall shortly return.

In this context, the question is whether the Nietzschean influence on Foucaldian genealogy is really so determining, and whether Foucault could not find elsewhere than in this unsuccessful parallelism with Nietzsche a way to legitimate his claims about the value of truth. Surprisingly, many aspects of his thinking about truth seem remarkably close to William James in this respect.[53] Indeed, neither James nor Foucault himself have an *ante rem*, absolute and objective, conception of truth: for James, an idea can only be "instrumentally true,"[54] that is, true in proportion to its efficacy. Correspondingly, truth is not a quality that belongs to ideas, a "stagnant property inherent in it. Truth *happens* to an idea. It becomes true, it is *made true* by events."[55] It is thus equally impossible to consider an idea metaphysically, as an abstract and purely theoretical representation, and to understand truth as adequation. As James shows, the hypothesis of a correspondence between a proposition and an independent reality is always an effect of retrospection, "reality" itself being no more than a mental construction whose interpretative nature has been progressively forgotten.[56] On the contrary, a true idea is above all defined by the dynamic that it creates in the domain of action, to the extent that one cannot separate it from its practical consequences, which, far from being exterior to it, constitute the criteria that allow its truth to be measured. For James, as for Foucault, that which is useful and effective becomes true: "Let me begin by reminding you of the fact that the possession of true thoughts means everywhere the possession of invaluable instrument of action; and that our duty to gain truth, so far from being a blank command from out of the blue . . . can account for itself by excellent practical reasons."[57] Most interestingly, one can also find in Foucault's work the echo of one of James's most famous passages, as a glance at the two following texts, the first by Foucault and the second by James, will show:

> Power never ceases its interrogation, its inquisition, its registration of truth: it institutionalizes, professionalizes and rewards its pursuit. In the last analysis, *we must produce truth as we must produce wealth, indeed we must produce truth in order to produce wealth in the first place.* (PK, 93; my italics)

> Our account of truth is an account of truths in the plural, of processes of leading . . . having only this quality in common, that they pay. . . . *Truth is made, just as health, wealth and strength, are made, in the course of experience.*[58]

Beyond the fact that both passages are centered on the analogy between truth and wealth, which is sufficiently unusual to be significant, James goes on (like Foucault himself) in an overtly nominalist sense and denounces what he calls the "rationalist trick" by showing that truth, wealth, and health are only retrospectively produced effects of language—which is exactly Foucault's thesis.[59]

Whether this shows a simple convergence of views or an influence by James, the Foucauldian definition of truth, such as is identifiable within the analysis of the human sciences, seems at least as close to pragmatism as to Nietzschean thought, for three reasons. Firstly, it shows truth as relative, historical, produced according to criteria that are neither intellectual nor objective. Secondly, truth is judged by its practical effects and draws its value from its efficiency. Finally, one already finds with James the very Foucauldian idea according to which truth is the object of a collective aspiration that energizes the social body: thus there corresponds to the "will to know" the theme of a "belief in truth itself, that there is a truth, and that our minds and it are made for each other—what is that but a passionate affirmation of desire [of truth], in which our social system backs us up."[60]

It is necessary nonetheless to note two important restrictions to this comparison. Firstly, the analyses of Foucault and James do not have the same theoretical range. For the latter, *all* truth is defined by its efficacy, whatever the subject concerned and without any distinction being made between, for example, the fundamental sciences, philosophy, or literature. James even uses the general character of his definition as an argument for treating all these domains as equivalent. On the contrary, Foucault concentrates his approach on the specific case of the human sciences, which gives his analyses a more limited scope. The second restriction concerns the status of *usefulness* itself: James understands and measures it in an objective way, as the heuristic power of a proposition (the more "economical," in the sense of Ockham's razor, and the more effective in resolving a problem, the truer). Correspondingly, usefulness has as practical criterion, the possibility of a "satisfying relationship" with experience.[61] However, according to James, such a "satisfaction" is neither arbitrary nor subjective: it depends on the set of beliefs and mental habits on the background of which the true idea is formed and with which it must harmonize itself.[62] Therefore, James can define objectively the conception of usefulness on which he grounds his definition of truth.[63] But Foucault understands usefulness *relatively*, by referring it to the specific "regime" through which truth is necessarily connected to power. Therefore, he fundamentally distinguishes himself from the author of *Pragmatism* by contesting the possibility of a *nonpolitical* definition of usefulness. This has the major consequence of making impossible the consideration of usefulness as an absolute criterion for defining truth, as it is only from power-knowledge that either can be thought.

This relativity of usefulness and truth has the greatest importance for Foucault's thinking, as it plays a very rich and ambiguous role. Positively, it constitutes the theoretical basis upon which Foucault establishes the possibility of a critique. As the later analyses of the Greek paradigm and its historical development will show, although truth always had to be useful, it was not always subjecting, but has become so only due to the development of a new power (biopower), which has progressively identified the political and social usefulness of individuals with the possibility of their being subjected. Thus, Foucault's subsequent history of subjectivity will reveal that truth was not necessarily or primarily connected to subjection, and that the emergence of this connection itself can be traced through the analysis of the historical understanding of usefulness generated by disciplinary power. In this sense, Foucault's deepest insight is not that truth is *per se* subjecting, but rather, more subtly, that subjection is the most recent form of the relationship between truth and power established by the regime. This discloses the possibility of other definitions (such as the Greek aesthetics of the self, in which truth operated as a subjectivizing, not subjecting, element) and opens the way for a critique. Thus, Foucault can use the relative character of usefulness to denounce the normalizing power of the human sciences, a denunciation whose aim is precisely to question the historical identification of usefulness and subjection that the analysis of power-knowledge had allowed him to reveal: "It's not a matter of a emancipating truth from every system of power (which would be a chimera, for truth itself is power) but of detaching the power of truth from the forms of hegemony, social, economic and cultural, within which it operates at the present time" (*PK*, 133; modified).

However, the hidden cost of this historicization of usefulness is the revival of a considerable problem. As already shown by our study of Foucault's borrowings from Nietzsche, Foucault again seems to fall prey to his own relativism. Indeed, although it allows him to recontextualize and critique the contemporary understanding of usefulness, this relativism also simultaneously closes off from Foucault any possible recourse to the universal and ahistorical perspective required from a foundational standpoint, and prevents him from convincingly justifying his preference for other modes of the functioning of truth. Foucault's relativism turns out to be the best and the worst of things: by historicizing the relationship of truth and power, it opens the possibility of a critique; but in doing so, it condemns the critique in advance to remain deprived of any objective foundation. Although Foucault's preference for specific values (those of the Greek "aesthetic of existence," for example, in which subjectivization was understood as a free and individual way of life) clearly indicates that his skepticism has limits, his own understanding of truth denies him any possibility of legitimizing incontestably the reversal of values that he seems to advocate, and exposes him to the accusations of "nihilism" often formulated against him.[64]

Nonetheless, it seems fair to say that Foucault's genealogy of the human sciences largely fulfills the requirements of the program originally established by *The Order of Discourse*. The elaboration of the power-knowledge paradigm, as well as the newly introduced notion of the "regime of truth," allow Foucault to form a quasi-pragmatic understanding of truth, which archaeology, concentrated on the discursive alone, was unable to see. But what are the consequences of these analyses for the archeo-genealogical question of the conditions of acceptability of truth? If the production of truth itself responds to the politico-economic imperatives specific to subjection, under what conditions will a discourse be "in the truth"? And how will these conditions, the latest avatar of the historical *a priori*, be distinguishable from those which define the regime of truth?

The Renewal of the Critical Question and Its Difficulties: The "Discursive Regime"

Foucault returns to the critical question in reference to the notion of the "regime," following a retrospective logic that explicitly refers to the archaeological problematic by underlining the existence of radical "ruptures" in the evolution of certain sciences, as for example in medicine:

> These are not simply new discoveries, there is a whole new "regime" in discourse and forms of knowledge. . . . But the important thing here is not that such changes can be rapid and extensive, or rather it is that this extent and activity are only the sign of something else: a *modification in the rules of formation of statements which are accepted as scientifically true*. (*PK*, 112; my italics)

According to this passage, the "regime" appears to be merely an avatar of the *épistémè*, being defined in the same terms and according to the same criteria (through reference to the "rules of formation of statements accepted as scientifically true"), as Foucault himself confirms by stating that "it was these different regimes that [he] tried to identify and describe in *The Order of Things*" (*PK*, 113). But the text continues by abruptly introducing an important modification:

> There is a problem of the regime, the politics of the scientific statement. At this level it's not so much a matter of knowing what external power imposes itself on science, as of what effects of power circulate among scientific statements, what constitutes, as it were, their *internal regime of power*, and how and why at certain moments that regime undergoes a global modification. (*PK*, 112; my italics)

We have thus moved from an epistemological definition, which up till now only referred to the "scientific procedures" involved in the evaluation of the truth content of discourses, to a political conception which coextensively connects the regime and power. However, following the genealogical logic already encountered in *The Order of Discourse*, Foucault does not give up the critical question; on the contrary, he presents the introduction of the concept of the "discursive regime" as a way of redeeming the "lacks" of archaeology:

But what was lacking (from my work) was this problem of the "discursive regime," of the effects of power peculiar to the play of statements. I confused this too much with systemacity, theoretical form. . . . This central problem of power, which at the time I had not yet properly isolated, emerges in two very different aspects at the point of junction of *Madness and Civilization* and *The Order of Things*. (*PK*, 113)

In accordance with the archaeological thematic, the regime thus concerns neither the "contents" of propositions (otherwise one could not distinguish the regime from that which it governs), nor their "theoretical form" (as it is not defined by a set of formal laws). On the contrary, the text indicates the necessity of attributing a specific level of existence to the regime by implicitly taking up the distinction, previously established by *The Order of Discourse*, between the acceptability and the predication of truth: "It is a question of what governs statements, and the way in which they govern each other so as to *constitute a set of propositions which are scientifically acceptable, and hence capable of being verified or falsified* by scientific procedures" (*PK*, 112; my italics). This point also resurfaces in the only passage of *Discipline and Punish* where Foucault refers to the *épistémè*. He begins by asserting the material dependence of the human sciences on the power-knowledge that "made them historically possible," as the analysis of disciplinary mechanisms allowed him to establish, and continues as follows: "If [the human sciences] have been able to be formed and to produce so many profound changes in the *épistémè*, it is because they have been conveyed by a specific and new modality of power" (*DP*, 305). Foucault implicitly maintains the necessity of distinguishing between the two different levels—the empirical level of the formation of the human sciences, on the one hand; and on the other hand, the epistemic level, where the "profound changes" (*bouleversements*) of the birth of a new power are indirectly felt. Like the *épistémès* themselves, the "regime" possesses a specific mode of existence, which volume 1 of *The History of Sexuality* will have the task of identifying.

It should be noted that the idea that the analysis of the discursive regime must take into account the "central problem of power" is not radically new *per se*. It was already expressed in *The Archaeology of Knowledge*, as well as in "Réponse à une question" (*DE*, 1: 690 ff.), although it played a minor enough role in both texts. Foucault had already asked the question of the relationship between medicine and what he then called "political practice," giving himself the task of discovering "how medical discourse as a practice concerned with a particular field of objects, being in the hands of a certain number of statutorily designated individuals, and having certain functions to exercise in society, *is articulated on prac-*

tices that are external to it, and which are not themselves of a discursive order" (*AK*, 164). Thus, if the discursive regime can be distinguished from its archaeological counterpart, the *épistémè*, it is not only because it refers to power, as this was already implied in 1969 by the necessity of relating medical discourse to nondiscursive practices; the difference between archaeology and genealogy is due, rather, to the problem of the *modality* of this articulation. Contrary to what *The Archaeology of Knowledge* suggested in mentioning "external practices," the connection of the discursive regime to power cannot be described as a relation of *exteriority*. On the contrary, the profound reciprocity between techniques of power and scientific discourses revealed by the analyses of the concepts of subjection and objectification allows Foucault to conclude that the regime that the subjecting discourses obey is itself formed *from within* by the demands of normalization, thus realizing the project of "replacing the regime of the production of the true and the false at the heart of historical analysis and political criticism."[65] Contrary to what the archaeologist thought, the predication and acceptability of truth are not independent, as far as the human sciences are concerned: to be acceptable, before even being declared true or false, a discourse must possess a normalizing potential, a fact that is revealed by the impossibility of understanding the formation of objects and discursive domains independently of techniques of subjection.

Foucault draws out the methodological consequences of this discovery in the long passage of *The History of Sexuality*, volume 1, where the four "rules of analysis" of discourses are stated. Although he is careful to mention that they are not "methodological imperatives," but "prudent prescriptions," some clues (like their number, which corresponds to the four archaeological domains) suggest that they more modestly echo the attempt in *The Archaeology of Knowledge* to erect the principles of analysis of statements.[66] Thus, the first two rules repeat in the same order the first two criteria for the analysis of the *épistémè* given by archaeology (the formation of the objects of discourses and the status of their sources), while the last two return to the question of the strategies specific to the discursive, which was the fourth angle under which the enunciative function was analyzed. It thus does not seem unreasonable to analogically attribute to the study of the forms of the constitution of discursive objects the same role for the definition of the regime as that which it played in the case of the *épistémè*, and to think that the functioning of the regime itself must be in part be understood from the formation of the objects of discourse. This is confirmed by a passage in *Discipline and Punish*, which reveals a tight correlation between the "new field of objects" and the appearance of a "new regime": "Beneath the increasing leniency of punishment, then, one may map a displacement of its point of application; and through this displacement *a whole field of recent objects, a whole new system of truth*" (*DP*, 22; my italics).

The first of the rules analyzed by volume 1 of *The History of Sexuality* allows the connection between the regime and the constitution of discursive objects to be developed through the example of sexuality: "If sexuality was constituted as an area of investigation, it was possible only because relations of power had established it as a possible object; and conversely, if power was able to take it as a target, this was because techniques of knowledge and procedures of discourse were capable of investing it" (*HS*, 98). Sexuality is not, therefore, a natural object, but the result of a process of constitution circularly involved with power relations, being supported by them (by being "instituted as a possible object") and reinforcing them (by permitting them to "take it as target"). As might be expected, one finds again in these themes a definition of objectification, as well as a description of the reciprocal relationship that it entertains with the techniques of subjection. Since both concepts only make sense in reference to their normalizing function, we can see better why the relationship of the discursive regime with power must necessarily be understood as internal. Indeed, if objectification is really one of the fundamental structures of the discursive regime (as it defines the forms of constitution of the objects of discourse), by definition the latter should take at least some of the characteristics of the former. Without identifying itself with either the discourses themselves or the techniques of subjection that make them possible, the regime thus relies on the *structural internalization of the disciplinary techniques and imperatives specific to objectification itself.*

This internalization is the deep reason for Foucault's rejection of the Platonic, Baconian, and Marxist models, as it renders doubly obsolete the idea of a relationship of opposition or of use between power and knowledge: firstly, by showing that the very structures that constitute knowledge have power relations as their conditions of possibility—those that aim at subjection; and secondly, by making it clear that they share the same normalizing ambition. This essential idea is confirmed in the following passage:

> "Sexuality": the correlative of that slowly developed discursive practice which constitutes the *scientia sexualis*. The essential features of this sexuality are not the expression of a representation that is more or less distorted by ideology, or of a misunderstanding caused by prohibitions; *they correspond to the functional requirements of a discourse that must produce its truth*. (*HS*, 68; modified)

One can measure here both the proximity of genealogy and archaeology (suggested by the return to the familiar theme of the "discursive practice"), and the distance separating them, as the "functional requirements" (which the text later numbers at four [*HS*, 68]) cannot be understood independently of the relations of power. This is particularly clear in the case of the first two functional requirements, which concern the formation of a theoretical object (sex) and of a corresponding domain (sexuality), and therefore directly refer to the movement of internalization described above. The last two stipulate respectively that any discourse on sex must firstly be able to serve as the foundation for an eventual resistance to power (the connection being then established *a contrario*), and secondly, be a determining factor in the constitution of the self as a subject, a "constitution" that was shown by the analysis of the two senses of subjection to possess, by definition, a political dimension. The "functional requirements" are not, therefore, internal theoretical necessities tied to the "form of systematicity" previously mentioned: the discursive regime of statements about sex is intrinsically governed by the normalizing strategies of bio-power.

The three other rules for the analysis of discourses laid down by the first volume of *The History of Sexuality* no longer define the study of the regime through reference to the formation of discursive objects, but by showing that it is the internal principle of distribution of the effects of the power specific to the statements considered. Thus, the second rule, that of "continual variation," analogically repeats the second criterion of analysis established by *The Archaeology of Knowledge*, that is, the study of "enunciative modalities": just as we should not start from the notion of the author in order to analyze discourses, but infer from the discursive itself a number of possible positions and functions for enunciation, likewise we should not ask "who has the power in the order of sexuality" (*HS*, 99), but analyze the effective "distributions of power" to which discourses give rise from their internal economy, their "interior regime of power" (*PK*, 112). In the same way, the last two rules, that is, the "double conditioning" and "tactical polyvalence of discourses,"[67] show that the study of the "world of discourse" (*HS*, 100) cannot be conducted in a purely theoretical manner, but must necessarily take into account the strategies of power that penetrate it. The same discursive elements can have opposing functions according to the type of distribution that governs them and the effects of power sought (for example, when in the nineteenth century homosexuals began to assert the legitimacy, even the "naturalness," of homosexuality, they did so precisely "in the same vocabulary, using the same categories by which were used to medically disqualify it" [*HS*, 101]).

The idea of the regime thus seems to play a double role: it allows the thinking of the mode of formation of discursive objects, and it defines the specific internal economy of a discursive practice, by which discourse "transmits and produces power" (*HS*, 101). From this perspective, the notion of the regime possesses two advantages over that of the *épistémè*. Firstly, it seems clearer and more coherent since it is elaborated from a smaller number of concepts. Foucault has learned from the mistakes of *The Archaeology of Knowledge*, which the multiplication of explicatory entities had entangled in the internal contradictions examined above. He shows himself now more faithful to Ockham's razor by only using a minimal number of new notions—in particular, in defining the discursive regime, he makes no further reference to the concept of the statement (using it only in its ordinary sense). Secondly, the concept of the discursive regime allows Foucault to ground the intuition expressed in *The Order of Discourse* in a still general form, according to which certain discourses possess in themselves "intrinsic" effects of power. Thus, in order to "appear as an element of knowledge," a discourse will now have to meet two conditions. Firstly, it must "conform to a set of characteristic rules and constraints, for example to this or that type of scientific discourse in a given epoch."[68] To this condition, archaeological in nature, a second requirement is added; it must be capable of "possessing effects of coercion or simply of encouragement specific to what is validated as scientific or simply rational."[69]

The interest of this analysis of the discursive regime is that it shows that these "effects" are generated by the structural necessities of the constitution and regulation of discourses within a specific discursive practice, and also by the subjecting purposes that determine the latter. "'Truth'—the specific power of discourses accepted as 'true'" (*PPC*, 112; modified), as Foucault can laconically declare. Although it defines truth from the "true," this definition is not tautological: there would only be a tautology if truth was understood purely epistemologically, as the formal property of true discourses. But by understanding truth as the *power* specific to these discourses, Foucault indicates the impossibility of considering the criteria of "scientific" discourses (which allow them to "accepted as true") independently of their political function. Thus, the apparent tautology in reality rests on an ellipse, itself justified by the *analytic*, rather than synthetic, relation that the definition of the discursive regime allows between the "true" statement and its effects of power.

Within this configuration it becomes crucial to determine the relationship of the discursive regime to what Foucault calls the "regime of truth." As we have seen, the latter must be understood in an empirical sense, as referring to material *loci* of production and diffusion (university, media, etc.), which presupposes that truth is assimilated to a commodity. By contrast, the discursive regime is understood both as the set of theoretical procedures (at whose center is objectification), through which a "discursive practice" can be constituted, and as the internal economy of the discourses that are so formed. It thus seems reasonable to think that the enunciative regime constitutes the specifically discursive element of the regime of truth, by comparison with the empirical conditions of the production of truth. This hypothesis is indirectly confirmed by the Foucault's analyses of the "apparatus" (*dispositif*), whose definition is nearly identical to that of the regime of truth:

> What I'm a trying to pick out with this term is, firstly, a wholly heterogeneous ensemble consisting of discourses, institutions, architectural forms, regulatory decisions, laws, administrative measures, scientific statements, philosophical, moral and philanthropic propositions—in short, *the said as much as the unsaid, such are the elements of the apparatus.* (*PK*, 196)

The text continues by explicitly using the notion of the "regime of discourses" and attributes it the function previously given to the *épistémè*:

> In *The Order of Things* my problem was to ascertain the *sets of transformations internal to the regime of discourses* necessary and sufficient for people to use these words rather than those, a particular type of discourse rather than some other type, for people to be able to look at things from such and such an angle and not some other one. (*PK*, 211; modified)

Another passage in the same text directly assimilates the *épistémè* and the discursive regime by showing that both constitute the specifically discursive element of the "apparatus," itself understood as "much more general case of the *épistémè*." Thus, "the *épistémè* is a specifically discursive apparatus, whereas the apparatus in its general form is both discursive and non-discursive, its elements being much more heterogeneous" (*PK*, 197). Henceforth, the originality of genealogy compared to archaeology would be to show the impossibility of understanding the discursive regime independently of a more general set of conditions concerned with the production of truth, without, however, identifying it with them or thinking about it as determined by them—which is why the discursive regime is one of the "elements" of the regime of truth and not its logical consequence or material product.

One can find an example of this complex relationship in the analysis of the "ritual of producing penal truth" (*DP*, 38) proposed by *Discipline and Punish*. Foucault shows that "certain rules had to be obeyed in establishing the truth" (*DP*, 36), and specifically defines the "rigorous model of penal demonstration" that governed the establishment of proof: the distinction between "true, direct or legitimate proofs," "indirect, conjectural, artificial proof," or again "imperfect or slight" (*DP*, 38), and so on.[70] That this "system of legal proofs" could be assimilated with the regime that characterized the judicial discursive practice of the time is suggested by several elements in the text; for example, the idea that the system constitutes a "*mode of regulation internal* to the absolute and exclusive power of knowledge" (*DP*, 37; modified) that has the production of truth as its aim. Although it can be defined on a purely discursive level, by reference to "formal constraints to legal proof" (*DP*, 37), this regime can only really be understood from what Foucault calls its "operative function"—the proportioning of the criminal's punishment according to the degree of perfection of the proofs provided. Thus a "semi-full" proof, as against a "full" proof, can entail severe punishment but not death. The regime is thus neither independent of power relations nor determined by them: it is, rather, a constitutive element of their functioning, as it allows, on the practical level, the forms of their application to be specified, and on the theoretical level, the exercise of power to be founded, by giving it the form of a meticulously defined and legal "arithmetic" (*DP*, 37). In this way it ensures *per se* the production and regulation of the effects of power coextensive with the discourse that it governs. However, this regime is not the only means of the production of truth, which also involves material techniques, the most spectacular of which is torture, this "discloser of truth" (*DP*, 55),[71] which accompany it in the material order and can even replace it. The tortured man who confesses his crimes supersedes all the other proofs as a "living truth" (*DP*, 38). In this sense, the discursive regime is only one element of a greater regime, itself centered on the production of truth in the judicial domain, a "general regime" whose close connection with the monarchic form of power is shown in chapter 2 of *Discipline and Punish*. Correspondingly, one might think that a given regime of truth would include several discursive regimes, differing according to the domains concerned. Thus, the *scientia sexualis* and criminology clearly have different objects and theoretical requirements but are both the products of the regime of truth specific to bio-power.

The principal advantage of such an approach is that it removes one of the major problems left open by archaeology: the connection of the *épistémès* to the material instances of the production of discourses. As we saw, this problem arose from the very approach of archaeology, which above all questioned the nature of the *épistémès* and was little concerned to connect them with "nondiscursive" practices. Genealogical reinterpretation escapes this difficulty to the extent that the discursive regime, although capable of being defined at its own level, internalizes both the aims and the techniques of subjection, which is why the discourses that it governs intrinsically possess the "effects of power" so often mentioned by Foucault. The discursive regime is one of the constitutive elements of the regime of truth (in the sense that it is an integral part of its functioning): it is determined by it (as it has as condition of possibility the techniques of subjection specific to bio-power), and reinforces it (as the various forms of knowledge that it controls induce the perfecting of these techniques). The relationship between the discursive regime and the regime of truth reproduces the circularity of power-knowledge itself, while being founded by it.

One might therefore conclude that Foucault's examination of the human sciences and the imbrication of the knowledge and power that gave birth to them, as well as the elaboration of the notions of "discursive regime" and "regime of truth," allow him to replace archaeology with a more accurate and coherent analytic model. However, at least three problems remain; the first and perhaps the least difficult is concerned with the extension that should be accorded to Foucault's claims. Indeed, we have seen that his analyses of truth and power only make sense in reference to the human sciences, and should therefore, *stricto sensu*, concern only them. However, the passages quoted above do not distinguish between the different domains where the predication of truth is considered pertinent; they assert in a global manner the necessity of understanding truth from its relationship with power. But it is clear that all types of truth do not conform with this model: mathematical propositions, for example, which are probably among the least subjecting and most lacking in direct effects of power (especially in the case of fundamental research), are nonetheless recognized as truths by Foucault, and even provide the strongest model for scientificity, as shown by *The Archaeology of Knowledge*. Insofar as they can be understood and demonstrated in themselves, they seem to contradict *de facto* Foucault's thesis that it is impossible to define truth independently of power relations. For the same reason, the case of mathematics indirectly questions the notion of a "regime of truth" by suggesting a nonpolitical paradigm for understanding the establishment of truth.[72] One can certainly understand why Foucault does not talk about it, but the existence of this counterexample perhaps shows the necessity of rethinking truth, of multiplying its definitions, and mostly of grounding the distinction between those that call for an overtly "political" approach and those that don't. Moreover, there is a similar problem in relation to power. As we have seen, the study of the disciplines in *Discipline and Punish* leads Foucault to criticize theories of sovereignty and to propose his own model, whose theoretical foundations are established in volume 1 of *The History of Sexuality*.[73] However it appears that the characteristics laid out in this text would be more pertinent to the description of the functioning of *contemporary* power than to understand power in general. For example, it is not certain that, in the case of the monarchic exercise of power in France during the seventeenth and eighteenth centuries, power did "come from below," or that the relations of power were "at once intentional and non-subjective" (*HS*, 94).[74] In this sense, the Foucauldian conception of power, like that of truth, seem to show a tendency to turn a particular case into a generality without much justification.

The second and perhaps more serious difficulty is related to the definition of the regime of truth itself. Foucault understands truth from a positivist perspective, as a content elaborated within the framework of "forms of hegemony, social, economic and cultural" (*PK*, 133),[75] according to the internal demands (themselves internally shaped by power) that are specific to each of the discursive regimes concerned. From this perspective, truth ends up being identified by metonymy with the "true" statements themselves (the reason why Foucault can adopt the materialist lexicon of "consumption" and "distribution" and speak of "truths" in the plural). The genitive ("regime *of* truth") thus receives an objective meaning, which understands truth as that which the regime governs and allows us to think. But in the *same* text Foucault also defines truth very differently, as "the set of rules according to which the true and the false are separated and specific effects of power attached to the true" (*PK*, 132; modified). Here, truth seems identified, not with any particular content, but with what allows the truth-value of the contents to be decided (the "rules"). It would then be necessary to give the genitive a subjective sense and, rather than defining truth from the regime, to understand the regime from truth as a "set of rules." For example, we could construe the regime as the way in which the rules are articulated among themselves in order to allow for the predication of truth.

Taken in itself, this idea would be quite sensible; but added to the preceding theses it generates two problems. Firstly, it is difficult to see how truth can be defined both as a content, as suggested by the definitions of the regime of truth examined above, and as the set of rules which allows the true to be defined. We are thus faced again with one of the major difficulties generated in relation to the notion of the "discursive practice" by the anthropological version of the transcendental theme, that is, the confusion between the constituting (truth as a set of rules) and the constituted (truth as a commodity). On top of this internal tension, the second problem is that this definition of truth as a "set of rules" appears very similar, if not identical, to that of the discursive regime itself. Indeed, the idea that truth permits the "separation of the true from the false" and the "attachment to truth of specific effects of power" takes up exactly the two criteria of acceptability described above (to obey the rules of scientificity valid at a given epoch, on the one hand, and to be endowed with the "coercive effects" that stem from it, on the other). Here Foucault seems to fall prey to another of the doubles of man, the regression in the order of the conditions of possibility exhibited by the concept of the originary. Indeed, it is difficult to see how accounting for a "set of rules" (truth) by other rules (the discursive regime) themselves defined in the same way as the first, could be enlightening. On the contrary, the enterprise seems doomed to the "homunculus" sophism, as it seeks to explain one element by others that in fact merely repeat its problematic characteristics.

This already delicate configuration is still further complicated by the fact that the *same* text adds another supplementary definition of truth: "'Truth' is to be understood as a system of ordered procedures for the production, regulation, distribution, circulation, and operation of statements" (*PK*, 133).[76] This conception is related to the preceding one, as it defines truth not as a content (which would be the true statement), but as that which allows it to be produced. Nonetheless, it differs from it to the extent that the notion of "procedure" appears more concrete than that of "rules" and therefore seems to refer to a set of material processes rather than to the theoretical operation of separating the true from the false—as suggested by the economic vocabulary of "production" and the "putting into circulation" of statements. Far from avoiding the two difficulties described above, this definition in fact generates a third one, in that it seems to identify truth (as a "system of procedures"), not with the discursive regime, but with the regime of truth itself. Beyond the fact that it makes it very difficult to know what Foucault's concept of truth is, this second assimilation has the unfortunate consequence of indirectly identifying the discursive regime with the regime of truth,[77] and thus of destroying the hypothesis of a regime of power *internal* to the field of statements—an idea that is nonetheless presented in the same text.

To these already considerable difficulties is added a third: that the idea of "power-knowledge" itself appears very problematic.[78] This concept too was established, by the Foucauldian analysis of the human sciences, to characterize the functioning of disciplinary power. However, Foucault once again generalizes his claims by stating that the existence of a coextensive relationship between knowledge and power is not simply a historical given, but a *structural invariant*: "We should rather admit . . . that power and knowledge directly imply one another; that *there is no power relation without the correlative constitution of a field of knowledge, nor any knowledge that does not presuppose and constitute at the same time power relations*" (*DP*, 27; my italics). This idea appears still more clearly in the following passage:

> However, I have the impression that there exists, I have tried to make appear, *a perpetual articulation of power on knowledge* [savoir] *and of knowledge on power*. It is not sufficient to say that power needs this discovery or that form of knowledge; the exercise of power creates objects of knowledge, makes them emerge, accumulates information, uses it. . . . *The exercise of power perpetually creates knowledge, and inversely, knowledge entails effects of power*. . . . Modern humanism is therefore wrong to separate knowledge and power. *Knowledge and*

power are internal to each other, and it is pointless to dream of a day where knowledge would cease to depend on power. *It is not possible that power can be exercised without knowledge, it is not possible that knowledge can be created without power.* (*DE*, 2: 753)

Even if one were to allow this generalization in the faith of analyses yet to come, this "perpetual articulation of power on knowledge" nonetheless would remain problematic because its status appears unresolved. Indeed, in certain texts Foucault defines it in a quasi-essentialist manner:

The subject that knows, the objects to be known and the modalities of knowledge must be regarded as so many effects of *these fundamental implications of power-knowledge and their historical transformations*. In short, it is not the activity of the subject of knowledge that produces a corpus of knowledge, useful or resistant to power, but power-knowledge, the processes and struggles that traverse it and of which it is made up, that determines the forms and possible domains of knowledge. (*DP*, 27; my italics)

Power-knowledge, far from being a contingent and historically given configuration, appears here as a metaphysical entity,[79] endowed with a quasi-transcendental function ("to determine the possible forms and domains of knowledge"). Admittedly, such a definition presents the advantage of allowing the relationship of the regime of truth to power-knowledge to be described in an apparently satisfactory manner: the former would have the function of defining the different "transformations" of the latter, so permitting the identification of its historical forms of functioning, a perspective in which the diverse Western regimes of truth would feature as particular historical variations of power-knowledge itself. But this definition of power-knowledge is problematic for two reasons. Firstly, although it does not necessarily imply a totalization or even progress, it nonetheless seems to reactivate the type of Hegelian schema so disliked by Foucault, in which power-knowledge would take the different historical forms that the analysis of truth regimes would allow to be identified. Secondly, and most importantly, it radically contradicts the genealogical approach adopted by *The Order of Discourse* by reintroducing the same essentialist perspective that it had attempted to render untenable, since the idea that power-knowledge could be a sort of essence definable in itself appears to return to exactly the sort of metaphysics that genealogy sought to combat by giving primacy to perspective and interpretation, against any essentialist ontology.

It is probably his own implicit recognition of these difficulties that leads Foucault *himself* to redefine the concept of power-knowledge in a radically different direction, adopting the overtly nominalist position that considers power-knowledge as an "analytic grid,"[80] a mere theoretical tool designed to clarify, within the problematic established by *The Order of Discourse*, the conditions of "acceptability" of a set of propositions: "It is a matter of describing a power-knowledge nexus which allows that which makes the acceptability of a system to be identified, whether it is the system of mental illness, of penalism, of delinquency, of sexuality, etc."[81] The idea of a "nexus" (i.e., etymologically speaking, of a "knot," an indissociable connection between two elements), symbolically illustrates the structural indissolubility of knowledge and power described above. The clear benefit of such an approach is that it avoids any metaphysics of power by rejecting in advance the idea that knowledge and power could be "entities" or "powers,"[82] or even "lunar, extra-terrestrial elements" (*DE*, 631). But the problem then is that Foucault appears to be passing from Charybdis to Scylla, as the "nexus" seems identical to the regime of truth itself: it "allows that which makes the acceptability of a system to be identified" and fulfils exactly the same function: to define the conditions under which "true" statements can be produced and considered as such. However, the concept of the regime of truth was only meaningful to the extent that it rested on the idea of an empirical articulation between knowledge and power (highlighted by the study of the human sciences and disciplines), whose functioning it made visible. If it turns out that this articulation itself is merely an "analytic grid," the notion of a regime itself becomes deprived of any foundation. Finally, establishing such a complex structure just to explain a mere "grid," beyond that it might appear to be rather sterile, would expose Foucault to another of the doubles of the transcendental theme, the regression in explanation that stems from the multiplication of identical explicative entities. As a result, the definition of power-knowledge remains caught between these two contradictory positions, excessive essentialism or nominalism,[83] which is perhaps the reason why later Foucault will progressively cease using the concept.

Despite these difficulties, the preceding analyses taken altogether suggest that the genealogical reinterpretation of the historical *a priori* is one of the most fertile elements in Foucault's work. As we saw, its greatest significance lies in the idea that the conditions of acceptability themselves cannot be defined from a epistemic standpoint alone, but are always already preshaped by the norms of power-knowledge, whose diffusion they in turn encourage. From this perspective, the attention given to *practices* in general (whether discursive or not) gives Foucault a rather effective way of escaping the archaeological blocks, and allows him to reinterpret his work around a single theme (the questioning of truth) while recasting his answer to the critical question in a much more elaborate manner.

Genealogy itself turns out to be a powerful methodological tool, in which three principal elements can be distinguished: firstly, a new paradigm to understand the relationship of knowledge and power from the coextensive connection between subjection and objectification; secondly, a more precise conception of truth, which understands it from a quasi-pragmatic perspective, through the functional demands specific to power-knowledge; and finally, the establishment of new concepts (such as "subjection") that will prove essential for Foucault's later work.

However, this somewhat optimistic picture must be qualified, as a critical examination of the genealogical texts shows many failures in Foucault's argument. The references to Nietzsche, although omnipresent, suffer from a lack of theoretical elaboration, which as a consequence deprives Foucault's genealogy, if not of its effectiveness, at least of the theoretical foundation which it needs philosophically. Correspondingly, Foucault occasionally succumbs to the (highly metaphysical) temptation of totalization, and unduly generalizes his analyses of truth and power-knowledge by giving them a reach that largely exceeds that which the examination of the problem of the human sciences can establish. Finally, most of the genealogical concepts (notably those of the discursive regime, the regime of truth, and even "power-knowledge" itself) display the same lack of coherence as their archaeological counterparts, and stand as new transpositions of the confusion between the transcendental and the empirical denounced with reference to the originary. For all these reasons, genealogy is partially marked by a return of transcendentalism, which is revealed in the reoccurrence of the aporia formerly identified by Foucault himself in reference to the doubles of man.

Nonetheless, it may be the case that all these criticisms are not (or are not any more) central. Indeed, from the course of genealogical studies it appears that Foucault's questioning of the relationship of truth and power progressively replaces the study of the *conditions of the possibility of truth* (its "acceptability") with the study of its *consequences* (its "effects of power"). Thus, although it is the genealogical avatar of the *épistémè* in the first volume of *The History of Sexuality*, the notion of the "discursive regime" is meant to study the action of discourses on *the subject itself* at least as much as to describe the rules of their formation. In this way, the archaeological theme of the conditions of possibility of truth becomes surreptitiously tied to that of the constitution of subjectivity, which, as the following section will show, will turn out to be the principal focus of the later Foucault's concerns. Henceforth he will fasten the critical question on the various historical forms taken by the knowledge of man, and analyze the effects on the subject of the truths whose historical conditions of possibility are defined by the various discursive regimes. From this perspective, the introduction of the architectonic concept of "problematisation"[84] will allow the author to retrospectively uncover the deeper aims of archaeology by connecting the historical forms taken by acceptability to the different modes of subjection. In a massive readjustment, the critical question thus will find itself set within a larger horizon, that of the "historical ontology of ourselves" (*MF*, 237), the subject to which I shall now turn.

Truth and Subjectivation: The Retrospective Stakes of the Critical Question

Introduction to Part III

Reading *The Use of Pleasure* reserves a considerable surprise for anyone who expects the program announced at the end of the French edition of the first volume of *The History of Sexuality* to be fulfilled,[1] a surprise perhaps as large as the long silence of eight years that separates the publication of the two volumes. A surprise in the style—the purified, measured introduction barely resembles the flamboyant descriptions of Borges's "Chinese" encyclopedia or the punishment of Damiens on the place de Grève. A surprise in the period studied—Greek and Roman antiquity, which Foucault had hardly touched on before. Finally, a surprise because of the almost total absence of any of the now familiar concepts of power, disciplines, or regimes of truth. While the theme of genealogy remains,[2] a set of new concepts appears: "problematizations," "ethical substance," "the teleology of the moral subject," and so on, all of which are aimed at allowing the analysis of what Foucault now identifies as the essential question—the "study (of) the modes according to which individuals are led to recognize themselves as sexual subjects" (*UP*, 5; modified). His analyses will therefore have a dual aim: firstly, to establish the theoretical foundations for such research, as attempted by the introduction to *The Use of Pleasure* through an examination of the subject centered on the opposition between the Greek ethics of self-constitution and the Christian forms of morality that demand submission to the law from the subject; secondly, to give the project a specific content by identifying the historical forms taken by this problematization of the self while analyzing the different practices through which it was effected—a preoccupation with practices that defines, as before, the specifically genealogical nature of this approach.[3] Foucault's central thesis is thus that since the subordination by Socrates of the *epimeleia heautou* (care of the self) to the Delphic imperative of *gnōthi seauton* (know thy self), the constitution of the self has had to occur through the establishment of a relation to truth, which induces a transformation of the *ethos* of the subject concerned through the use of specific techniques.

Surprising as it might appear, this recentering on the relationship between truth and the subject could be anticipated from the genealogical analysis of subjection: its second definition, as given by volume 1 of *The History of Sexuality*, involved *per se* the idea of a constitutive connection between truth and subjection, which retrospectively appears as a more restricted form of subjectivation. As we have seen, subjection was not only understood as the disciplinary submission of "subjects of obedience," but also as the production of a subject "*tied to its own identity by its conscience or self-knowledge*" (*MF*, 212; modified, my italics). In this second sense, subjection referred to the demand imposed on individuals to construct themselves through preestablished norms, and therefore to become "subjects" not only politically, but also by recognizing themselves within socially constructed forms of subjectivity, Foucault's fundamental idea already being that subjection can only "transform individuals into subjects" through "constraining them to produce the truth." Thus, "we must speak that truth; we are constrained or condemned to confess or to discover the truth . . . truth is the law" (*PK*, 93–94; modified). The relationship with truth was thus understood since the first volume of *The History of Sexuality* as a major principle of the construction of subjectivity, through a process exemplified in detail by Foucault's analyses of confession.[4] As Foucault himself explains very clearly in the introduction to *The Use of Pleasure* (*UP*, 5–11), the study of the "slow formation, during Antiquity, of a hermeneutic of the self" can effectively be understood as the retrospective elucidation of the major presuppositions of *The History of Sexuality*, volume 1, and as the opening of the negative model of subjection onto the wider horizon of subjectivation.

Although they adopt a different perspective by proposing a positive counterpoint to the analyses of subjection (in the form of a study of the practices and discourses of truth voluntarily put into play by the self-constituting subjects), the last two volumes of *The History of Sexuality* fully belong in the lineage of the first.

Careful to maintain the continuity of his work,[5] Foucault reconstructs his progress in the following way: "I have tried to analyze how areas such as madness, sexuality, and delinquency could enter into a certain game of truth, and also how, through this insertion of human practice, of behavior, in the game of truth, the subject himself is affected" (*PPC*, 48). The first part of this program ("to analyze how areas . . . ," etc.) corresponds to the archeo-genealogical enterprise, which, by revealing the conditions of possibility of "scientific" discourses and the way in which they are informed by power relations, was meant to give a retrospective account of the functioning of the "games of truth." The "genealogy of the subject"[6] no longer aims to examine the production of "true" discourses, but rather *their effects on the subject* ("how . . . the subject himself is affected").

Thus, the general task that the later Foucault sets himself is to discover "the relationships that can exist between the constitution of the subject or of the different forms of the subject and games of truth, practices of power, and so forth" (*FF*, 10; modified), and this, within the framework of a "history of subjectivity" (*DE*, 4: 213–14). Several questions therefore arise. Firstly, what precise role should be attributed to truth in the formation of subjectivity? Why should the relationship to the self necessarily pass through a relation to truth, as Foucault claims, and how should the different historical forms taken by this truth be analyzed? Correspondingly, how should the "games of truth" that produce and propagate it be understood? If they really define the conditions by which a truth can be accepted as such and have some effects on the subject, what can their relationship be with the old concepts of the historical *a priori*, the *épistémè*, or the discursive regime? How is the analysis of the acceptability of "true" discourses and their relationship with power taken up by the study of the problematizations of the self? In other words, what is the connection between the history of *subjectivity* and the project of a "history of *truth*" (*UP*, 3)? And if the "games of truth" are Foucault's last answer to the critical question, do they allow this last reworking of the archeo-genealogical perspective to escape the "return of the transcendental" so feared by the author?

To these general questions a more immediate one must be added. As we have seen, the real object of Foucault's analysis is not only the constitution of the self as a "subject of desire" (*UP*, 6), but the "historical constitution of the different forms of subject" *in general* (*FF*, 10), its modalities as well as its relationship with the games of truth. But if the "desiring subject" is only *one* of these "forms of the subject," is it legitimate to identify the analysis of *sexuality* with a history of *subjectivity in general*? It is likely that Foucault's inclusion of sexuality itself within the general category of "experience" is an attempt to neutralize this objection: but how then can this "experience" be understood, and how can it be the ground for such a shift?

FIVE

Truth and the Constitution of the Self

The Two Definitions of Experience

At first sight, the beginning of the introduction of *The Use of Pleasure* seems to pick up where volume 1 of *The History of Sexuality* left off, taking the question of "sexuality" as its point of departure and analyzing it in similar terms. Underlining, as he had eight years before, the recent appearance of the term at the beginning of the nineteenth century, Foucault returns to the archaeological idea that the study of sexuality must work at a specific level and cannot be identified with the level of "behaviors" or of "ideas." Thus, "the use of the word was established in connection with other phenomena" (*UP*, 3), of which the first two—"the development of diverse fields of knowledge" and the "establishment of a set of rules and norms . . . which found support in religious, judicial, pedagogical, and medical institutions"—indicate the domains studied by archaeology and genealogy, respectively. This is confirmed later in the text, where Foucault states that "as to the first two points, the work I had undertaken previously . . . provided me with the tools I needed" (*UP*, 4).[1] The third "phenomenon" concerns the "changes in the way individuals were led to assign meaning and value to their conduct, their duties, their pleasures, their feelings and sensations, their dreams" (*UP*, 4–5). Foucault concludes innocently:

> It was a matter of seeing how an *"experience" came to be constituted* in modern Western societies, an experience *that caused individuals to recognize themselves as subjects of a "sexuality,"* which opened onto very diverse forms of knowledge and was linked to a system of rules and constraints. What I planned, therefore, was a *history of sexuality as an experience, where experience is understood as the correlation, in a culture, between fields of knowledge, types of normativity, and forms of subjectivity.* (*UP*, 4–5; modified, my italics)

But while it is presented as self-evident, the idea of such an "experience" is radically new! Nothing in the "previously undertaken work" allowed us to predict such an addition. As we have seen, *The Archaeology of Knowledge* had rejected the idea of an "experience of madness" by referring it back to a "vast subject of history" itself denounced as an avatar of the transcendental subject. *The History of Sexuality*, volume 1, meanwhile, had no need of any such "experience" to account for sexuality as the "correlate of that slowly evolved discursive practice which constitutes the *scientia sexualis*" (*HS*, 68; modified), since the genealogical analysis of disciplines was enough to establish that the norms established by the latter were internally shaped by the slow formation of bio-power. Despite the serene and smooth tone adopted by Foucault, the addition of this third "phenomenon," defined by the way in which the individual "lends meaning" to his conduct, as well as the introduction of the notion of experience itself, constitute real and unexpected innovations.

But what is this "experience"? The way in which Foucault presents it is highly ambiguous. He describes the constitution of such an "experience" as when individuals had to "recognize themselves as subjects of a 'sexuality,'" which presupposes that this "experience" and "sexuality" itself are two different things (unless the sentence is to be tautological), and that the appearance of the second is one of the elements that allows the formation of the first to be understood. The only thing that can be said about this experience for the moment is that it concerns a necessary relationship between individuals and their sexuality (they were "*caused* . . . to recognize themselves as subjects of a 'sexuality'") and that therefore it should be analyzable in an archeo-genealogical way, that is, by reference to knowledge and power, as this experience involves "fields of knowledge" and a "system of rules and constraints."[2] But the next phrase, although apparently connected with the first by a relationship of consequence ("therefore"), actually makes the logical leap which consists in understanding sexuality, not as one of the elements which allow us to think this still undefined "experience," but as experience *itself*. Experience is then defined in a second sense as an objective (a "correlation"), anonymous and general structure ("in a culture"), which links together not two but three elements: the "fields of knowledge," the "types of normativity" (which echo the archeo-genealogical "fields of knowledge" and "system[s] of rules and constraints"), and the new and mysterious idea of "forms of subjectivity." This definition, far from being isolated, is used in numerous other passages, as for example the following, which describes experience as "understandings of a certain type, . . . rules of a certain form, . . . certain modes of consciousness of oneself and of others" (*F*, 335).

This "objective" definition of experience immediately raises two problems. Firstly, Foucault implicitly takes up again the problematic of *The History of Sexuality*, volume 1, and seeks to add a third dimension of analysis to the two elements in reference to which he had previously defined sexuality (the discursive regime and the power practices that inform it), which is confirmed by the emphasis on continuity in his presentation. But although genealogy was able to show—at least as concerned the human sciences—the coextensive articulation of knowledge and power, it is difficult to understand the "correlation" meant to unite the two first axes with the third. The latter seems different from the other two, if only because it does not refer to objective conditions, but introduces the reflective dimension of subjectivity—which is doubly confirmed by the strong presence, in the definition given by *The Use of Pleasure*, of the theme of "recognition" and the "certain forms of self-consciousness," mentioned above.[3]

This difficulty is accentuated *a contrario* by another passage, where Foucault indicates that his "problem" concerns

> the *relations* between *experiences* (like madness, illness, transgression of laws, sexuality, self-identity), *forms of knowledge* [*savoirs*] (like psychiatry, medicine, criminology, sexology, psychology), and *power* (such as the power which is exercised in psychiatric and penal institutions, and in all other situations which deal with individual control). Our civilization has developed the most complex system of knowledge, the most sophisticated structures of power: *what have this kind of knowledge, this type of power made of us?* (*PPC*, 71; modified)

Although two of the three "axes" of experience as a tripartite structure ("forms of knowledge" and "power") can be identified here, two major modifications are revealed: firstly, the theme of a "correlation" reappears indirectly (as "relations"), but is not itself understood as experience. On the contrary, the idea of an "experience" as a tripartite structure shines by its absence, as the "experiences" (among which, significantly, is sexuality, which *The Use of Pleasure* also referred to as experience, but as a name for the tripartition itself) are clearly identified as the elements to be related, not as the structure itself. Moreover, the three terms ("experiences," "knowledge" and "power") cannot have an equal status, as the first must clearly be considered the result of the two others, which form its conditions of possibility ("what have . . . made of us"). Experience is thus defined at the same time as an overall structure and as one of the elements supposedly united by this structure, which brings back the unwelcome memory of the regressions characteristic of the empirico-transcendental doubles.

Secondly, the definition of experience as a "correlation within a culture," empirically observable and independent of any particular subject, excludes the possibility of understanding experience phenomenologically—be it, schematically speaking, as the "experience of consciousness"[4] through which the latter dialectically progresses toward absolute knowledge, or as the ante-predicative evidence which, for Husserl, constitutes the condition of possibility of all judgment. Foucault's definition clearly seeks to break with the philosophical tradition that subordinates experience (be it as *Erfarhung* or *Erlebnis*) to subjectivity in order to give it an objective definition. However, the problem is that, while he rejects of idealist approach to experience, Foucault equally excludes the materialist hypothesis that would assimilate experience to the "concrete determinations of social existence" (*F*, 335) and define it as a set of objective conditions functioning according to a causal logic ("determinations"). One thus finds again, and surely not by chance, within the concept of experience the same ambivalence as that which governed the elaboration of the concepts of the historical *a priori* and the *épistémè* during the archeological period: the notion of experience can designate neither a set of material conditions serving as infrastructure nor a subjective process. But if this "correlation" must unite both objective (knowledge and power) and subjective elements ("forms of self-consciousness"), while being itself neither objective nor subjective, how can it be understood?

The beginning of *The Use of Pleasure* is therefore very problematic, sexuality appearing sometimes as an element of a still ill-defined "experience," and sometimes as this experience itself, understood as an objective tripartite structure composed of three "axes" ("forms of knowledge [*savoirs*]," "systems of power," and "forms within which individuals are able and forced to recognize themselves as subjects of this sexuality" [*UP*, 4]), a structure whose theoretical status therefore remains delicate. A way out of this impasse may consist in noting that the third of the above axes, the "forms of subjectivity," presupposes, in fact, another understanding of experience from which the structure itself could in turn be reinterpreted. Indeed, the preface to the English edition of the second volume of *The History of Sexuality* clarifies the nature of these "forms of subjectivity" by defining experience as the "correlation of a domain of knowledge, a type of normativity and a *mode of relation to the self*" (*F*, 333; my italics). The forms of subjectivity, therefore, refer to a certain type of relationship of the subject with himself, as *The Use of Pleasure* confirms by describing from the same perspective the "forms within which individuals *can and must recognize themselves* as subjects of this sexuality" or the "modes according to which individuals are given to *recognize* themselves as sexual subjects" (*UP*, 4, 5; modified). Moreover, Foucault's definition of "subjectivity" itself as "the way in which the subject *forms the experience* of himself" (*DE*, 4: 633; my italics) is enough to identify the relation to oneself as an "experience." The idea of "forms of subjectivity" thus presupposes *per se* that another meaning of experience is used, defining it through the quasi-Hegelian idea of a "recognition" through which individuals reflectively constitute themselves as subjects—a point to which I shall shortly return. This second definition is indirectly reinforced by numerous passages, such as Foucault's reference to "the experience *of* sexuality" as a "singular historical figure," or to "the experience *of* the 'flesh'" (*UP*, 5), since it is clear that the experience that has as its objects "sexuality" or the "flesh" cannot itself be understood as a tripartite objective structure (which would be redundant and senseless), but must rather be referred to the way in which the individual "could *experience* himself as a subject of a 'sexuality'" (*UP*, 5, 6)—that is, to experience as the reflective process of the constitution of the self.

Most importantly, one can show that this relationship of presupposition was present, however implicitly, in the main passage analyzed above. In it, Foucault described the constitution of an "experience" that, as noted above, could not be identified with sexuality, a fact that rendered the meaning of the rest of the text—in which sexuality was understood precisely as an experience (in the objective sense)—obscure. But the passage becomes clearer if one considers the "constitution" of this mysterious "experience" as the appearance of a particular historical form of experience as self-constitution. What Foucault means, then, is that a set of objective conditions ("sexuality"), definable by reference to the formation of "fields of knowledge" and a "new system of rules and constraints," progressively shaped from the inside the relationship of individuals to themselves in a particular domain, and thus necessarily determined experience as self-constitution.[5] This interpretation is confirmed by another assertion in the same sentence, which describes the said "experience" as being such that it "caused individuals to *recognize themselves* as subjects of a 'sexuality,'" and thus explicitly connects this "experience" to the theme of recognition. This is equally corroborated by the idea expressed elsewhere, according to which nothing can "allow for experiences (that is, for understandings of a certain type, for rules of a certain form, for certain modes of consciousness of oneself and of others) except through thought"

(*F*, 335). Significantly, even while experience is characterized as an objective tripartite structure ("understandings," "rules," "modes of consciousness of oneself"), "thought" is named as its subjective condition of possibility. "There is no experience that is not a way of thinking," as the text clarifies a little later on. Thus sexuality as an "experience" (in the objective sense) would describe the specific conditions from which was effected this historical determination of the self-constitutive relationship. It is in this sense that sexuality could represent, like other "experiences," like "madness," "sickness," or "delinquency," a "matrix" or "locus of experience" (*F*, 336). All of these expression equally presuppose the distinction between the two definitions of experience, since the experience of which madness is the "focus" or "matrix" can hardly be assimilated to madness itself as experience.

Thus the addition of this third element, the "forms of relationship to the self," considerably changes the perspective of *The History of Sexuality*. Indeed, experience as a relationship of "subjectivation" (*UP*, 29) will now constitute the backdrop against which sexuality as an (objective) "experience" can make sense. This "shift" (*UP*, 6), described at length in the introduction to *The Use of Pleasure*, is confirmed in other extracts by the general notion of a "history of subjectivity" (*DE*, 4: 633), or of a "genealogy of the subject,"[6] of which the "genealogy of the subject as subject of ethical actions" (*MF*, 240) is not the main theme, but, rather, one of its elements—an ordering that Foucault will elsewhere take up by stating that the "history of the care of the self" was "a way of doing the history of subjectivity" (*DE*, 4: 213). What must now be studied is the "constitution of the subject as object for himself" (*DE*, 4: 633), a constitution that the preceding studies gave other examples of, such as the "mad" or the "delinquent" subject.

Thus, by a curious movement of inversion, "sexuality," the former main object of an analysis in which the forms of relationship to the self were merely one element, now *itself* appears as only one of the possible forms of self-constitution— "a historically unique form of experience" (*DE*, 4: 636), as Foucault says. *The History of Sexuality* therefore must be seen as one of the "elements that might be useful for a history of truth" (*UP*, 6), a history centered on the notion of the "games of truth," of which the study of the "sexual subject" is merely one possible dimension:

> What are the games of truth by which man proposes to think his own nature when he perceives himself to be mad; when he considers himself to be ill; when he conceives of himself as a living, speaking, laboring being; when he judges and punishes himself as a criminal? What were the games of truth by which human beings came to see themselves as desiring individuals? (*UP*, 7)

As we have seen, the connection between this "history of truth" and the "history of subjectivity," mentioned above, rests on the definition of subjectivity itself as "the way in which the subject forms the experience of himself in a game of truth in which he relates to himself" (*DE*, 4: 633), a theme that in the introduction to *The Use of Pleasure* takes on the form of a study of "the games of truth in the relationship of the self to itself and in the forming of oneself as a subject" (*UP*, 6; modified). It is, therefore, the fundamental idea of a connection between subjectivation and truth, not the analysis of sexuality *per se*, which constitutes, in Kantian terms, the "keystone" of Foucault's work, as it alone allows a bridging of the gap between the archeo-genealogical study of the conditions of truth and the role that truth plays in the constitution of the self. But how can such a constitution be understood? And above all, what are its theoretical foundations? Foucault turns to this problem in the introduction of *The Use of Pleasure*, by attempting to refute transcendentalism one last time and to show the necessity, in order to understand the subject, of involving the model of a temporal and historical constitution, the nature and forms of which I shall now examine.

"Subjectivation" as the Constitution of the Self

In an often quoted passage from the introduction of *The Use of Pleasure*, Foucault carefully establishes an initial distinction between the first two levels of analysis, the "moral code" and the "morality of behaviours" (*UP*, 25, 26). The first is composed of "interdictions and codes" that can be analyzed formally and independently of any effective action; the second refers to the "actual behavior" of individuals, and only can be evaluated, *a posteriori*, by reference to the "prescriptive set" circumscribed by the moral code. Although Kant is never mentioned by name, this is clearly a transposition of the distinction established by the *Groundwork of the Metaphysic of Morals* between the moral law and actions that may or may not conform to it.[7] Just as Kant did before him, Foucault denies that morality could be understood solely by reference to the actions carried out, and therefore rejects "actual behavior" as being inframoral.[8] Morality must be defined, not through the conformity of the action with the codes, but in reference to the intention and the freedom of the subject, and thus, ultimately, to the way in which the will determines itself. "For what is morality, if not the practice of liberty, the deliberate practice of liberty?" Foucault asks, before adding elsewhere that "ethics is the reflective form assumed by liberty" (*FF*, 4; modified).[9] However, the difference between Foucault and Kant lies in the way in which this "practice of freedom" is conceived. For Kant, it is respect for the law alone that allows us to decide the morality of an action,[10] but as Foucault reminds us, the Greeks had very few codes and prohibitions. What mattered to them was not the relationship with the law, but the necessity of the subject determining and expressing, not only his will, but also his way of being through action. Thus to the Judeo-Christian understanding of morality, based on the relation of the subject to the law, Foucault opposes an ethics that can be defined from the "conduct" of the individual, so implicitly taking up the traditional opposition between act-centered morality and agent centered ethics.[11]

So a third level between codes and actions appears, allowing the Kantian opposition between action and the law to be superseded, a level concerned with the "manner in which one ought to constitute oneself as an ethical subject acting in reference to the prescriptive elements that make up the code" (*UP*, 26; modified). For Kant, it is the possibility of defining *a priori* both the moral law and the good will that allows the foundation of a universal and necessary moral law. Furthermore, the idea (expressed in *Religion Within the Limits of Reason Alone*) that it would be just as impossible for the will to systematically go against the law (which would be the maxim of a diabolic will) as it is for reason itself to become irrational, is enough to rule out the hypothesis that the "moral subject," in his *a priori* power of self-determination, could be the result of a "constitution." Being naturally endowed with reason is a sufficient condition for being able to be moral. As could be expected, the transcendental approach is enough, when defining morality, to exclude the necessity and even the possibility of taking into account the agent's mode of being, which can only be defined empirically and *a posteriori*. Thus Foucault doubly takes the opposing perspective to Kant by affirming the impossibility that the Greeks would have understood morality independently of the quality of the moral subject and have defined this quality independently of his actions. It is not intention alone that decides the moral value of an action, or more exactly, intention cannot be examined on its own—the mode of being of the agent must be taken into account. This is not definable *a priori*, but is the result of the constitution of the subject by itself. The real object of Greek ethics is thus the "kind of relationship you ought to have with yourself . . . which determines how the individual is supposed to constitute himself as a moral subject of his own actions" (*MF*, 238), a relationship that demands continual elaboration and experiences temporal variation.

So a subtle dialectic is established between the action and the determination of the self. On the one hand, the individual constitutes himself as a moral subject by means of the accomplishment of specific actions: "A moral action tends toward its own accomplishment; but it also aims beyond the latter, to the establishing of a moral conduct that commits an individual, not only to other actions always in conformity with values and rules, but to a certain mood of being, a mood of being characteristic of the ethical subject" (*UP*, 28). It is likely that Foucault is here implicitly referring to the Aristotelian thesis that virtue is perfected by its own use, demanding from the agent a permanent actualization that ultimately will make it habitual. Indeed, the idea that action determines a "mode of being characteristic of the moral subject" clearly evokes Aristotle's definition of *hexis* as a "permanent disposition" progressively acquired through the repetition of specific actions, as the *Nicomachean Ethics* says: "The virtues are induced and fostered as a result, and by the agency of the same sort of actions as cause their destruction, the activities that flow from them will also consist in the same sort of actions."[12] Thus one becomes more moderate the more consistently one abstains from excess, the braver the more one faces danger. The act does not completely disappear in its being effected but subsists by leaving its trace in the subject's potentiality as an *hexis*.[13] In this way, the modification of being that Foucault speaks about can only occur through the deliberate and reflective repetition of certain actions judged to be virtuous,[14] which in a passage from the quantitative to the qualitative slowly transforms the *ethos* of the individual.

On the other hand, action itself can only make sense within the global perspective of the ethical determination of the self in which it is inscribed and which it helps to form. As Foucault indicates it is an "element and an aspect of [the subject's] conduct, and it marks a stage in its becoming, a possible advance in its continuity" (*UP*, 28; modified). If the act is the *ratio essendi* of morality, morality is the *ratio cognoscendi* of the act, following the circular movement that, when one recalls that the "constitution of the self as moral subject" can only occur through moral actions, clearly appears in the following passage: "There is no specific moral action that does not refer to a unified moral conduct; no moral conduct that does not call for the forming of oneself as an ethical subject" (*UP*, 28).

Foucault's analyses of the constitution of the self therefore take place against the double background of an implicit argument with Kant and an indirect reference to Aristotelian thought. Nonetheless, the general aim of his strategy is certainly not a return to Aristotelianism, nor is it only the analysis of Greek ethics, but rather (as testified by the inclusion of the history of sexuality within that of subjectivity examined in the previous chapter) to establish the *general* possibility and necessity of work by the self on the self for its constitution as subject. This is clearly stated at the end of the introduction, where the author takes care to underline that "*every morality*, in the broad sense, comprises the two elements just mentioned: codes of behaviour and forms of subjectivation" (*UP*, 29), although the second is weaker in the case of "Christian morals." This idea is equally presupposed by the very form of the questioning that consists in asking "how, given the continuity, transfer, or modification of codes, the forms of self-relationship (and the practices of the self that were associated with them) were defined, *modified, recast, and diversified*" (*UP*, 31, 32; my italics).

Foucault's refutation of Kant therefore goes beyond a simple return to pre–"codified moralities," and shows that *even these* presuppose a self-constitution by the subject. Rather than a Foucauldian critique of Kant, this is, rather, a reread-ing or reinterpretation of what it means to be moral, which reveals, even at the heart of the moralities of the law, the need for an ethical problematization. Thus, the only passage that Foucault explicitly devotes to Kantian morality stresses not the *a priori* character of the moral subject, but rather the allegedly *internal* need for Kantianism of a "constitution of the self as ethical subject": "Kant says, 'I must recognize myself as universal subject, that is, I must constitute myself in each of my actions as a universal subject by conforming to universal rules.' The old questions were re-interpreted: 'How can I constitute myself as a subject of ethics? Recognize myself as such? Are ascetic exercises needed?'" (*MF*, 252). The inflection of Foucault's reading of Kant is particularly clear in the last of the ques-tions mentioned above, as it is doubtful that the question of the "ascetic exer-cises" essential to antiquity was central to Kant himself.

Following the subordination of the analysis of sexuality to the history of sub-jectivity, the analysis of the constitution of the ethical subject serves as the depar-ture point for a more universal reflection on subjectivation in general. Foucault indicates that "what I really wanted to do was to show how the problem of the subject did not cease to exist throughout this question of sexuality, which in its diversity does not cease to encounter and multiply it" (*PPC*, 253). The following extract is still more explicit: "My problem was to define . . . the set of processes by which the subject exists with its different problems and obstacles and through forms which are far from being completed" (*PPC*, 252; modified). But if the rela-tionship of the subject to itself must be understood as a necessary "constitution" (*FF*, 10), the main question is clearly how to understand this "set of processes," and therefore to define the famous "problems" of the subject. "Indeed it was nec-essary that I rejected a certain *a priori* theory of the subject" (*FF*, 10), declares Foucault, explaining this as follows: "What I refused was precisely that you first of all set up a theory of the subject—as could be done in phenomenology and in existentialism—and that, beginning from the theory of the subject, you come to pose the question of knowing, for example, how such and such a form of knowl-edge was possible" (*FF*, 10). Because it mostly rejects the idea of a "subject which, in its transcendental functions, would found experience and its significations," Foucault's critique seems to have in mind not so much phenomenology in gen-eral as Husserlian thought in particular,[15] as was already the case during the archeological period. The significance of Foucault's position is clear: against any transcendental temptation that would approach the question of the possible "forms of knowledge" *from* a theory of subjectivity, it is necessary to reverse the movement by questioning the role of knowledge in the *formation* of subjectivity.

However, insofar as the conditions of possibility of knowledge are no longer examined in themselves, one can notice here an important difference from archaeology and even genealogy. The meaning of the critical question is now tied to the fact that it allows the genesis of subjectivity to be understood by showing that truth plays a constitutive and positive role in it. Rather than the notion of a "foundational act," Foucault therefore prefers that of a temporal constitution in which any foundation can only appear as a historical beginning and not as an origin ("different foundations, different creations, different modifications" [*PPC*, 28–29]), as the following extract describes more clearly: "Men have never ceased to construct themselves, i.e. to continually displace their subjectivity, to constitute themselves in a multiple and infinite series of different subjectivities, which will have no end, and will never place us in front of something which would be man" (*DE*, 4: 75). This very dense passage rests on the implicit distinction between a self-constituting activity ("constituting oneself," "to constitute oneself") and the historical forms taken by this constitution ("to continually displace their subjectivity" or "a multiple and infinite series of different subjectivities"), a distinction whose main presupposition is the impossibility of assigning man a fixed essence ("something which would be man"). From this perspective, Foucault implicitly takes up the method of hyperbolic doubt, described at the beginning of the first *Meditation*, to express a "systematic skepticism in regard to all universal anthropologies" (*DE*, 4: 634), correspondingly describing the need to "test" "all that is proposed to us in our knowledge as having universal validity, about human nature, or categories which one could apply to the subject" (*DE*, 4: 634).

> The first rule of method in this type of work is therefore this: to dispense with universals as much as possible in order to interrogate their historical constitution (and especially also those of the humanism which would valorise the rights, privileges and nature of a human being as the immediate *a*temporal truth of the subject). (*DE*, 4: 634)

One finds again here the nominalist and historicizing reduction that led *The Archaeology of Knowledge* to critique the ontological realism of *The Order of Things*, now applied to the idea of human nature and founding the opposition between an essentialist definition of the "human being" (what Sartre qualifies as "classical" humanism)[16] and the notion of a subject stripped of any "*a*temporal truth."

But if man must constitute himself, how can this constitution be understood?

The passage quoted shortly above ("Men have never ceased . . . ," etc.) identifies it as a "continual displacement of subjectivity" into an "infinite and multiple series of different subjectivities." To constitute oneself is therefore "to establish different forms of relationships with oneself" (*FF*, 10; modified), *"to recognize oneself"* in certain "forms" (*UP*, 4; my italics). Another passage states that "to analyze what is termed 'the subject,' it seemed appropriate to look for the forms and modalities of the relation to self by which the individual *constitutes and recognizes himself* as subject" (*UP*, 6). The constitution of the self is presented here, therefore, as a reflective experience through which the subject seeks to stabilize his autointerpretative activity by giving himself an interpretation of what he is, an interpretation in which he can recognize himself and through which one of the possible historical "forms" of subjectivity specifies itself. Hence Foucault can define the subject, not as a "substance," which would both presuppose a static nature and deny the necessity of the movement of reflection by seeing the subject as an in-itself, but as a "form" (*FF*, 10), that is, as a set of characteristics that the individual, by constituting himself as subject, recognizes as his own.

Foucault's central idea is therefore that there is no natural subjecthood, but only a becoming-subject that constitutes itself through the mediation of forms in which the individual must recognize itself. Such a thematic clearly has Hegelian connotations, and reminds us of the *Erfahrung* through which consciousness determines itself in a series of apparently objective figures which it is each time led to recognize as its own, in the movement of the *Aufhebung*. Thus the preface to *The Phenomenology of Spirit* reminds us, while referring to the dialectic process, that the *"pure self-recognition* in absolute otherness . . . , is the ground and soil for Science or knowledge in general."[17] Nonetheless there are at least two differences between Foucault and Hegel: firstly, as Christian Jambet has remarked,[18] recognition does not take place between two consciousnesses for Foucault, but from self to self. Secondly, and most importantly, the self-constitution is neither understood by Foucault as a teleological dialectic, which would order the "forms of subjectivity" from a general perspective culminating in their unification/totalization, nor as the anticipation of the progressive realization of some essence of man. On the contrary, Foucault seems to adopt the Nietzschean perspective of the creation/destruction of the self by defining the creation of the "forms" as "the destruction of what we are, and the creation of something totally other, a total innovation" (*DE*, 4: 74–75). This insistence on an alterity that refuses any mediation ("totally other"), and on a novelty ("a total innovation") that would work like a new beginning, is sufficient to refute the perspective of an *Aufhebung*, according to which, following the expression of Solomon so dear to Hegel,[19] nothing would ever truly be "new under the sun."

Recognition appears, therefore, as a nondialectical movement through which the subject freely adopts an interpretation of what he is by identifying himself with a "form," the identification of the origin and nature of which is Foucault's main problem. From this perspective, one can understand the introduction in *The Use of Pleasure* of the notion of "problematization," the task of a "history of thought" being "as against a history of behaviours or representations: to define the conditions in which human beings 'problematize' what they are, what they do, and the world in which they live" (*UP*, 10). Problematization, judged by Foucault to be inseparable from the practices of the subject ("what he does") and from the "world in which he lives," thus describes the self-interpretative movement through which the subject understands his own nature ("what he is"). Following the Greek etymology (*problema*), it forms the theoretical "shield" that allows the subject to define himself through his actions in and relationships with the world.

By virtue of its interpretative dimension, and because it presupposes the impossibility of dissociating the subject from its activity and the worldly context to which it belongs, problematization could be taken to follow, if not the letter, at least the spirit of Heidegger's definition of *Dasein* as self-interpretative being,[20] which would implicitly be confirmed by the opposition (in the previous passage) between "problematization" and "representation." Nonetheless, this hypothesis is contradicted by another passage, which defines "thought" and "problematization" as follows:

> It seemed to me that there was one element that was capable of characterising thought: this was what one could call problems or, more exactly, problematizations. . . . Thought is not what inhabits a certain conduct and gives it its meaning; rather, it is what allows one to step back from this way of acting or reacting, to present it to oneself as an object of thought and question it as to its meaning, its conditions, and its goals. (*F*, 388; modified)

Thus, to the Heideggerian idea of a prereflective understanding immanent to everyday practices, Foucault prefers the notion of a reflective "problematization" ("standing back"), which demands an active elaboration of the self from the subject ("give oneself [one's conduct] as object of thought," etc.). There are numerous passages in *The Use of Pleasure* that stress both the active and the reflective aspects of problematization—for example, an "effective problematization *by thought*" (*F*, 388), or again an "*active* and intense problematization" (*UP*, 195; my italics).[21] The very manner in which Foucault formulates the project of *The History of Sexuality* is very explicit on this point, since it is aimed at discovering "the forms in which sexual behavior was problematized, becoming an object of *concern*, an element for *reflection*, and a material for *stylisation*" (*UP*, 23), all operations that presuppose both an activity and a reflective elaboration of the self by the self. Another passage is just as clear, specifying once more that it is not a matter of creating a history of behaviors, but "a history of the way in which pleasures, desires, and sexual behavior were *problematised, reflected upon, and conceived* in antiquity" (*PPC*, 256), thought itself being significantly defined as "freedom in relation to what one does, the motion by which one *detaches oneself from it, establishes it as an object, and reflects on it as a problem*" (*F*, 388; my italics). In all these cases, the emphasis is placed on the intellectual and reflective aspect of problematizations, which appear as indissolvably tied to the theme of self-consciousness.

However, problematization is not sufficient *per se* to define the constitution of the self. It must be accompanied by a set of practices through which the subject can modify himself in order to adhere to the "form of subjectivity" that was uncovered by and stimulated his problematizing activity, and in which he wishes to recognize himself. Thus the movement of self-constitution, of which problematization is a necessary but insufficient condition, should not be understood as a simple theoretical self-positioning in which the subject would seize itself reflectively through confrontation with a set of exterior objects: it entails a practical transformation of the being of the subject concerned. Experience as the constitution of the self is not only an intellectual process, but always induces an "alteration, a transformation of the relationship that we have with ourselves and the world, and in which so far we recognized ourselves without difficulty" (*DE*, 4: 46);[22] it is a "transformation of what we are" (*DE*, 4: 46). Notwithstanding the absence of any dialectic in Foucault's thought, this thesis once again appears close to the Hegelian paradigm, since for Hegel, too, experience cannot be understood purely theoretically, being defined as the dynamic process (the "path," as Hegel says) through which consciousness transforms itself by appropriating its own essence. However, although Foucault indicates the impossibility of understanding the constitution of the self independently of the modifications that the subject must perform on itself, his definition of the constitution of the self overall remains quite intellectualizing, in that it implicitly focuses on a conception of subjectivity as a free-determining will. His insistence on the importance of problematization and recognition as *voluntary and reflective* activities leads him to envisage the relationship to the body in a purely unilateral manner, as an action of the self on the self, where the body only appears as material for transformation while consciousness seems to be paradoxically reinstalled in the sovereign position that genealogy had criticized. This is a point that I shall come back to, since it generates major difficulties for the relationship between the history of subjectivation and genealogy.

The Presuppositions of the Foucauldian Conception of the Subject: Genealogical Difficulties

From these analyses, subjectivation can be defined as the result of two elements: firstly, the reflective process through which the subject forms an interpretation of what he is and recognizes himself in it; and secondly, the action through which he seeks to transform himself to conform with this interpretation, by means of the "reflective practices" described by *The Use of Pleasure*. However, two sets of difficulties arise from this, the first pertaining to the relationship between the subject and the individual, and to the definition of the subject itself. From the above, Foucault understands the notion of the "subject" either, in a nominalist way, as a "model of humanity"[23]—that is, as the means for the constitution of the self—or as the individual himself—the product of the reflective process of self-constitution of which he is the actor. The subject is thus understood in an ideal manner, as a "form," and in a substantialist sense, as the individual, once he has been "tied to his own identity by his consciousness or self-knowledge" (*MF*, 212; modified). Consequently, in order for the idea of a "genealogy of the subject" to be coherent, an analysis is needed of what the *individual* (as not yet formed subject) is as point of departure for subjectivation. However, such an analysis cannot be found in Foucault's work. The texts of the genealogical period, which are the first to treat the "problem of the subject," avoided this difficulty by putting the emphasis, not on subjectivation as the willful constitution of the self, but on subjection and therefore on techniques that bypassed reflectivity by manipulating bodies and not "souls." The individual appeared there as a sort of raw material, a "docile body," or even as the statistical "unit" upon which power relations fasten themselves. But as soon as the individual is considered within the framework of an analysis of problematizations, that is, inasmuch as he "constitutes himself," he must be capable of the voluntary and reflective activity required by the perspective of a self-recognition, which prevents him from being understood simply as a docile body. However, for Foucault, the reflexivity specific to self-consciousness seems to be the privilege of the *subject* and not the individual, as it is "being tied to his identity" through his "self-consciousness" or "knowledge" that characterizes the subject. But if it is neither the relationship to the body, nor self-consciousness, nor even the notion of "identity" or personal difference, what defines the individual? How can we understand it?

It is also clear that the individual, as the agent of the reflective constitution of the self by the self, cannot be identified with a "substance" or a neutral material, or even envisaged as a yet not fully formed subject (since the constitution of the self is not a dialectical process). One of the few passages where Foucault defines the individual distinguishes it from a "sort of elementary nucleus . . . on which power comes to fasten" (*PK*, 98), which is equally consistent with the idea that the individual is not a "substance." But the problem is that the passage goes on and reduces the individual to a simple "effect of power," a "relay" of power that "moves through the individual which it has constituted," power itself being "that which makes a body, gestures, discourses, and desires be identified and constituted as individuals" (*PK*, 98; modified). But how is it possible to understand, within this nominalist regression, the initial unity of this "body" and of these "gestures," as one can hardly believe that they should be understood purely atomically as radically dispersed elements? This hyperbolic application of Foucault's nominalism seems to end up in the dissolution of its very object. Thus, the individual features as the blind spot of the process of subjectivation, that which makes it understandable but which cannot be thought—perhaps significantly, occupying a position similar to that which Foucault formerly attributed to "man" in the contemporary *épistémè*.

Notwithstanding this difficulty in understanding the individual, the second problem, mentioned above, is that the considerable attention given by Foucault to processes of subjectivation presupposes a definition of the subject that is never explicitly formulated. One of the texts that comes closest is the extract quoted above, according to which "men have never ceased to construct themselves, that is to continually displace their subjectivity, to constitute themselves in an multiple and in a series of different subjectivities which will have no end" (*DE*, 4: 75). Paradoxically enough, Foucault proposes a definition of the essence of man as the only being without essence (in the metaphysical sense of the word), which is why it is constitutively impossible to find oneself "in front of something which would be man" (*DE*, 4: 75). Although Foucault insists on the interpretative and historical character of the definitions of man by invoking the multiplicity of forms taken by subjectivity ("infinite series . . ."), he does not contest the idea that this self-interpretative activity is itself specific to man, nor that it should be understood as the reflective constitution of the self by the self ("to constitute oneself"). To this extent, although he always criticized existentialism, he comes very close to Sartrian humanism by accepting three of its presuppositions: the absence of a fixed and determined essence for man, the rejection of the idea that the "self" could be "something which is given to us" (*MF*, 237), and the corresponding need for a reflective elaboration of oneself (which was already predictable from the theme of the "possibilities of organization of a self-consciousness" [*PPC*, 253], mentioned above).

Several elements corroborate this hypothesis. Another passage indicates that "what must be produced, is not *man as nature would have produced it, or as its essence prescribed*: we must produce something which does not yet exist and which we cannot yet know" (*DE*, 4: 75; my italics). But the very terms of this opposition strongly call to mind the beginning of *Existentialism and Humanism*, in which Sartre opposed so-called classical humanism, defined by the idea that "the essence of man precedes that historical existence which we confront in experience,"[24] with an existentialism for which "man is not definable [because] he is above all nothing, and will be that which he makes of himself."[25] Although he is careful himself not to pronounce on the relationship between existence and essence, and even avoids mentioning the question, Foucault implicitly aligns himself with the existentialist position according to which there is no "imprisoned nature" or "fundamental truth" of man (*DE*, 4: 75), and claims the necessity of the constitution of the self by the self. For an additional proof, there is the curious reworking of the archeological theme of the "death of man," now reinterpreted through the idea that by "transforming his own subjectivity, man has never found the limit of the destinies of man" (*DE*, 4: 75). Thus the "death of man" comes to describe, not the actual disappearance of "man" from the language-centered *épistémè*, but the theoretical impossibility of giving the subject a predetermined essence and of understanding subjectivation according to the pseudo-Hegelian teleological model: "When I speak of the death of man, I wish to put a stop to all those who would establish a rule of production, an essential aim in this production of man by man. In *The Order of Things*, I was mistaken to have presented this death as something which was taking place in our epoch" (*DE*, 4: 75). Finally and perhaps above all, Foucault's critique of authenticity itself confirms *a contrario* the idea of a reworking of the central theses of existentialism. This critique is formulated thus:

> In Sartre's work there is a tension between a particular understanding of the subject and an ethics of authenticity. . . . the notion of authenticity refers, explicitly or not, to a mode of being of the subject defined by his adequation to himself. However it appears to me that the relationship to the self should be able to be described according to the multiplicity of forms among which "authenticity" is only one of the possible modalities.[26]

Although he condemns its actual *modalities*, Foucault thus implicitly subscribes to the Sartrian idea of a "relationship to the self" processing a "multiplicity of [possible] forms." His problem, as indicated by a variant of the same text, is not to refute Sartrian existentialism, but to determine the *"practical and acceptable consequences of what Sartre said,"* or again to find a "practical consequence (of this) idea that the self is not pre-given to us" (*MF*, 237; modified). Although he opposes the moral understanding of authenticity with an aesthetic one, in which the subject is required, following Oscar Wilde's famous formula, "to create himself as a work of art" (*MF*, 237), Foucault accepts the ethical principle of a "self-creation" (*DE*, 4: 75), itself understood in reference to freedom—which is confirmed by the title of one of his last interviews, "The Ethic of Care for the Self as a Practice of Freedom."[27] However, the idea of self-creation as both a moral and aesthetic project is *in itself* a Sartrian theme; as Sartre had already claimed in 1947, "There is this in common between art and morality, that in both we have to do with creation and invention. We cannot decide *a priori* what it is that should be done"; and in response to a painting by Picasso, he said, "We understand very well that the composition became what it is at the time he was painting it and that his works are part and parcel of his entire life."[28] The individual projects himself into his work and in this very movement creates what he is. To be an artist is both to create a work and to be one's own work.[29] In the same way, this reversibility between the apparent exteriority of the work and the interiority of what Foucault calls the subject's "ethical substance" is, according to Foucault, precisely the major characteristic of the Greek "aesthetic of existence."

However (and beyond its highly paradoxically presupposing the very conception of the subject that archaeology had always violently criticized),[30] this return to Sartrian humanism is dangerous; because of the extent to which it gives the central place to human freedom and autonomy in the constitution of the self, it risks causing a regression beyond the results established by genealogy. Indeed, from a genealogical point of view the subject is the *point of application* (and not the creator) of the techniques of subjection that *Discipline and Punish* and *The History of Sexuality*, volume 1, sought to reveal. In this sense, the idea of a sovereign "self-consciousness" seems to contradict that of the genesis of forms of subjectivity within power-knowledge, a tension that generates an internal contradiction focused on "subjectivation" and its relationship to truth. Indeed, the previously cited texts refer the notion of subjectivation to the reflective activity (problematization), as well as to the practices through which the individual integrates a "model of humanity" that he recognizes as his own. Foucault's central idea is thus that the constitution of the self can only occur through a specific relationship to truth, as shown by the generic definition of "subjectivity" as "the way in which the subject forms the experience of himself *in a game of truth where he has a relationship with himself*" (*DE*, 4: 633; my italics). But the idea of a "game of truth" is highly ambiguous. It can be understood in a pseudo-Hegelian sense, as, on the one hand, the identification/recognition by the subject of what he really is, and, on the other, the transformations that follow. Following the movement which I shall examine in relation to the Greek paradigm, truth would be a self-induced ontological determination of the being of the subject, concerning only the relation of the self with itself. Foucault is probably thinking of such a hypothesis when, in the introduction of *The Use of Pleasure*, he suggests that subjects "recognize and confess themselves" as subjects of desire, "bringing into play between *themselves and themselves* a certain relationship that allows them to discover, in desire, the *truth of their being*" (*UP*, 5; my italics).

However, the more usual definition of the "game" of truth is quite different: "When I say 'game' I mean a *set of rules for the production of truth*. It is not a game in the sense of imitating or entertaining. . . . It is an ensemble of procedures which lead to a certain result, which can be considered in function of its principles and its rules of procedure, as valid or not" (*FF*, 16). But this definition cannot be understood from the individual perspective of the self to self-relation! On the contrary, it appears to echo, by taking them beyond the domain of propositions with scientific pretensions, the genealogical notions of "discipline" (as an "anonymous system" which includes a "*play of rules* and definitions" [*OD*, 59])[31] or of the "discursive regime" (insomuch as it concerns the "*rules of formation* of statements which are accepted as scientifically true" [*PK*, 112]). Another passage clearly takes up the archaeological problem of acceptability by defining games of truth, not as "the discovery of true things, but (as) *the rules according to which, in relation to certain things, what a subject can say is implicated* [relève de] *with the question of truth or falsehood*" (*DE*, 4: 633; my italics).[32] From this perspective, games of truth must be understood in a nonsubjective and anonymous manner, as defining the conditions of possibility of "true" discourses, thereby taking up the function previously given to *épistémès*. Significantly, Foucault elsewhere summarizes his work by stating that *The Order of Things* had the task of "discovering how the human subject entered into games of truth . . . which take the form of a science or which refer to a scientific model" (*FF*, 1).[33] He explains in another passage that he was concerned to analyze "these so-called sciences [the human sciences] as very specific games connected to the specific techniques which men use in order to understand who they are."[34]

More generally, the games of truth constitute the element from which to understand problematizations themselves.

> Problematization doesn't mean representation of a pre-existing object, nor the creation by discourse of an object that doesn't exist. *It's the totality of discursive or non-discursive practices that introduce something into the game of the true and the false and constitute it as an object for thought* (whether in the form of moral reflection, scientific knowledge, political analyses, etc.). (*PPC*, 257; my italics)

But within this context, problematizations have nothing to do with the intellectual activity of a self-constituting subject (they are not "representations"). Their definition as "discursive or non-discursive practices" clearly indicates that they should be analyzed in an archeo-genealogical manner—that is, without taking self-consciousness as point of departure. Just like the games of truth themselves, problematizations seem to provide a final answer to the critical question, as Foucault himself suggests, by taking up one last time the main problematic of *The Order of Things*. They allow superficial conflicts between different theories to be bypassed, "to rediscover at the root of these diverse solutions the general form of problematization that has them possible—even in their very opposition" (*F*, 389). Equally, another passage defines as an "effective problematization by thought" (*F*, 388) that by which archaeology had previously characterized the historical *a priori*, that is, "what makes [differing responses to the same difficulty] simultaneously possible: the point in which their simultaneity is rooted; the soil that can nourish them all in their diversity and sometimes in spite of their contradictions" (*F*, 389). In this context, problematizations should thus be understood as a "field" (a recurring metaphor in the archaeology) inside which acceptable propositions can be formed, as the following extract indicates: "What I would like to define in the next pages [is] not the 'doctrinal context' that might give each one [of the texts considered] its peculiar meaning and its differential value, but rather the 'field of problematization' that they had in common and that made each of them possible" (*UP*, 36, 37). But, once more, this "field of problematization" clearly cannot be understood from man's activity as a "thinking being,"[35] but only genealogically, that is, by reference to the practices that are its conditions of possibility. As Foucault himself says:

> The notion common to all the work that I have done since *Madness and Civilisation* is that of problematization, though it must be said that I never isolated this notion sufficiently. . . . In *Madness and Civilisation* the question was how and why, at a given moment, madness was *problematised through a certain institutional practice and a certain apparatus of knowledge*. Similarly, in *Discipline and Punish*, I was trying to analyze the changes in the *problematization of the relations between crime and punishment through penal practices and penitentiary institutions* in the late eighteenth and early nineteenth centuries. (*PPC*, 257; my italics)[36]

However, if games of truth and problematizations must be understood from an archeo-genealogical perspective, that is, from the power relations which give birth to them (thus, the truth games find themselves "in the institutions of power" [*FF*, 16]), then the theme of subjectivation is bound to take a quite different meaning from that of self-constitution, raising grave difficulties. Indeed, if the idea of an essential connection between "the constitution of the subject or the different forms of subject and the games of truth, power practices" (*FF*, 16) is wholly genealogical, it radically contradicts the notion of a reflective self-constitution in which the subject would stand as master of itself and author of the problematizations in which it recognizes itself. On the contrary, it gives the theme of constitution a passive dimension that prevents subjectivation from being understood solely as an active recognition, and therefore opens it to the unmasterable "outside" constituted by the power relations in which the individual always finds himself already enmeshed. This tension clearly appears in the following extract: "What I wished to show, is how the subject *constituted himself*, in this or that determined form, as a mad or healthy subject, as a delinquent or non delinquent subject, through a certain number of practices which were *games of truth, practices of power*, etc." (*FF*, 16). A similar form of this tension between activity and passivity underlies the idea that it is necessary to "wonder about the conditions which make it possible, *according to the rules of speaking truly or falsely*, . . . for a subject to *recognize the most essential part of himself* in the modality of his sexual desire" (*DE*, 4: 634; my italics). But the archeological analyses have shown that the subject does not know these rules, as it is constitutively impossible for him to thematize the *épistémè* to which he belongs. The Foucauldian analysis of subjectivity therefore appears to oscillate in a contradictory manner, between a definition of subjectivity as "self-creation," on the one hand, and on the other hand, the need, in order to understand the games of truth through which recognition itself operates, to go back to the practices of power of which subjects are not masters and are usually not even aware.

Foucault's new insistence on the idea of a reflective problematization and an active constitution of the self by the self, therefore, introduces into his work a very strong tension between two interpretations of subjectivation that are inherently conflictual. On the one hand, the subject appears as autonomous, as the source of the problematizations of what he is and as a free actor in the practices through which he transforms himself. On the other, he is shown by the genealogical analyses to be inserted into a set of relations of power and practices that are subjecting to various degrees, and that define the very conditions of possibility for the constitution of the self. Foucault's analysis of the subject is affected by this fundamental ambivalence insofar as it is very difficult to say if, for him, the subject is constituting or constituted—an ambivalence perhaps symbolized by the lack of any Foucaldian analysis of the difference between subjectivation and subjection. Because problematizations are internally shaped by the power relation that determines their acceptability, the central paradigm of a free self-constitution needs to be replaced within the framework of a wider conception that considers subjectivation genealogically,[37] through reference to anonymous practices of the power and truth games that defined the conditions of possibility for any subjective "problematization."[38] On the basis of these analyses, it becomes essential to determine whether Foucault's more detailed study of the Greek paradigm, in particular, and of the history of subjectivity, in general, will allow the tensions inherent to subjectivation to be resolved by clarifying the nature and genesis of the "forms" of the subject, or whether it will accentuate them.

SIX

The "History of Subjectivity" and Its Internal Tensions

As we have seen, *The Use of Pleasure* and *The Care of the Self* both seek to understand the starting point of the history of subjectivity by analyzing the forms taken by the constitution of the self in Greek and Roman antiquity. From this perspective, the Platonic paradigm appears to fulfill a double function: firstly, it identifies the structure of the recognition of truth by revealing its historical moment of birth, thereby also establishing that this recognition is pivotal to the constitution of the self by the self; secondly, the Platonic paradigm shows that, due to the weak institutionalization of power relations, antiquity is the only period of Western history in which subjectivation can be assimilated to a reflective constitution of the self by the self—which also might explain Foucault's metonymic insistence on this theme in his analyses of the subject. In this sense, the principal interest of the Greek model is that it allows us *a contrario* to "return through time further and further from the chronological framework" initially set, in order to "address periods when the effect of scientific knowledge and the complexity of normative systems were less" (*F*, 339). To the extent that exterior elements influencing the constitution of the self are found at their lowest level of development (the modern form of the State analyzed in *Discipline and Punish* hadn't yet developed), it is possible to isolate the relation of subjectivation in its first and purest form. However, as we shall see, the paradigm of self-constitution remains very ambivalent, an ambivalence which is worsened by the need to rein-scribe it within the framework of the history of power. Unfortunately, this will confirm the necessity of giving the concept of subjectivation a wider definition than that involved in the constitution of the self, and this will thereby revive the tensions that were revealed in the previous chapter.

The Role of Truth in the Constitution of the Self: The Ambivalence of the Platonic Paradigm

As he examines the forms taken by the constitution of subjectivity for the Greeks through the idea of the "care of the self," Foucault's essential question is to deter-mine how the *epimeleia heautou* causes the subject to enter into relation with truth: "Why do we care for ourselves only through the care for truth? I think that we are touching on a question which is very fundamental and which is, I would say, the question of the Western world. What caused Western culture to begin to turn around this obligation of truth, which has taken on a variety of different forms?" (*FF*, 15). The questioning bears both on the way in which the care of the self was annexed by the care for truth (". . . only through the care for truth"), and on the moment and causes of such an annexation ("What caused Western culture to . . . ," etc.). Foucault responds to this double interrogation with the theory that Platonism marks a major change in the history of subjec-tivity, as it indicates the moment where the care of the self became indissociable from the quest for truth. Platonic thought constitutes the turning point from which the *epimeleia heautou* was subordinated to the Socratic principle of *gnōthi seauton* (know thy self): "This concern for a beautiful existence was linked to the concern for truth-telling by means of care of the self in the work of Socrates at the dawn of Western philosophy" (*FF*, 109).

Foucault thus takes up and renews one of the central themes of *The Order of Discourse*—the Nietzschean idea that the first episode of the history of truth begins with Platonism. From this epoch onward, the care of the self becomes "the figure of thought which in Western antiquity united the subject and truth" by fusing the necessity for self-transformation and the search for truth, and thereby "linking ethics to the game of truth" (*FF*, 5; modified). But how can the "Socrato-Platonic" idea that "one can not care for oneself without knowing one-self" (*FF*, 5) be understood? And if it involves not only self-knowledge, but also the "need to know" (*UP*, 73) in general—"to know the things one does not know, to know that one is ignorant, to know one's own nature" (*UP*, 73)—what sense can be given to the notion of truth? What role can it play in the constitution of the self? How can the status and function of the practices of the self be understood from this point of view? Finally, how can all these elements clarify the meaning of subjectivation itself?

The last chapter of *The Use of Pleasure* shows how Plato inseparably connected "the use of pleasures and access to truth . . . , in the form of an inquiry into the nature of true love" (*UP*, 229). Foucault argues that the Platonic analysis of eros took the opposite form to the traditional problematization of love through a double displacement. Firstly, this problematization came to bear, not on the immediate object of love (the boy), but on the nature of love itself; secondly, this interrogation of the being of love led the subject to name its real object, truth itself. Thus what now characterizes true love is that it is "beyond the appearances of the object, a relationship to truth" (*UP*, 239; modified). Plato breaks with the tradition that opposed the activity of the lover to the passivity of the loved as an object of desire, by showing that, for both of the lovers, love is the "motion that carries them toward truth" (*UP*, 240). The real question is thus "to determine by what actual movement, by what kind of effort and work upon himself will the Eros of the lover be able to free itself and establish for ever his relation to true being" (*UP*, 243; modified). This new connection of *epimeleia* to truth leads the subject to seek to discover the truth of his own being, understood as a "ontological recognition of the self by the self" (*UP*, 88). Thus the *Phaedrus* tells us how the soul is led by love to contemplate the "realities which are outside the heavens," and so to the discovery of its own intelligible nature (*UP*, 88). Provided that it is true—that is, philosophical—love reveals to the subject his own essence and what he must consider as the real object of his concern—not his body but his soul, inasmuch as it partakes in the intelligible. In the same way, Foucault reminds us of the way in which the *Alcibiades* shows how a soul which contemplates itself in another soul (or in the divine element of another soul) will recognize their shared intelligible component in the "element of the divine,"[1] and thus reach an "ontological knowledge of the self" (*MF*, 248).

For the first time, the theme appears of a recognition understood as the identification by the subject of his own essence (his "divine component") and as the conversion through which his ethos will come to conform with that which he now knows to be his truth. This recognition is ambiguous insofar as, for Plato, it is the *general form of knowledge* (as *anamnesis*) and therefore does not merely describe the reflective operation by which the subject appropriates his own essence. Nonetheless, this is probably one of the sources for Foucault's previously analyzed claim that the constitution of the self can only occur through a specific recognition that in turn conditions the form taken by the constitution of the self. Thus, the double question of *Alcibiades* ("What is this 'self' which one must care for, and what does caring for oneself mean?")[2] receives a new answer in the idea that the care of the self is not care of the body, but of the soul, as the truest part of the individual. Henceforth, whoever desired to recognize their own nature as intelligible soul would be led to neglect their bodily requirements, and to adopt an ascetic lifestyle that would allow them to use the "eyes of the soul" more easily, thus closing the circle of the knowledge and transformation of the self. Recognition is therefore both what structures the relationship of subjectivation itself and the condition of possibility of a transformation of the being of the subject. It allows the constitution of the self to be understood both theoretically (as the intellectual recognition of the truth) and practically (as the "transfiguration" of the subject, a point to which I shall return shortly), which is why Foucault defines it as a "structural, instrumental, and ontological condition for establishing the individual as a subject" (*UP*, 89).

Two important points should be noted. Firstly, that the truth of the subject cannot be established in isolation. For Plato, the recognition of the soul by itself derives its meaning and importance from a more general knowledge of essences. The knowledge that the subject achieves of its own essence (as an intelligible soul) must be subordinated to a more general understanding of truth (which reveals, for example, the distinction between the sensible and the intelligible). As Foucault reminds us apropos the *Phaedrus*, where "the relation to truth plays a fundamental role," the subject can only understand "what the nature of the human soul in its truth is" (*UP*, 88) on condition of knowing about the "divine soul," and about the relationship between souls and bodies in general. The truth of the subject only makes sense, therefore, against the background of a wider understanding of truth itself, to which it is necessary to have access to be able to constitute oneself. Secondly, and reciprocally, the truth that the subject must recognize as its own is not a knowledge of the individual: the "self" concerned is not the individual in its particularity, but, on the contrary, the soul as the most excellent part of man. As Foucault notes, self-knowledge is "ontological," and not "psychological" (*MF*, 248):

> *This idea that one must know oneself, i.e. gain ontological knowledge of the soul's mode of being, is independent of what one could call an exercise of the self upon the self.* When grasping the mode of being of your soul, there is no need to ask yourself what you have done, what you are thinking, what the movements of your ideas or your representations are, to what you are attached. (*MF*, 249; my italics)

Therefore, it is structurally impossible for the individual to constitute himself as a subject "without constituting himself at the same time as a subject of knowledge" (UP, 86; modified), taking himself as an "object and domain of knowledge."³ Equally, the Platonic subordination of the *epimeleia heautou* to the Delphic imperative of the *gnōthi seauton*, far from introducing a refocusing on the individual in its particularity, demands, on the contrary, that the subject should relate the truth of what he is to a metaphysics that teaches him about truth in general. The subject can "only be what he must be through the knowledge of the truth itself."⁴ Only then will he be able to recognize adequately the object of his care and to transform himself through the knowledge acquired, following a complex movement, which Foucault summarizes as follows: "The movement of self-knowledge leads to wisdom. From this moment, the soul will be wise, capable of distinguishing true from false: it will know how to behave acceptably."⁵

The great novelty introduced by Platonism, therefore, is the idea that the constitution of the self entails a recognition which, by denying individual differences, makes the truth of the subject inseparable from knowledge of the general. Such a recognition introduces a transformation of the very being of the subject (hence its "ontological" quality) by means of specific practices—the "techniques of the self." Indeed, the answer to the question "What is the work which I must effect upon myself so as to be capable and worthy of acceding to the truth?" (MF, 251). is provided by the instrumental definition of the techniques of the self as "ethopoetic," that is, endowed with the "quality of transforming the mode of being of an individual, of transforming his *ethos*."⁶ Following the movement examined above, the ambition of these techniques is not to generate a knowledge of the self as an individual, but to incite the subject to deny his particularities in order to become "capable of truth,"⁷ and make him conform to that which he must recognize as being his own essence. Thus, the techniques of the self are a "set of practices by which one can *acquire, assimilate, and transform truth into a permanent principle of action*."⁸ This "transformation " is referred by Foucault to a gnosis itself defined as that which "always tends to transfer . . . to the act of knowledge [*connaissance*] itself the conditions, the forms and the effects of spiritual experience."⁹ The specificity of the gnostic structure of knowledge is therefore that it attributes to truth an intrinsic power in the constitution of the self: "There is, in the access to truth, something which leads the subject to his own fulfilment, something which leads his being to completion, something which transfigures him."¹⁰ To recognize the truth of what one is (for example an intelligible soul) does not only mean to know the truth theoretically: it means equally—and quasi-performatively—to become a true subject, that is to make truth the principle of the ontological "transfiguration" of the self by the self.

The traditional definition of truth as cognitive content is thus doubled, following the dual theoretical and practical process of the constitution of the self, by an ontological determination that turns truth into the result of the work on the self and understands it, in an almost Hegelian sense, as an achieved adequation between the being of the subject and the knowledge that he has acquired of himself—an adequation whose movement defines that of subjectivation itself. At the end of this movement, truth no longer refers to theoretical content alone, but to the very person of the subject, following "a process of becoming more subjective."[11] Truth is therefore not only what the subject must seek to know, but that which he must *be*: "The being of the subject is at stake: the price of truth is the conversion of the subject."[12] However, such a conversion (*metanoia*) must not be understood in the Judeo-Christian sense, and does not involve any transcendent God. It is the immanent conversion of the subject to himself, which allows him to harmonize his *bios* with his *logos* (*FF*, 108). Through the play of gnosis, truth finally becomes incarnated in the very being of the knowing subject, producing a perfect match between what the subject knows to be true and the truth of what he is. The true and truthful subject has thus become a Parrhesiast: "The ground of *parrhesia*, is this adequation between the subject of the statement and the subject of the action. . . . The subject which speaks is engaged, in the very moment in which he speaks the truth, to do what he says, and to be the subject of a conduct unifying point by point the subject to the truth that he formulates."[13] The Parrhesiast is he whose theoretical comprehension of truth is integrated with his behavior to the point of their no longer being separable. His very mode of being has become the living proof of his mastery of truth: the truth of what he knows has become the truth of what he is—"*Aletheia* becomes *ethos*,"[14] so realizing the "ontological constitution of the self by the self" initially evoked by *The Use of Pleasure*.

The Genealogy of Power and the Accentuation of the Initial Tension

Foucault's study of Platonism presents him with a double advantage: on the one hand, it allows the identification of the historical moment at which the relationship to the self became mediated by a relationship to truth, and on the other hand, it reveals the structure of the relationship of recognition as itself a fundamental element of subjectivation. However, the Platonic paradigm is very ambivalent, as far from confirming the general thesis that self-constitution is an autonomous and reflective activity, it reveals the impossibility of understanding subjectivation exclusively through the solipsistic model of the constitution of the subject by itself. Moreover, it shows that this impossibility was *already present* at the beginning of Western history and therefore is coextensive with subjectivation itself, ruling out any possibility of solving the previously mentioned tension between the history of subjectivity and genealogy by distinguishing between two successive models for the constitution of the self—an early, positive form of subjectivation (the Greek model) and a later, negative model (subjection). As we have seen, the agent finds himself *ab initio* confronted with the necessity of finding outside of himself both the universal truth in which he recognizes himself and the techniques that allow him to interiorize it. Foucault himself admits the existence of this originary passivity:

> If now I am interested, in fact, in the way in which the subject constitutes himself in an active fashion, by the practices of self, these practice are nevertheless not something that the individual invents himself. *They are patterns that he finds in his culture* and which are proposed, suggested and *imposed* on him by his culture, his society and his social group. (*FF*, 11; my italics)

Another text elaborates on the same idea, clarifying that "the experience that one can have of the self and the self-knowledge that one develops have been *organised by means of specific schemes [which] were defined, valued, suggested, imposed*" (*DE*, 4: 213; my italics) differently according to the societies and epochs considered. This is why the history of subjectivity has to be that of the "*models* proposed for the setting up and developing relationships with the self, for self-reflection, self-knowledge, self-examination, for the decipherment of the self by oneself, for the transformations that one seeks to accomplish with oneself as object" (*UP*, 29; my italics).

The hidden paradox of the Platonic paradigm, therefore, is that although it is apparently centered around the reflective and controlled activity of an "obviously free" subject (*UP*, 22), in fact it works *against* this understanding as it *structurally* involves a set of truths and practices that are not produced by the subject himself, but through which the subject must nonetheless transform himself. The constitution of the self cannot be understood anymore through the sole lens of the "creation of the self," described above: on the contrary, it is necessary to open the history of subjectivity onto the outside constituted by the genealogy of forms of power. As Foucault himself said, the "history of the different modes by which . . . human beings are made subjects" (*MF*, 208) is therefore inseparable from that of a "continuous statification of the relations of power . . . in the pedagogical, judicial, economical, and familial order" (*MF*, 224; modified), which produced a progressive "integration" of the practices of the self "into the exercise of pastoral power in early Christianity, and later, into educative, medical, and psychological types of practices" (*UP*, 11; modified).

If the genealogy of power is able to "create a history of the different modes by which, in our culture, human beings are made subjects" (*MF*, 208), it is precisely because it alone is capable of accounting for the transformations of these two *external* elements of the constitution of the self—the truths in which the subject recognizes himself and the techniques which are brought to bear on him. This is indirectly confirmed by Foucault's understanding that to carry out "the genealogy of the subject within Western civilization," it is necessary to study not only the techniques of the self, but also what he calls (implicitly referring to Habermas) "techniques of domination," whose specificity is that they are applied to the subject from the outside (the clearest example being disciplinary methods). But if it is necessary to "take into account the points where the techniques of the soul are integrated into the structures of coercion or domination,"[15] then it is clearly impossible to understand subjectivation from the subject himself, as the constitution of the self has to be totally reset within the framework of a history of techniques that were little by little "elaborated, rationalized, and centralized in the form of, or under the auspices of, State institutions" (*MF*, 224). Because of this, the history of subjectivity turns out to be affected by the same—if not worse—ambivalence as the Platonic paradigm. At first sight, it provides Foucault with the means of deepening and replacing his analyses of the human sciences within the wider context of subjectivation, and seems to confer a greater coherence on his work as a whole; but, in reality, it reproduces and accentuates the first tension between the idealist notion of a fully free constitution of the self by the self, on the one hand, and its genealogical deconstruction, on the other.

Apparently oblivious of this tension, Foucault states that the constitution of the self always had as its condition of possibility the constitution of a "field of true knowledges [*connaissances*]." Among these, in those used for subjectivation "the existence of man was in question," which made them especially "pertinent for the transformation and improvement of the subject."[16] According to Foucault, four main divisions in the history of the forms of subjectivation can be schematically identified: the Platonic turn studied above, the imperial period, the birth of Christianity, and the birth of disciplinary technologies and modern power. While a metaphysic of essences is what revealed to the Platonic subject his nature as an intelligible soul, and thus allowed him to properly identify the object of his concern, the truth used by the Stoic constitution of the self appears within "a theoretical framework as science, as, for example, in Lucretius' *De Natura Rerum*."[17] Taking up some of Pierre Hadot's theses,[18] Foucault establishes that the truth in which the subject must recognize himself becomes grounded in a cosmology that reveals to him the nature of the universe as logos, allowing him to recognize himself as a fragment of the "great Reason of the world": "It is not a matter of discovering a truth within the subject or of making the soul the place where truth . . . resides in. On the contrary it is a matter of turning the learned, memorised truth . . . into a quasi-subject which reigns sovereignly within us" (*DE*, 4: 362).[19] The fundamental structure of subjectivation remains unchanged during the Hellenistic and Roman periods, as the recognition of a universal truth remains the means and end of the constitution of the self. As for Christianity, while its development produced a profound transformation of the *contents* of the truths to be used for subjective self-constitution, it did not actually modify the *structure* itself: "The duty to accept a set of obligations, to hold certain books as permanent truth, to accept authoritarian decisions in matters of truth, not only to believe certain things but to show that one believes, and to accept institutional authority are all characteristic of Christianity."[20] In the same way: "To make truth of oneself, and to get access to the light of God, and so on, these two processes are strongly connected to the Christian experience. . . . those two relationships to truth were connected in such a way that they were almost identified."[21]

Finally, the key to the last stage of the history of subjectivity lies in the growth of the modern state, which for Foucault was accompanied by that of an administrative and institutional network that tended to both institutionalize the practices of the self and to produce new models of knowledge: "However great the isolation of a certain number of religious institutions might have been . . . there was an implantation, multiplication even and diffusion of pastoral techniques within the secular framework of State apparatus" (*DE*, 3: 551).[22] As we have seen in *Discipline and Punish* and the first volume of *The History of Sexuality*, in the case of the human sciences the "field of true knowledges" can only be analyzed by replacing truth within the epistemic and political framework defining the conditions of acceptability for each epoch. From this viewpoint, the principle lesson of the history of subjectivity is that it would become more and more difficult to separate the history of subjectivity from that of the progressive "epistemologization" of the knowledges used by individuals for their own constitution: "The truth obligation for individuals and a scientific organisation of knowledge; those are the two reasons why the history of knowledge constitutes a privileged point of view for the genealogy of the subject."[23]

It is from this retrospective standpoint that the analyses of *The Order of Things* attain their real polemical significance, as Foucault can retrospectively show that the new knowledges of man, whose epistemic conditions of possibility he had already analyzed, must now be identified with those that are used for the constitution of the self. Thus, "through these different practices—psychological, medical, penitential, educational—a certain idea or model of humanity was developed, and *now this idea of man has become normative, self-evident, and is supposed to be universal.*"[24] What is now demanded from the subject is no longer that he should recognize himself as an intelligible soul, as a part of the great Logos of the world, or as a sinning creature; but that he should define himself as a living, speaking, and working individual, conforming to the norms imposed on him by medicine, pedagogy, or criminology. It is no longer in "transcendental rules, a cosmological model, or in a philosophico-moral ideal" (*DE*, 3: 648) that the government of the self will find its foundations, declares Foucault, retracing the chronology in reverse, but in the "specific forms of rationality" (*DE*, 3: 648) defined by the social sciences. Henceforth, the subject "is led to perceive himself as mad, to see himself as ill, to reflect upon himself as a living, speaking, and labouring being" (*UP*, 7; modified).

Foucault's analysis of the confession is perhaps the best example of this imbrication of the birth of the various knowledges of man and the new forms taken by the constitution of the self. To the apparition of the "power mechanisms that functioned in such a way that discourse on sex . . . became essential" corresponds a new demand to "pronounce a discourse on sex that would not derive from morality alone but from rationality as well" (*HS*, 23–24). The decline of the Christian model, which connected the problem of sex to the thematic of sin and lust, was accompanied by the "objectification of sex in rational discourses" (*HS*, 33) which encouraged the individual to constitute himself as a subject, not through theological guidelines anymore, but in reference to the principles of the *scientia sexualis* newly constituted within the framework of medicine, pedagogy, and psychiatry. Thus individuals "were called upon to pronounce a discourse of truth concerning themselves, a discourse which had to model itself after that which spoke, not of sin and salvation, but of bodies and life processes—the discourse of science" (*HS*, 64). Although the constitution of the self must still operate through the mediation of a relationship to a general truth, this truth is now delivered by a science that "caused the rules of confession to function within the norms of scientific regularity" (*HS*, 65).

Following the logic examined in the Part II, confession reveals itself both as the method which allows the constitution of science, and as the privileged form of the transformation of the subject: "From the eighteenth century to the present, the techniques of verbalisation have been reinserted into a different context by the so-called human sciences in order to use them without renunciation of the self but to constitute, positively, a new self."[25] Thus a subtle dialectic between individual and general truth was initiated: the collection of individual truths confessed by subjects provided *scientia sexualis* with the material from which it could develop itself as a "science." Conversely, this science constituted the general framework from which alone could be generated the theory that prescribed what the individual must be in his particularity, and from which the model of normativity was derived, to which the subject—through the performative dynamic of confession—had to make the truth of what he is conform. The truth of the individual thus became the point of departure for the constitution of the science which alone could specify, from the perspective of a general theory, the ideal truth that would define the subject as "normal" while negating him in his very individuality.

According to Foucault, the rise of the human sciences resulted in the "constitution of a new subjectivity by means of reducing the human subject to an object of knowledge" (*DE*, 4: 74–75). As a result, far from confirming the hypothesis of an autonomous constitution of the self by the self, archeo-genealogy establishes the impossibility of understanding subjectivation as a free and reflective activity, since it makes clear that the initial ambivalence of the Platonic model was only reinforced through history, mainly because of the importance gained by the exterior elements within the structure of recognition. Thus the activity deployed by the subject to constitute himself has been progressively doubled by the appearance of disciplinary mechanisms that characteristically allow direct action on the body and not the "soul" of individuals, thereby eliding the very moment of recognition. Following the circular dynamic of power-knowledge, "*social practices* can come to create domains of knowledge [*savoir*] which not only give birth to new objects, new concepts, and new techniques, but also *give birth to totally new forms of subjects* . . ." (*DE*, 2: 539).[26] It is thus in this disquieting vision of a more and more normalized formation of subjectivity that the two definitions of subjectivation described in Chapter 5 (as the production of "subjects of obedience" and of subjects "tied to their own identity by consciousness or self-knowledge" [*MF*, 212]) converge. But as we saw, this strong thesis unfortunately contradicts Foucault's equally vigorous definition of subjectivation as the free constitution of the self by the self.

Although "it is not power, but the subject, which is the general theme of [Foucault's] research" (*MF*, 209), at the end of the day it is the history of power that holds the key to those of truth and subjectivity. Experience, whether it is identified as the relation of subjectivation itself or, on the contrary, as the set of elements that condition it in any given domain and time, can only be analyzed through a reflection on power, as this constitutes the domain in which the relation to the self must be reinserted since it externally determines its internal parameters. But by a strange irony, this history *by its very breadth* only accentuates the tensions inherent in the relation of subjectivation, which seems more and more torn between two irreconcilable extremes. On the one hand, it appears in Foucault's most theoretical texts as the active and reflective movement by which the subject "constitutes himself" by freely problematizing what he is. On the other hand, the history of subjectivity shows that this movement is only one element of a larger process that reinscribes subjectivation in a set of practices acting from outside the subject to constitute him in a passive and unreflective way. The apparition of the disciplines attests to the necessity of referring subjectivation to elements that are external to the recognition itself. Further still, the history of power reveals that this tension is *internal* to the very constitution of the self: the analysis of the Greek paradigm shows that, from the outset, this constitution took the form of a process of recognition in which the subject appropriates a truth which he must make his own by transforming himself but which he discovers outside of himself, and which archeo-genealogy discloses to be dependent on conditions of possibility other than himself. The apparent simplicity of the model of subjectivation as the production/appropriation by the subject of an interpretation of what he is, upon which many of Foucault's most theoretical passages insist, is thus contradicted by the conclusions of genealogy, which, by analyzing power practices, establish the impossibility of understanding subjectivation from the subject himself. Admittedly, this tension can probably be partially ascribed to the underlying influence of the Greek paradigm, which stressed freedom and mastery by referring the constitution of the self to the reflective activity of "obviously free men" (*UP*, 22). But it nonetheless remains true that the idea that subjectivation operates, by means of a recognition followed by a voluntary action of the self by the self, is afflicted *ab initio* by an intellectualizing character that contradicts the letter as much as the spirit of the genealogical method and that seems to revive at the heart of Foucault's analyses the idealism from which he had always wished to escape.

As we have seen, this danger crystallizes around the two key elements that are the question of experience, and the Foucauldian definition of the subject. As for the first, it has become clear that Foucault's definition of experience as a static and objective structure ("correlation") implicitly presupposes a dynamic conception of experience as a process of self-constitution centered on the idea of a founding recognition. But the passages quoted in the preceding chapters show that Foucault does not hesitate to juxtapose these two definitions. Thus sexuality, delinquency, or madness, are *simultaneously* understood as subjective "experiences" and as the tripartite objective "correlations" held to be the historical conditions of possibility for the experience of the self.[27] One could argue that this is terminological drift, not a fundamental problem, which a more rigorous use of the concepts could easily have avoided. However, the definition of experience as "correlation" presents *per se* two major difficulties. Firstly, it can only be understood in reference to the third of its "axes" (*UP*, 3–4)—the "forms of subjectivity" (another text mentions the "mode of relation between the individual and himself" [*F*, 334]). This gives rise to the problem that these "forms" *internally* reintroduce the subjective dimension which the idea of experience as empirical correlation was precisely meant to eliminate, resulting in the invalidation of the very possibility of an objective definition. Correlatively, this definition is characterized by a structure of inclusion that makes appear within it what is in fact its condition of intelligibility. Indeed, experience as "correlation" is characterized by the relationship that it establishes between "a domain of knowledge, a type of normativity, and a mode of relation to the self" (*F*, 333); but as shown in Chapter 1, the relationship to the self is exactly what the objective definition of experience derives its meaning from.[28] The self-relationship, therefore, occupies an untenable position, being both an internal content (as an "axis") and the external condition of possibility for the definition of experience as "correlation" (as the perspective which gives it sense). In this ambiguous structure, which confuses the constituted with the constituting, one can identify a new transposition of the first figure of the transcendental theme in its anthropological version, that is, the empirico-transcendental doublet.

Secondly, Foucault returns, even while repeating his implicit critique of Husserlian thought, to a pseudo-phenomenological conception of the subject as a being with a fundamental plasticity, bound to elaborate diverse problematizations that are historical interpretations of what he is. However, although he adopts the phenomenological idea that the subject is lacking any essence, Foucault examines neither the concepts nor the problems studied by phenomenology itself; on the contrary, he seems to wish to appropriate its conclusions without discussing its methods or difficulties. In particular, he never enquires about the relationship of recognition itself, whose existence and necessity he simply presupposes. But surprisingly, the implicit lesson of the history of subjectivity ends up being that this relationship itself should be considered as an *invariant*.[29] Indeed, Foucault's constant insistence on the historicity and plurality of the different understandings of truth, as well as the attention he gives the study of the historical development of their relations with power, have as paradoxical counterpart an ahistorical and monolithic conception of *recognition* as the agent of the constitution of the self. Moreover, in spite of the very detailed analyses of the historical "forms" of subjectivation suggested by Foucault, the subject of recognition itself remains enigmatic and turns out to be—just as "man" is in Kant's thought or the "individual" is for genealogy—the blind spot of Foucault's work.

Because Foucault reactivates the perspective of a constitutive subjectivity and understands the constitution of the self by means of the atemporal structure of recognition, strangely enough he seems to regress to a prephenomenological perspective, as most phenomenologists (such as Heidegger or Merleau-Ponty) made considerable attempts to bypass the notion of a transcendentally constituting subjectivity. Despite his efforts, his last work remains haunted by a pseudo-transcendental understanding of the subject, in which the structure of recognition, although experiencing different historical contents, nonetheless appears to function *in itself* as an unthematized *a priori*.

Conclusion

Whereas the critical question pointed, metaphorically speaking, upstream to the analysis of truth, the study of its role in the constitution of the self explores downstream to the "history of truth" planned by Foucault. In this sense, his work retrospectively appears as a diptych hinging on the central question of truth—as the author says, "My own problem has always been the question of truth, of telling the truth, the *wahr-sagen*—what it is to tell the truth" (*PPC*, 33), depending on whether truth is described according to its conditions of possibility or to its consequences. But unfortunately, if archaeology turned out to be incapable of providing an adequate answer to the problem of the conditions of possibility of knowledge, it seems that the history of truth itself is also fraught with structural tensions that its development, although retrospectively giving the archeo-genealogical enterprise its real object in the conditions of acceptability and predication, only exacerbates further.

It is worth pointing out, however, that the problems encountered by the late Foucault seem to stem from his understanding of the subject, rather than from the application of the genealogical method or even from the "reintroduction of the problem of the subject" *per se*. Indeed, the tension that animates his late texts principally arises from the idea that problematization would above all be an autonomous and reflective activity (since, although it is intrinsically "tied to a set of practices," these practices are understood as the "*reflective and voluntary* practices through which men not only seek to establish rules of conduct but also to transform themselves" [*DE*, 4: 545]). As we saw, a problematization is therefore a conscious interpretation by the subject of his own being, to which he seeks to conform by "modifying himself in his singular being" (*DE*, 4: 545). This has the unfortunate consequence of making the reflective activity of the subject the starting point for the constitution of the self and of defining practices in an antigenealogical way, as the simple application of an already formed and explicit understanding. The deep contradiction which drives the Foucauldian understanding of the subject does not result from the idea that the subject is deprived of any specific essence, nor from the use of the genealogical method, but from the definition of subjectivation as the reflective constitution of the self through thought.

But Foucault's work also presents a quite different definition of thought, which could at least partially resolve these contradictions: thought, Foucault says, is not "to be sought for only in theoretical formulations such as those of philosophy or science; it *can and must be analyzed in every manner of speaking, doing, or behaving*" (*F*, 334; my italics). In this second sense, thought does not refer to an intellectualized activity ("theoretical formulations"), but is on the contrary revealed as its implicit presupposition, which another passage indirectly confirms by mentioning the "systems of thought that have now become familiar to us, that appear evident to us and that *have become part of our perceptions, attitudes and behavior*" (*FL*, 282; my italics). Thought thus appears to designate an interpretation of the self and the world which is carried by the mode of being of the subject ("ways of saying, doing, behaving"), which preexists any conscious elaboration of what it is. It should not be understood in reference to the theoretical order of knowledge, but from habitual and nonreflective human practices. Foucault implicitly confirms this by describing his "attachment" to the principle that "man is a thinking being *exactly in his most mute practices*, and thought is not that which makes us believe in what we think nor admit what we do, but *that which makes us problematize even what we are ourselves*" (*DE*, 4: 612; my italics).[1] Thus, thought is immanent to our practices themselves, and these, far from being neutral or from making sense only from the reflective and voluntary activity of the subject (which would make us "believe in what we think" or "admit what we do"), intrinsically involve an understanding of what man and his relationship to the world are. From this perspective, any conscious interpretation by the subject of his essence ("to problematize even what we are ourselves") should thus be referred to "thought," which conditions it from the horizon of the practices it belongs to, a conclusion that is also drawn in another passage: "The study of forms of experience can thus proceed from an analysis of 'practices'—discursive or not—as long as one qualifies that word to mean the different systems of action in so far as they are *inhabited by thought* as I have characterized it here" (*F*, 334).

Given the homage paid by Foucault to Heidegger, quoted in the notes section of the Introduction to this book, one might speculate that these passages, as well as the theoretical framework that they bring with them, are of Heideggerian inspiration and that they establish an implicit dialogue with the first division of *Being and Time*. There are at least three reasons for such speculation. Firstly, thought is understood in a nonmetaphysical way; it is referred to everyday practices that are not necessarily objects of representation or conscious intentions (for example one of the "mutest" practices in a Christian society could be making the sign of the cross when entering a church). Foucault appears to implicitly take up Heidegger's critique of Husserl's claim that signification is primarily linked to the subject's intentional attitude;[2] he understands the formation of meaning by reference to the practices themselves.[3] Similarly, the allusion to "belief" (thought is not "that which makes us *believe* in what we think") could perhaps be understood as an argument against the Husserlian thesis that our understanding of the world works on the basis of a subjective set of beliefs. Secondly, to the extent that thought "inhabits" practices and preexists any conscious elaboration, it appears very to be close to the Heidegger's notion of the preontological understanding[4] that is implicitly involved by *Dasein*'s mode of being.[5] The definition of the subject as that which "'problematizes' what it is, what it does and the world in which it lives" (*UP*, 10; modified) seems to echo the well-known passage of *Being and Time* that states that *Dasein* is that which "understands itself in its being and that to some degree it does so explicitly."[6] Moreover, if *Dasein* really is for Heidegger the being which "in its being, has a relationship to that being," and is therefore an entity for which an "understanding of Being is itself a definite characteristic of Dasein's being,"[7] Foucault's claim is that the problematizations operated by the subject are that "through which being offers itself as what can and must be thought" (*UP*, 11; modified).[8] Foucault seems to regard thought as an analogue to the "understanding of Being"[9] immanent to human practices, which constitutes the ante-predicative horizon of intelligibility from which alone *Dasein* can reflectively thematize its own behavior and define what it is. Finally, the third common point with Heidegger is doubtlessly the idea that man is defined both by his self-interpretative mode of being[10] and by the absence of any fixed nature—provided, however, that one leaves aside the fact that the introduction of the concept of *Dasein* by Heidegger in *Being and Time* was precisely aimed at avoiding the use of the terms "subject" or "man,"[11] and correspondingly brackets the founding role attributed by Foucault to subjectivity.[12]

This idea that problematizations are immanent to practices seems to indirectly confirm Hubert Dreyfus's thesis, according to which "power" would be the Foucauldian equivalent of Being for Heidegger. This claim is founded on the observation that the two concepts have the same characteristic of opening a "limited field of possibilities." For Dreyfus, power establishes a "social *Lichtung*," which would be a more limited equivalent to Heidegger's *Lichtung* as the "clearing" from which objects and actions become available.[13] From this functional analogy, it would therefore be possible to establish a parallel between the Heideggerian history of Being and the Foucauldian genealogy of power, and the latter could therefore appear as a way of approaching the history of problematizations without reactivating the transcendental perspective of the constitution of the self. Indeed, the idea that human practices themselves support a non-reflective comprehension of the self and the world, on the basis of which all reflective interpretations are elaborated, would allow Foucault to understand problematizations independently of the intellectual activity of the constituting subject, and thus, by definition, to analyze subjectivation through the practices themselves—"techniques of the self" and "techniques of domination"—indifferently. It is perhaps in this sense that one can read the passage from the introduction of *The Use of Pleasures*, already partially quoted, which appears to echo these occupations by assigning to the "history of truth" the task of analyzing, "not the behaviours nor the ideas," but "the problematizations through which *being offers itself as that which can and must be thought*—and the practices on the basis of which these problematizations are formed" (*UP*, 11; modified, my italics). Clearly, "being" cannot be understood here from its metaphysical characteristics, as one can hardly see how otherwise it could "give itself" through problematizations (in the nonreflective sense defined above).[14] Correspondingly, the idea that being "gives itself" appears to echo later Heideggerian texts,[15] which understand the relationship of Being to man precisely in the form of a "gift." In any case, Foucault seems to distance himself from any traditional ontology (see Introduction) in order to adopt here a hermeneutic approach which seeks to "make Being speak"[16] inasmuch as it "can and must be thought," implicitly defining it, as we have seen, as the preontological understanding indissociable from all human practices and paradoxically presupposed by their analysis.[17]

The task of genealogy would then be to start from the practices themselves in order to articulate the different historical meanings taken by Being, thus considered as the understanding which "gives itself" in them and which they presuppose in their activity. Between the stages of the history of Being[18] and those of the Foucauldian history of truth, certain chronological markers are indeed quite close (the Greek world and the medieval, modern, and technological epochs for Heidegger; Greek and Roman antiquity, Christianity, modernity, and bio-power for Foucault).[19] Equally, the Foucauldian idea that to each of these stages of history corresponds a particular determination of the essence of man (as soul, as a part of the great Logos of the world, as a creature, as a docile body) appears, at least in its form, rather Heideggerian. Moreover, both authors have quite similar definitions of truth—for example, Foucault's analyses of dogma and the role played by theology in the constitution of the self at the beginning of Christianity are rather close to Heidegger's idea that in the medieval epoch the "real locus of truth has been transferred by Christendom to faith—to the infallibility of the written word and to the doctrine of the Church."[20] Finally, as Dreyfus points out, Foucault's denunciation of the "normalization" processes that are specific to the contemporary epoch calls to mind the Heideggerian analyses of *Gestell*,[21] especially as thematized in "The Question Concerning Technology."

Nonetheless, however interesting the comparison between Foucault and Heidegger, the assimilation by Dreyfus of "power" and Being appears problematic at least for three reasons. Firstly, Foucault's definition of power as what "structures the possible field of action of others" (*MF*, 221) refers this "structuration" to the idea of a "governmentality" itself understood not as "power" in general, nor as a quasi-epochal determination, but in reference to *individuals* themselves.

> It is free individuals who try to control, to determine, to delimit the freedom of others and, in the order to do that, they dispose of certain instruments to govern others. That rests indeed on freedom, on the relationship of self to self and the relationship to the other. . . . *The notion of governmentality allows one, I believe, to set off the freedom of the subject and the relationship to others*, i.e., that which constitutes the very matter of ethics. (*FF*, 19–20; my italics)

In the same spirit, the last texts devoted by Foucault to the question of government insist increasingly on the necessity of thinking power from individual action—which is the meaning of its generic redefinition as an "action upon actions" (*MF*, 222). Consequently, any "political" definition of power (for example, as "power over others") must be set within the context of an ethical understanding, as "power over oneself" (*FF*, 20). As Foucault says again: "If one addresses the question of political power by placing it in the larger field of governmentality . . . , *the analysis of power must be referred to an ethics of the subject defined by the relation to the self*."[22] The idea that power and government should always be fundamentally understood through the individual itself, and moreover in reference to human action and freedom,[23] is hardly compatible with the analogy between Being and power, since, for Heidegger, Being should not be thought from man, and even less from the "relation to the self."

Secondly, even if one leaves aside these later texts and keeps to the "political" definition of power, the "structuration" effected by power nevertheless remains distinct from the opening of a *Lichtung*. Indeed, Foucault seems to understand power from the Nietzschean idea of a play of forces, in which the political, although defined as a "field," is nonetheless understood as *immanent* to the relations of power themselves. Thus, Foucault asserts that "every power relation refers, *as its effect but also as its condition of possibility, to a political field of which it forms a part*" (*PK*, 189; my italics). The theme of the conditions of possibility ("that which makes it possible") can be interpreted, as Dreyfus does, in an "existential" sense, that is, in reference to the idea of a determination that would not be causal and would not affect actions themselves, but rather the possibilities implicitly open to action, within whose framework alone a decision could be made and an action taken. However, the "field" in question is doubly referred by Foucault to the very element which it is supposed to determine, both through a logical relationship of consequence ("as its effect") and by virtue of a relationship of belonging ("of which it forms a part"). One can certainly question the pertinence of such a definition, which once again seems to activate the structure of regressive inclusion already analyzed in relation to the notion of experience. But the point is that, whatever its validity, this conception of power results in *the negation of the Heideggerian theme of the ontological difference*, which by definition presupposes a division between the "clearing" and that which is revealed within it. Moreover, even if this passage were to be considered an exception, it still would remain that Foucault understands "government" polemically—in the etymological sense of *polemos* (combat)—as an unstable and violent field where the relationships of force permanently form and dissolve, which once again appears much closer to Nietzsche than to Heidegger.

Finally, the last reason why it is impossible to assimilate the Foucauldian "history of truth" to Heidegger's history of Being is that Foucault never questions *the nature of the understanding of truth belonging to each epoch*. He refers the constitution of the self to the different interpretations of what man is, which are each time inscribed within the frame of a more general theory—Platonic metaphysics, Stoic physics, Christian theology, the human sciences. But the truth through which recognition is held to work only appears in his analyses as a set of theses whose ontological presuppositions are never challenged. Although he is not a relativist,[24] Foucault does not wonder about the "essence of truth," and never considers the possibility of a first opening from which different historical understandings of truth could be defined. Consequently, the difference between truth as *aletheia* and the ontic understandings of truth[25] remains absent from Foucault's analyses, where, finally, truth appears only as a content. Correspondingly, the Heideggerian idea according to which each epoch of the history of Being continues a "destining"

(*Geschick*),[26] a form of disclosure which for each epoch determines the mode of apparition of beings, does not have a Foucauldian equivalent.

More generally, it seems impossible to justify the comparison I suggested myself between Foucault's "problematization" and Heidegger's preontological understanding. Firstly, as already seen, there are other Foucauldian definitions of thought (notably as "the act which posits a subject and an object"), including some—such as the idea that "thought *is not* that which inhabits a certain behaviour and gives it its meaning" (*F*, 388)—which directly contradict the statement analyzed above.[27] In the same way, the assertion that thought would be present in "the ways of saying, doing or behaving" of the individual, understands the latter as a "subject of learning, an ethical or juridical subject, *a subject conscious of himself and others*" (*F*, 335; my italics). At the end of the day, Foucault's idea is not that thought is a preontological understanding immanent to all human practices, but rather that it depends on the reflective activity through which the subject constitutes itself—by which we return to the difficulties examined in Part III. This fundamental ambivalence can be found again in the notion of "problematization," which is alternatively referred to a conscious act, to the practices themselves, or to what is formed "out of the practices." In this light, the continuation from the above passage is particularly significant: although Foucault has just stated that problematizations are that through which "being offers itself as what can and must be thought" (*UP*, 11; modified), he goes on to declare that "the archeological dimension of the analysis made it possible to examine the very forms of problematization; its genealogical dimension enabled me to analyze their formation out of the practices and of the modifications undergone by the latter" (*UP*, 11, 12; modified). However, if *archaeology* is what must analyze the "forms" of problematization, then, by definition, the latter must belong to the order of the *discursive*. This is confirmed at the end of the passage, which evokes the "problematization of life, language, and labour in discursive practices that conformed to certain 'epistemic' rules" (*UP*, 12). Henceforth, the possibility of interpreting problematization as a prereflective understanding immanent to practices, however seductive it might be, is in fact rather compromised.

Finally, when Foucault mentions the necessity of a "historical ontology" (*F*, 49),[28] he is always referring to an "historical ontology *of ourselves*," an ontology understood from the perspective of a self-constitution of the subject. The following extract is very clear on this point:

> In other terms, the historical ontology of ourselves has to answer an open series of questions; it has to make an indefinite number of inquiries . . . : How *are we constituted* as subjects of our own knowledge? How *are we constituted* as sub-

jects who exercise or submit to power relations? How *are we constituted* as moral subjects of our own actions? (*F*, 48–49; my italics)

In another passage, Foucault again takes up exactly the same idea by invoking the possibility of three ontologies:

first, an historical ontology of ourselves in relation to truth through which *we constitute ourselves* as subjects of knowledge; second, an historical ontology of ourselves in relation to a field of power through which *we constitute ourselves* as subjects acting on others; third, an historical ontology in relation to ethics through which *we constitute ourselves* as moral agents. (*MF*, 237; my italics)

But the theme of an "historical ontology of ourselves" seems rather problematic. The idea of an "historical ontology" is not contradictory *per se*; on the contrary, it seems to fit well enough within the hermeneutic perspective described above— which is the only one possible anyway, given Foucault's rejection of any essentialist metaphysics. This "historical ontology" could be read as reflecting on the ways in which the being of man has been interpreted historically, and would thus rest upon a genealogical analysis of the different problematizations carried by the practices themselves, depending on the epoch, insofar as the practices constitute the backdrop of any action and conceptual elaboration, and are endowed with a historicity relative to that of the practices themselves. However, this hypothesis is once again contradicted by Foucault's marked insistence on the theme of the self-constitution of the subject (the expression "we constitute ourselves" returns six times!). Because of this, problematization can no longer be understood as a preontological understanding and it returns to its more restrictive definition as a reflective and intellectual activity, which presents the double disadvantage of reestablishing the perspective of constitution and of invalidating the idea of a hermeneutic *ontology* itself. Once more, Foucault appears to be the victim of his own quasi-Sartrian insistence on subjectivity and consciousness. This sliding is particularly clear in the following passage, where Foucault describes the "games of truth and falsehood"

through which *being constitutes itself historically* as experience; that is, as something that can and must be thought. What are the games of truth by which *man proposes to think his own being* when he perceives himself to be mad, when he considers himself to be ill; when he conceives of himself as a living, speaking, laboring being; when he judges and punishes himself as a criminal? What were the games of truth though which man came to recognize himself as a desiring individual? (*UP*, 6, 7; modified, my italics)

Here again, the idea of a "historical constitution of being" could possibly have been interpreted in the hermeneutic sense examined above. But such a hypothesis is immediately contradicted by at least two elements. Firstly, the definition of being as "experience" has the implicit consequence (following the movement analyzed in the first chapter of the third section) of surreptitiously reintroducing a subject of this experience and therefore of thinking being, not through practices, but in reference to subjectivity. This is confirmed by the continuing text, which indicates that such a "constitution" should be referred to the reflective activity of the human subject itself ("when he perceives himself . . . when he judges . . . himself . . . came to recognise himself as a desiring individual"). Moreover, the reference to "games of truth"—which, as we recall, were themselves defined as "an ensemble of *rules* for the production of truth" (*F*, 16)—combined with the absence of any definition of truth as *aletheia*, prevents us conceiving "being" in reference to a preontological understanding, which, because it is by definition infraconceptual, could not be analyzed through "rules" or, even less, result from their application.

Despite the many attempts constituted by the ideas of the "*épistémè*," the "archive," the "discursive regime," the "games of truth," and "problematizations," Foucault was unable to give the old Husserlian historical *a priori* a new satisfactory version. On the contrary, he repeatedly struggled with the different figures of the anthropological doubles originally analyzed by the *Commentary*. Each time revived by these successive attempts, the tension between the historical and the *a priori* repeatedly eroded the courageous project of "historicizing" the transcendental (*DE*, 2: 371), as, ironically enough, the archaeologist rediscovered at the end of his itinerary the problem which initially served as his foil: the problem of the subject. Although he always desired to break away from it, and multiplied historicizing statements, Foucault was finally confronted again with the transcendental perspective, in the form of the idea of a free and autonomous self-constitution of the subject. Two possible courses were still open to him to escape the impasses of his theory of subjectivation: either to take his version of Nietzschean genealogy to its limit and renounce the idea of a conscious and voluntary constitution of the self by the self; or to establish the hermeneutic ontology which might have permitted him, by privileging his own interpretation of thought as that which "inhabits" (*F*, 335) action and the "most mute practices" (*DE*, 4: 612), to bypass the aporia tied to his intellectualizing conception of the subject. But, for lack of having taken either of these routes, the late Foucault was condemned to unwittingly obey the law he had stated long before in *The Order of Things*, which made each *épistémè* the insurpassable limit of those it rules, even—and perhaps necessarily most strongly—when they seek to break free from it.

Reference Matter

Notes

All sources are by Michel Foucault unless otherwise stated.

Introduction

1. See "The Unities of Discourse," in *AK*, §2, draft 1, and, above all, "What Is an Author?" in *LCP*, 113–38.

2. See also 54, where Foucault states that "what we must grasp and attempt to reconstitute are the modifications that affected knowledge [*savoir*] itself, at that archaic level which *makes possible* both the different forms of knowledge [*connaissances*] and the mode of being of what there is to know" (modified; my italics). See also 63, which is concerned with "questioning Classical thought at the level of what, archaeologically, *made it possible*" (my italics). See also 72–73, 132, 166, 205, where the historical *a priori* is each time defined, with regard to different domains, as the "*conditions of possibility*" of discourse. See also *DE*, 1: 498, where Foucault says that he is looking for "what *makes possible*, at a given time, the apparition of a theory" (my trans., but also in *FL*). See also *FL*, 58: "My problem could be stated as follows: How does it happen that at a given period one could say this and that something else has never been said? It is . . . the analysis of the *historical conditions* that account for what one says or for what one rejects." See also *AK*, 79: "We seek the *rules of its formation* in discourse itself"; and also chapter 5 of part 3 in *AK*. Finally (for the texts of the same period), see *OD*, 55, where there is mention of "*external conditions of possibility*" of discourses (all my italics).

3. This point was already made in *DE*, 1: 708: "What I want to make visible is the *set of conditions which govern*, at a given time and in a specific society, *the apparition of statements*" (my italics).

4. *DE*, 4: 631: Foucault specifies that "if he does belong to the philosophical tradition, it is to the *critical* tradition which is that of Kant," and continues by indicating that "one might call his project a *Critical History of Thought*." This paper was written by Foucault under the pseudonym of Maurice Florence.

5. *LCP*, 134; notably, the following passage: "The work of these initiators is not situated . . . in the space it defines; rather, it is . . . discursive practice that relates to their works as the primary points of reference."

6. "La Constitution d'un transcendental historique dans *La Phénomenologie de l'Esprit* de Hegel," cited in Didier Eribon, *Michel Foucault* (Paris: Flammarion, 1991), 47.

7. See, for example, *DE*, 3: 580.

8. A little lower in this source Foucault states his desire to "define a method of analysis purged of all anthropologism."

9. Notably—besides Marx himself—Althusser, Marcuse, Reich, and Fromm.

10. On this point, see, for example, *DE*, 2: 276. See also, *PPC*, 17–46.

11. On this point, see *MF*.

12. The three phases are represented by the three "archaeological" texts, that is, *The Birth of the Clinic*, *The Order of Things*, and *The Archaeology of Knowledge*.

13. *The Birth of the Clinic* mentions twice a "concrete *a priori*" (preface, xv, and 192 ["the historical and concrete *a priori* of the Modern medical gaze was finally constituted"]). Page 113 mentions an "essential *a priori*" that governs the repartition of the visible and the sayable. The notion recurs many times in *The Order of Things*, for example, xxii, xxiv, 157, 158, as well as in *The Archaeology of Knowledge*, which devotes section 3, chapter 5, to it.

14. The first appearance of the term *épistémè* is in the preface of *The Order of Things* (xxii), which then mentions it often. By contrast, it reappears only once in *The Archaeology of Knowledge*.

15. *The Archaeology of Knowledge* dedicates almost a whole section to this concept.

16. A little later in this work, Foucault insists that there is "no relationship, for me, with Kantian categories."

17. See also, on the same question, "Critique et *Aufklärung*," *Bulletin de la Société française de philosophie* 84, no. 2 (April–June): 35–63, 50 (does not appear in *DE*). All citations from this source are my translation.

18. "Critique et *Aufklärung*," 38.

19. Ibid., 49.

20. The same idea is taken up in *DP*, 27: "We should admit rather . . . that power and knowledge directly imply one another; *that there is no power relation without the collective constitution of a field of knowledge, nor any knowledge that does not presume and constitute at the same time power relations*" (my italics).

21. The denials are notable in an interview by Pasquale Pasquino, entitled "Précisions sur le pouvoir: Réponses à certaines critiques," *DE*, 3: 625–35. This is a point made by Jürgen Habermas.

22. Motivated by the desire for continuity, Foucault continues by declaring that although he had "more or less left side (the problem) in my first studies," he was nonetheless concerned to try "to follow the progress and the difficulties through its whole history."

23. The text continues by affirming the necessity of rejecting any "transcendental consciousness."

24. The theme comes up six times in two pages!

25. This passage is so well known and controversial that it might seem foolhardy to repeat it:

> Heidegger has always been for me the essential philosopher. . . . My whole philosophical development was determined by my reading of Heidegger. . . . I probably wouldn't have read Nietzsche if I hadn't read Heidegger. I tried to read Nietzsche in the '50s, but Nietzsche by himself said nothing to me. Whereas Nietzsche and Heidegger—that was the philosophical shock! But I've never written anything on Heidegger and only a very short article on Nietzsche. Yet these are the two authors who I've read the most. I think it's important to have a small number of authors with whom one thinks, with whom one works, but on whom one doesn't write. Perhaps someday I'll write about them, but at that point they will no longer be instruments of thought for me.

Heidegger is also mentioned in the same spirit in the following extract: "I was surprised when two of my friends in Berkeley wrote something about me and said that Heidegger was influential. Of course it was quite true. But no one in France has ever perceived it. . . . Paradoxically enough, Heidegger is not very difficult for a Frenchman to understand" ("Truth, Power, Self: An Interview with Michel Foucault," in H. Martin, H. Grotman, and P. H. Hutton, *Technologies of the Self: A Seminar with M. Foucault* [Amherst: University of Massachusetts Press, 1988], 12).

26. The expression is used three times on the same page. See equally *F*, 45–47.

Chapter 1: The *Critique* and the *Anthropology*

1. "Critique et *Aufklärung*," *Bulletin de la Société française de philosophie* 84, no. 2 (April–June): 47. All citations from this source are my translation.

2. Immanuel Kant, *The Critique of Pure Reason*, trans. N. Kemp Smith (London: Macmillan, 1929), "Canon of Pure Reason," 635.

3. As far as I can tell, the only paper published on this topic is S. Watson, "Kant and Foucault on the Ends of Man," *Tijdschrift voor Filosofie* 47, no. 1 (March 1985). In "What Is Enlightenment? Kant and Foucault" (in *The Cambridge Companion to Foucault*, ed. Gary Gutting [Cambridge, Eng.: Cambridge University Press, 1994], 159–96), Christopher Norris focuses on the relationship between Kant and Foucault from the perspective of texts that appeared much later, mainly, "What Is Enlightenment?" (*Magazine Littéraire*, no. 207 [May 1984]: 35–39). A longer version has been printed in *F*.

4. "Ni à un sujet en soi, ni au Je pur de la synthèse, mais à un moi qui est objet, et présent dans la seule vérité phénoménale. Mais ce moi objet, offert au sens dans la forme du temps, n'est pourtant pas étranger au sujet déterminant, puisqu'il n'est pas autre chose en fin de compte que le sujet tel qu'il est affecté par lui-même."

5. Kant, *Critique of Pure Reason*, "Transcendental Analytics," 1, 2, "Deduction of the Pure Concepts of the Understanding," 120.

6. "La naissance et le devenir des formes humaines."

7. "Une certain vérité critique de l'homme, fille de la critique des conditions de la vérité."

8. "Y avait-il dès 1773, et subsistant peut-être tout au fond de la *Critique*, une certaine image *concrète* de l'homme qu'aucune élaboration philosophique n'a pour l'essentiel altérée, et qui se formule enfin, sans modification majeure, dans le dernier des textes publiés par Kant?"

9. Therefore the contemporaneousness of the *Anthropology* with the whole of Kant's corpus is a clue to this. Foucault similarly reminds us (15) that the "moment of birth" of anthropological research—the beginning of the writing of the *Anthropology*—was about 1772, at the end of the precritical period, it would remain unfinished at Kant's death.

10. See 56, 80, 83, 89, 103, 108, 120, and 123.

11. "La question anthropologique *pose* en les *reprenant* les questions qui se rapportent à elles. Nous sommes au niveau du fait structural de la *répétition anthropologico-critique*. L'*Anthropologie* ne dit rien d'autre que ce que dit la *Critique*."

12. "La structure interne de l'*Anthropologie* et la question qui l'anime ont la même forme que l'interrogation critique elle-même."

13. *Anthropology from a Pragmatic Point of View*, trans. Mary J. Gregor (The Hague: Martinus Nijhoff, 1974), 21.

14. Ibid., §§7, 21, and §§43, 71.

15. Ibid., 72.

16. "Une prétention à connaître les possibilités et les limites de la connaissance: elle mime dans l'extérieur et dans les gestes de l'empiricité le mouvement d'une *Critique*."

17. "L'empiricité de l'*Anthropologie* ne peut se fonder sur elle-même . . . ; elle ne peut donc envelopper la *Critique*, mais elle ne saurait manquer de s'y référer; et si elle en figure comme l'*analogon* empirique et extérieur, c'est dans la mesure où elle repose sur des structures de l'*a priori* déjà nommées et mises à jour."

18. Especially in the following passage: "We must therefore make trial whether we may not have more success in the tasks of metaphysics, if we suppose that objects must conform to our knowledge. This would agree better with what is desired, namely, that it should be possible to have knowledge of objects *a priori*, determining something in regard to them prior to their being given." *Critique of Pure Reason*, 22.

19. Ibid., "Transcendental Analytic," 2, "Deduction of Pure Concepts of the Understanding," 125.

20. Ibid., 42.

21. Ibid., 44.

22. "Critique et *Aufklärung*," 41.

23. Respectively, "l'investigation du conditionnant dans l'activité fondatrice"; and "l'inventaire du non fondé dans le conditionné."

24. "L'*Anthropologie* suit le partage des facultés de la *Critique*; mais le domaine privilégié n'est plus celui de leur pouvoir positif, mais celui où elles risquent de se perdre."

25. "Forme de l'expérience et condition d'une connaissance limitée mais fondée"; "tentation d'un égoïsme polymorphe." There are other examples on the same page.

26. "L'expérience possible définit aussi bien, dans son cercle limité, le champ de la vérité et le champ de la perte de la vérité."

27. "La constitution du nécessaire dans le champ de l'expérience."

28. "Les possibilités dans l'order des conditions."

29. The *Logik* and the *Opus posthumum*.

30. "Marginale pour la *Critique*, et décisive pour les formes de réflexion qui se donneraient pour tâche de l'achever."

31. Cf. *Opus posthumum*, trans. Eckart Förster and Michael Rosen (Cambridge, Eng.: Cambridge University Press, 1993), esp. 218–56.

32. "L'unité concrete et active par laquelle Dieu et le monde trouvent leur unité."

33. "L'unité *réelle* dans laquelle la personalité de Dieu et l'objectivité du monde se rejoignent"; and "mais aussi cela seulement à partir de quoi l'absolu peut être pensé."

34. Foucault is most probably alluding to the following passage of the *Opus posthumum*: "God, the world and that which thinks both in real relation to each other: the subject as rational world-being. The *medius terminus* (copula) in judgment is here the judging subject (the thinking, world-being, man in the world" (231).

35. "S'affecte dans le mouvement par lequel il devient objet pour lui-même. . . . Le monde est découvert . . . comme figure de ce mouvement par lequel le moi, en devenant objet, prend place dans le champ de l'expérience et y trouve un système concret d'appartenance." This self-modification must be thought of *a priori*: cf. *Opus posthumum*, esp. 104, 106–7, 109, 117, 121–22, 126–27, 129–31, 134–36, 142, 149, 167, 191. It is the solution to the main problem of the *Opus posthumum*, that of bridging the "gulf" that lies between, on the one hand, the system of the metaphysical principles of the science of nature, which is determined by *a priori* principles, and, on the other hand, an empirical physics conceived of as a *scientia naturalis*. Kant is concerned with "bridging the unbridgeable gulf" (82) between the two "domains" and uniting in the single element of *philosophia naturalis*. Since physics itself cannot produce the means for such a passage, which then would be merely *a posteriori*, Kant's solution consists in finding a subjective principle that is "placed *a priori* at the foundation of physical investigations." This subjective principle is the subject as it affects itself *a priori*, since

> what is subjective in the determination of myself is equally objective by the rule of identity, according to a principle of *a priori* knowledge. There is only one space and one time, each of which is represented in intuition as an inconditional intuitive whole, i.e., as infinite. My synthetic *a priori* knowledge as transcendental philosophy is a transition from the metaphysical foundations of natural science to physics, i.e., to the possibility of *experience*. The first synthetic act of consciousness is that through which the subject makes itself an object of intuition: not logically (analytically), . . . but metaphysically (synthetically).

Kant can then define transcendental philosophy as "the system of pure idealism of the self-determination of the thinking subject through synthetic *a priori* principles from concepts; the subject constitutes itself through these principles into an object. . . . Transcendental philosophy is thus the . . . formal element of the theoretically-speculatively and morally-practically self-determining subject" (252). Cf. also: "I, the subject, am an object to myself, i.e. the object of my self."

36. "Un habitant du monde." The same expression recurs on 104, with the same meaning.

37. "Quant à l'homme, il est leur synthèse—ce en quoi Dieu et le monde réellement s'unifient—et pourtant il n'est par rapport au monde qu'un de ses habitants, et par rapport à Dieu qu'un être limité."

38. "Toute réflexion sur l'homme à une réflexion sur le monde."

39. "Les rapports empiriques et circulaires des immanences, au niveau d'une connaissance naturelle nécessaire."

40. "Anticipé sur la totalité et l'a prépensée précisément comme limite."

41. "Par sa répétition même, le niveau du fondamental, et de substituer à des divisions systematiques l'organisation des corrélats transcendentaux."

42. "D'acheminer l'*a priori* vers le fondamental."

43. To my knowledge, Hubert Dreyfus and Paul Rabinow are the only ones who have defined it, but they did so by identifying it with the "conditions that allow knowledge." Cf. *MF*. Gary Gutting (*Michel Foucault's Archaeology of Scientific Reason* [Cambridge, Eng.: Cambridge University Press, 1989], 200) has a similar approach: "Finitude as founding is the 'fundamental'; finitude as founded is the 'positive.'"

44. "D'inséparables transcendances."

45. "Le passage de l'*a priori* au fondamental, de la pensée critique à la philosophie transcendantale."

46. "Un accès naturel."

47. "S'affranchir d'une critique préalable de la connaissance et d'une question première sur le rapport à l'objet."

48. "Le champ d'une positivité d'où toutes les sciences humaines tireraient leur fondement et leur possibilité."

49. "Dans l'obédience de la *Critique*."

50. "Non seulement ce qu'il est, mais ce qu'il fait de lui-même."

51. Foucault defines the "pragmatic" as a kind of intermediary between the *a priori* moral imperative and a purely empirical means/ends calculus that would only be governed by the principles of efficiency and maximalization. The specificity of the pragmatic is that it "connects *homo natura* to the definition of man as a subject of freedom [articule l'*homo natura* sur une définition de l'homme comme sujet de la liberté]" (34).

52. "La dimension de liberté et de totalité qu'il ouvre fait qu'il n'y a d'*Anthropologie* que pragmatique, où chaque fait est repris dans le réseau ouvert du *sollen* et du *können*."

53. See the "Anthropological Didactic," I, 113: "The principle of the mind that animates it by *ideas* is called *spirit*."

54. "Le principe qui anime l'esprit par les idées, c'est le principe spirituel."

55. "Elle anticipe sur un schéma qui n'est pas constituant, mais qui ouvre sur la possibilité des objets. Elle ne dévoile pas en un mouvement 'ostensif' la nature des choses,

mais elle indique comment rechercher cette nature." The passage thus paraphrased is located on 550 of the "Appendix to the Transcendental Dialectic," "Of the Aim of Natural Dialectic."

56. Kant, *Critique of Pure Reason*, "Appendix to the Transcendental Dialectic," "Of the Aim of Natural Dialectic," 550.

57. "Fait se poursuivre la vie empirique et concrète du *Gemüt*."

58. "Arrache le *Gemüt* à ses déterminations."

59. "L'énigmatique nature de notre raison" (my italics).

60. Kant, *Critique of Pure Reason*, "Canon of Pure Reason," 1, "Final Purpose of the Pure Use of Our Reason," 630 (my italics).

61. "Quelque chose qui serait le noyau de la raison pure, l'indéracinable origine de ses illusions transcendantales . . . , le principe de son mouvement dans le champ empirique où surgissent inlassablement les visages de la vérité."

62. "Semble renvoyer la *Critique*, parvenue à son sommet, vers une région *empirique*, vers un *domaine des faits* où l'homme serait voué à une très originaire passivité."

63. "Ainsi, le rapport du donné et de l'*a priori* prend dans l'*Anthropologie* une structure inverse de celle quiétait dégagée dans la *Critique*. L'*a priori*, dans l'ordre de la connaissance, devient dans l'ordre de l'existence concrète un *originaire* qui n'est pas chronologiquement premier, mais qui, dès qu'il est apparu . . . se révèle comme déjà là."

64. "Ce qui est *a priori de la connaissance*, du point de vue de la *Critique*, ne se transpose pas immédiatement, dans la réflexion anthropologique, en *a priori de l'existence*, mais apparaît dans l'épaisseur d'un devenir où une soudaine émergence prend infailliblement dans la rétrospection le sens du déjà là."

65. "Une connaissance de l'homme, dans un mouvement qui objective celui-ci, au niveau et dans le contenu de ses déterminations animales; mais elle est connaissance de la connaissance de l'homme, dans un mouvement qui interroge le sujet lui-même sur ses limites, et sur ce qu'il autorise dans le savoir qu'il prend de lui-même."

66. Kant, *Critique of Pure Reason*, "Transcendental Analytic," 1, 2, "Deduction of the Pure Concepts of Understanding," 120.

67. Ibid., 2, 1, "Of the Paralogisms of Pure Reason," 328.

68. "La forme empirique et manifeste dans laquelle l'activité synthétique du Je apparaît comme forme *déjà synthétisée*, comme *structure indissociablement première et seconde*" (my italics).

69. "Limite *a priori* de ses connaissances."

70. Foucault had previously noted that "even the anthropological upon which we too often reflect, is alas actually a transcendental which pretends to be true at a natural level."

71. This inversion had already been described by *The Birth of the Clinic*: "The possibility for the individual being both subject and object of his own thought implies an inversion in the structure of finitude. . . . The anthropological structure that then appeared played both the critical role of limit and the founding role of origin" (197).

72. "Les valeurs insidieuses de la question "*Was is der Mensch?* sont responsables de

ce champ homogène, déstructuré, indéfiniment réversible, où l'homme donne sa vérité comme âme de la vérité."

73. Cf. *C*, 105: "One will lend to anthropology both the privileges of the *a priori* and the meaning of the fundamental, the preliminary character of the *Critique* and the completed form of transcendental philosophy; it will unfold without distinction from the problematic of the necessary to that of existence; it will merge the analysis of conditions and the questioning of finitude [On prêtera (à l'anthropologie) à la fois les privilèges de l'*a priori* et le sens du fondamental, le caractère préalable de la *Critique* et la forme achevée de la philosophie transcendantale; (elle) se déploiera sans différence de la problématique du nécessaire à celle de l'existence; (elle) confondra l'analyse des conditions et l'interrogation sur la finitude]." Cf. also 123: "One has tried to turn [the *Anthropology*] (which is nothing but another way of forgetting the *Critique*) into the field of a positivity from which all the human sciences would derive their foundation and their possibility, whereas in fact it can only speak the language of limit and negativity [On a voulu faire (de l'*Anthropologie*) (ce qui n'est qu'une autre modalité de l'oubli de la *Critique*) le champ d'une positivité d'où toutes les sciences humaines tirent leur fondement et leur possibilité, alors qu'en fait, elle ne peut parler que le langage de la limite et de la négativité]."

74. When he speaks about passive genesis—that is, the associative operation that gives us "the 'ready-made' object that confronts us in life as an existant mere physical thing" (par. 38, 78)—the "realm of the 'innate' *a priori*," or the "concrete *a priori*," which alone makes possible the analysis of the creation of the ego: "Only through the phenomenology of genesis does the ego become understandable" (*Cartesian Meditations*, trans. Doris Cairns [The Hague: Martinus Nijhoff, 1969], par. 39, 81).

75. Respectively: "Transcendental Aesthetics" and "Analogies of Experience."

76. "Ce qui ronge l'activité synthétique elle-même."

77. "Des synthèses déjà effectuées."

78. "In this Fold, the transcendental function is doubled over so that it covers with its dominating network the inert, grey space of empiricity; inversely, empirical contents are given life . . . and are immediately subsumed in a discourse which carries their transcendental presumption into the distance."

79. "Le réseau de contresens et d'illusions."

80. Respectively, "The Empirical and the Transcendental," "The Cogito and the Unthought," "The Return of the Origin."

81. "Le Geist, ce serait ce fait originaire qui, dans sa version transcendantale, implique que l'infini n'est jamais là."

82. "Le Geist est la racine de la possibilité du savoir. Et pour cette raison, il est indissociablement présent et absent des figures de la connaissance."

83. "Ce retrait, cette invisible et visible réserve dans l'inaccessibilité de laquelle la connaissance prend place et positivité. Son être est de n'être pas là, dessinant en ceci même le lieu de la vérité."

84. The expression is borrowed from Jacques Derrida, *Le problème de la genèse dans*

la philosophie de Husserl (Paris: PUF, 1990), 12. The notion of "primitivity" evokes the retrospective play by which mundane temporality can preexist its own constitution.

85. "Valoir comme une *Critique* libérée des préjugés et du poids inerte de l'*a priori*."

86. *Critique of Pure Reason*, 606.

87. The term appears in *Les progrès de la métaphysique en Allemagne depuis le temps de Leibniz et de Wolf*, trans. Louis Guillermit (Paris: Vrin, 1973), 107–8. The passage that Foucault refers is the following: "A philosophical history of philosophy is itself possible not historically or empirically, but rationally, i.e. *a priori*. Because, while it establishes the facts of reason, it does not lend them to the telling of a historical story, but draws them from the nature of human reason as a *philosophical archaeology*" (my italics).

Chapter 2: The Methodological Failure of Archaeology

1. Except in one instance, which I shall return to later, *OT* mentions the concepts of historical *a priori* and *épistémè* as if they had already been defined (see, for example, 168, 172, 206–9, 245, 257, 309, 310, 318, 344, 349, 364–66, 374, 378). The same phenomenon had already occurred in *The Birth of the Clinic* (192), where the concept of a historical *a priori* is evoked without any specific definition. As for *The Archaeology of Knowledge*, the chapter that is devoted to the *a priori* bears not only on this topic, but also on the "archive."

2. See especially "Sur l'archéologie des sciences: réponse au cercle d'épistémologie," in *DE*, 1: 696–731.

3. For example, Georges S. Rousseau: "Whose Enlightenment? Not Man's: The Case of Michel Foucault," *Eighteenth Century Studies*, no. 6 (1972–73): 283–86; Georges Huppert: "*Divinatio* and *Eruditio*: Thoughts on Foucault," *History and Theory*, no. 3 (1974) (a critique of chapter 2 of the order of things); Michel Pélorson, "Michel Foucault et l'Espagne," *La Pensée*, no. 152 (July–August 1970): 93–97, 131–38 (which argues against Foucault's interpretation of Cervantes' *Don Quixote*); and John Greene, "Les mots et les choses," *Social Science Information*, no. 6 (1967) (an attack on the role attributed to Buffon and Lamarck). Foucault responded to some of these criticisms in "Les monstruosités de la critique," *DE*, 2: 214.

4. Depending on whether one is dealing with a "problematic" idealism (such as Descartes') or an "idealist" one (such as Berkeley's). Cf. Immanuel Kant, *The Critique of Pure Reason*, trans. N. Kemp Smith (London: Macmillan, 1929), "Transcendental Analytic," 2, "Refutation of Idealism," 244; or "Transcendental Dialectic," 2, "Of the Dialectical Inferences of Pure Reason," 1, 4, "Fourth Paralogism: Of Ideality," 344).

5. Kant, *Critique of Pure Reason*, 348.

6. On 168, Foucault also mentions the "fundamental *necessities* of knowledge [*savoir*] that must be interrogated" (modified).

7. These differences are laid out in chapter 4 of *The Archaeology of Knowledge*, where Foucault is much more severe about the history of ideas than about that of the sciences.

8. This may be done, as in the history of ideas, from the perspective of a continuity

established by those "magical" notions, "influence" and "change," or from the perspective of the discontinuity described by Bachelard's "epistemic ruptures."

9. *AK*, 163: Foucault rejects the possibility of "a causal analysis [which] would try to discover to what extent political changes, or economic processes could determine the consciousness of scientists—the horizon and direction of their interest, their system of values, their way of perceiving things, the style of their rationality."

10. I am fully aware of the lack of precision in talking about "Marxism" (even though Foucault himself does so often, notably in "Critical Theory/Intellectual History," which repeatedly evokes "Marxism" in general), and I am conscious of the many readings of the *Contribution to the Critique of Political Economy*, in which Marx raised the problem of determination by stating that "the mode of production of material life conditions the process of social, political and intellectual life in general." But however different they may be, the "scientific" interpretation of these texts, which maximizes the role of economics by understanding determination in the form of a physical causality, and the so-called humanist reading, of Lukács, for example, which gives increasing attention to the feedback effects of the superstructure on the infrastructure, both agree in giving economics a decisive importance. Even Althusser, whose concept of "overdetermination" allows the massive model of economic determination to be replaced by a differential analysis of the specific contradictions of each social formation, and therefore allows superstructures a relative autonomy, recognizes that "in the last instance" it is the economic determination by the mode of production which is primary (*Pour Marx* [Paris: Maspéro, 1974], 111).

11. Although this is a somewhat dubious assertion, given the systematic character of archaeology described above.

12. Kant, *Critique of Pure Reason*, 194.

13. *OT*, xxii: "I am not concerned, therefore, to describe the progress of various forms of knowledge towards an objectivity in which today's science could finally recognise itself" (modified). This is obviously one of Foucault's attacks against the history of ideas; however, it also applies, although in a more nuanced way, to Bachelard (a good illustration of this normative side would be the distinction between *histoire périmée* [obsolete] and *histoire santionnée* [approved], in *L'activité rationaliste de la physique contemporaine* [Paris: PUF, 1951]).

14. Kant, *Critique of Pure Reason*, 194.

15. Hence the famous pages devoted to Buffon and Aldrovandi; cf. *OT*, 22–23 and 39–40.

16. Cf., for example, "Structuralism and Post-Structuralism," *DE* 4: 431–37.

17. The metaphor of the gaze is reminiscent of the preface, one of the only other texts in which Foucault expands on the nature of the historical *a priori*.

18. The investigation starts with the classical age and stops around 1832, when the "crisis of fevers" was solved.

19. The notion is suggested for the first time in *The Birth of the Clinic* (as a "concrete *a priori*," probably reminiscent of Husserl), on xv.

20. The subtitle of the book is "An Archaeology of Medical *Perception*," whereas that of *The Order of Things* is "An Archaeology of the Human Sciences."

21. There are identical definitions in many places, such as 90 or 96: "In the clinic, as in analysis, the armature of the real is designed on the model of language. The clinician's gaze and the philosopher's reflection have similar powers because they both presuppose a structure . . . in which the totality of being is exhausted in manifestations that are its signifier/signified, . . . in which the perceived and the perceptible may be wholly restored in a language whose rigorous form declares its origin. . . . *The world is for them the analogue of language*" (my italics).

22. Foucault then notes that "knowledge [*connaissances*] in the order of anatomo-clinical medicine is not formed in the same way and according to the same rules as in the mere clinic" (*BC*, 137).

23. Maurice Merleau-Ponty, *The Visible and the Invisible*, trans. Alphonso Lingis (Evanston, Ill.: Northwestern University Press, 1968), 3. One may object to this parallel, since the publication of the *Visible and the Invisible* (1964) was after that of *The Birth of the Clinic* (1963). However, numerous interviews testify that Foucault attended most of Merleau-Ponty's courses at the Sorbonne, and especially the ones bearing on the problem of language, to which he attached a special importance. See, for example, "Structuralism and Post-Structuralism," *PPC*, 21: "That, I think was a fairly critical point: Merleau-Ponty's encounter with language. And as you know, Merleau-Ponty's later efforts addressed that question. I remember clearly some lectures in which Merleau-Ponty began speaking of Saussure who, even if he had been dead for fifty years, was quite unknown, not so much to French linguists and philologists, but to the cultured public. So the problem of language appeared."

24. Merleau-Ponty, *Visible and the Invisible*, 126 (in reference to Lacan).

25. Ibid. The distinction between "speaking word" (*parole parlante*) and "spoken word" (*parole parlée*) (*The Phenomenology of Perception*, trans. Colin Smith [London: Routledge and Kegan Paul, 1962], 197) was Merleau-Ponty's response to the primacy given by Saussure to *langue* (language) over *parole* (speech), and therefore (indirectly) to structuralism. Against the idea that language could be studied as a purely formal system—like, for example, the concept of "value" in *The Course of General Linguistics*—Merleau-Ponty affirms the necessity of understanding the speaking word as an expressive act and "linguistic gesture," which transcends the order of constituted significations. The distinction between the two types of word is continued in the text, in which Merleau-Ponty describes the opposition between "secondary word" and "originary word."

26. Foucault evokes "clinical perception" or "medical perception."

27. An "archaeology of the medical *gaze*."

28. See also xi, xii, 29, 51, 52, 97, 105, 115, 118–20, 129, 135, 163, 166, 168, 170.

29. Merleau-Ponty, *Phenomenology of Perception*, 207.

30. The same observation applies to *The Order of Things*, which insists on the "ambiguous" character of Merleau-Pontian phenomenology without condemning it (321)—an ambiguity which, as is well known, was openly endorsed by Merleau-Ponty himself.

31. In *The Phenomenology of Perception*, Merleau-Ponty shows that perception can be thought only "once distinctions between the *a priori* and the empirical, between form and content, have been done away with" (222). *The Visible and the Invisible* refutes the notion of "a transcendental, intemporal order, as a system of *a priori* conditions," in order to think the "openness upon a natural and historical world" (85).

32. This is particularly clear at the end of the text, where Foucault anticipates *The Order of Things* by criticizing the apparition of the theme of "finitude."

33. Since, as shown by fundamental ontology, phenomenology need not be a philosophy of the subject.

34. This is indicated by the title of the work. Foucault states in *The Archaeology of Knowledge* that the title was ironical, a point to which I shall come back shortly.

35. Perhaps it is in this sense that one can understand the "raw" (*brut*) character of words mentioned several times in the text, and which seems curiously reminiscent of Merleau-Ponty.

36. Hence Foucault's analyses of the endless replication (*moutonnement*) of commentaries in chapter 2, section 4.

37. The "ordering of empiricities" by general grammar, the analysis of wealth and natural history.

38. Cf. *OT*, 311 (modified): "Language has lost that secret consistency which, in the XVIth Century . . . interwove it with all the things in the world; yet it has not acquired the multiple existence which we wonder about today; in the Classical age, discourse is that translucent necessity through which representation and beings must pass—when beings are represented to the mind's eye, and when representation renders beings visible in their truth. The possibility of knowing things and their order passes, in the Classical experience, through the sovereignty of words . . . which form a colorless network on the basis of which beings manifest themselves and representations are ordered."

39. Foucault summarizes this process in the following way: "The threshold between Classicism and Modernity . . . was definitely crossed when words ceased to be interwoven with representations and to spontaneously grid the knowledge [*connaissance*] of things. At the beginning of the XIXth century, they rediscovered their ancient, enigmatic density: though not in order to restore the curve of the world which had harboured them during the Renaissance, nor to mingle with things in a circular system of signs. . . . Since then, language only existed and still exists nowadays in a dispersed mode" (*OT*, 304, modified). Cf. also *OT*, 295–300.

40. Thus, Foucault claims that "from Bichat onwards, the pathological phenomenon was perceived against the background of *life*, thus finding itself linked to the concrete, obligatory forms that it assumed in an organic individuality" (*BC*, 153).

41. The comparison with Condillac is also expanded by means of an analogy between clinical symptoms and the action language (*BC*, 93 ff.).

42. One can find in *The Birth of the Clinic* many other passages that go in the same direction, for example the following: "One now sees the visible only because one knows the language: things are offered to him who has penetrated the closed world of words;

and if these words communicate with things, it is because they obey a rule that is intrinsic to their grammar" (*BC*, 115).

43. Cf. *OT*, 46: "The (legible) signs do not resemble (visible) entities anymore" (modified).

44. *Raymond Roussel* (Paris: Gallimard, 1963), 207–8.

45. A few years later, Foucault himself will claim—giving explicit credit to a paper written by Paul Veyne ("Foucault révolutionne l'histoire," in *Comment on écrit l'histoire* [Paris: Seuil, 1971], 203–42)—that he is trying to detect "the effects on historical knowledge [*savoir*] of a nominalist critique which is itself formulated by means of a historical analysis," a definition to which I shall come back ("Table ronde du 20 Mai 1978," in *L'impossible prison: recherches réunies par M. Perrot*, ed. Michelle Perrot [Paris: Seuil, 1980], 56).

46. The same theme appears in the "Réponse au Cercle d'épistémologie," *DE*, 1: 720–22.

47. See also, "Nietzsche, Genealogy, History," *LCP*, 142: "There is 'something altogether different' behind things: not a timeless and essential secret, but the secret that they have no essence or that their essence was fabricated in a piecemeal fashion from alien forms."

48. *Structural Anthropology* (London: Penguin, 1968), 62 (modified). Significantly, the opening pages of *The Savage Mind* (London: Weidenfield and Nicholson, 1966) state that "the thought we called primitive is founded on this demand for order. This is equally true of all thought" (10).

49. Cf. the Introduction to this book.

50. Martin Heidegger, *On Time and Being*, trans. Joan Stambaugh (New York: Harper Torchbooks, 1972). The expression is already present in Heidegger's early writings (cf. Jean Greisch, *Ontologie et temporalité: esquisse d'une interprétation intégrale de "Sein und Zeit"* [Paris: PUF, 1994], 27–29).

51. Heidegger, *On Time and Being*, 5–6.

52. I am aware that Heidegger's position toward metaphysics changed throughout his work. I am referring here to the conception of it he had during his middle period, that is, at the time of the Nietzsche lectures. On this point, see Michel Haar, *La fracture de l'histoire* (Grenoble: Jérôme Millon, 1995), esp. chap. 4 ("La métaphysique dans *Sein und Zeit*"); chap. 10 ("Le tournant de la détresse ou: comment l'époque de la technique peut-elle finir?"), and chap. 11 ("Achèvement de la métaphysique et nouveau commencement").

53. Heidegger, *On Time and Being*, 6.

54. Ibid., 24.

55. Analyzed, for example, in "On the Essence of Truth," trans. John Sallis, in *Pathmarks*, ed. Will McNeil (Cambridge, Eng.: Cambridge University Press, 1998), 114–54.

56. This text dates from 1938 (Martin Heidegger, "The Age of the World Picture," in *The Question Concerning Technology and Other Essays*, trans. William Lovitt [New York: Harper and Row, 1977]).

57. This point is expanded on by Hubert Dreyfus in "On the Ordering of Things:

Being and Power in Heidegger and Foucault," where he gives a more general analysis of the possibility of a correspondence between "Age of the World Picture" and Foucault's historical divisions (*Michel Foucault, Philosopher*, ed. Thomas G. Armstrong [Hemel Hampstead, Eng.: Harvester Wheatsheaf, 1992]). Equally, see Gary Gutting, *Foucault and Literature: Towards a Genealogy of Writing* (London: Routledge, 1992), 102–6.

58. Heidegger, "Age of the World Picture," 128. See also, 132: "Man sets himself as the setting in which whatever is must henceforth set itself forth, must present itself [*sich präsentieren*], i.e., be picture. Man becomes the representative [*der Repräsentant*] of that which is, in the sense of that which has the character of object."

59. Ibid., 133.

60. Martin Heidegger, *Kant and the Problem of Metaphysics*, trans. Robert Taft (Bloomington: Indiana University Press, 1997), 152.

61. *OT*, x: "[The archaeology] was not meant to be a search for a *Weltanschauung* but strictly a "regional" study."

62. Cf. Heidegger, "The Age of the World Picture," 139: "Descartes's interpretation of what it is to be and of truth first creates the presupposition underlying the possibility of a theory of knowledge or a metaphysics of knowledge." This theme is taken in up in several other places, for example, in *What Is Philosophy?* trans. William Kluback and Jean T. Wilde (New Haven, Conn.: New College and University Press, 1956): "*Certitudo* becomes the fixing of the *ens qua ens* which results from the unquestionability of the *cogito* (*ergo*) *sum* for man's ego. Thereby, the ego becomes the distinctive *sub-jectum*" (87).

63. Heidegger, "Age of the World Picture," 115.

64. Heidegger, *On Time and Being*, 9.

65. This point is analyzed by Aaron Kelkel, "La fin de l'homme et le destin de la pensée," *Man and World*, no. 18 (1985): 3–37. However, Kelkel's approach is mostly focused on Heidegger's thought.

66. Especially in the *Letter on Humanism*.

67. Foucault denies having "developed a theory" or inferring the analysis of discursive formations from a definition of statements that would serve as a foundation" (*AK*, 114 [modified]). However, in the same passage he confesses to "regretting not having achieved it yet," which is quite explicit about his intentions. Alan Megill notes in "Foucault, Structuralism, and the End of History" (*Journal of Modern Philosophy*, no. 51, fasc. no. 3 [September 1979]: 451–503) that *The Archaeology of Knowledge* is very close to a "discourse on method" in that it starts with doubting the empirical units and then tries to give them a foundation in chapter 3.

68. The historical *a priori* is defined in the last section of chapter 3 (§6), and the *épistémè* in the last section of chapter 4.

69. There are many complex definitions of knowledge [*savoir*] in *The Archaeology of Knowledge*. Perhaps the clearest and most concise can be found in Foucault's preface to the American edition of the text: "By *connaissance* I mean the relation of the subject to the object and the formal rules that govern it. *Savoir* refers to the conditions that are nec-

essary in a particular period for this or that particular type of object to be given to *connaissance* and for this or that enunciation to be formulated" (*AK*, 15).

70. These four aspects are studied in sections 2–6 of chapter 2.

71. Foucault insists that discursive formations won't necessarily coincide with the "old units," which is likely in the case of the analysis of wealth, for example.

72. See section 2 first, where the same movement is mentioned at a smaller scale.

73. Foucault introduced the theory of "thresholds" so as to be able to think diachronically, instead of synchronically, the becoming of each discursive formation, and to specify the level that is specific to the archaeology (the threshold of epistemologization). The four thresholds defined by *The Archaeology of Knowledge* are (from the lowest to the highest) the thresholds of "positivity," "epistemologization," "scientificity," and "formalisation" (see *AK*, 186–87).

74. See the definition of the *épistémè* as a "space of dispersion, an open and probably indefinitely describable field of relations" (*DE*, 1: 676). Remarkably, the epistemic space is not, *stricto sensu*, "discontinuous" but only *discrete*, since it leaves open and even requires the possibility of ordered relationships between the elements that belong to it. This is paradoxically attested to by Foucault's definition of "discontinuity," which sees it "not as a monotonous and unthinkable void . . . but as a play of specified transformations that differ from each other (each with its conditions, rules, level) and are linked together by schemas of dependence" (*DE*, 1: 680).

75. There is a similar definition in the "Réponse au Cercle d'épistémologie" (*DE*, 1: 719), which evokes the "regulated system of differences and dispersions, a four-tiered system which rules a discursive formation."

76. These "systems of rules" concern the formation of objects, enunciative modalities, concepts, and strategies.

77. As has been already shown in relation to *The Order of Things*, this negative definition of the *a priori* (as a "condition of validity for judgements") is clearly aimed at the Kantian conception of the *a priori* and at the normativity that is specific to it.

78. This definition repeats the tension that we already noted about the *épistémè*, between the diachronical (the "conditions of emergence," "principles" of transformation) and the synchronical ("law of coexistence," "form of the mode of being").

79. These definitions are located in section 2 of chapter 3, 92–103.

80. Foucault defines the statement as the function itself, for example, at 86–89, 107.

81. Foucault defines the statement as the element that the function allows us to identify, at 90, 98–100, 116–17.

82. Foucault does not deal with virtual systems, which is the reason why he is not a linguist, a logician, or a structuralist.

83. Nevertheless, Foucault alludes to the Husserlian conception of the *a priori* in many places. On top of the above mentioned extract, see, for example, *DE*, 1: 772: "I am not trying to study the beginning in the sense of a *primary origin*, a *foundation* from which everything else would be possible. I am not searching for that solemn first moment from which, for example, the whole of Western mathematics was possible. I am not going back

to Euclid or Pythagoras" (my trans., my italics). Moreover, *The Archaeology of Knowledge* itself rejects an *a priori* that would be

> a horizon of ideality, placed, discovered or established by a founding gesture—and one that is so original that it eludes all chronological insertion. [The "preconceptual level" which is specific to the archaeology] is not an inexhaustible *a priori* at the confines of history, set back both because it eludes all beginning, all genetic restitution, and because it could never be contemporary with itself in an explicit totality. (*AK*, 62)

Finally, Foucault devotes two pages to problems that are similar to those of *The Origin of Geometry*, in an interview by José G. Merquior (*DE*, 2: 165–66): "The problem [for Husserl] was to know . . . how geometry, for example, could follow for centuries this race for pure formalisation and be, at the same time, a science that could be thought in each of its points by an individual who could have an apodictic intuition of this very same science."

84. Published as an appendix in *The Crisis of European Sciences* (trans. David Carr [Evanston, Ill.: Northwestern University Press, 1970]), 353. The notion of a historical *a priori* recurs on 372–74, 377–78. About the relationship between Foucault and Husserl during the archaeological period, see Gérard Lebrun, "Note sur la phénoménologie dans *Les mots et les choses*," in *Michel Foucault, philosophe* (Paris: Seuil, 1989), 33–53. Lebrun notes (48) that "the historical *a priori* is a notion of Husserlian origin," but without any further clarification.

85. As opposed to "passive comprehension," which is mere repetition.

86. Edmund Husserl, *The Origin of Geometry*, in *The Crisis of European Sciences*, trans. David Carr (Evanston, Ill.: Northwestern University Press, 1970), 373.

87. Ibid., 374.

88. Ibid., 378. The passage continues as follows: "If the usual factual study of history in general . . . is to have any meaning at all, such a meaning can only be grounded upon what we can call here internal history, and as such upon the foundations of the universal historical *a priori*" (378). Hence the possibility of a "universal-historical" understanding connected to the "*a priori* of historicity in general" (372).

89. Thus, Husserl takes up the theme of the "variations" set in place by *Experience and Judgment: Investigations in a Genealogy of Logic* (ed. Ludwig Landgrebe, trans. James S. Churchill and Karl Amoriks [London: Routledge and Kegan Paul, 1973]), §87, by asserting that it would uncover a "component of universality," that is, the historical *a priori*.

90. As opposed to the so-called primary relations, which pertain to the nondiscursive (for example, institutional relations), and "secondary" ones, which refer to the ways—faithful or not—in which the former are reflected at the level of discourse. Discursive relations are specific in that they "treat discourse as a practice" (*AK*, 45) and can, in principle, be studied independently from the two other types of relations.

91. Cf. the preface to the English edition of *The Order of Things*: "What I would like to do, however, is to reveal a *positive unconscious* of knowledge: a level that eludes the

consciousness of the scientist and yet is part of scientific discourse, instead of disputing its validity and seeking to diminish its scientific nature [which is an implicit attack against Bachelard]. What was common to the natural history, the economics and the grammar of the Classical period *was certainly not present in the consciousness of the scientist*" (last italics mine).

92. This is a version of the "humunculus problem," which occurs when entities introduced to elucidate a concept reproduce its structure at a smaller scale, thus generating an endless regression.

93. This is "why so many things, said by so many men, for so long, have not emerged in accordance with the laws of thought or with a set of circumstances only . . . but by virtue of a whole set of relations that are peculiar to the discursive level; in short, why, if there are things said—and those only—one should see the immediate reason for them in the things that were said, not in them, nor in the men who said them, but in the system of discursivity, in the enunciative possibilities and impossibilities that it lays down" (*AK*, 129).

94. Moreover, as shown by Dreyfus and Rabinow (*MF*, 95–97), the archive generates the reactivation of another of man's doubles, the "Cogito and the Unthought," since Foucault claims the impossibility of the archaeologist "describing his own archive, since it is from these rules that we speak, since it is that which gives to what we can say—and to itself, the object of our discourse—its modes of appearance, its forms of existence and coexistence, its systems of accumulation, historicity and disappearance. The archive cannot be described in its totality" (*AK*, 130).

95. Significantly, these concepts disappear completely from the conclusion of the section, even though it is dedicated to the historical *a priori* and the archive, which evokes "the general theme of a description that questions the already said at the level of its existence: of the enunciative function that operates within it, of the discursive formation, and the general archive system to which it belongs" (*AK*, 131).

96. However, the term recurs a few times in Foucault's last writings, in passages that will be examined in the third section of this book.

97. The concept is mentioned three times elsewhere. It occurs in *DP* (305) and in *PK* (196–97).

98. If one excludes the *Order of Discourse*, which works as a transition, and to which I shall turn in the next section.

Chapter 3: The Reformulation of the Archaeological Problem

1. See, for example, "Two Lectures," *PK*, especially the second, 102 ff. See also the *Annuaire du Collège de France* (1976), where one finds a critique of Hobbes.

2. Foucault only very rarely mentions his old master; but the frequency with which he discusses the concepts of "ideology" and of "State apparatus" suggests that he is attempting to distinguish his approach from that of Althusser. See, for example, "Body/Power" or "Questions on Geography," in *PK*.

3. "The Repressive Hypothesis," in *HS*, pt. 2. See also "Two Lectures," in *PK*, lecture 1.

4. *Surveiller et punir* (Paris: Gallimard, 1979), back cover.

5. See "Critique et *Aufklärung*," *Bulletin de la Société française de philosophie* 84, no. 2 (April–June): 35–36 (all citations from this source are my translation); or "The Art of Telling the Truth," in *PPC*.

6. *Actualité* also means "relevance."

7. "Critique et *Aufklärung*," 39.

8. Ibid.

9. Foucault concludes "Critique et *Aufklärung*" by proposing to "take the path in the opposite direction now," and therefore to "carry the critical question towards that of the *Aufklärung*" (53).

10. This theme is equally taken up in 1968 in "Réponse à une question," and then in 1969 in *The Archaeology of Knowledge* itself, to which I shall return.

11. "Sur les façons d'ecrire l'histore," interview by Raymond Bellour, *Les Lettres françaises*, no. 1187 (15–21 June 1967).

12. Foucault criticizes what he calls the "historico-transcendental recourse: trying to seek, beyond all historical manifestation and point of birth, a project which would be withdrawn from any event," as well as the "empirical or psychological recourse: seeking the founder, interpreting what he wanted to say, detecting implicit meanings which silently slept within his discourse." See, equally, *PPC*, 23:

> For me, the problem was framed in terms not unlike those we mentioned earlier:
> is the phenomenological, transhistorical subject able to provide an account of the historicity of reason? Here, reading Nietzsche was the point of rupture for me.
> There is a history of the subject just as there is a history of reason; but we can never demand that the history of reason unfold at a first and founding act of the rationalist subject.

13. Friedrich Nietzsche, *The Will to Power*, trans. Walter Kaufmann and R. J. Hollingdale, ed. Walter Kaufmann (New York: Vintage, 1968), §§152–54.

14. "The Birth of a World," in *Philosophy and Truth: Selections from Nietzsche's Notebooks of the Early 1870's*, trans. and ed. by Daniel Breazeale (London: Humanities Press, 1979).

15. Thus, in *DE*, 4: 572, Foucault states that "words themselves are nothing else but interpretations," which clearly evokes the analyses of "On Lies and Truth in an Extra-Moral Sense" (*DE*, 1: 787) or the *Genealogy of Morals*.

16. This hypothesis is criticized by Foucault in *PPC*, 106: "Philosophers or even, more generally, intellectuals justify and mark out their identity by trying to establish an almost uncrossable line between the domain of knowledge, seen as that of truth and freedom, and the domain of the exercise of power. What struck me, in observing the human sciences, was that the development of all these branches of knowledge can in no way be dissociated from the exercise of power."

17. Francis Bacon, *Novum organum*, bk. 1, aphorism 3, in *Works*, ed. John Spedding (London: Longman, 1859), 4: 222.

18. "Critique et *Aufklärung*," 48–49.

19. To the best of my knowledge, one can find developed definitions of truth in only two particular texts in the period concerned: "Two Lectures" and "Truth and Power," both in *PK*.

20. See, for example, *DE*, 3: 184 ff.

21. See also, for example, *MF*, 208: "I would like to say, first of all, what has being the goal of my work during the last twenty years. It has not been to analyze the phenomena of power, nor to elaborate the foundations of such an analysis."

22. *PPC*, 23.

23. "Critique et *Aufklärung*," 49. The term is also used in *The Order of Discourse*.

24. On the contrary, *The Archaeology of Knowledge* was careful to distinguish between discursive formations and disciplines, defined there as empirical units; but here Foucault seems to abandon the distinction, conferring on disciplines the regulatory role previously accorded to discursive formations, as they are now held to operate "a permanent reactualisation of the rules" (ibid., 61).

25. The second form of the history of truth anticipates the thematic of *Discipline and Punish* and concerns "juridical forms and their evolution in penal law as a determined number of forms of truth" (see chapter 2 for the analysis of this form of truth).

26. "Critique et *Aufklärung*," 49.

27. As Etienne Balibar notes rapidly in "Science et vérité dans la philosophy de G. Canguilhem," in *Georges Canguilhem, philosophe, historien des sciences*, acts of the symposium of 6–8 December 1990, Paris (Paris: Albin Michel, 1993), 64.

28. Georges Canguilhem, "Galilée: La signification de l'oeuvre et la leçon de l'homme," in *Etudes d'histoire et de philosophie des sciences* (Paris: Vrin, 1983), 46.

29. This calls to mind Canguilhem's ferocious critique of the notion of "precursor," he "whom one knows after that he came before." But the idea described here is of a different order: it is not a matter of retrospectively reconstructing a fictive continuity between ideas or authors, but of showing that Galileo had actually anticipated a system whose proofs would only come later.

30. This idea is confirmed by the interview with A. Badiou, quoted by E. Balibar, where the philosopher affirms "that 'true knowledge' is a pleonasm; as is 'scientific knowledge,' and 'science and truth' also."

31. In introducing the theme of monstrosity, Foucault probably had in mind the numerous analyses consecrated to this subject by Canguilhem himself—for example, *The Normal and the Pathological* (New York: Zone Books, 1989), as well as "La monstruosité et les monstrueux" (published in *La connaissance de la vie* [Paris: Vrin, 1980], 171–84), from which the expression is drawn (172). The first line of this text reads as follows: "The existence of monsters puts into question the power of life to teach us order."

32. Translator's note: This is the author's pun; as it cannot be demonstrated it can only be shown or displayed—*monstration*, in medieval French.

33. Interestingly, these two statements themselves presuppose two others, the first of which is not discussed by Foucault; firstly, that the conditions from which one can judge the truth of a proposition are not dependent on its value as effective truth—that is, that truth, contrary to the Cartesian hypothesis, for example, has no particular evidence; secondly, that it must be possible to isolate a specific level at which to study these conditions—exactly the task that archaeology is assigned.

34. This suggests, of course, that ultimately acceptability should be understood in a political, and not purely epistemic, way. This is the core of the genealogical move—see the next chapter.

35. "Critique et *Aufklärung*," 49.

36. See equally the preface to the English edition of *The Order of Things* (xi), which defines knowledge (*savoir*) as the "rules of formation, which were never formulated in their own right," which are used to "define objects, form concepts, build theories."

37. This clearly indicates the opposition, within *The Archaeology of Knowledge*, between "global" and "general" history, as well as the points against Hegel scattered in this text and in *The Order of Things*.

38. Foucault's subsequent analyses of power will answer this point indirectly, as one of their aims is to show that predication reflects back on acceptability; therefore, whatever affects one will affect the other.

39. Foucault defined more precisely his debt to Nietzsche in *PPC*, 32: "My relation to Nietzsche, or what I owe Nietzsche, derives mostly from the texts of around 1880, where the question of truth, the history of truth and the will to truth were central to his work."

40. *Annuaire du Collège de France* (1971): 246.

41. See, for example, *The Will to Power*, §§87–91, 136–37, 146–50, 159; and *The Gay Science*, trans. Walter Kaufmann (New York: Vintage, 1974), §354.

42. It is likewise in this sense that he interprets the reasons that he read Nietzsche: "Now, as it happened, I had read Nietzsche in '53 and, curious as it may seem, from a perspective of inquiry into the history of knowledge—the history of reason: how does one elaborate a history of rationality? This was the problem of the 19th century" (*PPC*, 23).

43. Marcel Détienne, *The Masters of Truth in Archaic Greece*, trans. Janet Lloyd (New York: Zone Books, 1996). After a general introductory chapter, chapter 2 of Détienne's book begins exactly by examining the modes of discourse for Greek poets of this period.

44. Ibid., 67 (it is, of course, necessary to reverse the order of the last two functions to make the order match).

45. Ibid. The text continues: "Like the poet and the diviner, the King was also a master of truth. In such thought, truth is thus always linked with certain social functions. It cannot be separated from specific types of individuals and their qualities, or from a reality defined by their particular function in archaic Greek society."

46. Ibid., 74 (modified).

47. Ibid., 134. This theme is anticipated as follows: "This type of speech is an instrument of dialogue. It no longer depends on the interplay of transcendence religious forces

for its efficacy. It is founded in essence on social agreement manifested in either approval or disapproval" (99).

48. I am very grateful to Francis Wolff, whose seminar at the Ecole Normale Supérieure d'Ulm directed my attention to the forms of truth-saying in the Greek epoch.

49. It is interesting to compare this passage with the following extract in which Détienne discusses prophetic speech: "The speech of the divine and of oracular powers, like a poetic announcement, defines a particular level of reality: when Apollo prophesies, he 'realizes' (*krainei*)" (Détienne, *Masters of Truth*, 73).

50. See, for example, *The Will to Power*, §§1, 50 and 52, 106–10.

51. See Michel Haar, *Nietzsche et la métaphysique* (Paris: Gallimard, 1993); notably, the chapter, "La Subversion des catégories et des identités."

52. *Annuaire du Collège de France* (1971): 248.

53. Notably, see *The Will to Power*, §§112–13; *Twilight of the Idols*, "How at Last the 'Real World' Became a Myth."

54. Furthermore, even if one allowed without further discussion this quite considerable change, it would still remain true that there is no equivalent within Foucault's work to the many analyses (notably of the relationship of the will to power to the body, of the quality and orientation of forces and the establishment of perspectives) that in Nietzsche's thought establish the use of the concept and give it meaning. It could be objected that these themes will be later developed by Foucault, which is indisputable—as concerns the body and the notion of force at least. But they are then referred to *power*, not to the will to truth.

55. See Béatrice Han, "Nietzsche and the Masters of Truth: The Pre-Socratics and Christ," in *Heidegger, Authenticity, and Modernity: Essays in Honor of Hubert L. Dreyfus* (Cambridge, Mass.: MIT Press, 1999), 1: 23.

56. One can find a very short history of the development of the concept of the will in the West, which is referred to Schopenhauer's thought and its reworking by Nietzsche, in *DE*, 3: 604.

57. See, for example, *MF*, 104–17; Jeffrey Minson, *Genealogies of Morals: Nietzsche, Foucault, Donzelot, and the Eccentricity of Ethics* (London: Macmillan, 1985), 40–78; Gary Gutting, *Foucault and Literature: Towards a Genealogy of Writing* (London: Routledge, 1992), 119–46.

58. In "Nietzsche, Genealogy, History," Foucault shows that "truth, and its original reign, has had a history within the history" (*LCP*, 144), while insisting on the necessity of an "effective history" (*LCP*, 154).

59. See Foucault's critique of the "chimeras of the origin" and of "indefinite teleologies" (*LCP*, 144).

60. Foucault develops the idea that the "devotion to truth and the precision of scientific methods arose from the passion of scholars, their fanatical and unending discussions, and their spirit of competition" (*LCP*, 142).

61. Thus Foucault shows that "behind the always recent, avaricious, and measured truth, it posits the ancient proliferation of errors" (*LCP*, 143). See also *Annuaire du Col-*

lège de France (1971): 247, which develops the idea that "knowledge is an 'invention' behind which there is . . . a will to appropriate."

62. For example, *The Gay Science*, §§110, 123, 344, 347–49, 355; *Daybreak*, trans. R. J. Hollingdale (Cambridge, Eng.: Cambridge University Press, 1982), §§26, 327, 539.

63. One reencounters here the latent character of Socrato-Platonic nihilism as analyzed by Michel Haar (*Nietzsche et la métaphysique*, 10–14), more disguised and dangerous because truth is given in an apparently purely affirmative form.

64. See also *DE*, 1: 572: "This is why the interpreter is for Nietzsche the 'truthful': he is 'true,' not because he grabs a slumbering truth and articulates it, but because he states the interpretation that any truth aims at covering up" (my trans.).

65. *Annuaire du Collège de France* (1971): 247.

66. "Power-Relations Pass to the Interior of the Body," interview by Lucette Finas, *Quinzaine littéraire*, no. 247 (1–15 January 1977). The theme of fiction would be taken up again by Foucault, in 1978, in an interview with Daniel Trombadori: "People who read my work, particularly those to appreciate what I do, often tell me laughingly: 'Deep down, you know well that what you say is only fiction.' And I always reply: 'Of course, there is no question that it could be anything else but fictions'" (*DE*, 4: 44).

67. This definition will be repeated in almost identical terms in *PK*, 117: "And this is what I would call genealogy, that is, a *form of history which can account for the constitution of knowledges, discourses, domains of objects, etc.*, without having to make reference to a subject which is either transcendental in relation to the field of events or runs in its empty sameness throughout the course of history" (my italics).

68. "Critique et *Aufklärung*," 52 (my italics). Despite the parallelism suggested by Foucault's text, the notion of "strategy" operates in his work rather as a tool for analysis than as a complete and distinct method.

69. This is also confirmed by Foucault's insistence on the necessity of connecting archaeology and genealogy (see, for example, in *PK*). *The Order of Discourse* had already specified that: "The difference between the critical and the genealogical enterprise is not so much a difference of object or domain, but of point of attack, perspective, and delimitation" (*OD*, 72).

70. For example, see Vladimir Propp, *Morphology of the Folktale*, 2nd ed., trans. Laurence Scott, intro. Svatava Pirkova-Jakobson (Austin: University of Texas Press, 1968).

71. Such as, "It is raining," "I am tired," and so on.

72. *Annuaire du Collège de France* (1971): 248.

73. It is exactly this type of discourse, however, that Nietzsche attacks; his critique, therefore, is more radical than Foucault's. See, for example, *The Gay Science*, §§123, 344, 347–49.

74. One finds a mention of the case of mathematics in *FF*, 16.

75. This is also one of the questions addressed by Dreyfus and Rabinow to Foucault at the end of their work (*MF*, 294–95), where, however, it remains unanswered.

76. *Annuaire du Collège de France* (1971): 245.

Chapter 4: The Genealogical Analysis of the Human Sciences

1. See, for example, *DP*, 26 ff., and *HS*, 92 ff., as well as the last chapter of this book, which is totally devoted to bio-power.

2. See, for example, the deployments specific to disciplines, the most emblematic of which is the panopticon (*DP*, 195–228), or the technique of confession discussed in *HS*, 67.

3. Such as one can find, for example, in "Critique et *Aufklärung*" (*Bulletin de la Société française de philosophie* 84, no. 2 [April–June]), where Foucault describes the existence in all societies and all epochs of a "power-knowledge nexus." All citations from this source are my translation.

4. This point is developed by Michael Donnelly in "Michel Foucault's Genealogy of the Human Sciences," *Towards a Critique of Foucault*, ed. Mike Gane (London: Routledge and Kegan Paul, 1986), 15–32.

5. See, for example, *HS*, chap. 2, and *PK*, 92 ff.

6. This concept has been the object of many studies, notably: André Bové, "The End of Humanism: Michel Foucault and the Power of Disciplines," *Humanities in Society*, no. 3 (Winter 1980): 23–40; S. Breuer, "Foucault and Beyond: Towards a Theory of the Disciplinary Society," *International Science Journal*, no. 41 (1989): 235–47; William E. Connolly, "Discipline, Politics, and Ambiguities," *Political Theory*, no. 11 (1983): 29–52; Jeff Goldstein, "Foucault Among the Sociologists: The 'Disciplines' and the History of Professions," *History and Theory*, no. 23 (1984): 170–90.

7. Plato, *Republic* 374 ff.

8. Plato, *Gorgias* 493a ff.

9. An indirect confirmation of this point can be found in a paper first given in Japanese in 1978, which was not available when this hypothesis was formulated (*DE*, 3: 537), where Foucault distinguishes three possible meanings for the idea that the philosopher during antiquity was an "anti-despot": firstly, as a "philosopher legislator," like Solon, who "defined the system or rules according to which, in a city, power must be exercised"; secondly, as a "philosopher pedagogue," an "adviser to the prince who teaches him wisdom, this virtue, that truth which will be able, when he has to govern, to restrain the abuse of his power"; and thirdly, as a cynic, "who says that after all, whatever the abuses that power could heap on him or others, he, the philosopher . . . will remain independent of power: he will laugh at power."

10. See also: "I wonder whether the opposition between philosophical reflection and the exercise of power does not better characterize philosophy than its relationship to science, since after all, it's been a long time that philosophy can't play the role of a foundation for science anymore" (*DE*, 3: 537).

11. One can find very interesting analyses of Foucault's relation to the Frankfurt School by Axel Honneth, "Foucault et Adorno," *Critique*, no. 471–72 (August–September 1986): 801–15; David Couzens Hoy, "Power, Repression, Progress: Foucault, Lukes, and the Frankfurt School," in *Foucault: A Critical Reader*, ed. D. Couzens Hoy (Oxford: Basil

Blackwell, 1986), 69–106; and B. Smart, *Foucault, Marxism, and Critique* (London: Routledge and Kegan Paul, 1984), esp. 122–36.

12. "Table ronde du 20 mai 1978," in *L'Impossible prison: Recherches réunies par M. Perrot*, ed. Michelle Perrot (Paris: Seuil, 1980), 47.

13. *PPC*, 28: "True, I would not speak about one bifurcation of reason but more about an endless, multiple bifurcation—a kind of abundant ramification."

14. On Foucault's differences from Habermas, see, for example, his declarations in "The Ethic of Care for the Self as a Practice of Freedom," an interview by H. Becker, R. Fornet-Betancourt, and A. Gomez-Müller, in *FF*.

15. See especially page 104 and following of the same conference, where Foucault shows how the political theories of law were constituted in reference to the model of royal power, the question being both to legitimize it and to give it limits. One can also find in *Discipline and Punish* an analysis of the monarchical representation of power, notably from 47 to 129, where a synthesis is proposed.

16. *PK*, 97: "A second methodological precaution urged that the analysis should not concern itself with power at the level of conscious intention or decision; that it should not attempt to consider power from its internal point of view and that it should refrain from posing the labyrinthine and unanswerable question: 'Who then has power and what has he in mind?'"

17. Francis Bacon, *Novum organum*, bk. 1, aphorism 3, in *Works*, ed. John Spedding (London: Longman, 1859), 4: 47.

18. Francis Bacon, *In Praise of Knowledge* (1592), in *Letters*, vol. 1.

19. Francis Bacon, "Valerius Terminus: Of the Interpretation of Nature," in *Works*, 3: 222.

20. It consists of thirty-six Brothers, the first twenty-one of whom are divided into five groups charged with collecting information, which is then transmitted to the "Compilers," then to the "Lamps," to the "Innoculators," and to the "Interpreters of Nature," before arriving at the "Dowry Men," who decide if the knowledge thus formed should be used and for what ends.

21. Karl Marx, *Idéologie allemande* (Paris: Editions Sociales, 1968), 79.

22. Marxists such as Althusser, whom Foucault was close to at the beginning of his career, in opposition to the so-called humanist trend, illustrated by Lukacs.

23. See also "Two Lectures," in *PK*; in the second lecture there Foucault implicitly criticizes Althusser's "scientific" Marxism.

24. See also *PK*, 58: "What troubles me with these analyses which prioritize ideology is that there is always presupposed a human subject on the lines of the model provided by classical philosophy, endowed with a consciousness which power is then thought to seize on."

25. See, for example, *PK*, 122: "The State can only operate on the basis of other, already existing power relations. The State is superstructural in relation to a whole series of power networks that invest the body, sexuality, the family, kinship, knowledge, technology and so forth. True, these networks stand in a conditioning-condition relationship to a kind

of "meta-power" which is structured essentially round a certain number of great prohibition functions; but this meta-power with its prohibitions can only take hold and secure its footing where it is rooted in a whole series of multiple and indefinite power relations that supply the necessary basis for the great negative forms of power."

26. *PPC*, 118: "Since the 19th century, the critique of society has essentially started with the nature of the economy, which is effectively determining. A valid reduction of 'politics,' certainly, but a tendency also to neglect the relations of elementary power that could be constitutive of economic relations."

See also *PK*, 88, where Foucault criticizes the Marxist conception as redisguising an "economic functionality of power. 'Economic functionality,' to the extent that power has essentially the role both of maintaining the relations of production, and of redirecting a class domination that the development and modalities specific to the appropriation of the forces of production had made possible; political power, from this point of view, finds in economics its historical reason for existence." On the contrary, "the inseparability of economics and politics is not due to a relation of functional subordination, nor to a formal identity, but to another level which it is clearly necessary to uncover" (modified).

27. See notably the analyses of the Rasphuis of Amsterdam in *DP*, 121 ff.

28. See also, "La Politique de la santé dans les établissements du XVIIIe siècle," in *Les machines à guérir: aux origines de l'hôpital moderne; dossiers et documents* (Paris: Institut de l'Environment, 1976); *DE*, 3: 13–27.

29. Friedrich Nietzsche, "The Oldest Moral Judgements," in *Daybreak*, trans. R. J. Hollingdale (Cambridge, Eng.: Cambridge University Press, 1982), bk. 2, §§102, 59.

30. See also *DP*, 215: "'Discipline' cannot be identified with a single institution or apparatus, it is a type of power, a way of exercising it, involving a whole assemblage of instruments, techniques, procedures, levels of application and targets. It is a "'physics' or an 'anatomy' of power, a technology."

31. One can find other examples of this complementarity on pages 162, 186, and 296.

32. See also *HS* (107), where Foucault states that the establishment of *scientia sexualis* is connected with "an intensification of the body—with its exploitation as an object of knowledge and an element in relations of power."

33. *DP*, 128: "What one is trying to restore in this technique of correction . . . is the obedient subject, the individual subjected to habits, rules, orders, an authority that is exercised continually around him and upon him, and which he must allow to function automatically in him."

34. *HS*, 85: "Confronted by a power, i.e., law, the subject who is constituted as subject—who is 'subjected'—is he who obeys."

35. Thus: "The entry of the soul onto the scene of penal justice, and with it the insertion in legal practice of a whole corpus of 'scientific' knowledge [would be] the effect of a transformation of the way in which the body is invested by power relations."

36. This is the idea defended by Paul Veyne in an article entitled "Foucault révolutionne l'histoire," (*Comment on écrit l'histoire* [Paris: Seuil, 1978], 203–42). Foucault himself takes it up on his own account by affirming his desire to travel the "circle of 'objec-

tivation' of those elements that historians consider as given objectively (the objectivation of objectivities, so to speak)" ("Table ronde du 20 mai 1978," in *L'impossible prison*, 55–56). Explicitly referring to Veyne, Foucault would redefine his research as an attempt to reveal the "effects on historical knowledge of a nominalist critique which is itself formulated through an historical analysis."

37. See on this point *PK*, 59: "If it has been possible to constitute a knowledge of the body, this has been by way of an assembly of military and educational disciplines. It was on the basis of power over the body that a physiological, organic knowledge of it became possible." See also *DE*, 3: 587–88.

38. Thus, "the acceleration of the productivity of the body has been, I believe, the historical condition for the development of the human sciences, sociology, psychiatry" (*DE*, 3: 587–88).

39. The panopticon is described in detail in the chapter of *Discipline and Punish* devoted to it, as well as in "L'Oeil du pouvoir," the preface to the edition of Jeremy Bentham's work. See, for example, the following extract: "The panopticon functions as a kind of laboratory of power. Thanks to its mechanisms of observation, it gains in efficiency and in the ability to penetrate into men's behaviour, knowledge follows the advances of power, discovering new objects of knowledge over all the surfaces on which power is exercised" (*DP*, 204). One can find analyses of the panopticon in, for example, Jeffrey Minson, *Genealogies of Morals: Nietzsche, Foucault, Donzelot, and the Eccentricity of Ethics* (London: Macmillan, 1985), 55–57, 97–100 and 106–10.

40. Columbus challenged his advisors to make an egg stand unsupported. When they failed he broke the bottom to make it stand.

41. On this point, see *DE*, 3: 521: "With the appearance of the discipline in the space of the hospital and because it is possible to isolate each individual . . . , the individual emerges as the object of medical knowledge and practice."

42. See also *DE*, 3: 551: "All the great disciplinary machines (barracks, schools, workshops and prisons) are machines that allow the individual to be circumscribed, to know what he is, what he does, what can be done with him. . . . The human sciences are forms of knowledge which make it possible to know what the individuals are, what is normal and what is not. [Disciplinary mechanisms] turn the individual, his existence and his behavior . . . into an element which is relevant, necessary even, needed for the exercise of power in Modern societies. The individual has become an essential object for power. Power is all the more individualising because, paradoxically, it is more bureaucratic and has been annexed by the State."

43. This paradox is analyzed by François Ewald in "Michel Foucault et la norme," in *Michel Foucault: lire l'oeuvre* (Grenoble: Jérôme Millon, 1992), 201–22.

44. This concept would be developed through the analyses of bio-power, to which the last chapter of *The History of Sexuality*, volume 1, is consecrated. I'll return to this point later.

45. Remember that *The Archaeology of Knowledge* stated that they have not reached the fourth threshold of epistemologization.

46. See also the following passage, just as explicit: "The psychiatric apparatus was not made to cure, but to exercise a pre-determined power over a certain category of individuals" (*DE*, 2: 772). On the connection between the development of medicine and disciplinary techniques, see *DE*, 3: 735, notably the following passage: "Medicine as the general technique of health, even more than as the care of the sick and the art of curing, occupies a more and more important place in administrative structures and in this machinery of power which never ceases, in the course of the 18th century, to spread and affirm itself. The doctor roots himself in the various *loci* of power."

47. *Annuaire du Collège de France* (1974): 295–96 (my italics).

48. If further confirmation is needed, see *HS*, 112, which states that the families' concern about Charcot's intervention was unwarranted, as the therapist only intervened "in order to return them to individuals who were sexually compatible with the family system."

49. One finds a very similar definition in the following extract, originally published in Japanese: "The productions of truth cannot be dissociated from power mechanisms, both because these mechanisms of power make them possible and encourages them and because these productions of truth have effects which tie us, which attach us" (*DE*, 3: 404).

50. The idea of a "political economy" clearly refers to the preface of *A Contribution to the Critique of Political Economy* (Moscow: Progress Publishers, 1970), 19. See also the following extract: "There are effects of truth which a society like the Western society—now one can say world society—produces at every moment" (*DE*, 3: 404).

51. This expression is probably an ironical allusion to Schopenhauer, who in "The Supplements to the First Book" of *The World as Will and Representation* (New York: Dover, 1966), 2: 160, describes "man's need for metaphysics."

52. This lack is coherent, given the absence in Foucault's thought of the concepts of the will to power and the Dionysian.

53. The idea that Foucault had a pragmatic understanding of truth is briefly explored by Richard Rorty (in reference to Dewey) in an article entitled "Method, Social Science, and Social Hope," in *Consequences of Pragmatism* (Minneapolis: University of Minnesota Press, 1982), esp. "Ungrounded Hope: Dewey Versus Foucault," §§4, 203–8.

54. William James, *Pragmatism* (New York: Longman Green, 1928), 58.

55. Ibid., 201 (my italics).

56. For his thesis, extremely close to Foucault's, see *The Meaning of Truth* (Cambridge, Mass.: Harvard University Press, 1975), esp. 222–23.

57. James, *Pragmatism*, 202.

58. Ibid., 218 (my italics).

59. Ibid., 220–21: "It is a case of the stock rationalist trick of treating the name of a concrete phenomenal reality as an independent prior entity, and placing it behind the reality as its explanation. . . . In the case of 'wealth' we all see the fallacy. We know that wealth is but a name for concrete processes that certain men's lives play a part in, and not a natural excellence found in Rockefeller and Carnegie, but not in the rest of us."

60. William James, *The Will to Believe* (New York: Dover, 1956), 9.

61. James, *Pragmatism*, 58: "Ideas . . . become true just in so far as they help us to get into satisfactory relation with other parts of our experience. . . . Any an idea upon which we can ride, so to speak; any an idea that will carry us prosperously from any one part, linking things satisfactorily, working securely, simplifying, saving labour; is true for just so much, true in so far forth, true *instrumentally*."

62. Ibid., 216: "Our theory must mediate between all previous truth is and certain new experiences." On the same question, see, David Lapoujade, *William James: empirisme et pragmatisme* (Paris: PUF, 1997), esp. 50 ff.

63. Although it might be argued, of course, that the criteria for such an objective definition, such as "a satisfying relationship," are themselves dubious.

64. Accusations of nihilism have been made, notably, by José G. Merquior, *Michel Foucault, le nihilisme de la chaire* (Paris: PUF, 1986). This is equally (in part) the critique formulated by Charles Taylor, in "Foucault on Freedom and Truth," in *Foucault: A Critical Reader*, 69–102. For a defense of Foucault's conception of value, see Béatrice Han, "Nietzsche and Foucault on Style: The Limits of the Aesthetic Paradigm," in *Nietzsche, Postmodernismus, und was nach ihhen kommt*, ed. Endre Kiss and Uschi Nussbaumer-Benz (Cuxhaven, Ger.: Dartford-Junghans, 2000).

65. "Table ronde de 20 mai 1978," in *L'impossible prison*, 47–48.

66. The four archaeological domains are the formation of objects, the enunciative function, the formation of concepts, and the formation of strategies. See *AK*, pt. 2, §§2–6.

67. The first indicates the necessity of taking into account within the analysis of the formation of discourses a play between two different scales, that of local "tactics" and that of "collective strategies." The second insists on the necessity of understanding the signification of discourses not as fixed and autonomous, but through their function and their own particular effects of power.

68. "Critique et *Aufklärung*," 48.

69. Ibid.

70. The text gives further examples.

71. See equally page 35, which states that the "tortured body is first inscribed in the legal ceremonial that must produce, open for all to see, the truth of the crime."

72. Or, if not nonpolitical, at least less political.

73. Essentially in chapter 2 of *HS*, "Method." One can find similar analyses in "Two Lectures," *PK*, lecture 2, 92 ff., and (to mention two others) in "Power and Strategies," in *PK*; and *DE*, 3: 423 ff.

74. This is a point that Charles Taylor criticizes in "Foucault on Freedom and Truth," in *Foucault: A Critical Reader*.

75. The examples given are, as we have seen, the university, the army, and the media. One can find an analysis of the functioning of the university in "A Conversation with MF," interview by J. K. Simon, *Partisan Review* 38, no. 2 (April–June 1971): 192–201; and also in "Rituals of Exclusion," in *FL*.

76. See also *DE*, 3: 407: "By truth, I do not mean a sort of general norm, a series of

propositions. I mean by truth *the collection of procedures which allows in every moment and every individual to make statements which will be considered true*" (my italics).

77. This confusion could be connected to the fact that the discursive regime and the regime of truth have both, in different places, been identified with the *épistémè*.

79. Several commentators have noted this point, mostly by insisting on the difficulties created by Foucault's understanding at the political level. See, for example, Nancy Fraser, "Foucault on Modern Power: Empirical Insights and Normative Confusions," *Praxis International* (1981–82): 272–87; Mark Philp, "Foucault on Power: A Problem in Radical Translation," *Political Theory*, no. 11 (1983): 29–52; Jeffrey Minson, "Strategies for Socialists? Foucault's Conception of Power," in *Towards a Critique of Foucault*, 106–48; Paul Patton, "Taylor and Foucault on Power and Freedom," *Political Studies*, no. 37 (1989): 260–76.

79. This is one of the criticisms that Jürgen Habermas addresses to Foucault, however briefly, in *The Philosophical Discourse of Modernity* (Cambridge, Eng.: Polity, 1987), chap. 9, "The Critique of Reason as an Unmasking of the Human Sciences: Michel Foucault."

80. "Critique et *Aufklärung*," 48.

81. Ibid.

82. Ibid.

83. The question of essentialism is discussed in an article by Gary Wickham, "Power and Power Analysis: Beyond Foucault?" in *Towards a Critique of Foucault*, 150–79.

84. Thus Foucault states that "what serves as a form common to the work I've done since *Madness and Civilization* is the notion of *problematization*, though I had not yet sufficiently isolated this notion" (*FL*, 295).

Introduction to Part III

1. A total of five volumes are projected there: *The Flesh and the Body, The Children's Crusade, The Wife, the Mother, and the Hysteric, The Perverse*, and *Populations and Races*.

2. Genealogy is mentioned from the beginning of the introduction of *The Use of Pleasure*.

3. Cf. *UP*, 5: genealogy is meant to "analyze the practices by which individuals were led to focus their attention on themselves."

4. See, for example, page 60: "The obligation to confess . . . is so deeply ingrained in us, that we no longer perceive it as the effect of a power that constrains us; on the contrary, it seems to us that truth, lodged in our most secret nature, 'demands' only to surface."

5. This is a constant preoccupation for Foucault. See, for example, "Politics and Reason," in *PPC*; the interview by Daniel Trombadori in *DE*, vol. 4; "Subjectivité et verité," in *DE*, 4: 213; the introduction to *The Use of Pleasure*; the preface to the *History of Sexuality*, in *F*; "Foucault," in *DE*, 4: 632–36; "The Return of Morality," in *PPC*.

6. Darmouth lectures (Autumn 1980), *Political Theory* (May 1993): 223.

er 5: Truth and the Constitution of the Self

1. The passage is the following: "The analysis of discursive practices made it possible to trace the formation of disciplines [*savoirs*] while escaping the dilemma of science versus ideology. And the analysis of power relations and their technologies made it possible to view them as open strategies, while escaping the alternative of a power conceived of as domination or exposed as a simulacrum" (*UP*, 4–5).

2. The position of the two commas—"an 'experience' came to be constituted in modern Western societies, an experience that caused individuals to recognize themselves as subjects of a 'sexuality,' which was accessible"—indicates that the antecedent of the relative pronoun is experience itself, not sexuality.

3. The theme of "self-consciousness" had already been introduced by the idea that subjectivity rests on the "organization of a self-consciousness" (*PPC*, 253).

4. The preface to *The Phenomenology of Spirit* (trans. A. V. Millar [Oxford: Oxford University Press, 1977]) carries the subtitle "On Scientific Cognition." Hegel gives a first analysis of the idea of experience in the introduction, notably in the well-known passage of paragraph 86: "This *dialectical* movement which consciousness exercises on itself and which affects both its knowledge and its object, is precisely what is called *experience* [*Erfahrung*]" (55).

5. Thus, Foucault always insists on the idea that individuals "were led to," or "are given to," or "had been brought to" recognize themselves as "sexual subjects."

6. Darmouth lectures (Autumn 1980), *Political Theory* (May 1993): 22.

7. Immanuel Kant, *Groundwork of the Metaphysics of Morals*, trans. Henry J. Paton (London: Routledge, 1991), 63–65.

8. Thus, having "set aside" actions "contrary to duty" and those which "accord with duty, yet for which men have no immediate inclination" (ibid., 63), Kant concludes his analysis of those for whom there exists an "immediate inclination": "Such an action of this kind, however right and however amiable it may be, has still no genuinely moral worth . . . for its maxim lacks moral content, namely, the performance of such actions, not from inclination, but from duty" (64).

9. Foucault also shares with Kant the idea that moral behavior presupposes a rational conception of action (the "reflective form," the "reflective practice"), which excludes from the moral field any determination by sensible inclinations.

10. "An action done from duty has its moral worth, not in the purpose to be attained by it, but in the maxim according which it is decided upon. . . . Duty is the necessity to act out of reverence for the law" (Kant, *Groundwork of the Metaphysics of Morals*, 65–66).

11. As is pointed out by Julia Annas (*An Introduction to Plato's Republic* [Oxford: Oxford University Press, 1981], chap. 3), those who emphasize the act understand the virtuous action by referring it to a set of preestablished prescriptions, while those who emphasize the agent, on the contrary, attach little importance to "duty" and define virtue itself from the conduct that a virtuous man adopts.

12. Aristotle, *Nicomachean Ethics*, trans. J. A. K. Thomson (Harmondsworth, Eng.: Penguin, 1976), 94 (2.2.1104a ff.).

13. See also *Nicomachean Ethics* 5.9.1134a; 6.13.1144a.

14. In the sense that to be virtuous an action cannot be unreflective, and needs a "deliberation." On *proairesis*, see *Nicomachean Ethics* 1112 ff.

15. Husserlian thought, at least as it was understood by Foucault. See "Critical Theory/Intellectual History," in *PPC*.

16. Jean-Paul Sartre, "The Humanism of Existentialism," in *Essays in Existentialism*, ed. Wade Baskin (New York: Citadel Press, 1993).

17. Hegel, preface to *Phenomenology of Spirit*, 14 (my italics).

18. Christian Jambet, "The Constitution of the Subject and Spiritual Practice," in *Michel Foucault, Philosopher*, ed. Thomas G. Armstrong (Hemel Hampstead, Eng.: Harvester Wheatsheaf, 1992).

19. Georg Wilhelm Friedrich Hegel, *Reason in History*, trans. H. B. Nisbet (Cambridge, Eng.: Cambridge University Press, 1975), 45. It could be objected that Hegel quotes Solomon's saying precisely to indicate that the movement of the Spirit is not a "self-repetition"; but it remains, nonetheless, that the different stages of the process of the determination of the Spirit only derive their meaning from their to inscription in the dialectical movement inside which they can never, by definition, constitute a radical beginning.

20. Martin Heidegger, *Being and Time*, trans. John Macquarrie and Edward Robinson (Oxford: Basil Blackwell, 1995), 32, §4.

21. There are many other similar passages; for example, the following at the beginning of the conclusion of *The Use of Pleasure*: "Thus, in the field of practices that they singled out for special attention (regimen, household management, the 'courting' of young men) and in the context of the discourses that tended to elaborate these practices, the Greeks *questioned themselves* about sexual behavior as an ethical problem. . . . Restricting oneself, as I have tried to do here, to the *prescriptive discourses by which they attempted to reflect on and regulate their sexual conduct*, these three focuses of problematization appear to have been the most important ones by far" (*UP*, 249 [my italics]).

22. One notes the presence of the theme of recognition.

23. "Truth, Power, Self: An Interview with Michel Foucault," in H. Martin, H. Grotman, and P. H. Hutton, *Technologies of the Self: A Seminar with M. Foucault* (Amherst: University of Massachusetts Press, 1988), 15.

24. Sartre, "The Humanism of Existentialism," 27.

25. Ibid., 28 (modified).

26. Translator's note: This is my translation of Foucault's revised answer in the French edition (*Michel Foucault, un parcours philosophique* [Paris: Gallimard, 1984], 331). For the original reply, see *MF*, 237.

27. Foucault's criticism of authenticity seems rather feeble, for two reasons. Firstly, Sartre completely admits the possibility of a multiplicity of forms to understand the relationship to the self—as the analyses of bad faith attest *a contrario* (*Being and Nothingness: A Phenomenological Essay on Ontology*, trans. Hazel Barnes [London: Routledge, 1989],

chap. 2.1–3). Secondly, what distinguishes authentic behavior from other forms of behavior is precisely the fact that it refuses that forms of self-relation should be prescribed by pregiven social roles. Thus there is no contradiction between authenticity and self creation. The "adequation to oneself," insofar as it is authentic, should not be understood as the integration of a fixed mode of being which would stop the dynamic of self-creation, but, on the contrary, as the very movement by which the self freely projects itself toward itself, while refusing any conformism and resolutely accepting the fact that it has no essence.

28. Sartre, "The Humanism of Existentialism," 49.

29. On this point, see Béatrice Han, "Nietzsche and the Masters of Truth: The Pre-Socratics and Christ," in *Heidegger, Authenticity, and Modernity: Essays in Honor of Hubert L. Dreyfus* (Cambridge, Mass.: MIT Press, 1999), vol. 1; and Han, "Nietzsche and Foucault on Style: The Limits of the Aesthetic Paradigm," in *Nietzsche, Postmodernismus, und was nach ihhen kommt*, ed. Endre Kiss and Uschi Nussbaumer-Benz (Cuxhaven, Ger.: Dartford-Junghans, 2000).

30. On this point see Gary Silverman, "Jean-Paul Sartre vs. Michel Foucault on Civilizational Study," *Philosophy and Social Criticism*, no. 5 (1978): 161–71.

31. The French word for "game" and "play" is the same: *jeu*.

32. One can find a rapid analysis of this notion in V. Gracev, "Foucault et les jeux de vérité," in *Michel Foucault: les jeux de vérité et du pouvoir* (Nancy: Presses Universitaire de Nancy, 1994), 41–50.

33. The passage goes on to suggest that there are other games of truth, "like those that can be found in institutions or practices of control."

34. "Technologies of the Self," in *Technologies of the Self,* 18 (modified).

35. "Truth, Power, Self," 10.

36. The use of the passive mode ("was problematized") reinforces both the anonymity of problematizations and suggests that they have been imposed on subjects rather than invented by them.

37. Although Foucault's last interviews point in the direction of such wider conceptions, he died before he could address these issues.

38. This ambivalence was implicitly presupposed by Foucault's definition of subjectivation, given above, which understood it as "the process which results in the constitution of a subject, or more exactly of a subjectivity" (*PPC*, 253 [modified]). However, this affirmation, just like the old Pythian formula, is actually highly ambiguous, as this "process" could just as well refer to the active problematization/recognition of the subject by himself as to the history of the objective conditions, which can either define internally the circumstances in which recognition occurs by influencing the understanding of truth itself, or exert an external influence on the subject, for example by taking his body as point of application, as in the case of disciplinary practices.

Chapter 6: The "History of Subjectivity"

1. "L'herméneutique du sujet," *Concordia: Revue internationale de philosophie*, no. 12 (1980): 50.

2. Ibid., 48.

3. Ibid., 64.

4. Ibid., 65.

5. Ibid., 50.

6. Ibid., 59.

7. Ibid., 46.

8. "Technologies of the Self," in H. Martin, H. Grotman, and P. H. Hutton, *Technologies of the Self: A Seminar with M. Foucault* (Amherst: University of Massachusetts Press, 1988), 35 (my italics).

9. "L'herméneutique du sujet," 46.

10. Ibid.

11. "Technologies of the Self," 35.

12. "L'herméneutique du sujet," 46.

13. Ibid., 67.

14. "Technologies of the Self," 35.

15. Darmouth lectures (Autumn 1980), *Political Theory* (May 1993): 203.

16. "L'herméneutique du sujet," 60.

17. "Technologies of the Self," 35.

18. Pierre Hadot, "Réflections sur la notion de culture de soi," in *Michel Foucault, philosophe* (Paris: Seuil, 1989), 267.

19. In an article entitled "Ethics as Aesthetics: Foucault, the History of Ethics, and Ancient Thought" (in *The Cambridge Companion to Foucault*, ed. Gary Gutting [Cambridge, Eng.: Cambridge University Press, 1994], 115–40), Arnold Davidson compares in a similar fashion the position of Foucault to that of Pierre Hadot and Jean-Pierre Vernant.

20. "Technologies of the Self," 40.

21. Darmouth lectures, 211.

22. See also, *DE*, 3: 656; and "Sécurité, territoire, et population," *Annuaire du Collège de France*. In these, Foucault retraces the genesis of the "great economies of power" in the West. Also see *DP*, 126 ff., and *DE*, 2: 742.

23. Darmouth lectures, 223. One notes once again that it is the "history of knowledge" in general here that plays the role of the "privileged point of view." It is clearly impossible to understand the constitution of the self from a theory of the subject.

24. "Truth, Power, Self: An Interview with Michel Foucault," in H. Martin, H. Grotman, and P. H. Hutton, *Technologies of the Self: A Seminar with M. Foucault* (Amherst: University of Massachusetts Press, 1988), 15 (my italics).

25. "Technologies of the Self," 49.

26. The text continues as follows: ". . . in the 19th century, a certain knowledge

[*savoir*] of man, of individuality, of the normal or abnormal individual, within or out-side the rule, a knowledge which, in truth, was born from the social practices of control and surveillance. . . . This knowledge was not imposed on a subject of knowledge [*con-naissance*], was not proposed to him, neither was it impressed on him, but it *has given birth to an absolutely new type of subject*" (my italics).

27. See pp. 133–138.

28. This structure of inclusion is particularly clear in the following extract: "Not that sexuality cannot and should not—like madness, sickness, or criminality—be envisaged as a locus of experience, one which includes a domain of knowledge, a system of rules, a model for relations to the self. Indeed, the relative importance of the last element rec-ommends it as a diving thread for the very history of this experience and its formation" (ibid., 338).

29. A very interesting article by Rainer Schürmann ("Se constituer soi-même comme sujet anarchique," *Les études philosophiques* [October–December 1986]: 451–72) notes that "the concept of subjective self-constitution . . . is an invariant" (461). Nonetheless, Schürmann assimilates "subjectivation" and self-constitution (466), which does not appear to be justified, without articulating and analyzing the problem.

Conclusion

1. This is a reworked version of "On the Genealogy of Ethics."

2. A criticism that is not without problems, since, strictly speaking, it would only apply to pure logic.

3. This theme is developed by Hubert Dreyfus in *Being-in-the-World: A Commentary on Heidegger's "Sein und Zeit," Division 1* (Cambridge, Mass., MIT Press), 2 ff. One can also find an analysis of Heidegger's critique of Husserl in a book by J. Greisch, *Ontolo-gie et temporalitie: esquisse d'une interprétation intégrale de "Sein und Zeit"* (Paris: PUF, 1994), 44–61.

4. This theme is introduced in section 5 of *Being and Time*: "The understanding of Being belonging to Dasein develops or decays along with whatever kind of being Dasein may possess at the time" (Martin Heidegger, *Being and Time*, trans. John Macquarrie and Edward Robinson [Oxford: Basil Blackwell, 1995], 37); also in *Kant and the Problem of Metaphysics*: "We understand Being yet we lack the concept," which insists on the ante-predicative nature of the preontological: "The being of Being, which is understood pre-conceptually in its full breadth, constancy and indeterminacy is given as something com-pletely beyond question" (Heidegger, *Kant and the Problem of Metaphysics*, trans. R. Taft [Bloomington: Indiana University Press, 1997], 155). The same idea is taken up in "On the Essence of Ground," where Heidegger states that any questioning already presupposes an "understanding of Being that guides and illuminates in advance all comportment towards beings," a nonthematized comprehension that "has not yet been brought to a concept" and which one can name "pre-ontological understanding or ontological in the

broadest sense" (in *Pathmarks*, ed. Will McNeil [Cambridge, Eng.: Cambridge University Press, 1998], 104).

5. See, for example, section 31 of *Being and Time*, where "understanding" (*Verstehen*) is defined in nonepistemologically and defined not as a form of knowledge, but as the second existential structure (along with mood and "discourse" [*Rede*]): "The disclosedness of understanding, as the disclosedness of the for-the-sake-of-which and of significance equiprimordially, pertains to the entirety of Being-in-the-World" (182). The following paragraph shows, in the same spirit, how any behavior presupposes a nonreflective and antipredicative interpretation (*Auslegung*), itself rooted within comprehension. However, most importantly, the fundamentally projective dimension attributed by Heidegger to preontological comprehension has no equivalent in Foucault.

6. Ibid., 32.

7. Ibid.

8. Page 7 had already expressed the very similar idea that "being is historically constituted . . . as something that can and must be thought."

9. Martin Heidegger, *Nietzsche*, trans. David F. Krell (San Francisco: Harper and Row, 1987), 4: 218; quoted by Michel Haar in *Heidegger et l'essence de l'homme* (Paris: Jérôme Millon, 1990), 121.

10. See, for example, *Being and Time*, §5: "To be sure, its ownmost being is such that it has an understanding of that being, and already maintains itself in each case as if its being has been interpreted in some manner." Nonetheless, this understanding cannot be assimilated to a reflective elaboration. See also *Kant and the Problem of Metaphysics* (159): "Man is a being in the midst of beings in such a way that for man that being which he is himself and that being which he is not are always already manifest."

11. This point is analyzed by Michel Haar in "La pensée de l'être et l'éclipse du moi," in *La fracture de l'histoire* (Grenoble: Jérôme Millon, 1994), notably 50 ff.

12. This major restriction is probably one of the strongest reasons to reject the analogy. Foucault's early antihumanism is, as we saw, quite close to Heidegger's, but his final insistence on the subject seems difficult to conciliate with the later Heidegger's shift from *Dasein* to Being.

13. Hubert L. Dreyfus, "On the Ordering of Things," in *Michel Foucault, Philosopher*, ed. Thomas G. Armstrong (Hemel Hampstead, Eng.: Harvester Wheatsheaf, 1992), 81 ff.

14. From this perspective, one may think of the Heideggerian critique of the "Four Theses on Being," formulated in section 4 of the *Basic Problems of Phenomenology*, trans. A. Hofstadter (Bloomington: Indiana University Press, 1982).

15. See, for example, Heidegger's introduction to "What Is Metaphysics?" trans. Walter Kaufmann, in *Pathmarks*, 284; or his "Letter on Humanism," trans. F. A. Capuzzi, in *Pathmarks*, 239–76.

16. Ibid., 311. Obviously, the idea of an hermeneutic can only make sense provided that the latter is understood independently of its original historical signification as an exegesis searching for the hidden or vanished meaning of a specific corpus of texts—a

conception of hermeneutics that Foucault himself rejected from the start by criticizing the "monotonous repetition [*moutonnement*] of commentaries."

17. This thematic of the "hermeneutic Circle" is laid out in section 32 of *Being and Time*. But the theme appears from the third part of section 7, where Heidegger, while distinguishing the three principal meanings of the word, is careful to move away from the "derivative" epistemological definition that understands it as a "methodology of those human sciences which are historiological in character," an allusion to Dilthey.

18. Traced, for example, in Martin Heidegger, "The Age of the World Picture," in *The Question Concerning Technology and Other Essays*, trans. William Lovitt (New York: Harper and Row, 1977); but above all in "Nihilism as Determined by the History of Being," in *Nietzsche*, 4: 197–252.

19. The idea of the closeness of the two chronologies has been examined principally by Samuel Ijsseling, in "Foucault with Heidegger," *Man and World*, no. 19: 413–24. The relationship between Foucault and Heidegger has equally been examined by Aaron Kelkel: "La fin de l'homme et le destin de la pensée," *Man and World*, no. 18 (1985): 3–37. Nonetheless, this second article takes as point of departure essentially the question of anthropology and humanism, and is above all centered on Heidegger.

20. Heidegger, "Age of the World Picture," 123. The rest of the text is just as explicit, and indirectly insists on the institutionalization of truth: "The highest knowledge and teaching is theology as the interpretation of the divine word of revelation, which is set down in scripture and proclaimed by the Church. Here, to know is not to seek out; rather it is to understand rightly the authoritative word and the *authorities* proclaiming it" (my italics).

21. This is a theme that has particularly been analyzed by Hubert Dreyfus, in "On the Ordering of Things: Being and Power in Heidegger and Foucault," in *Michel Foucault, Philosopher*.

22. "L'herméneutique du sujet," *Concordia: Revue internationale de philosophie*, no. 12 (1980): 64 (my italics).

23. Thus, Foucault indicates that power cannot be defined merely from its "institutionalized forms," and most notably not from an analysis of the State: "It is certain that in contemporary societies the State is not simply one of the forms or specific situations of the exercise of power—even if it is the most important—but that in a certain way all other forms of power relation must refer to it. *But this is not because they are derived from it*; it is rather because power relations have come more and more under State control" (*MF*, 224 [my italics]).

24. See Chapter 3.

25. One can find an analysis of these two understandings of truth in, for example, "The Essence of Truth," in *Pathmarks*; or in *What Is a Thing?* trans. W. B. Barton, Jr., and Vera Deutsch (Chicago: Henry Regnary, 1967).

26. Martin Heidegger, "The Turning," in *Question Concerning Technology*, 37.

27. See p. 189.

28. See also *MF*, 237.

Index

In this index an "f" after a number indicates a separate reference on the next page, and an "ff" indicates separate references on the next two pages. A continuous discussion over two or more pages in indicated by a span of page numbers, e.g., "57–59." Passim is used for a cluster of references in close but not consecutive sequence.

Atopia: Philosophy, Political Theory, Aesthetics

Béatrice Han, *Foucault's Critical Project: Between the Transcendental and the Historical*

Gregg M. Horowitz, *Sustaining Loss: Art and Mournful Life*

Robert Gooding-Williams, *Zarathustra's Dionysian Modernism*

Denise Riley, *The Words of Selves: Identification, Solidarity, Irony*

James Swenson, *On Jean-Jacques Rousseau: Considered as One of the First Authors of the Revolution*

dad, age 93 and mom, age 80

Barcelona, Spain

Pere Noel, my adopt father, Godfather, and Uncle

friend Renee and me, MBA garduate

THIRTY-FIVE YEARS OLD TO FORTY-FIVE YEARS OLD

Through Tribulations Come Peace and Joy—If you weather the storm

On the last ownerships transition, I was still the Met Lab Supervisor, and I had three technicians reporting directly to me. Within a year, the company started to lose production and began to lay off employees. During that time I lost my supervisory title, but I was doing the same exact job with more responsibilities. I firmly believe that the president of the division made a terrible mistake, which he caught when it was almost too late. I had the nerve to bring that to his attention in an employees meeting. He did, outside of the meeting, admit that he made the mistake. What was it? The company was sold because the previous administrators could not manage well and were really managing with mediocrity. The president still left them in control even after purchasing the company from the previous owners. When he realized that he made a disastrous mistake, he had to remove the general manager and a few of his "disciples." Within the first year, I had a new manager and a supervisor, who I'll name Bob. Bob was a great guy, so it did not bother me to have him as a boss. He knew that I was the best metallographer in the industry, so he treated me as such. We developed a great relationship, and as of today, we remain friends. I was always an exempt salary employee since my first year in the company. There a number of employees who were also exempt, which comprised of all the supervisors, the foremen, and the Level III's. The new management changed everyone to a non-exempt salary status but me. Those individuals were able to keep their salary intact and were getting paid for overtime, but not me. I honestly worked my *derrière* off for those guys. It means, I worked ten to twelve hours weekdays, most Saturdays and Sundays, and did not get paid a cent more. That was not right. Maybe my status was not changed for the Affirmative Action Program report (AAP), because I was the only Haitian in the company at that time. Please note: this is simply an assumption.

My lack of formal education was being used to hinder my advancement. Even though there were a number of people who did not have a college degree, I was the only one that was picked on. During that time I was dealing with some tough times, even when my mother was at home for seven months to help us. Every day was like hell; nevertheless, I dealt with it because I knew that we were going to be fine after we had the baby. How did I break the news to her? Well, when the day to tell her came I invited Max, a good friend of mine and Joey's godfather, who was also a licensed physician, and another good friend of mine, Pastor Mirbel, to come over for the breaking news. I asked my mom to take Joey into his bedroom, and Kettline was sitting in a rocking chair. The atmosphere was very tense, I didn't know what to expect because Kettline had already been through a lot. As I also mentioned, six months after we got married her grandfather died. Six months after the death of grandpa, her biological father died. That meant only her grandmother was left, who was the only woman she knew that was left in her life, now how do I tell her that her grandmother had passed also? I took a deep breath and I said, "Keke, we have bad news." She said "What happened?" I said, "I'm afraid we have something to tell you and it doesn't look good." Her response was, "Please don't tell me my mom is dead." I said, 'Yes,' she passed. She lost it. Honestly, I felt so relieved. Then Max took over. We both had and still have so much respect for Max. So it was not a bad thing to bring him home because I knew Kettline would listen to him. So after Max managed to restore order, after a while, her first question was, "Where is Joey?" I said, "He is with my mom." Then I asked my mom to bring Joey, which was a great consolation to Kettline. Max explained to her why I could not tell her. She agreed, but she told me she would appreciate it if I took time to go to Haiti for grandma's funeral. I also regret that I did not go. We moved on, but we both were so depressed. Thank God that my mom was around, so we managed through good days and bad days to stay alive. During that time, I was also going through some tough times at work but I still managed to have fun with Kettline and Joey. There was a time, I would say, a little bit past two months, my mom suspected that Kettline and I were pretty much aroused. On doctor's order, we were not to have any sexual relations until the baby is born. This is to say that we were going through one year without intercourse. Mom had a message for us: "Guys, listen, you need to wait for three months or more before you could be sexually active, because Kettline's body needs this time to get back to normal. Any sexual contact can cause some types of abnormal female problems." We laughed at her, but we took her advice seriously. I told Kettline that the reason why my mom told us that was for her not to extend her stay, in case Kettline gets pregnant while Mom is in Ohio. In May of 1987, Kettline, Joey, and I were on our way to New York for the college graduation of my brother Paul. For the first time in the seven years that we had been going to and from New York, I drove for only an hour from Painesville, and Kettline drove the rest of the trip. I was so sick that I sat in the backseat throughout the trip.

In the middle of June Kettline started feeling more depressed; I didn't give it too much thought because I thought it was the after-birth effects. To our big surprise, she went to see our family doctor for depression. The doctor asked her to see an obstetrician immediately. Guess what? She was already a month and a half pregnant. We could not believe that because it took a lot of fertility treatment before she got pregnant with Joey, and now, just overnight, she gets pregnant with Ricky. I was so glum that a friend of mine, Pastor McVicker, took me out to play golf. In the third hole, he told me we should call it quits, because he felt that I could not play. I am pretty sure he said to himself, he is not worth the time. So he asked that we finish the game at another time. Our glum situation was not because we were not happy to have the children so close, but the fact that Kéké had already been through so much during the first pregnancy and the death of her Grandma. As a matter of fact, we did go through the same thing again. Even though she was to move out of the house only to go to the clinic or to the hospital, she had no choice but to travel to Haiti to request an American visa for her biological mom to come live with us during the pregnancy. She went there, met with the American Consulate, and applied for a two-week visa for her. Although it was always very difficult for somebody who did not have a healthy bank account, or governmental backups, to be granted a visa, Kettline's mom got her visa with no sweat. While Kettline was in Haiti she started bleeding, which forced her to fly back to the United States the next day. So I met with them in Miami to bring them back to Painesville safely. The following day after her arrival, I took her to her to see her doctor who immediately sent her to the hospital for a procedure. From that point, the difference between the two pregnancies was that Kettline was hospitalized for four days. Without going further, at the end we were blessed with our second son. He, Richard Philippe (Ricky), was born on March 1, 1988.

A month or two after Ricky's birth, something happened which pushed me to pursue a formal American education with a strong drive. The manager of my department had five employees, including myself, who reported to him directly. During the performance review period, the manager gave a 5 to 7 percent raise to the other four employees and he gave me a 2 percent raise. Ironically, I had an excellent review. I did not have the same raise as the other guys simply because I dressed with expensive clothes and I drove a nicer and better car than them, including the manager. That meant I did not need money. Those were the words of the manager to me. I knew the other ones got the higher raise because the Supervisor himself told me prior to getting my review that I was to receive a big raise since I was the last person to be reviewed. So, I was expected to receive the same raise or better, because I was the best that they ever had. It did not happen. The band continued to play on. Another time, I was performing a metallographic analysis on a specimen for "Hot Tear." A brief explanation of metallography: it is the science that studies physical properties, structures, and components of metals and/ or alloys, typically using microscopy. Microscopy is the technical field of using microscopes to view samples or objects that are not within the resolution rage of the normal eye. There are three common types of microscopy: Optical, Electron, and Scanning Probe Microscopy. I have used most optical microscopes, from the oldest to the newest. I was privileged to use one of the first long-arm microscopes, Metallograph, made by Busch and Lomb. I have also, later, used a new design digital microscope with a charge-coupled device (CCD) camera to examine samples and images shown directly on a computer screen without the need of expensive optics such as eyepieces. These machines can help to perform examination of specimen at a magnification of 2000X, and even higher. I don't mean to brag, but I was one of the top metallographers in the aircraft engine parts industry.

During the examination process, I found a defect that was somewhat unusual and I was not able to identify it. I called the engineer who requested the job to help define the defect; the engineer was a metallurgical degreed engineer. He could not define it. So I called the manager of the department, who also had a metallurgical degree, he also could not help to define it. Then we called Dr. ChuChu, a PhD in metallurgy in the research and development department, for help. We spent hours and hours trying to identify the defect; even the "good doctor" could not identify the defect. As a way of coming to a decision, we called it "URO" (Unidentified Remained Object.) That was used against my ability to perform my duties. Why do I go to that extent to explain the precedent event?

Let me tell you why.

I came to realize that I was being used. I did not get paid like the other employees in my category. Remember that I said that I was not getting the same raise as my peers. I called the human resources director and sat a meeting to discuss my situation. The HR director came into our plant from the corporate office with her secretary. A meeting was held in the HR office in our plant. Present were the HR director, the department manager, the plant human resources representatives, the director secretary, and myself. The purpose of the meeting was to discuss a possible salary augmentation for me. Even though I was no longer the supervisor of the department, I was nevertheless responsible for the exact same tasks prior to the demotion. My new title was Metallurgical Laboratory Technician. So the director passed a survey ranks and pay rate for different technician levels: Level I, Level II, and Level III with their degree of abilities and responsibilities. Then she asked me, "How do you rate yourself?" I said, proudly, "Level III." The director turned to the manager and asked him the same question. The gentleman said, "Level II." So, the director told me that I got paid well and that my salary was within the range. I asked the manger, "If I am a Level II Tech, who is the Level III? Because the company has to have a Level

III to release metallurgical examination works that are requested by customers' specifications." Then I added, "As far I know, I am the only Tech / Metallographer that you have." The director asked him to explain why I was a Level II but not a Level III. He told her that I could not identify a foreign material defect, which was found in a "Micro" (Mounted specimen for microanalysis), and a Level III would have been able to do it. I stood up and said, with a loud and angry voice, "Sir, with all due respect, you are pathetic to say something like that. Don't you remember that Dr. ChuChu, the engineer responsible for the job, yourself, and I could not identify the foreign material in the Micro, so we called the defect, 'URO' (Unidentified Remained Object.) So, does that make all of us a Tech Level II or me only?" I waited for an answer, and I did not get one, then I said, "That is what I thought." Then I left the office, slammed the door shut, and went back to the lab. I could have got fired for insubordination. Why did I not get fired? I think I was right, but I did not have any reason to slam the door shut. God let bad things happen to good people so they can see his glory. He always has a purpose and a good plan for his children. The HR Director could clearly see that the manager was not too sure about what he was saying. Although my reaction was not Christian like and certainly not professional, she allowed them to do the right thing. Two weeks later I was called into the HR office for a meeting. Present were the plant manager, the HR Rep, my manager, and myself. The purpose of that meeting was to give me a fifteen-minute performance review, an awesome merit of increase, and a letter that said that I was a good and loyal employee, and that I did an impeccable job. *Praise to the Lord.*

On my next and formal review, I asked the manager why I could not get my title back—Met Lab Supervisor—which could have been a kind of promotion. My request was denied because of my lack of formal education. One of the reasons I left my job in Haïti while I was working for the American Embassy because I got promoted and they would not pay me the money that my prdecessor was making or even put me at the bottom of the range.

When I asked why, the response was that they were doing me a favor in giving me the opportunity to work for the U.S. government; because I barely spoke English, I did not have an American education, and I did not know the American culture. So, I had to make a decision. At that time I resigned my employment to come in the U.S.A to pursue an American education. Now, I faced another "mountain," which appeared to be higher than the one in Haïti. I asked myself, "Do I quit?" The answer was, "No, I can't." So, I made a different decision. I decided to go back to school full-time. Prior to beginning school, I told the manager that I knew that my going to school would not make any difference, because it was always going to be depends on who you know and who you work for. I also let him know that there were few employees who did not go to college and that were promoted to higher levels. His answer to me was, "You are on the tree, but you are on the wrong branch." I never really looked, nor asked, to find out what he meant by that.

In September 1988, I went back to school full-time. I took a few preparatory courses for the first six months, and then I moved into the real deal. In June of 1991, I graduated with an AAS (Associate in Applied Science) at Lakeland Community College. My manager was one of our graduation's guests. In May of 1993, I received a BS (Bachelor of Science degree at Myers University). Once again, my manager was there at the graduation ceremony. Shortly after my graduation, the supervisor of the department had found another job and gave his resignation. The position, once again, became available. In an effort to regain my title, I submitted my résumé for the job. I was supposed to have an interview, let's say on a Thursday morning at 10:30 a.m. Early on that morning I got a phone call from the HR office and found out that the job was going to be put on hold. Therefore, my interview was cancelled. Next thing I knew, another department supervisor, whom I will call Tom, was transferred to the Met Lab as Supervisor. Who was Tom? The Company had acquired a number of companies in the greater Cleveland areas during the years of 1985 to 1987. Tom was a longtime employee of one of the companies purchased. It happened that the active plant manager was previously the plant manager where Tom worked. Tom quit the other company because he was upset for a reason that will not be mentioned in the book. Through some connections he got hired as a process engineer in my plant. He worked for a few months and took some time off for personal reasons. Upon his return, he got transferred to my department as my boss. Please note: he was a gentleman who did not know a thing in metallurgy and certainly nothing in metallography. I liked the guy to begin with, not knowing if he were going to make my life difficult, I accepted him as my boss. Besides, I didn't have a choice. First thing he asked me to move out of my office so he could move in. Then, he began to micromanage me. Can you imagine someone who is totally ignorant of what you are doing and wants to micromanage you? Everything that I said or will say about my working experience ordeal is to make a point that one must endure great pains to receive great favors. To begin with, Tom asked me to tell him every day what I was doing, and he told me when to take my break and lunch; it got to a point where he also told me to tell him when I go to the toilet. I began to get upset, and "butt heads" with him. Since I wanted to pursue an advanced degree, I told him that I wanted to go back to school to get an MBA. He explained that the company was not going to pay, nor reimburse, me for the school's cost. I asked why. He told me that the company does not need an MBA to perform the job that I was doing. I said, I knew that and it could be clearly seen. Then I said I was going to get the MBA to be more diverse in the company. I went to the manager of the department and asked for the same thing. He, too, told me that the company would not pay for me to earn an MBA. At that time, I pointed the Affirmative Action Program (AAP) law to them, which clearly asks the employer to help their employees become more skilled and marketable, especially the minorities.

The manager could not resist my point, so they let me begin the MBA program. After a number of trials and humiliations, Tom wrote a note to all techs and copied the manager; in his note he requested that all technicians, which included me, to work mandatory every other weekend for three months. To explain how ridiculous the guy was, I used to work every Saturday and most of the Sundays after church. I found it so stupid for him to make such a request from me. I asked him why he was doing that. This is what I said exactly: "Why are you doing this to me? You 'damn well' know that I am here every weekend, without having been asked by you or anyone. And you also damn well know that I don't get paid for overtime. What is the matter with you?" He said to me, "Not only can I mandate you to work every other weekend for the next three months, I can also mandate you to work weekends the entire year." I told him that he could not. I thought that it was time to speak with the department's manager about the ordeal. Please keep in mind that those two were good friends and were playing golf every Saturday. I brought the issue to the department manager. He basically told me not pay attention to Tom because he was a "stubborn" fellow and at times he can be pretty frustrating. But the manager let me believe that he was going to talk to Tom.

No one ever came back to me with a solution. My misery had just begun. Tom began to criticize everything I did, and he started to monitor my work closely. We were having a problem with one of our orders; the parts were to be soaked in solutions mixed in the lab. That was one of the reasons that we were to work every Saturday: to wash the parts and blow-dry them after soaking. The test was experimental, because no one knew if the process worked or not. So one day, Tom was having a discussion with me about coming early to wash the parts. I told him that I was not going to be able to make it that particular Saturday. The other tech, who was a good friend of mine, volunteered to work in my place. Tom insisted that I was the one who should come. I told him that he did not know what we were doing and that he would not even know whether I work that Saturday or not, for a few reasons: One, no one knew if the process worked or not. Two, he especially did not know what we were doing and did not even know what kind of solution that was used to soak the parts in. I also told him to take it easy because I could embarrass him badly. I let him know that he needed to understand that he would not know if I were to mess him up. He told me that if I did anything wrong and that he caught it, he would fire me on the spot. I asked him if it was a threat. He said, no, it was a promise. Prior to that, I had brought many complaints to the HR representative and to the acting general manager. No one had done anything about it except telling me not to worry about Tom and that I was going to move up and I was not going to be reporting to him anymore. They even asked me to go apologize and make peace with him. I did. During the process, I told Tom that I liked him and that I wanted him to work with me. He told me that he will work with me his way. I told him that I accepted the condition, but I would appreciate if he could stop threatening me with his *"fire you"* and the *"mandatory"* stuff. He said, "I am not threatening you. I promise I will fire you." I replied to him, "I know you cannot fire me and you know you cannot fire me. So, let's no longer talk about it." Then I walked away. When I got home that evening, I explained the situation to my wife; she told me that was going too far and that I needed to document those threats and have them put on my personnel file. So I did. The same day I gave the "threats" documents to the HR rep, I got a phone call, from her, telling me that Almondo, (I change the name to protect the person identity) an HR guru at the mother company, wanted to see me concerning my complaints. I called Almondo and I set an appointment to meet with him. I met with him and we discussed the situation in his office and then we had lunch outside the plant. Nevertheless, Almondo took notes and told me to go ahead and he will be at my company in the afternoon.

At about six o'clock, the department manager paged me and asked me to come into one of the conference rooms. What happened was that Almondo had made a request to remove Tom from the Met Lab and to have me report directly to the manager. At the time I got paged I was outside of the plant talking to another employee. I did not want to leave the plant because I knew Almondo was coming over, and I habitually worked long hours. After the meeting was over, Almondo wanted to let me know what had happened and wanted to tell me in front of the staff. Prior to have me page, he asked the manager if he thought that I was in the plant. The manager told him that, "Knowing Joel, he is still in the plant." As I was going through the front door to go to the conference room, Tom was going out. I said "Hi" to him and he responded as if he were on another planet. What I did not know was that the dude had just been demoted. I thanked Almondo and, for diplomatic reasons, I thanked the HR representative and the manager as well. It was a big relief. The next day I moved back into my old office. From there I would become a good friend of Almondo. I think that God let all these things happen so I could write this book to help and teach others to "stay put and let God." All the time, God is good! He allows bad things to happen to us so our purposes can be fulfilled.

I don't think what happened to me during those times has anything to do with the company, past or present owners, nor do I blame the company for the ordeals and the embarrassments that did and will come up during the course of my working life. Now, when I weigh or balance what the company did to and for me, I have much to be grateful and thankful for than to have any resentment against it. I have acquired three college degrees and I paid only for books. The company paid in full for all my tuitions and other related professional educations. I often tell everyone, "Your education is the only thing that you own and the only thing you take to with you to your grave." Yes, I am grateful and thankful to the company.

As I mentioned earlier, I have always had, and still do have, a habit of working most Saturdays and some Sundays if I am in town. Take a look at the following incident: One Saturday, around July 1995, I had two technicians working in the Metal-lurgical Lab. A friend of mine, Michelle and her husband from Conneaut, Ohio, invited us (Kettline and me) over for a cook-out. Before going there, I went first to the job to check on the tech that was working in the morning. I was planning to go back and check on the second shift guys. After the cookout, I went to the job at 9:30 p.m. When I got there, I decided to park my car right in front of the building, where all the executives and other important people always park, instead of in the employees park-ing areas. I deliberately parked my car sideways, meaning I took two parking spaces. Then I proceeded to the front door, because at that time, I had the front door key. That decision could have cost me my life. The building is located right across from a post office. So anyone who was in the post office parking lot could clearly see my car. Five minutes later, after I entered the building, I was paged by a security guard; I picked up the page only to find out that the plant facility manager, who lived in Madison, Ohio had called the guard to find out if I were in the building. When he confirmed that I was, he asked the guard to tell me that the police department was looking for me. So I immediately called the manager. I asked him if it were true what I heard, because they had a habit of "pulling my chain," he said, "Yes, it is true." Then I asked him if he knew why the police were asking for me, he said, "No." He continued, "Buddy, I am not kidding with you." I paused for a few seconds, wondering why the police department would want to see me. I said to myself, *it is not possible; some-body is pulling my chain.* Everyone in the plant had a way of kid-ding with me. So I called the police department, someone from the station answered the phone, and I told that person that my name was Joel Esperance, and I work for that particular company. Then, I told the person that I heard the city police were looking for me, and to let them know I was at my workplace and that

I was available to answer their questions. The person on the other line, which I assumed was a police woman, replied: "Don't worry about it Joel, we know you are Haitian, thank you for the call." Then she hung up. I said to myself, *what the heck does my being Haitian have to do with me getting a phone call from the city police department, inquiring about me?* So I called the plant manager and I asked him what exactly the police wanted from me. He told me that a cop asked him if he knew someone by the name of Joel Esperance, and he said yes, he's Haitian. The cop asked, "Does he work for the company?" He said, "Yes." Third question, "Is Joel allowed to enter the building through the front door?" The facility manager said, "Yes, Joel is allowed to go to the front door, and he is one of the company's supervisors." All of this was because of the fact that the cop was parked across the street, saw me pull in the parking lot and enter the building through the front door. I imagine the police officer didn't see me, Joel Esperance, enter the building. He saw rather, a "black man" enter the front door. So he automatically ran a background check from my license plate number. So, he gets my name and now wonders what my right was? *Does the 'nigger' have the right to go in there through the front door?"* the white police officer probably thought.

In 1996, I talked to the General Manager about a career change; I asked him if I could be trained to work in the inventory control and product schedule. He gave me some non sense answers and a crazy assignment where I would come to work everyday at 6:30 in the morning to 7:30 to find parts that were missing through the process. I had done that for almost three months, nothing was done, and the manager did not even talk to me again so I stopped doing that. Meanwhile, the dude who was my manager got laid off, and I began to report to the quality control manager. Another friend of mine, who is probably still working for that company, became the acting general manager under Doctor Edison's supervision. Doctor Edison was a veteran in the company and the industry as well. I call my friend James for anonymity. I went to James and told him to help me move up in the organization. I even told him that I would make extra time to take courses and seminars that could have helped. He asked me to talk to Dr. Edison, which I did. Dr. Edison asked me to write an objective plan and to come back to see him so he could guide me through it. So, I did. I prepared the plan with the help of Dr. Sears, who was the dean of the MBA program at Baldwin Wallace College at that particular time; I had just begun my MBA program. The idea worked out perfectly because that was an assignment for the program. We were to create and develop a mastery program on a project or a goal that we wanted to obtain. With the help of Dr. Sears, I did my assignment with the desire to become a Production Control Account Manager in two years. In the following weeks, I forwarded the project (report) to Dr. Edison. He took a look at the plan, made some corrections, and gave me his blessing. I then submitted it to the vice president, acting manager, HR, and my direct boss. I would like to share the plan with you. In case you have a dream, a project, and/ or a goal that you would like to achieve, you may find this to be useful to you. Here is the "Mastery Plan."

"A spirit with a vision is a dream with a Mission" N. Peart
Personal Mastery Paper
Joel Esperance
2/17/97

I am presently working at XY&Z Company, as a Materials Control Lab Supervisor, a job that I have held for 16 years. My personal vision is to be qualified to assume the position of a Production Control Account Manager in two years (Approx. March 1999). My efforts to pursue this vision have currently led me to business graduate studies at BW.

- *What does this vision represent to me?*

- *What value and benefit that I will attain upon achieving this mission?*

1. *Self-image and Tangibles*
   Marketable
   Better career
   Satisfaction
   "Mucho dinero"

2. *Work and status*
   More Responsibilities
   Play Key Roles
   Perceived Differently

3. *Self-actualization*
   Excitement
   Commitment
   Fully Engaged
   Achievement
   Effectiveness

Skills required by my Organization to Attain This Goal are:

- *Knowledge of PC systems—Computer literate / Knowledge of plant operations / personalities and Communication skills*

Customer interfacing

Interplant relationships (Foremen, Operators)
- *Ability to plan, set priorities, obtain results in Production*
- *Ability to schedule and integrate a variety of operations necessary for Shipments, Transportation, and Supplies*

Shipments, transportation, and pick ups

- *Production and production control floor experience. (2 years min) Knowledge of cost accounting - System and work standards - How they relate to (1) earned standard hours (2) plus sales dollars (3) scrap control*

I have the determination and the patience to pursue this vision. My desire and my positive attitude will help tremendously in the process. I came in the United States in 1979 with this vision in mind, yet I did not take it seriously. Twenty years later, my dream will come true.

The above statement showed my strengths.

My weaknesses consist of:

Verbal communications:

- *People sometimes have difficulty understanding me at glance. I speak too quickly and my accent does me no good, although it is fascinating and lends style to my approach.*

Self-control:

- *I am an extremist. I find it difficult to be in the middle. When I set a goal, I usually do not stick with it.*

Adaptable:

- *I experience stress. I frequently worry that I might fail. Maybe I try too hard. I need to reduce my stress level. Mr. Richard Boyatzis provides some competence models for effective management performance, which I will use.*

Competencies that I need to develop and implement toward my personal vision, in the next two years, are as follows:

Verbal communication and Use of oral presentations Self-control in terms of discipline, Stamina and adaptability –

Action Plan to Develop These Competencies:

Verbal Communication and Use (Oral Presentation:

Starting in March, I will be working with a Speech Pathologist and Speech Therapist on a bimonthly basis. I will develop the ability to speak more intelligibly and precisely. I will assess this from my Therapist's feedback and from peers' evaluations. I am looking to complete this program in a year. (Completion date is approx. March 1998). I will ask one question in each course session and I will make a verbal presentation in each course, even if there are no such activities. This will help to reinforce my confidence with regard to public speaking. This process will be ongoing throughout two years.

Self-control in Terms of Discipline:

I will prioritize my daily activities by using the "to do" list in the Priority Management Organizer and stop procrastinating by sticking to my plan. Starting March 1st, I will read a business-oriented book or similar organizational literature for fifteen minutes each night. I will document the time that I start the book to the time I finish it. I will complete my papers and my presentations before the deadline for all courses in the next two years.

Stamina and Adaptability:

I work long but flexible hours and I find it hard to control my stress level. I have made an effort at coping with it. My action plan is starting in March; I will prioritize my daily working activities. I will perform one task at a time. I have taken a Priority Management course, and believe that I have not used the principles properly. I will commit myself to schedule time on the Plan Page for appointments and meetings, schedule time to sleep and routine activities. Work on my Activities Page to assign priorities and schedule time. Finally, I will schedule time for "B" activities and personal life. I will reduce my level of stress and be more organized by doing so.

By implementing this competency plan, I will feel more confident about myself professionally and I will be perceived differently by my peers. I will have better tools to balance and control my time to deal the three external environments: Family, works, and school, which have great potential to affect my life and mission. I will use these competencies to attain my goal. I will devote my time, talents, and resources to this mission.

Action Plan to Attain the Vision's Requirements

Knowledge of PC systems & Computer Literate:

The next two courses that I will be taking are Mgmt. Science1: Computer Models and Information Systems for Management. I will use two or more concepts or models in each course to fulfill these criteria. The timetable is June 1997.
Knowledge of Plant Operation / Personalities:

I will use two or more concepts or models in the Operation Analysis course toward the above requirement and I will speak to my Instructor about my vision and the criteria to attain it. Hopefully the professor will lead me in the right direction. The timetable to complete this step is: approx. February 1998

Ability to Plan, Set Priorities, Obtain Results in Production:

I will use two or more concepts or models in the Marketing & Marketing Inf. Systems course to help achieve the above step. I will also develop some techniques based on some of the theories in the course. If the content of this course is not sufficient, I will use my Self-control action plan toward the above requirements. The timetable is approx. November 1997

Ability to Schedule and integrate a Variety of Operations Necessary for Shipments, Transportation, Supplies; and Knowledge of Cost Accounting Systems and Work Standard:

The American Production and Inventory Control Society (APICS) is a much better tool for me to achieve the vision. I will join the organization and take the required courses for my certification. I will also participating in their monthly meeting to gain interface contact and confidence in speaking in public. Couple with this experience,

I will use two or more concepts in the following courses: Accounting & Finance Management, Financial Management, and Operation Analysis as a guide to write a plan for my company about production control and scheduling. The timetable is July 1998.

Then I will present the plan to my boss and the General Manager, I will explore the possibility of working for few hours each day in the Production Control Department to obtain Production Control

Floor Experience: The time table is September 1998 to start, complete in February 1999.

I will use systematic thinking throughout the duration of the action plans. I will stay focus and committed. I will conduct self-audits every 6 months to measure my progress and make adjustments if necessary. I will also solicit input from associates to confirm my evaluations.

Prepared by: Joel Esperance

After I submitted the plan to the executives, quite frankly, nothing happened for the first three months. Then the vice president of the organization asked me to quit the MBA program to get an APICS (Association of Purchasing and Inventory Control Schedule) to become a Certified Inventory Control Schedule Manager. I was about to do that, but a friend of mine, who will become my boss in the next couple of years, advised me not to quit the program. I am glad that I took his advice. Early in 1997, a new general manager was hired. I did not waste any time; I requested a meeting with him to talk about career advancement. He was not too receptive to my request. I came to realize that no one was going to help because I was the only metallographer (technician) they had and I was one of the best around. I kept pushing, because I was not going to let go. At one point, I was given a shot at a second shift superintendent position. I declined because I did not think that the job was parallel to my goal. I continued with my plan, and I sent an updated copy to everyone. We were in the middle of July and it was time for my annual review; I was excited. I can say that I was happy and thought I had a much better chance to grow. At that time, I had not one, but two degrees, I was liked by the President and vice President and the top HR Manager was in my corner. It's worth it to say, I knew my job and was good at it. The company was converted to land-based products from turbine/airfoils products. So we were making large parts, which was an overall challenge. The whole plant was to be renovated to accommodate the new products. I was also to change and update some of my equipment. After sampling the small parts for metallurgical examination, we were practically using a mount press to embed them in epoxy or Bakelite. At that time, we used one and a half or a two-inch diameter micro frame and we were to move to "Monster Micros", which were three and a half diameter wide and one and a half inch high. I was so busy; I had to find a photographic place and a place to "Blanchard grind" the monster micros before we could polish them. I managed to reduce a five-day turnaround time from both places, to a next-day delivery, and sometimes the same day. I was happy that for once, things were going good for me and that my new boss was a savior. I thought he was a godsend who came to rescue me from tough times. Psalms 34:19 "A righteous man may have many troubles, but the Lord delivers him from them all." *"Le Malheur atteint souvent le juste, mais l'Eternel l'en délivre toujours."*

Still, I was about to face another mountain and a very deceptive one. The above verse does not shield you from running against adversities and deceptions, but it let you know that your Lord will see you through them all. *"Just let go and let God."*

At the end of July, 1997, I met with my boss for an annual performance review. As always, I had an excellent review and a 10 percent raise. Then the boss dropped the bombshell. The so-called "savior" told me that starting Monday morning (I had the review on a Friday) there would be a posting in search of a Metallurgical Laboratory Supervisor. I asked him where I was going. He said that I was to continue to work in the lab and report to the new supervisor. I was stunned. I said, "Hey Boss, after working so hard and so much, that is all you have to say. You gave me an excellent review, which means that I am capable of doing the job, and besides, I am the only 'whatever' you want to call it that is in charge of the lab and who has been since the beginning." He was about to say something, I interrupted him and said, "I have not finished yet." I continued, "What you just did, meant that you washed your hands and wiped them on a dusty floor." This was a Creole proverb *(ou lave main ou epui ou souyel ater)*. What I meant was, he gave me a great and beautiful review and slapped my face with that news. I was very angry.

He said that he was not finished yet and that he was going to tell me that he had something good on his mind for me. I told him, "Baloney, you had nothing on your mind for me." And I told him that he was the last person in the company I thought that would ever treat me like that. Then, I told him that I had to leave because I had a meeting with the manager of the Blanchard Grinding place for a cost reduction.

Upon my return, I made it clear to the GM and HR Manager that I was going to bid on the job, and they better make sure that whoever gets the job knows the job well, and had the same or more seniority that I have.

Sometimes in the afternoon the GM called me in his office and apologized for the way I was told about the idea of bringing someone in the lab. He gave me a baloney excuse that the whole reason to hire a supervisor for the lab was the fact I wanted to move out of the lab for a more challenging position. So, they did not want that to happen without having someone to run the lab. I told him that it would have been better if I were told that there was an intention to hire someone to replace me in the event I found a job. And that someone would report to me for the time being. I also told him that I thought that I was through with those kinds of humiliations. Anyway, the GM promised me that they were not going along with the process anymore, and that I was going to remain in charge of the lab until a position became available to me. I accepted his apology but I lost interest in working for those kinds of "dudes." They just killed my spirit. I called Amondo and I asked for an appointment to talk to him. I met with him in the next couple weeks. I explained to him what happened to me in the company. He asked me if I would not mind working in the HR area. My response was, "I always wanted to work in HR. In fact, after what happened to me up there, I certainly would not like it to happen to someone else. And the best place for me to be, in order to stop that kind of nonsense, was in HR." Almondo told me that there was an opening in the HR department, and he could not promise that I was going to have it, but he suggested me to apply for the job. So I happily did. Two weeks after I interviewed, I got a phone call from the VP of the company, who asked me to come to see him. I went to his office and he gave me the best and the biggest news of my entire working life. I got the job. Unfortunately, they did not know what I was going through. I was asked by the VP not to tell anyone, including my manager, because no one knew yet. I called Almondo to thank him for his continuous help. He told me that he could not wait to have me as part of his group. Getting the job was like having someone taking a heavy load off my shoulder and throwing it in the river. I was praying for the days to pass quickly so that I could begin my new job.

Within two weeks, the VP told my manager about my transfer to the other plant. My manager asked the HR Manager to put a posting up for the Met Lab Supervisor. The HR Manager said to him, "What about Joel?" He asked the HR Manager if she did not hear that Joel was going to work for Almondo. The HR Manager said, "No. When did he bid on the job? And besides, there was not any HR job positions posted here. So, the HR Manager, Suzette, was furious, because she was pretty close to getting that job a few months before. To this day she does not feel comfortable with me; she thinks that I took her job. Anyway, the job was posted. Most people in the company kept asking what was going on. They asked me directly if I were going to get another job, or if I was going to be the official Lab Supervisor. I felt bad because I was not allowed to tell anyone. I had to ask for permission to talk to my closest friends and a few other managers. By the way, I was the only salaried employee that left the company in good terms and did not have a "going away" party. We had received a few applications for the job. I was the main interviewer as well as, of course, the HR Manager and my boss. We made an offer to a young, degreed metallurgical engineer, with two years of experience in metallography. I asked my manager for a release time. He told me that I was not going to leave until the new guy got trained. Ironically, the guy who was going to be my boss, needed five months of intensive training just to go by. Oh! By the way, I was his trainer.

Almondo was pushing to have me released. I was finally released on condition that I continued to train the guy for another three months, part-time. I am not kidding you, one day I met with the guy to help him with a "set up" and a hands-on practice. He said to me, "Joel, I think that I am going to resign from the position. I said, "Man. Take a hold of yourself, you have been through the bad weather already, things are getting better. One day, looking back, you will not believe that you wanted to quit." I talked to him and gave him some encouragement; I promised him that I was not going to let "My Lab" down. I loved the lab. I kept that baby cleaned at all times; it was the only place in the whole company that had the best housekeeping. The lab's floor was always clean and shined just like a supermarket floor. Sometimes, I referred the lab as my "supermarket." Two years after the gentleman got hired; he was still having difficulties in operating the lab efficiently. Why those things happened? Was it because I was not liked, not fit in the club, my accent, and my skin color? I don't want to think so. What I don't hesitate to say is this: I have tried, and I am still trying very hard, to not let these negative thoughts get bother me. However, I do believe that the prejudice is alive and well in this country.

As for an example that skin color is not the reason: In 1987, I had to attend a seminar at North Carolina University. The engineering secretary made arrangements for my trip, including car rental. She said that she had a big surprise for me. I asked her to tell me about it; she said, "I'll tell you this, 'All black guys love to drive big cars.'" I still did not get it. At the airport, I went to the car rental area, and yes, I got a big surprise. A long and brand

new Lincoln Continental was reserved for me. I took a few minutes to understand the mechanisms to operate the car.

Anyway, one afternoon, while driving around, I could not
find my way back to the university. I kept getting deeper in a few
secluded white folk neighborhoods. After a good half an hour
driving around, I could not get out of the residential areas and I
had a course starting soon, so I had to make a decision. I began to
look around for any individuals who might be wandering around
their front yards or anyone passing by. A few houses down the
block I was in, I spotted a gentleman, about forty-five or fifty,
raking leaves in his front yard. I slowed down and I turned toward
his driveway very slowly. I took a look in my review mirror, I saw
people that stepped out of their front yard facing the gentleman's
house. I was scared, but I could not stop the car nor turn around.
I pushed forth; the gentleman moved back as I was getting closer
to him. People, about three men and four ladies, all white, actually got out of their yards and moved in the street. I said a word of
prayer, and the worst part was that Joey was only a couple months
old. When I realized that the man was so scared, I stopped at a
distance of fifteen feet away from him. I got out of the car and
I left the door open just in case. I have always, and to this day,
wear a suit jacket when I am on a business trip. So that particular
day, I was professionally dressed with the exception of a tie. As
I got out of the car, I am not kidding you, the man held the rake
handle so tight that I believe if I were to move one step closer, he
would have broke the handle. I looked at him and I said, "Good
evening, sir." I did not give him a chance to answer, I continued,
"I am attending a seminar at North Carolina University, and I
am lost. Would you please tell me how to get out of here and
find my way to the university?" He paused for two seconds, and
asked me, "Where're you from?"

"Ohio." I responded.

He said, "No, what country you are from?"

I said, "Originally, I am from Haïti. Haïti, West Indies."

He smiled and waved at his neighbors, saying, "He is Haitian. He is from Haïti. He gets lost." Then he began to give me some directions. While he was trying to explain how to get out, he made a gesture like forget it. He told me, "You know, just follow me, I am going to take you there. It might be too confusing for you." Can you imagine, the man left what he was doing and hopped in his car and led me to the university. The same ignorance, as when I got to my job from the front door. The questions that were asked, "Do you have a Joel Esperance who works for you? Does he have the right to enter the building through the front door?" You remember also the answer, "Yes, and he is Haitian?" I could have given you more tangible histories to show that the racism in the country is very minor, but the ignorance is what is killing it. I firmly believe that instead of *racism* we have a problem of *fear:* fear of rejection and acceptance. I will tell about this in my next book.

FORTY-FIVE YEARS OLD TO FORTY-NINE YEARS

Life at Peak and Life at Rapid Descent

There are, in my opinion, five distinct stages in the workforce that employees experience, which can have a huge impact on their life. And there is, in my opinion, and maybe for all workers, one of the stages that is very detrimental to the life of any employee. I will cover all the stages and in particular the worst one. The stages are as follows:

Being hired–Being promoted–Being resigned–
Being retired–Being fired.

Work is a physical or mental effort or activity directed toward the production or accomplishment of something. Something that one is doing, making, or performing, especially as an occupation or undertaking; a duty or task that is usually done in exchange for money. Work is usually defined as a "job or employment."

A job is a regular activity performed in exchange for payment, especially as one's trade, occupation, or profession, or a position in which one is employed.

Employment is a contract between two parties, one being the employer and the other being the employee.

An employee is defined as: "A person in the service of another under any contract of hire, express or implied, oral or written, where the employer has the power or right to control and direct the employee in the material details of how the work is to be performed." (American Heritage Dictionary)

Let's talk about the stages:

1) Being hired: Looking for jobs can be very frustrating. Only about 5 percent of people obtain jobs through the "open" job market—consisting primarily of help-wanted ads on the Internet and in print publications. Twenty-four percent obtain jobs through contacting companies directly. Twenty-three percent obtain jobs through such means as employment agencies, college career-services offices and executive-search firms. Forty-eight percent, nearly half, obtain their jobs through referrals–word of mouth, which we call "Networking." *Source: U.S. Department of Labor, 2001. (www.quint-carees.com)*

My experience in human resources, somewhat, conquers the Department Labor survey about the 5 percent of jobseekers can obtain employment through ads posted on papers. I read from an article, from www.career-intelligence.com, about search tactics that 95 percent of jobseekers and human resources professionals use employee referrals, networking, and personal contacts to find jobs. I can understand why it is stated 95 percent in the article comparatively to the Department of Labors' survey: the 24 and 23 percents mentioned above are both products of Referrals/Networking. Everyone knows that the ratio between vacant position and candidates available is extremely high. There is no question about it. Anyone is delighted to get hired. Especially if that someone were looking for a while, as most people do. If anyone who was unemployed or gets out of school gets a job with no sweat, that person should consider herself or himself very blessed. Qualified or not, skilled or not, educated or not, it is not that easy to get jobs. I have to make it clear that I am talking on a job-exempt level, $45,000/$50,000 and up. In the early chapters, I explained how thrilled I was when I got my first job as a messenger, and I felt the same and even more ecstatic when got my jobs in NY and OH. I don't have to elaborate anymore because enough has been said.

2) Being promoted: It is one of the most gratifying rewards an employee can get. Encarta World English Dictionary defines promotion as follows: "Advancing somebody in rank–Raising somebody to a more senior job or a higher position or rank–Moving somebody to the next grade–Supporting or encouraging something: to encourage the growth and development of something." As much as we know it is not always true that one gets promoted because of hard work and accomplishments, it is also a reward for an employee who is willing to go above and beyond the call of duty. Most people receive gifts, flowers, and of course more money. People are proud and should be proud of themselves when a promotion is received. It is their direct hard work, efforts, and ambitions that made it possible to get rewarded.

3) Being resigned: There are two types of resignations: voluntary and involuntary. I am going to talk about voluntary resignation due to the fact that involuntary resignation if a form of "firing", but an employer who wants to treat their employees with dignity asks the employee that is in trouble to resign so he or she can save face. An employee resigns usually for a better position or to pursue other endeavors. People don't always quit their jobs for a better job, because the grass on the other side may be deceitful. Sometimes it could be the worst mistake one could make. Leaving a present job is like taking a freefall. You never know how and where you are going to land. I had the chance to experience this feeling; it turned out to be the

best decision that I ever made in my working career. I cannot describe the level of my joy when I found out that I was selected for the human resources position. Even though later on I found out that I was the second choice, which was hard to swallow. I will go back to discuss what happened in the process and continue to unfold my working dilemmas while working in that position.

4) Being retired: This is the best feeling among them all. As for the resignation, there are also two types of retirements: voluntary retirement and involuntary retirement. Employees can be forced to retire either for health reasons or to take an early retirement. I am only talking about voluntary retirement to make my point. Working in general is not fun; but it is the most common rewarding element in human life. You get a paycheck every week or every other week. As a human resources professional, I faced, on a daily basis, all kind of emotions as well as content and disgruntled employees at the workplace. Most of the time, disgruntled employees are those who work because they have to, not because they like to. The best emotion has always been when an employee is retiring. Months before the retirement date, the retirees begin to express their feelings: I plan to cruise, to travel the world; things that they could not do because of work obligations. I had the privilege to work with a number of employees; I prepped their retirement documents and gave them great retirement parties. Most of those people were at an old age and worked a lot of overtime, so they had put a tremendous amount of time at work. Sometimes they worked seven days a week for a period of time. So approaching the retirement date was like they were promised a $1,000,000.00 in couple months and the money was guaranteed. Think about this, after retirement, the employee would not have to be at work at certain times, meaning he/she would not have to wake up at certain times. Oh! What a great feeling.

5) Being fired: "You're fired," is the favorite theme of the "Apprentice" television show hosted by the mighty developer,

Donald Trump. There is no substitute for the word "fired," no matter how you say it or put it; it is hard and difficult to swallow. No one likes to get fired. I hear this term: "You don't get fired, you fired yourself." I personally don't buy it. I never have and never will. As I mentioned above, there are all kinds of employees, good and bad, but we all know that there are also all kinds of employers, good and bad. Nowadays, employers are spending a lot of money toward employee relations and diversity training programs. One reason, and probably the most important reason, is to minimize the risk of having disgruntled employees. Most employers also do not follow through and evaluate their employees' behavior after those trainings. At the same time, employers continue to put a lot of stress on employees to get products out of the door. Employees under pressure make mistakes. Stressed employees get sick more often, get upset more often, and so forth. No one, like I said before, likes to get fired. Obviously, people who have never been fired cannot understand the anguish of being. That goes for the one who gets fired and the one who does the firing. Even when a company downsizes, employees who get affected are embarrassed and are often asked if they can come back at night to pick up their belongings. I am well aware that there are people who have received numerous disciplinary actions and counseling before their termination. That does not mean those people wanted to get fired or they fired themselves. I know people who got fired; I sat with employees who were getting fired, and I sometimes had to fire employees. Not once during my thirty-two-plus working years, of which eight plus years I spent in a human resources function, have I seen or known someone who was happy at the time they got fired. I don't have to give examples of violence that occurred in workplaces after employees got fired. Much violence occurred in workplaces because of fired and disgruntled employees and most of us are aware of them.

For the sake of my book, and the purpose of why I wrote the book, I am glad to say, "I sat where the folks who got fired, with the exception of those who committed violent crimes after their termination as way to release their frustration, sat." I lost a job after I worked for the company for twenty-five plus years. For legal matters, and a separation agreement that I signed, I would say that my separation with the company was mutual, but I can tell you that I felt and lived the same pain, the same embarrassment, and the same emotion as the ones who get fired. I will talk about the story and what I have learned in a later chapter. Yes! Getting fired is hard.

When I began to write this book, I did not know that I would be losing my job. So my plan was to talk briefly about the five above stages in the working life and move on to talk about my experience and feeling about my resignation/promotion and/or my transition from the materials control to human resources within the same corporation, but a different company. My separation from the company led me to experience the fifth stage described above, which leaves me no choice but to tell you about that emotion as well.

So let's talk about quitting a job for another one, or should I say, resigning from one job for another one. While working as a materials control laboratory supervisor, I applied for a human resources representative position within the same corporation, as I mentioned in the previous chapter, and got the job. I could not describe the level of my joy when I found out that I was selected for the human resources position. Painfully, but gracefully, later on I found out that I was the second choice for the job, which I considered a low blow, because I thought I was the prime and ideal candidate for the position. Gracefully, I was blessed to get the position, which was what I wanted. I should not be feeling disappointed for being the second choice. Let me go back to discuss what happened in the process and continue to unfold my working career dilemmas. Remember, I want you to know that, *I sat where you sit, I have been through what you are going through, and I am living through it so I could tell you about it, and you, one day, will tell someone else that you sat where they sit.*

The job was offered to the other candidate and for whatever reason, she declined it. Therefore, I benefited from her refusal. Why did I feel disappointed? As I stated before, I was not who I am today, a man with courage and wisdom. And I did not put God first. Otherwise, I would have known that everything happens for a reason and to fulfill a purpose. We often ask God for something and want it done our way. God does not work like that. Moreover, I was so miserable in the previous job; I suffered so many humiliations, and I received so many deceptions that I wanted to leave at any price. So getting a job was a godsend to me. I thanked God, the GM/VP, and the HR Manager for the opportunity. I received the job offer in the last weeks of October 1997. Right after I got the news, I felt like I was carrying a heavy load of materials on my back and it fell off. It took me almost six months before I could get transferred to the other plant to begin my career.

During the transition time, I was privileged to participate in the 1997 Christmas party that was hosted by the new plant. I was introduced to a number of employees as the new team member of the company. Just the fact I attended the party was a great victory and an honorable compensation and I enjoyed myself very much. I began the new job on March 8, 1998. When I worked in the Materials and Metallurgical Laboratory I was always dressed nice and upper-casual; I did not have to wear a tie unless we were going to receive customers and/ or visitors. On my first day at the new job I dressed way up. I wore a light green suit, a white long sleeve shirt with cuff links, and a very nice and well-matched tie. I began the new job with a lot of pride, I held my head so high that I felt the need to bend a little each time I had to go through a door. There were a few employees from the former plant that left before me to join the new plant; I met with them during my orientation. I regained my self-esteem and composure. I did have to fight very hard to not let anything take away my burning desire to be a success. I was not going to compromise my work ethic, nor let anyone to take away my dignity. Quite frankly, I began to lose my self-confidence and the drive to succeed while I was in the other company. As I said before, my life was miserable, and at times, I wanted to quit, but thank God that quitting was not an issue and will never be. Getting the new job was the greatest thing and the greatest relief of my live. I considered myself a true "comeback kid." Throughout life so far I kept coming back, and as you continue to read the book, you will agree with me that I am a "survivor boy." I am not through yet. Anyway, I was led to my office; I had an enclosed office. Oh! While I was working in the other plant, I had just purchased, for the first time, a brand new office chair, very classy; it was an executive one, I was not about to sit on a lousy chair. Oh no, not Mr. Joel Esperance, no sir! Let me tell you the history of the first chair: From October 1980 to August 1997, I have always shared an office with someone; either my manager or a technician. During that time, I never had a good chair or a new chair. A few other employees, including some engineers and technicians, were constantly waiting to "loot" a fired supervisor or manager's office for a better desk, chair, and other office furniture that were better then ours. It's just like riots you see on television after a dictator gets killed or ousted from their countries and, for example, when there are some contro-versial issues in the states such as the Rodney King situation in L.A. People always used those occasions to loot, burn cars and buildings, and destroy small business properties. Those times were really fun and we could not wait for any guy who happened to have nice furniture in his office to get fired or resigned. Some time around July of 1997, I was at my prime time in the company, so I profited the occasion to ask for better furniture. The request was gratefully granted. I bought a very expensive desk; I can tell you right now that my desk was one of the most expensive and the nicest desks of the entire plant. The desk had to be very stable and solid because an $80,000.00 machine was to be placed on it. Then I told my boss I had to have a chair that matches the desk. With no sweat I had it. I had the chair for only two months when I found out that I got a new job which means I was going to have it for six to seven months. So, when it was time for me to leave the company, I asked the manager if I could take the chair with me, he declined my request and he told me that the chair will stay in for my successor. My new office was nothing compared to the old office, for I was in a large room with my equipment. But the new office was somewhat private, which offered more of a bureau style. The desk was old and small like "Je vendais a crédit" *(I sold at credit)* with a chair which belonged not to the previous person who occupied the office, but the previous, previous one. The ceiling tiles were stained with watermarks. I automatically made a request to my new boss—A new chair similar to the one that I left in the other plant, if it was not the exact mark and model—A 6 x 3 foot desk with a matching credenza. I got the chair right away, but unfortunately not the desk. I waited for almost a year before I could get the complete desk set. My first day as a HR Representative was fantastic. The company has two plants, the main plant and an offsite plant. I would be the HR Representative for the Offsite Plant for seven plus years straight. On my first day, I met all first and second shift employees who were working that day from both plants. I met the third shift people within my first week.

June, 1998 was a great month for us, not because my wife was born on June 5, but because of some great events that occurred in both of our lives. We both graduated from the same college, Baldwin Wallace College in Berea, Ohio; Kettline's graduation was on Friday and my graduation was the Saturday of the same week. She proudly obtained her B.A. and I obtained my MBA. On that same Saturday, right after my graduation, which was in the morning, we moved into our brand spanking new house. What a month! The completion of my MBA was probably the best thing I have accomplished. A little bit before a year passed, I got transferred to the satellite plant, which was acquired to alleviate the compactness of the main building and to accommodate and facilitate a better environment for the employees. They were about three hundred employees in the building around April

2006. And I was in charge of all HR functions for that building. During the fall of 2000, I gave a speech on my twentieth anniversary with the company about *gratitude* and *thankfulness* in their Annual Awards Banquet Party celebrating employees' five, ten, fifteen, twenty, twenty-five, thirty, and thirty-five years of services. Up to that point and with all the ups and downs, I was still very grateful and thankful to the company. Going back to my previous life, nothing could be worse than what I have already survived. *"All things work together for good to those who love God in according to His purpose. Romans 8:28"* *(Toutes choses concourent au bien de ceux qui aiment Dieu. Romain 8:28.)*

That particular year, 2000, was very important for me; I celebrated three nice and meaningful occasions of my life at once: twentieth wedding anniversary, twentieth work anniversary, and the twentieth anniversary of living in Ohio. It was also the year that the company had proudly defeated an aggressive union-organizing attempt. I played a vital part in the process. That experience, and the observation of defeating the union's attempt, helped me to develop and implement an Employee Relations Program and Practice that transformed the plant into a "Trust and Open Communication" based organization. During the implementation of the program, which was not an easy task, I came to realize that most of us are taking things for granted in the U.S. I am especially talking about in the world of work. Employers do not appreciate and do not manage the "manpower " as they should. And employees do not appreciate either the fact that employers give them opportunities to proudly earn a living. In a specific way, the program was entitled "Supervisors and Employees Relationships," which I thought could bring light between the two parties. At the beginning of this chapter, I defined "Job/Employment" as: *A job is a regular activity performed in exchange for payment, especially as one's trade, occupation, or profession, or a position in which one is employed. Employment is contract between two parties, one being the Employer and the other being the Employee.* This is to say that the employer works hand-in-hand with the employee(s); there cannot be one without the other, even when one said, "I am a self employer." He or she is both.

I feel compelled to attach a copy of the program for your review. I am confident that those of you who are either employers or employees will greatly benefit from it. Please enjoy!

Employee Relations Principles for
Human Resource Professionals

Title: Supervisors and Employees Relationships

As employees continue to be more educated, it is becoming more of a challenge for organizations to develop good relationships between supervisors and employees. This practice would enhance productivity and would avoid or eliminate possible lawsuits.

Many companies tend to ignore the importance of employee relations in their organizations. Until we as members of the human resource community come up with strategic measures to develop and maintain a good relationship among supervisors/managers and employees, organizations will continue to pay a higher cost. Whereas employees would be dissatisfied and that would generate a negative attitude, which in turn would create more stress.

There is no another alternative or any substitute for good "employee relations" in any organization in this world. There are "good" and "bad" employees in any organizations, but when the importance of employee relations is ignored; good employees became bad and bad ones become worse. I intended to write this paper to provide some key information, which would help to promote functional guidance to organizations and their employees. This paper will address the importance of good supervisor/employee relations, how the ignorance of them can be costly, and the benefits and rewards to organizations and employees.

a. *Relationship Development—Employee relations is the most important tool in determining how to communicate more effectively and appropriately with fellow employees. Each one of us is involved in a number of relationships that are*

169

important to us to a certain degree. Unfortunately, there is no specific procedure or guideline for a perfect relationship, but by understanding the importance and what elements make up the relationships, we would benefit.

b. *Competent Relationships—Any relationship takes a lot of time and understanding to build. Building a relationship is not an easy task, it is like building a house where the foundation must be laid first before you can add the frame. The strength of an house depends on how firm its foundation is. Therefore, a lasting relationship depends on a solid foundation as well. The foundation of competent relationships is the characteristics of the supervisors and the employees, the relationship, and the relational history of each other.*

c. *Interpersonal Conflict—Conflict is a common type of communication. You cannot have any relationship without conflict. Conflicts arise for different reasons. Some of those reasons are different goal setting, unrealistic expectations, and false perceptions. However, conflicts are good for a relationship. Regardless of how conflicts arise, they make the relationship stronger, especially when they are managed clearly and productively.*

d. *Employee Relations - There is a great deal of difference between employee appreciation initiatives and employee relations. Because an organization provides employee assistance, occasional parties, and other benefits, that does not mean the organization has an employee relationship program. Employee relations require good understanding, time, and hard work to build. Employee relations involve both employee and supervisor/manager relationships.*

As stated before, the business world is changing rapidly. Therefore, management is focused more on the tangibles because they are easier to manage than employee and supervisor/manager relationships. According to Charles Gibson, PHR, "The current thinking of most Human Resources professionals is that Human Resources professionals should be an advocate for employees and a partner to business … Human Resources professionals must be involved in assisting operations to achieve its goals. Human Resources profes-

sionals must also serve as a legitimate employee advocate." The following are some behaviors that employees expect from Human Resources professionals per Mr. Gibson:

- *Someone who is interested in and works for fair treatment of employees.*

- *Someone who is interested in employee problems and attempts to resolve them.*

- *Someone who is interested in employee morale and tries to improve it.*

- *Someone who believes that employees should be treated with respect and dignity and who works toward that end.*

I found out that the above behavior expectations of the employees from Human Resources Professionals are reasonable. I spent seventeen-plus years listening to unfair complaints from fellow employees. I always thought that HRP should be the employees' advocate. Unfortunately, it did not work that way. Nevertheless, when I became an HRP, I found that organizations have their expectations from HRP as well. I decided to become an HRP to help find solutions to the employees' problems. I practice the saying "Don't do to others what you would not want to be done to you." I firmly believe that all HRPs should be interested in and work for fair treatment of all employees. They should be able to apply the above behaviors mentioned by Mr. Gibson. I would like to add; HRPs are the conscience of any organizations. Therefore, it should not be difficult for them in representing the employees.

There are a number of elements that are available to build good employee relations. Mr. Gibson gave some of the elements in his article published by Society for Human Resources (SHRM) Management. Here they are: communication relationship, ethics, fairness, perception, expectation, and conflict resolution. I will decipher them as follows:

- *Communication Relationship—Communication is the device that connects two people or a group of people's thoughts* together. It is also a two-way ongoing conversation to achieve common goals. A communication relationship, on the other hand, "is the communication's style in which the interdependence is based on symbolic exchange." Communication-relationship is the best element in employee relations.

- *Trust*—Trust is a mutual agreement. It is said, "If someone does not trust, they cannot be trusted." Without it, there cannot be any relationships. That is something supervisors and employees should earn from each other. If employees do not trust supervisors, or vice versa, the flow of communication will be affected.

- *Ethics* - Ethics, per Webster's New World Dictionary, is the system or code of particular persons, religions, groups, and professions. Employees need to understand and support the ethical standard of their supervisors and managers. Just as much, supervisors and managers need to understand the employees' ethical standard. If not, they will indirectly question each other's motives. This can be stressful for both employees and supervisors, which will affect productivity.

- *Fairness*—"Fairness simply means that all employees are treated the same, under the same circumstances. No favoritism should be shown. No one likes to be second best. This does not mean that superior performance should not be rewarded." This quoted directly from Mr. Gibson's article. His definition is very clear.

- *Perceptions*—Perceptions are hard to erase and are the closest thing to reality. Employees will form their opinions on what they perceive or believe to be true. That is why it is important to develop employee relations where there could be a sincere flow of communication. Employees need to be informed on any activities that occur in the organization. Otherwise, Employees' uncertainties may hinder their productivity level and will affect performance.

- *Expectations*—Expectations are somewhat related to ethics. Employees need to know the ethical standard of their supervisor so they can know what to expect from them. "No one likes surprises unless they are good surprises." Deceptions are the results of false expectations or goals.

- *Conflict Resolution—Conflicts arise in all relationships and all organizations. As I stated before, conflicts are healthy for any relation, as long as they are managed clearly and productively. When you manage conflict, it avoids excessive stress, so that the employee's performance is not affected.*

- *Failure to apply the above factors or to pay attention to employee, supervisor, and manager relations can be costly to any organization. The following are the consequences of such failure: Unionizing, employee absenteeism, and lawsuits.*

- *Unionization—Unionization limits management's ability to manage, which causes the organization to be less profitable. Employees seek to bring in a union to represent them because they don't trust management. Unionization can be avoided if organizations practice the factors involved in employee relations and are truthful to the employees.*

- *Employee Absenteeism—Employee absenteeism drives up the cost of doing business. Absenteeism is the most important impact of a failure to develop good employee relations. It creates the following costs: increased employee benefits, replacement workers, training, and overtime. Employees miss work usually when they are dissatisfied.*

- *Litigation—"Defending against litigation for allegations of wrongful employment actions drives up the cost of doing business, and could result in criminal, civil, and financial penalties. Supervisor/managers should take this seriously. In many situations, individual supervisor/managers can be found individually responsible and held accountable in a criminal or civil action." This is quoted directly from the Mr. Gibson' article.*

Employee Treatment—Employees' treatment is the most tangible aspect of employee relations. HRPs and supervisors need to make sure that employees are recognized. Some companies do a good job at recognizing their employees. They have different programs: rewards for the best suggestions, a dinner for no lost time, dinners or food certificates for good performance. They also have

Employees Assistance Program (EAP) and other employee assist-
ing programs. But still, do not have effective employee relations.
Supervisors need to treat employees with respect and dignity. Let's
not wait for a specific occasion to let them know that they are as
important as everyone else is. Once in a while, bring them into the
office; ask them, "How are things?" Ask them, "If there is anything
that I can do for you?" That is what treatment is about.

Summary

What is the cost of an effective employee relations program? The
answer is; having an effective employee relations program is
less-less costly than time and financial assets. Many organiza-
tions maintain that they have an employee relations program, but
these programs are not being effective. Some organizations prac-
tice the rule "If it's not broke, don't fix it." Organizations these
days ignore HRP's recommendations, to implement programs that
could be beneficial to them.

Organizations need rules, communication of the rules, ongoing
communication about matters of importance, and the right people.
Short-term initiatives and incentives should not be confused with
the long-term rewards of building good employee relationships. If
we know and believe that employees are not only the best assets
of the organization, but they are people, and we treat them with
dignity, respect, and fairness, then we can claim that our employee
relations efforts are on the way.

By: Joel Esperance, Human Resources
Representative, June 12, 2002

Since I give you, employers and employees, a taste of my
employee relations program, I would like to give everyone a taste
of my "triple twenty" anniversaries, the "gratitude and thankfulness" speech that I gave at the Annual Company Banquet, and
also at my church in the 2001 New Year's Eve service. Yes, I
feel compelled to display the speech here, but you will have the
pleasure to read the church version of the speech. Please enjoy:

Good evening! By ways of introduction, I am Joel Esperance.

I have a lot to thank God for this evening. People often take things for granted, especially things they should be thankful and grateful for. Being thankful and grateful are not a one-time event, but rather a lifetime matter. Folks, would you please indulge me for a few minutes while I express my gratitude and thankfulness? My family has been blessed beyond comprehension. This year God showed his grace and his mercy tangibly to us. Kettline and I had the opportunity to celebrate 20 years of marriage. I am honored to be a member of Calvary Fellowship Baptist Church and also serve on the Trustee Board. I attended several schools and universities, but never acquired a degree. During that time, I continued to improve my technical and academic knowledge. I would be doing an excellent job throughout the year, but when my review time came, my boss reminded me that because of my formal education, I would not be able to get promoted. Meanwhile, I kept seeing other employees getting promoted without a college degree. On February 14th, 1987, we had our first son and March 1, 1988, we had our second child. The same year, after an annual review, I told my boss, "This is the last year for you to tell me this story of formal education. I am going to school, starting this fall." Which, I did. In June, 1991 I earned an associate degree, in June 1993, I earned a bachelor degree, and In December 1998, I earned my Masters in Business Administration. I am presently working as a Human Resources Representative.

Now, I can proudly say, with the grace of God, the voids are being filled. However, I am still working on the English part, which seems to be a lifetime process. When it comes to the American culture, I do have a problem with one of its aspects, which changes the meaning of the word "gratitude", and makes it difficult for someone to be grateful and thankful without being perceived as a "brown-noser." This perception not only stops people from being grateful to others but sometimes to God. I certainly earned a lot of credits to achieve my goal, which helped me be where I am today. But, I also certainly did not do it all by myself; first of all, I have to thank God and I have a lot of people to thank and be grateful to. I would like to take this opportunity to express my gratitude to Fellowship Calvary Baptist Church as a whole and to a few of the people who helped me make it this far. I want to thank my wife, Kettline, for her spiritual and moral support, and for allowing the time to pursue my education. I am very grateful to my sons, Ricky and Joey, for their continuing love and support. I am grateful to Pastor Gerard Pierre Mirbel, a good friend of mine, for allowing his family to take care of my children while Kettline and I were going to school. I am grateful to my best friend, Dr. Max Pierre Gaujean, who taught me that the words {discouragement, impossible, low self-esteem} were only found in the dictionary of fools. I am grateful to pastor Doug and Mrs. Reeder for their spiritual guidance to the boys and for giving me the opportunity to serve on the Trustee Board of our church. Thanks to Pastor Paul and his staff for their support and appreciation for my family, and thanks to all of you for your kindness and your patience in allowing me the time to show my appreciation and for the opportunity for my family and I to be part of this great church. On behalf of my family and I, we are looking forward to serve our purposes with commitment and loyalty. In conclusion, I want to say as the Apostle Paul said in the book of Philippians 3:13 and 14. "Brothers, I do not consider myself yet to have taken hold of it. But one thing I do: Forgetting what is behind and straining toward what is ahead."

Once again THANKS.

Happy New Year and God bless you all.

It is said that in anyone's working life, if one has three bosses that he or she can call friends, that person is one of the luckiest employees in the working world. Up to 2002, I thought that I was one of the luckiest employees, but the working nature proved me wrong. I have worked for three men that I could call friends. They were Dick, Bob, and Almondo. They were all great bosses and good in their own ways. I will be talking only about the last boss for the sake of the following episode that I am about to explain.

I met Almondo, a sharp man, around 1992; he was working for another plant, as a senior executive, and oversaw the plant that I worked for in Ohio. He was a very impressive fellow; whenever he came to the plant, he was always highly dressed. I mean, he wore white shirts, nice ties, and nice suits. He would always leave his suit jacket in the office and walked around. The first time I saw him, I said, "When I make it to the top, I want to be just like him." At that time, I thought it was easy to get to the top. Anyway, I was inspired by him to do well. He was very humble and acted with good manners. He was very dedicated and committed to the company. He was a great inspiration to most employees and especially to those who worked directly for him. I am speaking from experience. Almondo was a man of integrity. In terms of communication, he is a great communicator and listener. Even when he administered a disciplinary action, he did it with ease and with compassion. He had a way of setting the tone when reprimanding a subordinate so that there were no hard feelings afterward. Something is going to happen that will put a stain in our relations, which will, at the end, break the relationship for good. I had my faults, but Almondo also had his, and I know one of his and probably the worst one. Nevertheless, even though he possessed these many good qualities and was a great academic and social educator, he was a *paranoid freak*. His paranoia was very apparent, and because of that, it was also very difficult for him to accept criticism. I was very close to him; we would have lunch at least three days in a week. We were really living like blood brothers. If I did not say this before, I owe him a lot of credit, because without him, I would not have gotten my MBA. He encouraged me to go for it. I have said all of this to describe the beginning of our friendship. I have already written about a level of humiliation, frustration, and betrayal I endured and survived during my working career to this point. I will continue to give you more learning events throughout the book. The following one will prove the ramifications of someone being paranoid and how that can affect someone else's life.

A month before my fiftieth birthday I had a conversation with Almondo about career advancement that did not go well. As a result, he did not come to my anniversary party, which occurred on April 19, 2003. I did talk about him and showed him in a picture with me, since I was presenting people who made an impact in my life. Life continued, and we moved on. I should have known that we were no longer friends but *boss* and subordinate.

In December 2003, approximately seven months after my fiftieth and glamorous anniversary, the "Big Five O", an event occurred which could have made us both, Almondo and myself, enemies for life, but did not. I will be writing about it later. Almondo, as I said before, would genuinely help his subordinates improve their academic studies, boost their confidence level, and treat them with respect. To my knowledge, the company was not setting up for succession planning, and Almondo did not have on his agenda to prepare a representative to replace him one day. My working career was always like a "rollercoaster"; the kind that moves upward, backward, sideways, and twists alternatively. Despite that, I have always tried to enjoy every good time around the bad times. Allow me to go back a few years prior to my fiftieth birthday and up to the last month of 2003. I earned a bachelor's degree in business and industrial management in 1993. I was forty years old. If you remember, I was told by one of my bosses that not having a formal education was the reason that held me back from getting promoted. The boss who told me that was in fact one of my graduation guests. I took a break from school to regroup, and in the fall of 1995, registered at Lake Erie College in a two-year program toward a master's degree. I completed two courses, then something came up, which required that I spend more time at home. So, I dropped out and restarted in the following fall at Baldwin Wallace College. I completed the program in December 1998, but I did march in the graduation ceremony of June 1998. Obviously, 1998, was a great year for me, I have already talked to you about the excitements of getting a promoted, graduating, and moving into our brand new house that we had built.

1999 was very challenging work-wise; I moved to a different plant, which could be considered as a promotion. I was responsible for the whole HR operation. I had some difficulties, since that was the year before 2000, which meant people did not pay attention to what was happening. Everyone was concerned about what might happen on December 31, 1999; people were trying to be prepared for a possible computer catastrophe. Everyone talked about nothing but Y2K; are we going to have enough food, water, or electricity? Will it be the end of the world? So, there was nothing else or anything more exiting to talk about. In reality, 2000 was a great year, much different and funnier than the year before. Kettline and I were doing much better, financially speaking, so, in July 2000, Kettline, the boys and I went on our first boat trip (cruise). That trip was extremely fantastic and fun. It was not the cruise that made the trip magnificence, but the combination of the whole trip. I have already mentioned sometime ago that we had and always have had a very small and probably the strongest Haitian community. We lived like a big family. In the community, most are medical doctors, and a few engineers, educators, business professionals, pastors, and university students. No matter how and when we are together, there is always a homogeneous mixture. You would never hear anyone talking about his/her profession or being somehow and somewhat condescend to each other. It does not matter of how big or how small one's house is, everyone feels comfortable over at anyone's house. It does not matter how bad the weather is, when we are invited to a party or a family event, everyone will be there. It does not matter where a son or a daughter is getting married, we would be there.

In or around July 2000, one of my friends, Dr. Jean-Daniel Policard's daughter, was getting married in Jacksonville, Florida. Kettline and I practically knew the girl since she was eight years old. We were invited to the wedding, so we profited the occasion not only to travel there, but also to arrange our vacation to cruise around the Caribbean Sea. We scheduled a five-night cruise with the main destination being the Grand Bahamas. Almost everyone in the Haitian community went to the wedding. The wedding was on a Saturday, we flew down there on Friday morning because there was a magnificent dinner party for those of us who arrived from far away. The plan was, on Sunday after the wedding, we would leave Jacksonville to go to Cape Carnival to board the cruise ship en route to the Grand Bahamas. On Sunday morning, as we traveled with two of our friends, Drs. Max and Emmelyne Gaujean, we had to take them back to the airport, which was the opposite way, so they could go back home to Ohio. Anyway, we took them to the airport and drove back by the house where we stayed and took the road in the direction of Cape Carnival. Let me back up for a moment; in Jacksonville, we stayed over at my sister Nicole's house. At the airport we rented a car to go over to her house; my sister and her husband were not going to be home. So, my sister knew that I liked to drive her 740 IL BMW; she left the car for me with a full tank and even set a CD with Latino music in too. This tells you that the car we rented at the airport was sitting in their drive way still Sunday morning. I had a ball.

Anyway, let me tell you what happened to us. Kettline took a wrong "MapQuest" direction for Cape Carnival to begin with; she put the right street address but put Orlando instead of Cape Carnival. So, we took our time driving to Orlando. Arriving in Orlando, we began to look for the place. In fact we did find the street but could not see any dock, or ship, or anything that like as if we were at the right place. So, we went to a shop nearby to ask for some information. Unfortunately, we found out that we were about one hour driving distance from where we were supposed to be, and one hour and fifteen minutes exactly before the final embarkation. This means we were in deep, deep trouble. The car was not running well, and we were to return it prior to embarking on the ship. It took us a good ten to fifteen minutes to find the right road to go there. Therefore, we were at fifty-five to sixty minutes from departure time and a one-hour driving distance. We began to freak out. I told Kettline the only way we could make it was if I drove over a hundred miles per hour, she asked me to drive ninety instead, so I compromised; I drove at hundred miles an hour. Sometimes when she was busy talking on a cell phone to find a place to park or to return the car, I exceeded the mileage limit; I went 110 miles per hour at times. The boys were in the car; that was insane. The truth was, we wanted to go on the trip so much that we looked at it as part of the affair; we viewed it as an adventure. We made it at last; we were given the authority to leave the car in the cruise ship parking area at no extra charge from the car rental people. We were also the last four people to board the ship. Ironically, I was supposed to meet with one of my brothers and he also got lost because he was the one who gave us the address to begin with. The deal was that we would meet him at the boat dock to give him some cash. Since the guy is a preacher I think he was praying that we would also get lost so we would make it at the same time and he could get his cash. My brother and I made it three minutes apart. Anyway, I gave him his cash, got on the boat, went directly on deck where we were getting safety instruction, and zoom, we left port. That was the most enjoyable trip the family had together. From there we decided, upon returning to the United States, the whole family will need to go to Europe.

Indeed we took a trip to Europe in summer 2001. That was our first long and memorable trip. Let me say that the trip was very fun because we traveled first class from Chicago all the way to Paris, France. There, we had the pleasure to visit four other countries: Switzerland, Italy, Germany, and Spain. Sometimes people are afraid to give God the glory that He deserves, because, as I stated in my thankfulness message, other people perceive them as: Brown nose, bragging, show off, etc.. I would like to add that all of these trips were first class travel. Thanks to the Lord Jesus Christ. That was our best year in many ways and shapes. The next time we are going to enjoy will be my fiftieth birthday party on April 2003. It would be again the best of the best; I will have so much fun with my family and my friends, which you will read about later. Unfortunately I will also, at the end of the year, experience my worst nightmare, which you are also going to read about later.

FORTY-FIVE YEARS OLD
TO FIFTY YEARS OLD

Dark Secret, Eloquent 50th Birthday party

Through my married life I have encountered, and continued encountering, a series of problems with my wife. It always appeared that we had a good married life, but if people could see inside, they would have a better understanding. We chose not to let people interfere in our private life though things were still not, okay. Our love for each other seemed to not want to let go.

For some reasons, things were escalated to their worst stages in the year of 2002. That particular year, I faced some tough challenges. Our problems have never been transparent, as I said above, and because of that we continuously received compliments from family and friends for the way we lived our married life. Or should I say, the way we seemed to live our married life. One of our friends, a prominent lawyer, divorced his first wife after seeing the way Kettline and I were living and loving each other. Although we have had a lot of problems, they never seemed to escalate to the point that people from the outside could interfere. I am not about to divulge my married life in this book. Once again, I want my readers to know that, I sat where they sit, and I want everyone to know that everyone has his or her own problems, only we do not know and see them. Therefore, I want to take a few minutes to talk about one of the incidents that happened in our lives and I thought that clearly demonstrated that we indeed have a serious marital problem.

On August 5, 2002, three days after our twenty-second marriage anniversary, it was a quiet evening. Kettline, the boys, and I were all in the master bedroom when Kettline and I began a conversation about a family matter. At some point during the conversation, I said something that caught her off guard, and suddenly she blew up. She went crazy and totally overboard. She even said that one of us had to leave the house. I did not respond to her nonsense talk. She screamed and yelled for hours, she asked everyone to leave the room and she locked herself in the bedroom. She would be spending the next five days without talking to anyone in the house. I got a little bit upset and I said to myself that I needed to come up with a decision. My decision was to have a divorce, but one of my brothers, Jarman, a few months prior to that event, called me from Haiti, where he was a resident at that time in a mission field, to talk to me about a dream that he had about me. He told me that in his dream he saw that I was going to have a lot of problems in my marriage and that I would want to divorce my wife. As a word of advice, he told me not to get a divorce or ask for a divorce without contacting him or possibly coming to see him in Haiti. So, I decided to go to Haiti to meet with my brother. I talked to Kettline, for the first time in five days since the incident, I told her that I was going to Haiti to meet with Jarman. I did not tell her why I was going to see him for. In Haiti, I met with Jarman and we discussed the situation. As a result, we decided that it was not worth it to break the marriage at that time. He gave me a few pieces of advice. His advice was from life experience and on the Bible's principles. I left Haiti and felt like I was on a mission. Kettline picked me up at the airport. She was very relaxed and poised. I got into the car, kissed her good evening and asked her about the boys. She told me about them and asked me about Jarman and Mary, my sister in-law. We had a normal conversation. Somewhere along the road, I told her that it was imperative that I talk to her about our married life. She said, "When do you want to do that?" I said, "Right this moment." Without her saying anything, I began to tell her that, "I see no reason for our marriage to break. However, we have to look at it differently since we are two different people anyway." I continued, "Kettline, our problem is not a big deal or a complex one. We have to understand that we are different and because of that we are seeing things differently, which does not mean that we cannot live a good married life. We are simply not compatible; things that you like are not what I like. When you would want to do something, may not be the time that I would want to do it. Having said that, we need to respect each other's opinion and try to understand each other. We need to be optimistic instead of being pessimistic. Then I said, "I would also want you to know that, according to the Bible, I am the head of the household, and that I want to be and feel that way." I also told her that I believed I was the only king not happy in his kingdom. She listened to me very carefully and made no comments. She told me that everything I said was okay with her, but she did want to know if my brother equipped me with those words. She did not say it in a nice way but more or so in a sarcastic way. Anyway, we agreed that we were going to mutually respect each other and work together to save the marriage. One of the examples that I can give you that we worked on is this: I love watching television and Kettline likes to read. Each night before we go to bed; Kettline would want to read and I would want to watch TV. Of course, the TV sound would interfere with her reading, so, she would ask me to get out of the room or shut off the TV, which I did all the time. Guess what? I ended up getting upset to make her happy. Upon our conversation, Kettline proposed to buy a headset for me as a way of accommodation, so while she is reading I could watch TV without disruption. In that case we were both happy, because we were, and are, able to do what we want to do and actually stay in the same room. Many other adjustments were made after that one instance. I could have given more "for-instances" that happened in later times, but as in every relationship and every marriage, Kettline and I keep on pressing. As a fighter, I lived through so I can tell others that, *I sat where they sit.* It is unfortunate that my marriage and my career are much paralleled. *"Je ne mourrai pas, mais je vivrai, Et je raconterai les œuvres de l'Éternel. »* *Psalms* 18:17 (I will not die but live, and will proclaim what the Lord has done.)

At the beginning of 2003, Kettline told me that she would want to give me a birthday party that would stay in my memory till death. Yes, it was indeed going to be my fiftieth birthday. Before I get down with the party, let me remind you that I made a big mistake, sometime around February or the beginning of March, when I talked to my boss about his attitude toward his subordinates. I hope you remember that. I paid a heavy price for that mistake at the end of 2003, and I was punished. That year was the best and the worst of my live. "The Beauty and the Beast"

First, I am going to tell about the Beauty, and then about the Beast.

The birthday party, of course, is the beauty. I have a lot of friends in the greater Cleveland area, and our parents and family are scattered all over the U.S. and around the world. To begin with, we wanted to invite as many people as possible to the party. So we put a list of invites together, and we came out with 485 people; which includes friends and families, Kettline's side and mine. We did not think we could afford to feed that many guests at $35 to $45 per person. We cut the list down to three hundred, which was still too many. So we came up with a new strategy, choose the closest family and friends. The process was not that easy because we had to make sure that we would not hurt too many people's feelings. What we did was invite all Haitians in our community, those who lived around and near, which included Cleveland, Akron, Columbus, and Toledo and, of course, Chicago, New York, Pennsylvania, Georgia, and Canada. Then we invited our close working friends, which included bosses and peers. We invited friends that were not close to other friends that we had. For instance, I invited only three families at work besides my coworkers. And Kettline did the same. Our final list contained 230 people all together, in which 188 invites came into the party. One of the reasons that some people did not show up was that the party occurred during the time that our country was getting back at Iraq. So, they were afraid to fly outside of their home states. Anyway, we had people that came from eight different states and four different countries. Let's go back for a moment, we sent the invitation out, and began to look for a place to rent or a party center that could accommodate our guests. We ended up using Lakeland College Catering group and their facility. And as a graduate of the college, I got a 10 percent discount on the food, room, and hours used. Besides that, I managed to get them to come down from $38.00 per person to $31.00. The party took place on April 19, 2003, one day after my birthday date. The party was incredibly magnificent. Some activities included but were not limited to: A videotape played showing my different stages of personal growth, from teen to actual life. Some of those pictures are in this book. Kettline sang this song by Celine Marie Claudette Dion, "Because You Loved Me." And the song was written by Diane. Joey, my older son, played the Godfather song with his saxophone, *(Parlez plus bas, car on pourrait bien nous entendre)* and Ricky, my youngest, played a couple songs on the piano, "Largo" and "Fur Elise." Most of my friends either played songs or said something about me in the party. Unfortunately, some people that wanted to be there were not; Jarman, my old boss Almondo, and my biological parents. My folks were not in shape to travel that far at that time. I always look for opportunity to give, God and people who have helped me, thanks and let them know how I value them. I gave my speech of gratitude and thankfulness. In my speech, I talked to the invites about a thought that made me feel at that point, one of the most blessed people on earth. Please allow me to share the thought with you:

Two years prior to the party, I was visiting Jarman in Haiti. The next day of my arrival there we went downtown Port-au-Prince to run some errands. That particular morning, we were on our way to the bank, where I had to meet with a friend of mine, the famous Mrs. Suzanne, who was one of the dignitaries at the bank. Mrs. Suzanne is the sister of one of our friends, Dr. Jocelyne, who used to live in Ohio, and part of the Elites Haitian community. On the way to the bank, I met several people who knew me; some were old friends at school, some were people I knew at work, (American Embassy/USAID), and some were acquaintances. Believe it or not, in the bank itself, I met a few other friends besides Suzanne. I had my meeting with Mrs. Suzanne and we left. As we were leaving the bank, my brother started laughing and he said, "Joe, when I die, there will be about fifty people at my funeral, but when you die, I will have to rent the Cleveland Indians Jacob Fields to have your funeral." I asked him why he said that. He answered, "In two and a half hours, you met more people who know you than I met in the past two years that I have been living here." It never dawned on me until a year after. When I worked as a human resources representative I went to almost every funeral service of an employee or employee's loved ones that died. Some of those funeral services were attended by only parents and close family members, some were attended by parents, family members, and friends, and at times, and depending on who had passed, there may be parents, a lot of family members, hundreds of friends, and others. I firmly believe that the best way to measure a person's life is at his or her funeral. So my birthday party confirmed that the statement made by my brother was true. I truly realize that I have a lot of friends, and I am a blessed man. It maybe sounds weird or you may think that I am self-centered; I don't think so. I am just telling you that I do believe that when I die, there will be a lot of people, at least a thousand, at my funeral services.

My birthday party was eloquent; our guests were all quality people. We received so many compliments from the catering manager and their staff for the affair. Everyone was dressed to kill; the music, the dances, and the whole program was excellent. I have a picture album of the party that I travel with everywhere I go. It is so beautiful and precious to me. I would like to share with you some of my birthday wishes and friendship statements that were made at the party by a number of invites. More particularly, one of my friends, Dr. Comoche Lamothe, took time to prepare a speech to give at the party; for some reason, he did not give it. He handed it to me after the party. I read it and I made a promise to him that one day, most of the people that were in the party would have a chance to read it as well. So, in a way to keep my promise, I attach it here, so all my readers as well as my family and friends have the chance to enjoy it. Oh! Since he wrote the speech in French, I have translated it in English so everyone can enjoy it. It printed in the book in French and in English. First, let's me share with you Dr. Lamothe's speech, then the statements.

Dr. Comoche Lamothe's speech:

Mon Cher Joël;

L'événement que nous célébrons ce soir a beaucoup de poids dans la balance de l'amitié et de la fraternité. En effet, il y a de cela un demi siècle, dans notre Haïti alors attirante, tu naquis avec tous les atouts et toutes les bénédictions nécessaires pour grandir, aimer la vie et viser la réussite. Tu y es parvenu et je t'en félicite.

Chers parents et amis de Joël;

Il suffit de rencontrer Joël une seule fois pour découvrir tout de suite qu'il est un leader, un amateur infatigable et aussi un rassembleur inné. Dans un monde aussi difficile nous avons intérêt à nous laisser prendre dans les filets de sa joie continuelle et de nous laisser capter par l'exemple de son amitié. En mon nom propre et en celui de ma femme, je te remercie Joël pour ton esprit de partage sans égoïsme si souvent exprimé à notre endroit. Je t'exhorte à continuer de faire de chaque jour de ta vie une raison de fêter. La pensée de Ralph Emerson traduit bien ta définition de la vie; il dit: "WITHOUT THE RICH HEART, WEALTH IS AN UGGLY BEGGAR" En effet, si dans les poches de Joël il n' ya peut être pas de millions, il porte dans son Cœur un trésor fait de belles qualités gracieusement mis à la disposition de son entourage.

Maintenant, J'invite tes parents et amis à associer leurs pensées aux miennes pour t'exprimer en une seule voix les souhaits que tu mérites bien: Santé et Paix intérieure, Bonheur en toi et autour de toi, Succès dans tous les domaines et aujourd'hui Sagesse.

> *TRES HEUREUX ANNIVERSAIRE,*
> *mon ami et AD MUTOS ANOS*
>
> *Dr. C. Lamothe, Cleveland*

Avril 18, 2003   *50 ans >>>>>>>> 100 ans >>>>>>>>>>*

Translation:

Dear Joel:

The event that we are celebrating this evening has a lot of weight in the balance of friendship and fraternity. Hence, there is a half century in our then very attracting, Haiti, you were born with all the assets and all the blessings necessary to evaluate, appreciate life, to aim at the success.

You reached that point and I congratulate you.

Dear parents and friends of Joel;

It is enough to meet Joel only once to discover immediately that he is a leader, an untiring amateur, and also an assembler fundamental. In such a difficult world we have interest to let us take in his nets of continual joy and to let us collect by the specimen of his friendship. I, and on behalf of my wife, I thank you, Joel, for your sharing spirit without selfishness that you often express toward us. I exhort you to continue to make each day of your life a reason of celebration. A thought from Ralph Emerson, an author, correctly translated your definition of life; it says: "Without the rich heart, wealth is an ugly beggar." Indeed, if in Joel's pockets there are not millions; he carries in his heart a treasure, which made of beautiful qualities graciously available to his entourage.

Now, I invite your parents and friends to associate their mind's spirits with mine so we can wish you in one voice all the best wishes that you so well deserved: Health and Inner Peace, Happiness in you and around you, Successes in all Domains and today Wisdom.

> HAPPY BIRTHDAY, my friend;
> AD MUTOS ANOS
>
> Dr. C. Lamothe, Cleveland

April 18, 2003   50years >>>>>> 100years >>>>>>>>

My birthday party left an engraved and significant notch in my life. Would I like it to be the last? No, but any other birthday was and will be greatly appreciated and considered to be just the grace and mercy of the God Almighty—Omega-50 has been personalized on my license plate since 2003. I joke about it; I tell most of the people that my life ended at fifty and past fifty it is a new beginning, which I am living with thanks and gratitude to my God.

Besides the remark of Dr. Lamothe, I selected few other thoughts and whishes, I wish I could write them all, from family and friends at my birthday party celebration. I love my friends very much. Note: I deliberately did not have them translated; not because of selfishness, but so they can keep their original, spiritual, and personal feelings.

Joël,

La vie est comme un livre ou chaque anniversaire marque le début d'un chapitre fascinant.

L'amitié s'inscrit aussi au grand livre de la vie. Des pages de précieux souvenirs qu'on se remémore avec plaisir.

Nous te souhaitons beaucoup d'autres années à fêter, une santé agréable, et plein de bonnes choses.

Joyeux anniversaire

Avec affection
Gérard, Valery, et Inès————-

Joel,

"Life is a highway, as the years go by, sometimes the road is level, sometimes the hills are high, but as we travel onward to a future that's unknown, we make each mile we travel a heavenly stepping stone" (Helen Steiner Rice).

Happy birthday to our good friend Joel! May your 50th be ever so blessed you have been a cherish friend for many years. We are looking forward, not only for today but many more to come.

Your good friends,
Dick and Donna————

Joël,

L'amitié est comme pour les grandes âmes

Bonne fête
Dr. Yves, Leyda, et les enfants————

Joel

50 is youthful and savory and smart. It's confident witty. And, man, it's got heart. It's sexy (extremely)! It's strong (like an ox)! It's sensible (sort of like good cotton socks)!

50 is relaxed. It's an age with a view. It's here. And it's now. And it's perfect on you.

> *Happy Birthday,*
> *Drs. Evelyne and Charles——*

Dearest Joel,

Happy Birthday, we wish you another 50 years with good health, happiness, and the Lord's blessings. We love you very much.

> *Love,*
> *Dr. Renault, Fifi, and Manmie*
> *Anne——*

Dear Joel,

We are very fortunate to be part of this special occasion. Our friendship has been our blessing for all those years and we are looking forward to the coming years.

> *God be with you.*
> *Vicky and Dr. Daniel———*

Dear Joel,

For your 50th Birthday, we asked the wise man on the mountain the secret of a long life, and the longer we'd like to pass a long words of wisdom to you, "Keep breathing as long as possible."

> *Dr. Eddy and Marie-Beth——*

Joel,

Your birth age says you're 50, but everything about you screams "40"

> *Happy Birthday and enjoy.*
> *Toni*

Joel,

*I hope you have a great 50ᵗʰ birthday! Don't be upset by turning
50—Remember it is a bonus just waking up every morning—
God Bless-*

Linda————-

Joel,

*Happy Birthday I hope you have a wonderful day and a great
party; remember you are only as old as you feel. I hope you have a
happy and healthy upcoming year.*

Jenn————

As a way to say a big thanks to my wife, Kettline, and more
particularly, because she really did a nice job, I offered to take
her back to Europe. She really loves going to Europe, especially
Paris, France. I told her that not only was the trip to thank her
but it was also to celebrate our twenty-fourth wedding anniversary. She graciously accepted the offer. We invited the boys to go
with us, since we always travel with them. For the first time, they
declined to go on vacation with us. As a matter of fact, they told
us that it was time that Kettline and I should enjoy each other's
company. Keep in mind that our anniversary is August 2. At the
end of July 2003, we hopped on the plane and *zoom*, we launched
for Europe.

On our first trip to Europe, we stayed over at families' houses
in France and Switzerland, and in hotels when visiting other
countries. That time, instead of staying with family, we decided
to book a hotel in Paris, but we did not have too much of a choice
in Switzerland, because one of my sisters lives in Geneva. So we
stayed over at my sister's home while visiting. We flew straight to
Paris and we stayed there for five days. The first night, we stayed
in a brand new Courtyard Hotel by Charles De Gaulle Airport
and we transferred to another Courtyard Hotel that is located
fairly close to "Arc de Triomphe et les Champs Elysées" (Arch of
Triumph and Champs Elise), in Neiue. Neiue is one of the Paris

Heights. We did have a lot of fun in Paris. One day, we decided to go for a long train ride; we purchased a one-day pass, and we hopped on a train without knowing where we were going. After we sat in the train for a good hour, it made a complete stop. Everyone on the train, which was not that many anyway, was asked to get out because the train was at it final destination. At that time we were already out of our travel areas, even though we had a one day-pass, but we were supposed to stay in certain locations. Guess what? Without knowing it, we were right at Disney World of France. As tourists, we bought two discounted tickets, because it was about 4:00 p.m., so we did not have to pay the full price. We had a great time there. The ironic thing was the fact that we had never been to one of the USA's Disney World.

The following day, we left Paris to go Switzerland, where we spent a few days at my sister's house. Then we went back to Paris for one last night. I cannot complete this story without telling you what happened to me in Paris. On the morning of our departure, Kettline had to deliver a package that she brought for a friend; we did not have the time to see the friend in Paris, and we decided to mail it to him. The post office was not too far from the hotel, so we walked down there. At the post office, we took a number and waited to be served. After a good fifteen minutes of waiting, Kettline told me that she had to go back to the hotel so she could finish packing our belongings. Kettline left and I stayed. Shortly after, I was called and served. I left the post office to go back to the hotel, which was not supposed to take any more than ten minutes walking. Man! Oh, Man! I walked twenty minutes, thirty and approaching forty. I began to panic. I got lost completely. Meanwhile, Kettline had already finished and called a taxi to take us at the airport. By then, I was lost for a good hour going to an hour and fifteen minutes. I really began to lose it; for some reasons the French are not like the Americans when giving directions. Every time I asked for directions, I got myself in a bigger mess. And also, there was no taxi available in the area that I was in. I was so worried, not because I got lost but because it was our departure day and we were pressed for time. Thank God I spoke with a couple gentlemen who told me where I could go and wait for a taxi. They also let me know I was very far from the hotel. I went up there and waited; suddenly, a taxi stopped right next to me and the cab driver asked me if I were the man who was looking for a taxi. I said, "Yes, and who told you that I needed a taxi?" He said he was in the area and a couple of guys told him that I was looking for a taxi.

Poor Kettline, she thought that something bad had happened to me. Anyway, the first cabdriver that came to pick us up had to leave. She called another one by faith. I finally made it more than an hour and a half later from the time I was supposed to be there to begin with. I explained to Kettline what happened and without taking any more time, we hopped in the taxi and went to the airport. Kettline took a stab at me for getting lost in Paris, and we chatted about the good times we had and how much we enjoyed our vacation. Oh, well, we had a ball in Europe. Of course, we missed our flight; we ended up flying back in coach. Not only were we uncomfortable, we also could not get a flight to Cleveland via Chicago. That flight was bound to Miami. Unfortunately, arriving there the plane could not land because the weather was not cooperating, so we went all the way to the Bahamas where we circled the area a few times until we were permitted to land in Miami. We waited in the Miami Airport for approximately two to three hours. Then we got on another plane to go to Cleveland. We made it there shortly after midnight. In Cleveland, one of my friends, Pastor Pierre, came to pick us up at the airport. At the same time he had one of his friends who he was supposed to drop off at the bus station to go to Alabama. When we got home ourselves, like I said, it was past one in the morning. That was when we realized that the gentlemen that was with Pastor Pierre had left with Kettline's suitcase. In that particular suitcase were Kettline's undergarments. Pastor Pierre and I left automatically and went back to the bus station; fortunately, the gentlemen had not left yet. We were able to exchange the suitcases. By that time, Kettline and I were running on twenty-seven hours of no sleep. So you can imagine how exhausted we were.

That same morning we got home, as I was getting in the garage, I suspected that my BMW had been used. So I asked Pastor Pierre if he had used the car for some reason, he said no, but he believed his son had used it. So I didn't say anything and went on with my business. In the following days, a few of my neighbors told me that my house was like a Grand Central Station; cars were moving in and out, meaning all three cars, of the garage. So we began to suspect there was some kind of privilege abuse.

So I asked the boys if they had used the cars for some reason and of course, they told me that they did not use our cars, but used theirs. Later during the day I found out that indeed the boys—Pastor Pierre's son, my brother-in-law Gerard's son, and my sister's kids, coupled with my two boys—were excessively misusing the cars and also that they were staying out late, sometimes until two o'clock in the morning. I also found out the boys did not personally use Kettline's and mine, but they let the other kids use them. So, I lost it. I was extremely angry and so was Kettline because we were very disappointed. At that time the boys were sixteen and fifteen. They were punished appropriately, and I then promised them both that they were not going to be punished by their daddy that way anymore. I have not had any stupid arguments like that with them since. The other kids were not disciplined; only Joey and Ricky were, which means only my family suffered the consequences.

As I began to regroup from that event, I found myself in a bigger mess, and that was the mess that I mentioned earlier while I was telling you about my old boss. As I promised, I will explain what happened, but I won't be able to go into full detail, due to the fact that I am no longer working for the company and I signed a separation agreement that does not permit me to do so. Early in December 2003, while I was working, I had to sit down with a fellow employee for a counseling session. Just for the record, I would like to summarize the event that took place on December 3, 2003, to be precise.

On Tuesday, December 2, 2003, it was brought to my attention that an employee was implicated in an inappropriate behavior in the plant's parking lot. After talking with my manager concerning the event, it was agreed that I would talk with the employee. So, in the afternoon, I met with the employee in my office to discuss the issue. I told the employee that the reason he was in the office was to talk to him about this note. The note contained information about what happened. I handed it to him. He read it and told me that it was not true. I simply told him that he was not being disciplined nor being accused of anything, but if he were acting in that manner, he needed to stop because that could cost him his job. He admitted that he did it. Then he asked me what I was going to do with the note, I told him that I would keep it "on file," and in the event that the issue resurfaced, it could be used to show that we had that conversation. End of that conversation.

In the evening I received two phone calls from another fellow employee requesting that I call him back no matter what time. So I did call him at 11:30 p.m. on my way from work to home. The employee asked "What the hell" I was doing. The phone call was in reference with the issue that I dealt with that afternoon. I told him that I was not going to discuss an employee's business with another employee. He started cussing and hung up the phone. I called him back asking him if he hung up or the phone call dropped. He said, "Your damn right I hung up on you." I asked him to let it go and then we could discuss the matter the following day. He once again hung up on me.

On the following day, I made a bad decision that I thought was the right one. I decided to pull myself away from everyone that I was close with. I felt that I was losing respect from coworkers because I was too friendly. I called a number of employees that I used to chat with in a friendly way, both young and old, black and white, male and female, and told them that I was not going to be too friendly anymore, and that I would continue to do my job professionally as I used to. I was very emotional and some of them were too. I made a terrible mistake by saying, during the course of my conversation, that there was no one in the company that could make me do any stupid thing to jeopardize my job and my married relationship. What I was thinking or what was I drinking? I admitted that I lost it. I was under a lot of pressure, but what is right is right. And I added, "Besides, I don't want to be any one of you here." One of the employees went and told a couple of other employees about my statement. They decided to retaliate against me. One of them called Almondo, my boss, and told him that she wanted to talk to him. Then later the same employee called him back and said that it was no longer important to talk to him. There was an event that required Almondo's presence in the plant early in the morning. So he went there before a shift change; there he found out that there were a number of employees that were talking about someone getting me upset and that I kind of lost it yesterday. That troubled Almondo and he decided that it was important that he talk to the employee anyway. After their conversation, Almondo began an investigation automatically, alone with one of the associates in the department. No one said or brought a complaint of any sort against me. Remember that I told you that Almondo was very upset at me early in the year.

Almondo had conducted a seventeen-day investigation and interrogated about thirty-five employees to see if there were any wrongdoing from my part and if he was not in any way implicated in that thing. Since I was a close friend of his, he was worried that employees would put his name into the mess. When he did not find any, he got to come with a decision. He came with an unprofessional conduct verdict and I was put on a final warning. This final warning would stain my professional career for a long time, if not forever. In the next two years, this will resurface and I will not like it at all. I continued to work for Almondo for almost two years after that event. At first, we were very distant from each other and the situation was very weird. I managed to retain and maintain a friendship with Almondo, despite the pain and agony the event inflicted upon me. I firmly believed that I was going to lose my job. Since then, I began to look for other opportunities, and I made Almondo aware that I was looking. I always believe in telling the truth even when I know the consequences will be severe. Of course, we were good friends and he did not want to see me leave; and at the same time, he was no longer comfortable having me in the department as a short-timer. Besides, no believers should have any reserve and should not complain when they are mistreating or suffering, because God never used someone that did not go through though adversities. Roman 8:31 "What then shall we say about these things? If God is for us, who can be against us? " At one point, Almondo called me in his office and asked me when I was going to leave. I told him that I would leave when I found a job. I have to say that Almondo and I tried very hard to save what ever was left from our friendship. We remained friends for a short period of time, but down the road, and because the wound was not healed properly, we will be separated again in the future. I will explain when I get there. Prior to that event, I contradicted a decision that Almondo made and at the same time, I questioned his authority. Because of that he did not come to my birthday party, but the entire staff came. I mentioned his name in my speech as one of the greatest friends that I had. I really meant it.

FIFTY-ONE YEARS OLD TO FIFTY-TWO YEARS OLD

Life after Fifty

Almondo called me a second time asking if I was still leaving the company and when I thought that I was going to make the move. That was when I began to realize the friendship was not coming back and that it was about to take a drastic turn. At that time, it was imperative that I did something. Then I said, "That too shall past." I started to think about some strategies.

Meanwhile, things were deteriorating rapidly. Almondo lost his trust in me, and anyone in the office could see that we were not the same. Now, you need to remember that I was dealing with a guy who was and probably one of the best executives in northeast Cleveland's history. Sometime later, I went on a trip to Florida, so I could get a break from the heat. That trip was going to be the windbreaker for the situation that I was living in and it would provide effective tools to build a way out. That way out will bring us back together and the friendship will be rebuilt stronger, at least for a year.

On the way back from Florida, I picked up a leftover copy of USA Today at the airport and I began to read some articles in the business section. A picture from the paper caught my eyes; I could tell the man in the picture was a top executive. For further description, he was a black man in his early fifties. The gentleman in the picture happened to be John W. Thompson, Chairman of the Board and CEO of Symantec Corporation. According to the article, John Thompson, a black man in the United States, had the luxury to fly a company's private plane, and not only that, he had the full control to divert or land the plane from a route to any other and legal routes without any questions ask. Unfortunately, I don't have the original article, so I cannot elaborate on it. Besides the newspaper, I did some research on the Internet; I was able to find some information about Mr. Thompson.

After finishing my homework, I said to myself, "Joel, you just found the perfect tool to work on Almondo." What I meant by this was to boost his ego to go higher and leave the plant. My intentions were very honest. I really wanted to help him move up. We had talked about that for many, many years prior to the incident. By the same token, I also wanted to get him out since I could not yet find a new job. Anyways, this move will be great at the beginning, but at the end, will be very costly to me. Maybe I should leave then, or have him get me out. Why do I say that? You will find the response in the next chapter. I also thought if we were not working together and being in the same parent company, we would get along fine and our friendship could be saved. I really love the guy, as I said time after time; Almondo is a good man and can be one of the greatest friends that one can have. Unfortunately his paranoia, at times, takes control of his intellectual capacity. My strategy did work. You will see. First,

I shared the thought with a very good friend of mine, Polie, who was also my confidant and my friend for life. I explained to her that I could use the article to get Almondo to make few phone calls to see how he could go ahead in the corporation. Polie knew about the ordeal and the tension between Almondo and me. She had already told me that, in her opinion, to continue working with Almondo was unpredictable. You know, I did not want to really leave the company and besides, I had already called most of my working contacts and other networking accesses. Those efforts were unproductive. Quitting was not an option. So, Polie told me that the article was the best way to convince him of making a move.

I knew that Almondo had some good contacts in the corporation and was well viewed and well respected from the peers and the top executives because of his loyalty and his passion for the company. At one point, Almondo and I were two of the most loyal employees in the company. I have to say, once again, Almondo is a very intelligent man and has ample expertise in the industry. Honestly, he was not performing at his best, because the company was not challenging his potential. His biggest problem was the fact he did not want to step on anyone's toes. He was always afraid to make a move, worried about losing his job or worried about if they, his higher ups, really like and respect him. If he lost his job, would it be easy to find another job? Would his age and race be negative factors? I used to discuss these scenarios with him all the time. I honestly did not think those scenarios would matter. After all, I found out that maybe he was right. In any way, shape, or form I don't want this book to appear to be or have any negative connotations, nor have a controversial aspect of age, race or sex. I just want to say it the way it is; "If it looks like a duck and walks like a duck, it is a duck." There is no other way around it. I called Almondo and asked him for a private meeting. We met in his office. I showed the article to him and asked him to read it. Then I asked him to answer this question, "What does this guy have that you don't?" Of course he read it but did not answer the question. Then I asked him, "Do you think this guy is more intelligent than you?" He said, "I don't know, Joel." Please note, Almondo, is very humble and he would not put himself above anyone. I finally said to him, "You know what the guy has that you don't?" He said, "No." I told him he has guts. He takes risk, he is not afraid of losing what he holds. Then I told him that it was about time that he seeks higher ground. I reassured him that he has the potential and the connection to get there. Our conversation was mutual. We discussed a few points, which would not be necessary to broadcast in the book. I urged and begged him to work on it and I asked him to make it clear that he would want to move up in the company, and that he thought it was time, and that he was serious about it. I remember clearly how uncomfortable he was in building a plan of action to tackle the idea. He was afraid that he would be perceived as a "brown noser." That particular day, our friendship was somewhat renewed and the sandy trust started to also renew and reclaim. It was not two weeks after our conversation, Almondo was already on a plane on his way to an interview. Before a month, he landed a perfect job and he was out. I thought talking Almondo out was going to be to my advantage, but it was not. I was going to find out later that he was really looking out for me. Almondo was my protector and I did not, consciously, take his advice to heart. If I never talk to Almondo again, I would regret that I never sat down to tell him how I really felt. I hope by reading this book, he realizes how much I am hurt. I have to say, and I have said before, I am forever and I will be grateful and thankful to him. I love the guy very much. If I had to, I would take away only one thing I said of Almondo: "I will take a bullet for Almondo." At the time I said that, I really meant it. God knows. I firmly believe that his action was purely because of his paranoia and a way to save his job in case I was really involved in the scandal. I hope that he forgave me as much as I forgave him. Keep in mind, I did not say that I forget what had happened. In the following chapter, I will draw more attention at the forgiving and forgetting concepts. Most of the time people get hurt because of disappointments. If your level of expectation is high, or if you put your trust in friendships, you are more likely to get hurt. I have learned that I have to place my hope in God and not in man. Psalm 118:8, "It is better to take refuge in the LORD than to trust in man." By the way, this verse is the center verse of the Bible. I wish that I could have learned from someone else's mistake; but instead, I learned from my own.

As with everything in life you have a problem, you solve it, and another problem shows up. Not knowing what was ahead, I made a few adjustments as I rearranged my plan. It began to work accordingly; what it did not do, because I didn't think of it, was leaving the past behind. Apparently, Almondo got over it, but I never finished, forgot, or sincerely forgave the fact that I was so hurt about what had happened. Yes, Almondo had left, which could have been a positive mark for a new beginning. No, it was not. It is written, "You cannot have a new beginning if you don't finish with the past." It is very important to understand the concept of "Forgive and Forget" and how they work together. By no means do I want to preach or teach about forgive and forget. I simply want to give my own viewpoint and the way I understand the concept myself. I clearly remember an argument with Almondo where I was very angry and disrespectful. Almondo calmly said to me, "I am not going to talk with a madman. I refuse to." Wow! How powerful! Still to date, I keep hearing this phrase, on and on again. Yes, it was powerful.

There are so many books written about "forgive and forget." So many preachers, teachers, lectures, and talk show hosts talk about this. One of the common questions asked when someone is hurt: "How can you forgive when you can not forget?" If I knew what I know today about the power of *forgive* and *forget* I would not suffer what I suffered prior to that point and I would not have to deal with it in the following years.

This is how Wikipedia defines *forgiveness* and *forgetting:*

Forgiveness is typically defined as the process of concluding resentment, indignation or anger as a result of a perceived offense, difference or mistake, and ceasing to demand punishment or restitution.

Forgetting (retention loss) refers to apparent loss of information already encoded and stored in an individual's long term memory. It is a spontaneous or gradual process in which old memories are unable to be recalled from memory storage."

Furthermore, I have done some research and Googled both terms. The following are a few of the findings. I only wish that I followed them all, honestly I would be better off today. I am hoping that you, my readers, follow them all.

- Forgiving is letting another know that there is no grudge, hard feelings, or animosity for any wrongdoing.

- Forgetting is putting these behind you; they are no longer brought up and no longer remain a barrier to your relationship.

- Forgiving is letting the other person know that you accept genuinely the remorse and sorrow for actions or words that hurt or disappointed you.

- Forgetting is promising that these acts, whether of omission or commission, will not be resurfaced again.

- Forgiving is accepting the sincerity of apology, sadness, and regret expressed over a grievous personal offense; make it enough to clear the air.

- Forgetting is your allegiance to let go of anger, hurt, and pain over this offense.

- Forgiving is the highest form of human behavior that can be shown to another person.

- Forgetting is equally as high a human behavior; it is letting go of the need to seek revenge for past offenses.

- Forgiving is the act of letting go of provisional ill will, dissatisfaction, or the repugnance that arises from the break in your relationship.

- Forgetting is bridging this gap in the relationship, eventually strengthening it against such a break in the future.

- Forgiving is the compassion, and the kindness virtues by which you give others a chance to know that they are certainly the children of God upon whom a mixture of graces and blessings have been given and that actual or past offenses are no longer a block that prevent goodness and value to stand out.

- Forgetting is the act of support, encouragement, and corroboration that leads you to assist another person to reconstruct, and reinstate a loving, kind, strong relationship with you, others, and the society where abilities, gifts, and skills are openly treasured and reciprocated.

As I said before, I was carrying the anger with me as I was trying to deal with the present structure, and besides, the company was going through a drastic change that started a few months prior to Almondo's transfer and it continued after he left. Those changes ranged from staff members, and included the HR manager slot. That means that I had to go through a lot of adaptations; and things were weird and scary. I have to admit that it was not the company that was the problem, even though the change of management was a norm, but the fact that I did not forget what had happened or, more likely, I did not let go of the past. How can anyone move forth, when he/she lives in the past?

Forgiveness without complete forgetting is no forgiving. The Bible puts it this way:

"For if you forgive men when they sin against you, your heavenly Father will also forgive you, but if you do not forgive men their sins, your Father will not forgive your sins."

Matthew 6:14–15 (NIV)

It is not the forgetting that is the problem, it is the anger that associates with the impact of the offense inflicted upon you by the offender. Stephen Arterburn and David Stoop wrote an article in the Men's Devotional Bible (NIV), and I will quote the last paragraph of the article: *"If a man buries his anger inside, he is only storing up pressure for a later implosion (hurting himself) and/ or explosion (hurting others). If he doesn't bring his anger the surface and deal with it someday, somewhere, somehow it will express itself in an out-of-bounds manner, and somebody will get hurt."*

During my time working in the metallurgical laboratory, I used a number of acid solutions and mixed chemicals, and I have seen and experienced a lot of chemical reactions. Those experiences lead me to compare anger and acid reactions. For example: If you store acid in a container, after a while it will eat the container and it will attack and destroy anything that it comes in contact with. I was an angry man. Therefore, I could not focus on what really was happening around me. I was dissatisfied, discouraged, and my level of anxiety was growing rapidly. I began to talk crazy, especially when things were overlooked; I would argue with my supervisors and became upset with them at times. Yet despite all this, I still managed to get my work done in a timely manner and most of the time I worked long hours. I asked upper management to reassign or to transfer me to another department. I was not granted this request. So, I began to look for other opportunities within the cooperation. I just did not like working there anymore. I remember sitting in my office one bright morning. It was about 10:45 a.m. and I felt like I was having a heart attack. I was sweating, my arms were tingling, my vision started to blur, and my knees were shaking. I prayed and waited for about fifteen minutes in order to compose myself. Then I left the office without saying anything to anyone, and went straight to the emergency room. When I got there, I told the front desk nurses that I was having a heart attack. Rather than dealing with my immediate problem, they instead told me to have a seat and someone would be with me in a moment. I waited for forty-five minutes; no one asked me any questions so I left the hospital. Right across the hospital was my cardiologist's office, so I went to see him. But, while I was in the emergency room waiting, my mind went back to the time when I witnessed a friend of mine who died right in front of me with a massive heart attack in an emergency room; he was forty-seven years old. You may wonder how that happened. I will tell you.

It was somewhere in mid July of 2004. My friend, whom I call Jack for the sake of privacy of identity, and I worked together in the early eighties for a few years until Jack left the company to work for another company. We were reconnected in June 2004. Jack worked third shift in the production department. On a Tuesday morning, I met him at the front door; he was smoking a cigarette while talking with a coworker. He did not look good at all. I asked him what he was doing out there. He told me that he was not feeling well and that he was waiting for his fiancée to pick him up. I took him to my office and had him sit down. We had a long conversation; we talked about what happened in the last eighteen years. I found out that he had three daughters, including a set of twins. Then I found out that less than six months prior to that event, he was hospitalized for heart problems. I asked him if it were crazy for him to continue smoking. He told me that he was going to quit, but he could not promise when. I urged him to go to see a doctor as soon as he left the office. Well, his fiancée came and they left. Jack did not come to work on Tuesday night, so I called him on Wednesday morning to find out how was he doing. Jack told me that he did not go to the doctor's office because he wanted to rest. On Wednesday evening, around 7:30 p.m., I received a phone call from Jack who told me that he was not feeling well and that he was going to the emergency room. Jack also let me know that there was a chance that he would miss another day of work. I told him to not worry about the job and to take care of himself, I would let his lead person know. Then I told him that I would come to see him at the hospital. At that particular time, I had a few guests over; I could not just get up and leave. As soon as my guests left I went straight to the hospital, which was about two miles from my house. At the hospital, I met Jack and his fiancée, whom I will call Lina, in a consultation room. Jack's blood pressure was very low. The blood pressure machine he was hooked on read 79 over 58. I told him that his blood pressure was too low and that I believed he should be hooked on a heart-monitoring device. Jack told me that the hospital personnel knew about his blood pressure status and that they were waiting for a cardiologist to come and check him out. I made nothing out of it, since he was in the hospital, and to be precise, in the emergency room. We started a talk about our friendship of twenty plus years. We talked about good times and bad times, about our kids, our working life, and our religions. Jack, who was also a good friend of my brother Jarman, had a chance to see him and hear a sermon that Jarman preached around one week prior. The sermon's title was "Do you have mildew in your life?" We talked about the message and Jack told me that he would need to remove some mildews in his life, and that he could not wait to find out when Jarman would make a comeback in Ohio so Jack would have another chance to hear him preach again. I made a huge mistake that night; I could have used that opportunity to lead him to Christ and I did not. I knew that he was not a Christian. That is one thing that I have to live with for the rest of my life. Okay, we changed the topic a little bit after fifteen to twenty minutes. One of Jack's employees had lost her mom and the funeral services were on Thursday morning. Jack realized he would not be able to attend them, and asked me to apologize to the employee and her family, and that he would follow up with her later during the week. Then he asked me if I was going. "Certainly," I replied to him. Then, I said to Jack and

Lina, "Tell me about you." Jack told me that Lina was his fiancée and got along with his daughters and his family very well.
They had been living together for a good five to six years. They
talked about how and where they met, the house they bought,
etc. I thought for a moment, and I said, "Guys, you know, if
something would have happened to my son Ricky, I mean, if he
dies, I would feel so devastated, not only because he passed, but
because I know what could have made him the happiest child in
the world; and I did not do it." Jack, who was a little bit tired,
turns his head toward me and with a weak voice, he said, "What
is it, buddy? What could have made him happy?"

"A dog; he always asks, since he was five years old, for a dog,"
I replied. Both Jack and Lina told me that I should buy my son
a dog. I laughed and I said, "I don't think so." We switched the
conversation about their lives in Painesville, Ohio, because they
had just moved to Ohio a little over a year earlier. They talked
about their new house purchased in Painesville, Ohio less than
six months earlier, their large outdoor Jacuzzi with six seats that
had not been installed yet, and their plans for the future. They
wanted to have Kettline and me over for dinner. I paused for a
minute, then, I asked Jack why he did not marry Lina after living with her for five years. Jack told me that he is scared because
of his first marriage, but he loves Lina very much and that also
he feels great about her. Lina, on the other hand, saw no reason
at all that holds them to get married. "We talked about it, but
we have not decided on a date. Well, I should say, on what year."
said Jack. " For some reason, I told them, sometimes, it is best to
do the right thing at the right time, and the right time is now.
We always put things on hold, only to find out that it is too late.
Jack gave me a few reasons why they were not married. Well
I left that part of the conversation alone. Jack was silent for a
moment as if he were thinking about something. Then he said,
"Hey buddy, would you get the bottle of Sprite on the floor and
pass it to me, please?" The bottle was half full, I guest he probably
brought it with him. I picked it up and passed it on to him. He

drank the remaining portion at once and he handed me the bottle, which I threw out to a small garbage can in the corner of his bed. He burped couple times, and he said, "Oh! G! I was thirsty." He got quiet again for a minute, as if he went into a deep thought. As he came out of it, he said, "Hey, buddy, I tell you what. Let's make a deal: If you buy Ricky a dog, I will marry Lina." It was then almost 9:00 o'clock. I replied, "Oh no! I can't buy him a dog." Then I continued: "It is not really because I cannot, I just don't want to buy a dog, because I would be the one to take care of it after all." You should see the look in Lina's eyes. If one would have to interpret or define that look, the interpretation would have been: "Joel, you are a total idiot. How dare you pass up a deal like that? Not only could you have made your son happy, but I would also have the chance to get married." Instead, she said, "Joel, you should consider buying the dog for Ricky, knowing that could make him so happy." As she was talking, Jack said, "Hold it! I will not be able to marry Lina in December." I asked him why. "I will need to file for income tax as a single, so I can get the maximum cash return," he replied. "Okay," I said. A couple seconds later, Jack got very quiet and turned his face against the wall opposite to Lina and he closed his eyes. On the bed, he was in a reclined position, I would say in an angle of 135 degrees. Lina was standing on his left side holding his left arm and gently rubbing down his forearm to his hand. I was standing at his right side. Less than thirty seconds later, his left arm in a rapid motion, jerked from Lina's hands. It was as if he received an electrical shock. Simultaneously, he sat straight at a perfect ninety-degree angle with his arms planted at his sides. Everything happened so quickly and at the same time. His head went from left to right and right to left repetitively with his mouth opened, gasping for air. Lina and I called for help. A couple nurses showed up and began to talk with Jack and few more hospital personnel arrived and they took him to another location. We waited for thirty minutes in a private room inside the ER area, when the head nurse came to ask us if Lina was Jack's wife. Lina told the nurses that she was his fiancée and that he was divorced. The nurses asked if his mom was around or any other close family. I asked why. The nurses said that he was not responding and that thing does not look good, but they are still working on him. Then she said, "I will keep you guys informed." She left us in the dark. We both did not think about death, because you cannot just stop talking with someone and that someone drop dead right in front of you. Ten minutes later, a doctor walked in and said, "We did everything we could. We lost him." Jack is dead.

I did not want to stay in the hospital after I thought about this tragedy. I left the hospital and went across the street to see my cardiologist, Dr. Espinosa. I did not have an appointment, but Dr. Espinosa told his staff that it was okay to let me see him. He examined me and ran an EKG and a stress test. Thank God! He found nothing wrong with my heart. He knew about the amount of stress I was under and that I just lost a friend, should I say, witnessed my friend's death, he sat me down for a counseling session. He told me that my symptoms were most likely the result of stress and having witnessed that gentleman's death. Therefore, my visit to him was more out of fear than an actual heart attack feeling. I went back to work and continued my normal routing.

FIFTY-TWO YEARS OLD TO FIFTY FIVE YEARS OLD

The University of Adversity–First-time Unemployed in my Working Career

Adversity is a state of hardship or of misfortune. It can be as small as locking your car with the key inside or leaving your office keys at home; it can also be a big thing like losing a family member or losing your job of twenty-five years. It can as well be having your house foreclosed or something as huge as going through a divorce, it can be going through a lengthy period of financial hardship or working in a job that you are completely dissatisfied with. Any problem in life can be described as adversity, long-term or short-term; it depends on how we take it or how we deal with it. If we are able to turn our adversity into a challenge instead of becoming depressed and distressed when things don't go our way, the smaller problems won't be a problem at all and the larger ones will be easier to deal with. It can be also described as persecution or bad luck, such as your house being burned, as well as unnecessary and unforeseen trouble resulting from an unfortunate event. In one sentence, adversity is anything that makes our life miserable. In this chapter, I will tell you about the troubles I suffered and endured during 2005 and 2006. I wish I knew the spiritual definition of *adversity* and the concept of the "University of Adversity." According to the Bible, every leader God used for his glory was tested and did go through hardship and severe adversity. Therefore, as we are going through hardship we need to know that God is preparing us to receive a blessing He has stored for us. Besides, adversity is quite often the element that cleanses our lives. For instance, we so often become occupied with what, in essence, amounts to insignificant and useless things. They become built up around us like fences or walls, so we can't normally control ourselves. Then adversity pushes itself into our lives. In my case, as I mentioned several times, my level of anger, frustration, and not being able to forget and forgive were my walls.

My level of frustration was getting higher and higher in March 2005. Maybe because I realized that I was no longer under Almondo's shadow. I lost my security blanket. Maybe his advice started to sink in, and maybe I realized he was looking out for me. Maybe I was in denial or I was so upset that I could not think. Maybe I was confused. Why was I so frustrated? I was making more money than I had ever made in my life. Ironically, as I was reviewing the rough edited manuscript of the book, I realized that I was making one third of that salary. Guess what? I was not going though any adversity. I was loved and respected by 85 to 90 percent of the people I worked with and for. Even while I was going through tough times, I was privileged to give advice to staff managers and VPs. A VP named me, "The most loyal employee in an entire plant." The president concurred. I was trusted by a number of GM/VPs that are today presidents and CEOs of big corporations. If I were to simplify everything to its simplest expression, it would be: "I was blessed." But, I did know that.

Having explained all of that, why I was so miserable? The answer that I can come up with is, I was blinded by anger; and as I said before, everything that was overlooked and overwhelming was getting on my nerves. I could not control the hostile environment. So I began to focus on my inner person: I began to see myself as a protector, a defender, and I would go farther to say, I began to see me as an activist. That was when "hell broke lose" and I was at war. I believe, among other things, my ordeal started around the month of September 2004. Throughout the book, I made mention about my personality. I always want for others to be treated with respect and dignity and to have the same opportunity as I have or better. I never felt comfortable to receive when my companion or my fellow workers don't. I prefer others to have more than I. I love people! By now, it should not be a surprise to you. People are so selfish that at times they will go to the extreme of getting themselves hurt or making themselves suffer instead of letting others benefit from something good they deserve.

Let me tell you a joke as an illustration: There were a few men who were walking in a desert, and they met a genie. The genie told them that it would grant any wishes they asked for with one condition. Each will have to bring a companion and the companion will in turn receive a double portion. Each gentleman came back with one companion and asked for their wishes. One of them was so selfish that he did not want his companion to have more than him, so he approaches the genie and asked that he be beaten halfway to death. That was a joke, but let me be real with you. Selfishness is a horrible thing. I am going to choose Haiti, my native country, but this example of selfishness is everywhere and being demonstrated mostly by capable people and affluent people. As in Haiti, these Haitians have high education, mostly educated abroad, money, businesses, high ranks, fame, etc. It is very common for the rich folks to live in the same neighborhood as middle and lower classes. This is to say that the roads are unpaved and there is a lack of electrical power. There was a time when people had a few hours of electricity in any given day. And before the "cell phone" age, telecommunication was a dilemma. During rainy seasons, it is a catastrophe. The roads are getting worse, power failure lasts longer, and house phones can take weeks to restore. Do you think that these affluent folks would put their resources/finance together to get these problems solved? No! Their thinking is this: If they solve the problems, middle classes and lower classes would also benefit from the results. Instead, they buy SUVs, and/or four-wheel drive vehicles; they buy powerful electrical inverters/generators that can produce enough electricity for the whole fortress and for many hours. As I said, before the cellular telephone age, they bought long-range "Motorola Walkie-Talkies." It is so unfortunate for people to go to these lengths to differentiate themselves from others. Those rich people would rather drive in the mud, see a pile of trash, smell all kinds of debris, and subject themselves to all kind of maladies just because they don't want others to feel or to enjoy a good time, especially, at their expense. I don't condone these types of behaviors. I firmly believe that people who display these ugly styles, often condescend to others, especially the unfortunate. It troubles me and I cannot take it. I refuse to. One of the best accomplishments in my career was to be in four different college graduations of four minority co-workers, four young black Americans that I encouraged to go back to school. Can you imagine if every one of us were to encourage four other people to do well, how great the world would be? I love people, all kinds of people. Every time I have a chance to talk to other folks, I always try to make a positive impression on them and let them know how important they are.

Two to three years prior to the month of September 2005, a co-worker was in my office for counseling. There I found out that she was having problems with her fourteen-year-old boy. She explained the extent of the situation and how it was interfering in her work. She was a second shifter. On a daily basis, the boy left the house immediately after she left for work to wander around the streets. Apparently, he was involved in drugs and other crazy things. The mom had to leave work from time to time to go to police stations to get him. As usual, she was a single mom with other children. That particular day, I gave her an advice that she did not like at all. As a matter of fact, she was very angry and did not talk to me for days. What did I say? I quoted her a verse in the Bible: *"No temptation has seized you except what is common to man. And God is faithful; he will not let you be tempted beyond what you can bear. But when you are tempted, he will also provide a way out so that you can stand up under it."* 1 *Corinthians* 10:13. Then I defined "The Way Out" for her. I told her that God is allowing her to see the direction that her child is taking, so He is preparing her to accept the out come. Then I bluntly told her that in a situation like this she would need to purchase a good life insurance policy on the boy. "Oh no, you did not say that, Joel," she angrily responded. She busted out crying and left my office. I felt bad, but I at the same time, felt compelled to say that to her. Not only did I feel compelled to tell her that, but also I knew she was not in a good financial position and that she would have some difficulties to bury the kid in the event that would have happened. Seriously, there are a number of people who have had a lot of legal problems with their children, and because of that, those parents have depleted all their funds. Then, they would sell every asset and even at times borrow money to bail their children out of jails and guess what? Most of those children ended up dead. Brutally murdered! The parents shamefully have to beg for money to burry them. My statement will, in a few years, become reality. Listen to this:

On Wednesday, September 14, 2005, I went to represent the company at the funeral of an employee's son, where Bishop C.M. Jenkins was to deliver the eulogy. The deceased was a sixteen-year-old who had died of a self-inflicted gunshot wound.

There were approximately 150 young men and women at the funeral. They were dressed mostly with long T-shirts with the picture of the deceased and the letters "R.I.P." inscribed on the back or the front of their shirts. I was hoping that the preacher who would deliver the eulogy was someone I knew, because I felt a burning desire to speak with the clergy. I thought for a few minutes and I asked the gentleman who sat next to me if he knew who the bishop was and to point him out to me. He pointed him out. I was surprised to see that he was not a "big guy", not to say that bishops are big, but that was the picture that I had in mind. I saw a well-fitted fellow, dressed in black, with a white shirt and a red tie. According to my culture, no one goes to a funeral with anything red. After pacing myself for a good five minutes, I got up and went to him and said, "Bishop, I am simply a messenger; you need to do whatever it takes to touch the hearts of these youngsters. If, through the Lord, you can save 25 percent of them, God will give you 25 percent more blessing." He smiled, and said, "You just have to pray for me, brother. Just pray for me." During the eulogy, Bishop Jenkins constantly repeated this phrase: "What happened to this young man is not stopping here. It is not finished with you, but you can finish with it." Before his conclusion, he asked, specifically, to all young people, "Who is next?" Then he repeated one more time, "It is not finished with you, but you can finish with it." He finished his sermon with this powerful statement: "It is time for youths and young adults to put an end to the traditional way of thinking and doing things, and to get 'out of the box,' to grow and to prosper, to take education seriously, and to stop the nonsense." Amen! Suddenly, most parents went out to look for their young ones and brought them in the church. You should have seen that, young people were coming from everywhere to go near and around the casket to pledge that they would not let their friend die in vain and that they would change their behaviors. The deceased was the son of that employee that I told to buy life insurance on that particular boy. I leave it up to you to guess about the financial impact. Bishop

Jenkins and I have met several times on a regular basis to come up with ideas to help young people at risk. As a result, Omega-5 International, Inc., was founded. It is a nonprofit organization with the purpose of meeting the educational, emotional, and cultural needs of youths and young adults, primarily in the U.S.A, but also around the world. Get the youngsters involved in their community, schools, and educational programs, and to eliminate fear of acceptance or rejection issues from other ethnic groups, specifically to enhance morale, self-esteem, and to build character and values. During the period of getting information and collecting data to build the organization, I developed the hidden passion and compassion within me and brought them out. Other people began to notice that I was no longer tolerant of certain behavior toward the less fortunate. I wanted to solve everyone's problems, I wanted to be at the hospitals, cemetery, hire everyone, and feed everyone. Honestly, I wanted to save the world. At times, I would take the oxygen mask off my face and place it on the face of the person sitting next to me, and get suffocated. This is hypothetically speaking. I don't really have to tell you how I felt going through those motions. I was affected by anything and everything. Previously, I have mentioned how anger reacts. I made an analogy of an acid reaction with anger reaction. I explained that if you put acid in a container for a long period of time, it will destroy the container and run out. Then it will destroy everything that it comes in contact with. The same goes for anger; you keep it inside of you, it will destroy you and come out. Then, it will destroy everyone that it comes in contact with. I am struggling to put my thoughts together. This chapter is one of the most difficult chapters for me to write. It took me a long time to write this chapter because I was wondering why I thought I was different from everybody, and why I felt that I was a rescuer? There is no doubt about it; God was preparing me to receive something big that He has planned for me. When will I get it? I don't know. One thing that I do know, God is always on time.

Therefore, I am taking each day as it comes. Adversity is like a university; you gradually conquer the graduation steps one at a time. As you claim the steps, the challenges become more apprehensive. It requires a higher level of resistance, and as you get closer to the end, you begin to feel better. What keeps me going, besides the faith I have in Jesus Christ, is the fact that I know the longer you are suffering or the longer you have been in a bad situation, you are halfway out. No need to look back. I have been procrastinating in dealing with this chapter, because I keep thinking that tomorrow will be better. I will get a job offer, I will get back on my feet, I will get a gigantic opportunity, and then I will feel more comfortable to write about what I went through instead of what I am going through. I just need to face it. And that is exactly what I am going to do. Let's go back to September 2005. Please remember the state of mind that I was living in. Remember the level of frustration and how sensitive I was toward certain behaviors. At the end of the month, my supervisor had a one-on-one meeting with me as he wanted to exchange ideas. Great! He began the meeting by bringing the drastic, ugly taint, and cancerous incident that occurred in December 2003. I said, "No, you didn't say that? You did not want to start the meeting this way? No, you didn't." Before he could answer, I told him that the meeting was over. I was so loud that a supervisor two offices down the hall came and knocked on my office door to calm me down. You know what was so amazing? The supervisor smiled and calmly said to me, "You need to be able to control your emotion if you want to advance to the next position." The acid came out and destroyed the trust that he had in me. Why I did not get fired I don't know. That was one more negative notch in my future with the company. The supervisor, prior to that incident, had much respect for me and in a wink of an eye lost it all. How could he continue to respect and trust me. I will not go through other things that had happened in between. At the same time my marriage was in limbo. I was having drastic problems with my spouse. I did not even want to go home at times.

I was trying to accommodate everyone's situation, I wanted to hire everyone, I thought I could solve everyone's problems. As a result, my financial means was deteriorating rapidly. I was under tremendous pressure and I was very unhappy at my job. I unfortunately became short-fused. I would yell at people for no reason. I had so much anger in me that I would talk in condescending ways to my peers and even to my superiors. Anyone who knows me will tell you that I was not the same person.

I tried to direct my energy toward Omega-5 in quest of fairness and education for the unfortunates. In March 28, 2006, after a heated argument with a third party vendor, I was asked to go home and think about my continuing working with the company. On April 7, 2006, I signed a mutual separation agreement and parted ways with the company. I will not be able to go into details about the separation process. For the sake of this book, I would say, yes it was mutual, but not pleasant. You remember in the previous chapters I wrote about the different feeling in a working career. I always thought that getting fired from a job was like getting flushed through a commode, but I honestly did not get upset or angry. Legally, I was not fired, but technically, I was. It did not surprise me. A number of people knew that I was unhappy. Therefore, it was not a surprise to them. I felt like I was taking a free and everlasting fall. I talked to Kettline and the boys and I told them that I would be taking some time off and starting my own business or when the time comes, I will have to make a few phone calls and I will get a great job. Ha! Ha! Ha! Take a seat.

You know I like to talk, to brag, and to show off, but I don't do these things to upset or to annoy others. I love to predict things, especially, when I talk about my future. My level of confidence is so high that people construe me to be arrogant. It is often very difficult for me to tell others that I behave that way because of my belief in God. Yes, I was so sure that I would get a job with no sweat. I wanted to spend my fifty-third birthday in a foreign land. Kettline and I decided that we should go to Japan. We did have a choice between Sidney, Australia and Tokyo, Japan. That alone troubled people around us. We were constantly asked the following questions: Where do you guys get this money? Why do you guys travel so much? Were you guys royalty in Haiti? I found the last question very ridiculous. As I mentioned above about my bragging, I told people that we always travel first-class. This is not to "pull their legs" we, most of the times, travel first class.

Please allow me to tell you what had happened to us one time at the Hopkins Airport in Cleveland, Ohio, I believe it was summer 2002. We were going to Amsterdam for our wedding anniversary celebration. Our tickets from Cleveland, Ohio to London, England, were first-class and purchased at a family-discounted price. For the sake of the incident, the tickets' cost $486 a piece, roundtrip. Then we purchased regular first class tickets for the rest of the trip, London to Amsterdam, roundtrip. Kettline and I dressed up very royally, top notch. We got our luggage checked in and we went to the boarding area, where we were to fly from Cleveland to Chicago, first leg. Right after the first call for passengers to board, we heard our names called to go to the airline's front counter. There we found out that we were not able to travel that particular period with the type of tickets we held. Wow! We could have canceled our hotels reservations but not the roundtrip tickets from London to Amsterdam. I told Kettline we are going to make a few phone calls at the airport and nothing happened. We asked the ticket agent what would be the cost for a regular ticket? We precisely asked for coach. We were told $1,256.00 per person. Meanwhile, the plane for our connection had left and we would not be able to connect with the Chicago flight. Then Kettline said, "Should we stay or should we go to another country?" I replied, "Oh, no, you did not say that." I told her, "When Joel left home, he told his kids and friends that he was taking his wife to Amsterdam to celebrate our wedding anniversary. Is that right?" Kettline said, "Yes, but.." I interjected, "Cé Kapab qui fè, pa kapab pa fè." "Non-Capable cannot do what capable can do." Because we could no longer travel that day, it was too late, we purchased two roundtrip coach tickets for $1,098 a piece for the trip and we spent the night at the airport hotel and flew the next day. Today, I call this stupid. Anyway, my wife and I left for Tokyo a couple days after I left the job, for over three weeks. I took time to research different avenues. I pushed Omega–5 and I did some teaching, and I explored the idea of buying a franchise form LMI, (Leadership Management Institute, based in Texas.) The cost was $30,000. Kettline had cold feet. I spent some time visiting my parents down south and made a couple trips to Haiti researching for this book.

In August, I decided that it was time to go back to work; I began to make a few phone calls and at the same time sent some résumés out. Guess what? Most of my so-called friends wrote back only to find out why I called them for. Without exception, they did not want to deal with me. People were still working and changing jobs for better positions or better living. I joined a group of executives that were either laid off or fired from their previous employments. We met on Wednesdays at a library in the greater Cleveland area. It was amazing to hear story after story about how easily people could lose a position. The worst stories were the well-paid guys who left a solid and concrete managerial position for VP or president positions just to get fired after a few months. It was really a great group of well-educated and professional people with a great pool of knowledge. The majority of jobseekers were MBAs and PhDs. I believe the group is still meeting at the same place. From time to time I receive an e-mail from a member of the group announcing that he or she has landed a good job, and that particular member automatically began to lobby for other members. We would joke about our ages and often some of us would color our hair for younger looks at an interview. Before joining the group, I remembered that a few years prior, I was offered a position from a local health equipment and medical devices manufacturer, I did not bother to look at it because I never dreamed of leaving the company that I worked for. It happened this way: A co-worker left the company and went to a small and privately owned company as an HR Manager.

While there, he felt that the opportunity was not the right fit for him, he began to look for other opportunities. He interviewed at that local company. For some reason, he thought that I would be a better fit for the job. He told the hiring manager to give me a call. So she did, and during our conversation, she told me that the position is mine if I wanted it. I would have to come and chat with her management team for formality. I asked her what was the amount budgeted for the position? She told me that is was $60,000 a year. I arrogantly told her that I would not waste her time and mine to interview for position that pays less than $80,000 a year plus an annual bonus. The conversation stopped right there. Unbelievable! Shamefully, I called the company later to find out if the hiring manager was still working there. Sure enough, she was. I asked to speak with her. She thought I was still working, she was happy that I called to say hello. When I told her that I am calling in quest of any vacant positions in her company because I was not working, she quickly reminded me that she did not have any $80,000 openings. I humbly apologized for my previous behavior and I told her that I would take an entry-level position. She was a much better and greater person than I was; she says that she did not have anything at that moment, and she kindly excused herself and said, "Good luck, my friend." I continued to send résumés out and attended executive search meetings with no success. I called a friend who used to work with me many years ago after his engineering college graduation. He owned a pretty good-sized company, and he asked me to come to see him. I did; we met and discussed some possibilities. We both realized that I would not be able to work for him, so he called a good friend of his whom I knew as well. He told him that I needed a job. The other gentleman, without hesitation, asked me to come to his office so we could discuss a good possibility. I went to see him, indeed, he offered me a job. From his office that was in another building than the one I was supposed to work in, he called the manager over there, and told him that he was sending me to talk with him about the position. Then he told me to call him on Thursday afternoon to discuss the salary. Oh! The whole thing happened on a Wednesday. Wow! I thanked him and left.

The same day, I met with the manager of the department, who told me where my office would be and what my assignments would be. He even apologized for being able to provide an upbeat office with new furniture and equipment to me; knowing that I came from a big company and he had seen my old office once. I could not wait for later in the afternoon; I called the gentleman at 2:00 p.m. He did not pick up, nor call back. I persisted to call, to finally found out that the position was no longer needed. Imagine yourself that you were in a position of power, where everyone needed you, where you helped so many, at every level, only to be constantly humiliated just because the table turned. It hurt! Hurt! Hurt! That happened on many occasions. I have to admit that I did have some good leads and at times I made it to a second interview, but could not land.

Searching for jobs is one of the most tortuous elements in anyone's life. Being an HR professional looking for a job, I imagine, since I have never been in jail, is like a police officer being in jail. A human resources manager, as I said again and again, is a company backbone and the conscience of the organization. People are at your mercy, they need you, and now you are at someone elses mercy. What upset me the most was the fact that the HR people that are currently employed, do not think that they too, could be on the other side. Not that I wish that, but I know the feeling. That also goes to the employed managers. You cannot really imagine how someone feels until you sat where they sit. As I am striving to finish this book; there are so many people that are out of jobs. There was a time that losing a job was a bad thing; you lost your job because you are a bad employee or you did something wrong. Today, people are out of jobs for no reason, just the fact companies are in limbo. You remember that I talked about the different sensations of losing a job. Nevertheless, there was a time that when you lost a job, you could get another one.

Today, getting laid off, quitting, and getting fired are like getting hit by a truck.

While I was still out of job, in the middle of the month of October, one Sunday afternoon, Kettline asked me if I had a good weekend. I said, "Yes." Then, she said, "Are you ready for bad news?" I asked her if my mom or dad went "bye bye?" She said, "No, I lost my job last Friday." I replied, "You cannot be serious." "Jo, I am dead serious." She said. Then I asked her why she did not tell me on Friday. She told me that she wanted me to enjoy the weekend. Contrary to how she reacted from my misfortune, I should not say "my misfortune" because it was our problem to begin with. Unfortunately, in her thoughts, she believed that I was doing or acting worse than what I explained to her that has happened. First, I was very unhappy at my job for about a good two and a half years. Second, I was not secretive about wanting out. Third, I was asked to go home to think, if I really wanted to continue with the company, and management was to do the same, meaning did they want to keep me on board or if I really wanted out. Fourth and not the last, I saw it coming. On top of it all, Kettline was not on my side. She would most of the time condemn me before I got convicted. I find myself saying most of the time to my boys and some close friends, "If I ever found myself on a trial for something or a crime that I did not commit, the prosecutors or the plaintiff lawyers called for a key witness, and that witness happens to be my wife, I would automatically stand up and put my hands behind my back so they could slap the handcuffs." I know it is awful to make such a comment in a book. Please remember that I am talking, and was dealing, with the most adversities in our lives. And certainly, I am not exposing my wife; I just wanted to make a point. Kettline, because of the ups and downs, more downs than ups, she would blame me for everything. I have done things that were not quite well, but nothing degrading to my family or my friends. And besides, how would I be able to write this book if my marriage were perfect? Nevertheless, this book is not about my marriage relationship, but what I learned in order to survive in this world thus far, and how much God, my God, has brought me through. I often compare my life with Joseph, son of Jacob. Just for the sake of the argument, a little bit of Joseph's history will help.

Joseph was the son of Jacob and Rachel. Rachel who could not get pregnant and was of old age, God blessed her with Joseph, in accordance with Genesis 30ᵗʰ vs. 23. "She *became pregnant and gave birth to a son and said,* "God has taken away my disgrace." He was his *father's favourite son. At a young age, he had two mysterious dreams that not only he told his brothers and his parents, but he interpreted them for them.*

Joseph's first dream was about his brothers. "Listen to this dream I *had: We were binding sheaves of grain out in the field when suddenly my sheaf rose and stood upright, while your sheaves gathered around mine and bowed down to it. His brothers said to him,* "Do you intend to reign *over us? Will you actually rule us?*" And they hated him all the more *because of his dream and what he had said.*" Genesis 37:6–8 *(New International Versions)* Red Flag!

Joseph's second dream was about the whole family. First he told his brothers: "Behold, I have dreamed a dream more; and, behold, the sun and *the moon and the eleven stars made obeisance to me.*" And he told it to his *father and the brothers together. His father rebuked him, and said unto him, 'What is this dream that thou hast dreamed? Shall I and thy mother and thy brethren indeed come to bow down ourselves to thee to the earth? Do you expect your whole family to come and bow down before you?'*" Genesis 37:9–10 (King James Version) More Red Flags!

Joseph was sold by his brothers, whom he looked everywhere for, so he could deliver the food that their father sent to the on the field. A man found Joseph wandering around in the fields and asked him, "What are *you looking for?*" He replied, "I'm looking for my brothers. Can you tell *me where they are grazing their flocks?*" "They have moved on from here," *the man answered.* "I heard them say, 'Let's go to Dothan.' "So Joseph *went after his brothers and found them near Dothan. There, his brothers sold him to some passers-by (Ishmaelites), because of jealousy. The Ishmaelites, upon arrival in Egypt, had sold him to Potipha, an officer of the*

Pharaoh of Egypt, as well as the captain of the Guard. Genesis 37:15–17 (New International Version)

Joseph was a slave in Egypt, but His Lord was with him there and the Lord made him a successful man. Joseph was a man of integrity, a man of character, everything he did was in God's favour. Joseph's master, Potiphar, saw this and gave favour to Joseph and made Joseph the overseer of his house and all that he had. While in charge of Potiphar's house he got tempted by the master's wife. But he refused and said to his master's wife, "Look, my master does not know what is with me in the house, and he has committed all that he has to my hand." 9 *There is no one greater in this house than I, nor has he kept back anything from me but you, because you are his wife. How then can I do this great wickedness, and sin against God?" Because of his faithfulness to his master, but more preferably, to His God, he ended up in prison.* Genesis 39:8–9 (New International Version)

Joseph was in prison for two years when Pharaoh himself had two dreams that bothered him. No one could help interpreting his dreams. Then someone remembered that Joseph had gift of interpreting dreams. So he told Potiphar about Joseph. So Pharaoh sent for Joseph. Then, he was taken to the Pharaoh. Joseph told Pharaoh that he did not have the power to understand dreams, but God does and He would give an answer through Joseph, which He did. Potiphar was amazed at what God had revealed to Joseph to tell him. He went from being a prisoner to the second most powerful man in Egypt.

Joseph made ruler in Egypt. The King and his staff were so impressed with Joseph's wisdom they decided to appoint him leader over all these things. The number one ruler of Egypt, Potiphar, said to Joseph, You shall be in charge of my palace, and all my people are to submit to your orders. Only with respect to the throne will I be greater than you." Genesis 41:40 (New International Version)

Joseph lived to be one hundred and ten years old. His body was embalmed and buried in Egypt.

I made reference to Joseph's life with mine because God is always at my side. No matter what is happening in my life I always think positively. I love the Lord with my entire heart and He knows it. He made me this promise that is stick on my mind: *"Because he loves me," says the* Lord, *"I will rescue him; I will protect him, for he acknowledges my name. He will call upon me, and I will answer him; I will be with him in trouble, I will deliver him and honor him. With long life will I satisfy him and show him my salvation."* Psalm 91:14–16 (New International Version) Kettline and I were getting deeper into depression and the atmosphere was getting more rigid.

After Kettline was able to convince me that she really lost her job, I said, "Now, what is next?" We called the boys and let them know that it was not only Dad but Mom also had lost her job. It was a sad afternoon. I told Kettline that she would need to file for unemployment as of the next day and that she would need to take a few days to relax her mind before beginning to hunt for jobs. Knowing how I felt, because I have sat where she then sat, when I took the time off to go to Tokyo, for a few weeks, I automatically proposed to her that we take a vacation. Kettline, who thought that I was not going to make or would take the news with such of a positive attitude, was very astonished. When I lost my job, as I said before, Kettline did not take it well; she thought that I was letting go for something else, instead of for what I told her had happened. Sometimes in life, God lets bad things happen just to prove a point. The point I think He wanted to make was to show Kettline not to be so quick to judge. It was a devastating blow for her, because she did not see it coming. I was very supportive of her and I explained to the boys the severity of the ordeal and I also told them not worry because the Lord was, and always will, be at our side. The following week, I believe, after Kettline lost her job, we were on our way to Cancun, Mexico. We had a fabulous time in Mexico; we enjoyed a seven-night and eight-day all inclusive trip there. Although we had traveled a good portion of the world, the trip to Cancun was probably one of the best, if it were not *the* best. You probably read this before: *"Après le beau temps, c'est la pluie."* After the good time is the bad time.

Back to reality, now we both are looking for jobs, each day we wake up with hope that today is it. Unfortunately, we would be looking for a long period with no luck. Come November, I was pretty discouraged, I had called all people on my rescue database and I had used all resources that I thought were available to me. By then I switched to outer states and even overseas, still nothing came my way or on Kettline's side. I could no longer concentrate on OMEGA–5, because the organization not only was a non-profit, but there was no positive movement of getting up and running. I began, like any other person, to ask, "Why me, why is this happening to me?" I also asked God. "What do you want me to learn from this? Is there anything good out of it? Most of the times I would fake it, like nothing was happening or I would be happy from the outside, but on the inside I was suffering so badly. More questions kept coming: Will I be in this situation forever? How far will this go? Secretly, I began to look for answers in the Bible. I came up with the following Bible verses:

> *For men are not cast off by the Lord forever. Though he brings grief, he will show compassion, so great is his unfailing love. He does not willingly bring affliction or grief to the children of men.*
>
> *(Lamentations 3:31–33)*

> *No temptation has seized you except what is common to man. And God is faithful; he will not let you be tempted beyond what you can bear. But when you are tempted, he will also provide a way out so that you can stand up under it.*
>
> *(1 Corinthians 10:13)*

> *I only know that in every city the Holy Spirit warns me that prison and hardships are facing me. However, I consider my life worth nothing to me, if only I may finish the race and complete the task the Lord Jesus has given me—the task of testifying to the gospel of God's grace.*
>
> *(The Apostle Paul in Acts 20:23–24)*

Have mercy on me, LORD, for I am faint; heal me, LORD, for my bones are in agony. 3 My soul is in deep anguish. How long, LORD, how long? Turn, LORD, and deliver me; save me because of your unfailing love. Among the dead no one proclaims your name. Who praises you from the grave? I am worn out from my groaning. All night long I flood my bed with weeping and drench my couch with tears. My eyes grow weak with sorrow; they fail because of all my foes. Away from me, all you who do evil, for the LORD has heard my weeping. The LORD has heard my cry for mercy; the LORD accepts my prayer.

Psalm 6:2–9 (New International Version)

In you, O LORD, I have taken refuge; let me never be put to shame; deliver me in your righteousness. Turn your ear to me; come quickly to my rescue; be my rock of refuge, a strong fortress to save me. Since you are my rock and my fortress, for the sake of your name lead and guide me. Free me from the trap that is set for me, for you are my refuge. Into your hands I commit my spirit; redeem me, O LORD, the God of truth.

Psalm 31:1–5 (New International Version)

I meditated on the above verses almost everyday. I did not talk too much about what was going through my mind, because I did not want to disturb Joey and Ricky. And I also did it to bring Kettline to the same stage that I was. I trusted the Lord. I took it one day at a time and let tomorrow worry about itself. As it is written, *"Do not worry about tomorrow, for tomorrow will worry about itself. Each day has enough trouble of its own. Matthew 6:34"* (New International Version NIV).

I continued to check my e-mail as if I were waiting for an important note that was promised to me. Of course, every day was a deception. Thank God that we had some money in reserve, so we were burning the fat. From time to time, we would take a short trip so we would not go crazy. In December 2006, we went to Florida for a few days to visit Kettline's folks. There I met a gentleman that either worked for a radio station or owned the station. He was a native of Haiti and a close cousin of my wife. I discussed some possibilities of getting a spot on the air in his station. He let me believe that it would not be a problem; I would just have to make it in. Upon our return, I discussed the idea of having a radio talk show in Miami with Kettline. I always nourished the idea to educate my fellow Haitians about *respect, integrity, and character*. To avoid some controversies, I do not mean that Haitians have no respect, integrity, or character; I was simply looking at a big picture and on an administrative level. I wanted to talk about human rights, and how and why to give is better than to receive. Our country, which is supposed to be a "world-wonder," is one of the most devastated and corrupted countries in the western hemisphere. I wanted to talk about respect for others and treating them as we wanted to be treated. I wanted to talk about having compassion for the country and our fellow Haitians. I wanted to explore the fact that I am Haitian and had a great education and did well in the U.S. that might help others to do the same. I saw the need to answer questions that my fellow Haitians have. I wanted to educate them about how to get a job. You're probably laughing at me talking about how to educate people to get jobs when my idea to go to Miami was due to the fact that I could not get a job myself. Let me explain, if I may; as a human resources professional, I have hired and trained a number of people. So I could and can give words of wisdom to prospective employees on how to conduct themselves and, based on their skills, what kind of jobs they would need to look for. I could not get a job because I was looking for a high paying job. I did not take the first few positions that were offered to me. They were rejected because the salary was not what I was looking for. Then, I had in mind that God wanted me to learn something. As of today, I still do   not get what He wanted me to know. I am still waiting to do His will. I have endured a high level of humiliations, deceptions, and calamities.

I can tell you what I learned, but not what I think God had for me to learn. I have learned to take the first job offer when you need one. If it is not the ideal one, keep looking, because it is easier to get a job while you are working than when you are not. I have learned that the friends that you thought you have were only your friends while you were working or while you were doing well. I have learned to accept what I cannot control. I have learned to humble myself. I have learned to forgive and forget. I have learned that you do not get time spent back. I have learned your family is all you have, no one else.

Then came Christmas, the holiday that we love to celebrate; Christmas was always the best time of our lives. Kettline and I, most of the time, would buy gifts for everyone. We would go over to some friends' houses and they would come over to our place. The Cleveland "Gangs" are the best Haitian Community in the world. We were a group of friends who lived like families. When we got together, there was always a homogenous mixture. On Christmas Eve, we would gather over at the Gaujeans, on Christmas Day, over at the Beauvais, some time in between, over at the Labastilles, on New Year eve, over at the Esperances, and on New Year day, over at the Policards. That was always the ritual. For some reason, Christmas 2006 and New Year 2007 were not up to par. Pastor Pierre, one of my best friends, sent a chain e-mail to me and at the beginning of the chain, it says, "By Rev. T.D. Jakes." I do not know if someone quoted T.D. Jakes and made it a "chain e-mail" or if is originated from him. I am using it as a reference to make a point. I let things that were bothering me go.

People can walk away from you,

let them walk. Don't try to talk another person into staying with you, loving you, calling you, caring about you, coming to see you, staying attached to you. Your destiny is never tied to anybody that left. The Bible said that, *"They went out from us, but they did not really belong to us. For if they had belonged to us, they would have remained with us; but their going showed that none of them belonged to us."* 1 *John* 2:19 niv *(New International Version)*

People leave you because they are not joined to you. And if they are not joined to you, you can't make them stay. Let them go.

It doesn't mean that they are bad people, it just means that their part in the story is over. And you've got to know when people's part in your story is over so that you don't keep trying to raise the dead. You've got to know when it's dead. You've got to know when it's over.

This is what Rev. T.D. Jack had to say, *"Let me tell you something. I've got the gift of good-bye. It's the tenth spiritual gift, I believe in good-bye. It's not that I'm hateful, it's that I'm faithful, and I know whatever God means for me to have He'll give it to me. And if it takes too much sweat I don't need it. Stop begging people to stay. Let them go!!"*

If you are holding on to something that doesn't belong to you and was never intended for your life, then you need to:

LET IT GO!

If you are holding on to past hurts and pains

LET IT GO!

If someone can't treat you right, love
you back, and see your worth..

LET IT GO!

If someone has angered you

LET IT GO!

If you are holding on to some
thoughts of evil and revenge

LET IT GO!

If you are involved in a wrong relationship or addiction

LET IT GO!

If you are holding on to a job that no
longer meets your needs or talents.

LET IT GO!

If you have a bad attitude

LET IT GO!

If you keep judging others to make yourself feel better

LET IT GO!

If you're stuck in the past and God is trying
to take you to a new level in Him

LET IT GO!

If you are struggling with the healing
of a broken relationship

LET IT GO!

If you keep trying to help someone who
won't even try to help themselves

LET IT GO!

If you're feeling depressed and stressed

LET IT GO!

If there is a particular situation that you are so
used to handling yourself and God is saying 'take
your hands off of it,' then you need to..

LET IT GO!

Let the past be the past. Forget the former
things. GOD is doing a new thing for 2007!

LET IT GO!"

Amen.

After I read the above e-mail, I made the final decision that I was moving to Miami to open a radio talk show. I brought it up to Kettline; she agreed with me and I called an airline and I booked a flight for Miami. Yes, it was a one-way ticket. I was to leave on February 1, 2007, at 8:30 a.m. A week after I bought the ticket, I got a phone call from my sister Nicole of Jacksonville. She advised me that she gave someone my phone number and that someone was to call me in the evening, No, I was to call the person myself. What is it about? The person who called Nicole was Patricia; please note I changed the name for privacy protection. Patricia's husband belongs to a fraternity of affluent people in Jacksonville, which my brother in-law, Dr. Marvin Wells, is also a member. Nicole had not seen or talked to Patricia for over three years. So it was bizarre to get a phone call from her. Patricia asked Nicole if she knew someone educated in the U.S. who also spoke French. She explained to Nicole that she was hired as consultant for a college in Jacksonville that was applying for a government grant to bring some Haitian businessmen, and possibly some from Santo Domingo also, into the college for a business management program development. So it was required that they have a Coordinator with a degree in business and that also speaks French. Nicole told her about me. Without taking another minute, she asked Nicole to call me and have me call her immediately. So I did. Next thing I know I was on a plane going to Jacksonville. I met with Patricia and the college staff for a session and guess what? I made the one-way trip to Miami, but I did not stay there. I was in Jacksonville working as a consultant and then I was hired by the college to run an outreach program. That was in March 2007 and Kettline got her dream job at the Florida Baptist Convention Center, in the beginning of February 2008.

FIFTY-FIVE AND HOLDING

An Intimate Reflection about my Atrocities and my laments at the end of 2008

The year of 2008 was hard-hitting for me and I think God let me go through some tough and sad events so I could be an example for others to not quit when things are not going the way they are supposed to go. There is a phenomenon that I cannot explain, and if I have to write, or if I am going to write another book, it will be about having so many good memories, before tragedy strikes. On the other hand, why have good times before bad times? At the end of the year, I lost four great friends through death.

In April 2008, I found out that my contract with the college was not going to be renewed, but I was hoping to find other opportunities within. Therefore, I did not worry much about it. Not only that, the contract was going to end October 15, 2008, which gave me a window of six months to land another job or possibly transfer to another campus. One of the reasons I was not stressed about it was the fact that I had so much faith in my brother in-law. I knew he would give me a job, at least while I would be looking for a better opportunity. In fact, that did happen. I began with the college situation because it was the starting point of my tragic journey. My adopted Dad, Père Noël, was battling cancer and he was not doing well in the month of April either. I took some time off to go to see him in San Francisco, California. I wanted to plan the trip for the following month, but I found out that Père Noël was getting worse, so I flew to San Francisco at the end of the month. I got to the airport around 12:30 p.m., I rented a car, and I was on my way to Petaluma, where he lived, and which is about an hour's drive from the airport. When I arrived at the house, my adopted sister Nicole, please don't forget that I also have a biological sister Nicole, met me outside of the house to tell me that Dad was not doing well at all. "It seems that he was waiting for you," She told me. "What do you mean by that?" I asked her. She said, *"Misié pa bon di tou." (He is not well at all)* I got in and I saw him sitting on a couch. Before I could say hello, he told me that he no longer belongs to me anymore, a slang way to say that he was going to die. I tried to encourage him by saying everything will be okay. Then I kissed him on his forehead as usual. He was still in his pajamas. He told me that he could not breathe. I asked him if he wanted me to do anything. He asked me to take him to the hospital. I told Nicole that Dad wants to go the hospital. Nicole said to wait for her husband to come in, so he could stay in the house with the kids. I asked her what time she expected her husband to come. "About 7:00 p.m.," she said. It was around 2:00 p.m. and I said, "I am sorry, we need to take him now." She agreed. We quickly washed him up and dressed him, just in case he would have to be admitted. The hospital was not too far from the house. It took us approximately fifteen minutes to make it. At the hospital, they wasted no time to get him in the emergency consultation room.

A couple hours later, the emergency room doctor asked to speak with us. Nicole was a little bit scared and asked me to go speak with the doctor alone. The doctor told me, had I not brought Dad in this afternoon, he wouldn't have made it. Then, she said that Dad is seriously ill. The cancer spread everywhere and his heart is failing rapidly. At that time, his heart was functioning at 25 percent of the normal rate. She let me know that they were going to admit him, but be aware that his life expectancy was two to three months. Just like that! Père Noël was not going to get back in his house anymore. However, I explained to Nicole what the doctor had said and told her that I had a feeling that Dad was not going to get back home. I spent a good week with him, going back and forth from the house to the hospital. We chatted a lot. He did not know how severe his situation was. My dad had a lot of confidence in me and often said I would be the one to make his funeral arrangements, even though he made sure that he planned for the cost for whenever that would happen. My adopted siblings did not buy the doctor's diagnosis, but I took time to make all funeral arrangements before I left San Francisco, and left the information with my adopted brother in-law and Nicole. I asked my brother, Renel, and my sisters to make an effort to go spend at least one week with him at home or at the hospital. Oh! I am glad they all did.

Back home, I got busy working and looking for future employment opportunities. Père Noël was getting more bad days than good ones. And job hunting was also taking a toll on me. Come August, I got very frustrated because I did not see any signs that I was going to get any opportunities from the college, and at that time I was trying to build an organization that could help most fellow Haitians to have more socially and economically educated and have respect one another. That organization's purpose was:

> *to meet the educational, social, and economical needs of Haitian descendants around the world, to advance morale, promote enlightenment, empowerment, and the cultural heritage of Haiti*

through various educational, economical, and social activities and recreational programs.

Unfortunately, the organization was not able to fully develop because I could no longer allocate anytime for it. Mid September 2008, I began to experience a high degree of tribulations and atrocity. And I will continue to endure tragedy after tragedy for the last four months and those moments will hurt me emotionally, psychologically, financially, and physically. I will lose four great and important friends in my life and they will pass away approximately one month from each other. They were close to me, they loved me unconditionally and they showed it too. In some or many ways, they have impacted my life. As I am writing this section, I had to pause for a moment to think about those mysterious events. Not only did my folks die one month after each other, but they died in such order:

By the length of time I knew them; by age, younger to older; and the degree of memories and closeness. I don't want to inflict any pain to my readers, but I just want to stick with the title, '*I sat where you sit*' and I survived them all.

> *Ms. Myriam died on 09/21/2008, she was 29.*
> *Pastor Chery died on 10/30/2008, he was 58.*
> *Dr. Gaujean died on 11/21/2008, he was 79.*
> *Pere Noel died on 12/25/2008, he was 82.*

I feel compelled to tell about these painful steps into my life that I went through for five consecutive months.

Myriam Morrisset-Saint Jacques

On September 14, 2009, I received a phone call from a great friend of mine, Pastor Olian Saint Jacques of St. Petersburg, Florida, to regretfully announce the sudden death of his brother in Port-au-Prince, Haiti. I met Pastor Saint Jacques in mid-February 2008 through Pastor Gaston Compas of St. Petersburg, Florida.

I made a special trip to St. Petersburg to see him. At his house, I met his wife, and his three daughters: Angie, the oldest; Mimi (short for Myriam), the middle; and Claire, the youngest, as well as pastor St. Jacques, who told me that he also has a son. The son was not at the house at that time. I was embraced by the whole family. I had a great fellowship, which included lunch. His daughters were extremely polite and hospitable. The oldest had been graduated a little bit over two years from college, Mimi just graduated and Claire was in her fourth year. I spoke with them about their dreams. Mimi was the most talkative and very charismatic among the sisters. She told me that she was the "black sheep" of the family. I made fun of her by calling her "typical PK" because I am one of them. She was full of life and very beautiful. I remained in contact with the family. Pastor St. Jacques was an affluent member of the organization that I was building in Jacksonville. I called Pastor Saint Jacques on Tuesday, September 16, 2008 inquiring about funeral arrangements for his brother and finding out when he was going to leave for Haiti. He told me that things were getting worse. I asked myself, *what could be possibly worse?* The guy is already dead! Then I thought, *maybe he does not have money for the burial.*

I asked him if there was anything he would want me to do for him. He said, "Brother Joel, my daughter Mimi is in the Intensive Care Unit and we don't know what is going on." "Oh boy, how long she has been there?" I said. "Last night and she has been in a coma since," he replied. I was so shocked. I said to him, "God is good, everything will be okay." We discussed the funeral arrangements and I told him that I would call him on Wednesday, God willing, to check on Mimi. Then I prayed with him and said goodbye. The following day I called him as I promised. Mimi was still in the coma. Pastor asked me about what to do. Should he stay home or should he go to Haiti for the funerals? It was a tough call for me. My advice was probably not good. We never had a chance to discuss it thereafter. Anyway, I came up with a cultural or rather a psychological piece of advice.

I told him to go ahead and make a reservation to go to Haiti on Friday the nineteen, bury his brother on Saturday and come back on Sunday, September 21. This was only if Mimi remains in the coma. The motive behind my analysis was if Mimi were still in a coma, he would not be able to do anything for her; and, if he does not go to Haiti to bury his brother, it would haunt him for the rest of his life. That was by experience, I have been haunted for not going to Haiti in the funeral of my brother Jean-Claude, who passed in July 1985. To this day, my conscience still bothers me. Why? Because there will never be closure. So, Pastor Saint Jacques told me that he would make a decision on Thursday night; it would depend on her current status. He did make a reservation for Friday. There was no change on Mimi's status, so Pastor left early on Friday, September 19, 2009 for Port-au-Prince, Haiti. He buried his brother on Saturday, September 20, and on Sunday, September 21, 2009, he went to Haitian airport very early in order to catch his flight back to U.S. While waiting for departure at the airport, his daughter died in the hospital at 11:00 a.m., exactly two Sundays prior to her death, I visited her father's church in St. Petersburg; she sat two rows ahead of me. She took a look behind her and saw me there, she stood up right away ran toward me to say hello. She had the best smile on her face, and insisted that I had lunch with her family after church. After the service, she went up to the podium and began to sing with her brother, Olian Jr. and her little sister, Claire. They sang several short songs, while her husband of five months was playing the church's organ. She was so happy and wanted to live so much. Unfortunately, she did not know that she had only less than fifteen days to live. No one knew. Who could imagine, at that time, a young lady full of energy could have been expired, on September 21, 2008? She was twenty-nine years old.

Pastor Aurel Chery

Early in the month of January 2008, I was waiting in the administration building at Florida Community College at Jacksonville to get the elevator to go to my office on the second floor. Suddenly, I heard a deep voice with an accent much thicker than mine. "Teacher I need to speak with you." I turned my head toward the voice's direction. There he was, a man with a very dark complexion, gray hair, thick salt and pepper eyebrows, stocky, but well built with a bright smile with white teeth, looking at me. I automatically knew he was Haitian. He reminded me of the typical "Big Chat" Bacha, or Rich or well fed Haitian men. I said, "Good morning to you, Sir. What do you want to speak with me about?"

"Teacher, I would like to teach French here," he replied. I shook his hand and asked him if he were Haitian. He said yes. We exchanged names and we had a short conversation. He was taking English as a second language and he had been in the United States for a little less than a year at that time. I asked him to come to see me in my office, so we could discuss his intention. Although I knew that he would not be able to teach in the school, I saw some potential for the future. *"Vouloir c'est pouvoir."* (Where there is a will, there is a way.) That was the way we got connected.

Pastor Aurel would come to visit every time he had class and sometimes he would just stop by to say hello. He was a remarkable human being, a man with a deep voice, a very friendly guy. Pastor Chery would brag about his education as a lawyer and he would add to it that he attended the *"Institution D'Arts Dramatiques,"* that is, somewhat equivalent with public speaking institute. He did not need a microphone to speak to an audience. He knew how to use his diaphragm so he could be loud and clear. On several occasions, when he visited me at the college, I constantly asked him to lower his voice. He had a sincere and honest smile. Then he would say, "Joe, I am sorry, man." He continued by explaining some events, where he would give a speech, and how profound they would be. In particular, he would bring the event where he attended the funeral service of a friend of his. He was to make a reflection about the deceased. He asked me to stop whatever I was doing, or if we were walking somewhere in the college hallways or in the streets, so he could recite a portion of his speech for me. He would be so excited about the impact and the reaction of the affected friends and family of the deceased. He wanted to learn so much, he thought that he could teach French for the college while he was taking some English courses. He was always in good spirit. Regardless of how my days were, every time Pastor Chery stopped by, I had a brighter day. I told him from time to time, that he reminded me of a great friend of mine, whom I talked already about his relationships with me in Ohio, Pastor Pierre, and how God wanted me to have another close Christian friend. Pastor had a daughter who lives near Orlando, Florida with her family. He went to visit her from time to time, and make a point to call me over there. I met his wife, a great woman of God. His daughter and her family knew everything about me without having met me. Pastor told them so much about me so when I talked to them over phone, they talked to me as someone they knew years ago.

In the month of July, Pastor Chery went to St. Petersburg to visit an Assembly of God church, which happened to be the church my family in St. Petersburg, goes to. There he met with Dad, Mom, and my sisters. He had a good time with them and was so happy to have the chance to meet them. He could not wait to see me to tell me about this meeting with my parents and my sisters. They were very happy to meet him as well. In mid-September 2008, I did not see Pastor nor speak with him for a while. I was so preoccupied that it did not dawn on me that I did not see or talk to him. Between my unstable work situations, my dad in San Francisco, who was getting worse in his cancer battle and a trip to St. Petersburg to attend Pastor Saint Jacques older daughter's wedding. Yes, his older daughter got married about a month before the death of his second daughter, who was married five months before she passed.

On September 29, 2008, around 11:15 a.m., I got a phone call from Pastor Chery. I asked where he had been. Before he could answer, I followed with, "Are you in Orlando?" He told me that he had been hospitalized for a little bit over two weeks. "Okay, but are you in Orlando?" I replied. He said he was in Jacksonville and at the Shands Memorial Hospital. I asked for his room number, and I told him that I would be right there. The hospital is located around the college area, approximately one or two miles away. I left my office immediately for the hospital. When I arrived there, I met with Pastor and his wife. Of course, he was in a hospital gown and with possibly fifteen different tubes inserted in his body. They were everywhere. I asked what the diagnosis was. He told me that he was not sure. I left it alone and we talked about other things. I asked him if he was aware about Pastor Saint Jacques' loss. He said he knew and that he could not go to the funeral because he was already in the hospital. I kidded with him about opening a church in the area and he could teach me to become an assistant pastor. He was laughing so much that he got tears in his eyes. He and his wife both, they were not themselves that day, but they did not tell me too much about the situation except that Pastor was not feeling too well; he was having some digestive discomforts. Had he not been in the hospital or had the tubes in him, I would say he looked perfectly well. He did not lose weight nor did he appear to be hurting. At the time, I could see that he was a little bit scared, which I think is a normal reaction when you are in the hospital and doctors have ordered several tests on you. It was time for me to leave; I asked them if I could pray with them. Of course, they accepted and I prayed. As I was leaving the room, a doctor came in with a gentleman who speaks Créole as interpreter. Pastor Chery did not speak English well and the doctor wanted to make sure that he understood his situation. Pastor Chery was well educated, but they could only find someone who speaks Créole not French to translate for him. All Haitians speak Créole.

The doctor said hello and told pastor that he wanted to talk to him in confidence and that he brought a translator with him so he could understand clearly. Then the doctor asked that I leave the room for privacy. Pastor Chery told the doctor that he would want me to stay because I am part of the family and he would feel better to have me there. Through the interpreter, the doctor asked him if he were told what he had. He did not answer. He sighed and rolled his eyes. The doctor continued, "You know you have cancer?" He said, "Yes, but I wasn't told about its status." The doctor said, "It is pretty severe and the prognosis is not good. Do you know how long you have to live?" "I have no problem and no fear. I am ready when God is," he replied. The doctor paused for a minute. Pastor asked him, "How long do I have?" "Well, I am glad that you mentioned God. Based on my experience with the kind of cancer that you have and the degree of how it extended in the system, two to three months," he responded. I could not feel my legs. I sat down immediately. I looked at Pastor's face. It seemed that he was calm and emotionless. His wife was panicked and very emotional. The doctor went on explaining the follow-up details and let him know that he would be discharged; there was nothing that they could do anymore. I don't want to go farther. He was discharged the following day, September 30, 2008, and he passed on October 30, 2008. What was so unreal and so moving to me was, in one month, I have never seen a strong man with so much energy, so much will to live; a man with a golden and powerful voice, a well educated and articulated human being, dilapidated right before my eyes. His weight and his voice were the most noted. In his last days, he could not even whisper. I got a phone call from his wife on the 28th early in the morning telling me that she had him taken to the hospital because he fell into a coma. I was on my way to see him in the afternoon, I got on his floor, and I decided that I did not want to see him. I was spiritually weak and I was afraid that he would expire in front of me. Eight hours later he expired, on October 30, 2008. He was fifty-eight years old.

Dr. Max Pierre Gaujean

Max was the man with many titles; he was the Dean of the Haitian Community in Northeast Ohio, a medical doctor, an elder, a judge, a father, a godfather, an uncle, a brother, a husband, a boy scout, an advisor, etc., but he was known mostly as Doctor Max and a great friend. I met Max around Thanksgiving week of 1984 through another friend, Lucrèce Mio. Please keep this in mind, *Thanksgiving week;* I will end this passage with it. I have already explained how I met Mio in the same year. Mio took us over to Max's house the following Sunday after Thanksgiving Day. Kettline and I met with his family that Sunday afternoon with exception of his son. From that day, we stayed closed to the end. Max was indeed the greatest friend anyone, any human being, would want to have as a friend. He was loyal, honest, respectful, a man with integrity, a man of character, humble, but yet a simple man. He was sincere, genuine, *"Ou Gasson san fasson,"* a man of hospitality, and a man who loved everyone unconditionally. Max worked very hard, most of the times in the hospital and his two personal clinics, nights and days, but yet, always made time to visit his friends. He would be available at anytime you needed him, rain or shine. Max was highly respected and loved by everyone in our Haitian community and everyone in the communities that he lived and worked. From the day I met Max, our friendship never stopped growing until the day he passed. The first piece of advice Max gave me was when I invited him to come to our apartment for a visit. After seeing his house, I automatically felt that I needed to warn him about the size and the condition of my apartment. I lived in a small and barely furnished place. Max told me up front: "If you invite someone into your house (Appt.) for a visit, it means this person is a friend. So if this someone is coming to your place to see and judge what you have or where you live, this person is not your friend and therefore, he or she should not be in your place to begin with." *"Choses dites, choses faites"* Max and his family came to visit and I tell you frankly, I had never seen people feel so comfortable at my place before. They were so happy and we had the best time ever, and nothing was going to change when God blessed us with a fairly big and nice house. Early in 1986, Mom was visiting with us; Max was supposed to come to the house for some reason. By the way, he talked me into buying a house, which I did. Not only did he advise me to buy it, but he put time aside so his lovely wife, Dr. Emmelyne St. Germain-Gaujean, and he could go house hunting with Kettline and me. We bought a nice little house in Ohio in December 1985. I had to go somewhere, I took Mom with me, and I don't remember where Kettline was, before we left the house, Mom cooked something for dinner and left it on the stove. Knowing that Max was coming, I left a note at the door, in case he showed up and we are not back. Mom was worried about that, and she pressured me to get back before he showed up. Unfortunately, while we were approaching the house, I noticed Max's car parked in front of the house. I told Mom that Max is at the house. She was a little bit upset that the doctor came while we were out, which she called disrespectful. We should be home to receive him. To my surprise and my mom's biggest surprise, when we entered the door, the doctor was sitting calmly at the table eating his food. That day, I knew that Max was not a fake and he was ingenuous. Later on he became my older son's godfather. Among all advices that I got from Max, I always like to pass this one out to others, *"Vous n'êtes pas le premier et vous ne serez pas le dernier."* (You are not the first and you will not be the last) Later on from time to time, I would hear this motto from my pastor, Dr. Jeanette C. Holmes-Vann, *"And This Too Shall Pass."* Regardless of the situation that you are in, you are not the first and you won't be the last and this too shall pass. Do you see how they flow?

In the mid 2000s Max began to fight an illness, which he did courageously; peacefully, he remained very optimist throughout the adversity, never complained, never asked "why me," and still was visiting friends and family for each occasion. When I left Ohio in early 2007, it was hard to leave my family, my friends; my biggest pain was leaving Max behind. Max and I had developed a bond that we would call each other every week and when things are not well in his family or mine, we would communicate on a daily basis. Early in 2008, I found out that Max was in the hospital in New York, so I flew there to visit him. There he was still Max, even though doctors were doing all kind of tests on him, he managed to keep a strong spirit. We talked for a moment, and then they came to get him for more tests. Then, I said goodbye to my friend and I would talk with him another time, but that was the last time I was going to see my best friend alive. As I told you to keep in mind, "Thanksgiving Week" Max passed on November 21, 2008 to be precise. He was seventy-nine years old.

I was honored and privileged to speak at his funeral service. I feel compelled to insert the actual speech in my book. It is in French, but I would translate it for my English speaking readers.

Cher parents et amis:

Dans les annales de l'histoire, Il y a au moins 3 grands évènements qui ont toujours inversé le cours de l'existence. Il s'agit première-ment la naissance, celle-ci nous permet de faire la connaissance d'un monde jusqu' ici inconnu. Deuxièmement, il y a le mariage, qui est un acte dans lequel deux personnes s'unissent pour constru-ire une vie harmonieuse. Troisièmement, il y a la mort, qui est la fin du cycle de l'existence terrestre. La mort nous arrache toujours le fruit de nos entrailles et de nos durs labeurs. Comme c'est le cas d'aujourd'hui, elle nous arrache un être cher et précieux.

Vous êtes sortis en divers endroits, certains de très loin, d'autres plus près pour venir assister aux funérailles du Dr. Max Pierre Gaujean, notre cher Max, notre doyen, et mon compère.

Max sé té yon bon gason, li té zanmi tout moun, épi li té yon bon zanmi. Sé té yon nèg lè ou bò té koté 1ou pa santi ou ta al lwen, ou pa santi ou ta kité1. Li té yon moun simple é humble. » Max té toujou répond «présent » a l'appel quit té gain la pli, nège ou tè sèche. Li toujours la.

Nous sommes réunies en ce moment pour rendre un dernier hommage à notre cher Max et pour nous rappeler comment il nous a marqué par son amitié, son amour, et sa façon d'être. Car cet homme non seulement était un bon mari, un bon père, un bon frère, un bon oncle, un bon parrain, un bon médecin, mais il était l'ami de tout le monde. Oui, il était le bon ami de tout le monde. Max était un homme hospitalier et sincère. Et Si je devais ajouter, je dirais, Max était un homme RICHE, un Elite. Et s'il vous plait, cette richesse n'a rien à voir aux biens matériels, Mais plutôt a les valeurs fondamentales qu'il possédait, telles étaient: le Respect, l'Intégrité, le Caractère, et l'Honnêteté.

R-espect
I-ntegrite
C-aractere
H-onnette
E-lite

Au moment où nous faisons notre adieu à Max, nous devons nous rappeler par sa mort comment l'espèce humaine est fragile et comment notre issue est inévitable, seul Dieu est éternel. Mes amis, la mort pas gin préjuger ni discrimination, li pas avertir qui lè, qui gen, et qui coté lap pren nou. Cépendan, nou tout qui la a, gin ou rendévou. L'essentiel : nou pas connin qui date, qui lè, qui coté, et comman. Question nou doué mandé tèt nou: Are we ready? Are we ready?

Max nous a précédé dans le voyage, mais nous qui sommes encore sur cette terre, nous devons inspirer de lui notamment par sa façon de faire les choses, d'encourager les gens, c'est la meilleure façon de continuer son œuvre pour qu'il soit toujours vivant à travers nous.

Chers Parents et amis implorés, soyez réellement réconfortés ce jourd'hui, parce que moi-même qui vous parle, je sens réellement que notre ami est encore vivant. Le juste Juge ne manquera jamais de lui donner ou je peux dire, lui récompenser pour les biens, les efforts, et les œuvres qu'il avait opérés sur cette terre.

Parce que nous étions tous au ciel, Dieu nous a envoyé sur la terre et nous devons remonter au ciel. "C'est justement" Ne pleurez pas! Ne pleurez pas! Max n'est pas mort. Au delà du firmament, il y a une autre vie. Cette vie est réservée pour nous les bons chrétiens, rappelons nous bien, Max était un bon homme, un bon chrétien. Enfin, ayez confiance, un jour vous le verrez tel qu'il était.

Que Dieu vous bénisse, qu'il vous conserve la vie, parce que nous sommes pèlerins et voyageurs. Disons! Permettez-moi de vous dire, Max n'est pas mort.

Diable, tout équip la, nous pap di ou au revoi, pacé qué ou ap toujou avec nou, min nap di-ou allé en pè. Nap pren soin Emmeyine pou ou. Oh ! Pa fatigué-ou, ninport koté nou yé, si gain mangé map mangé pou rou é si'm pa la, Michel ap mangé pou rou.

"Diable," I love you and I am going to miss you so much.

English Translation of the Speech:

Dear parents and friends:

In the annals of history, there are at least big events which always reverse the course of existence. First, there is birth, which allows us to know and to get acquainted with a world that still to date remains unknown to us. Second, there is the marriage, which is an act in which two persons unite to create a harmonious life. Third, there is the death, which is the end of the cycle of the existence terrestrial. Death always snatches from us the fruit of our entrails and of our hard labors. As it is today's case, it snatches from us a dear and precious being.

You came out from various places, some from far away, others from near to attend the funeral services of the Dr. Max Pierre Gaujean, our dear Max, our Dean, and my best friend.

Max was a good and a very friendly man, and mostly a compassionate man. Whenever, you were in his mist, you would not want to leave. He always made you feel so comfortable. He was humble and kind. Max was there for everyone, he was never too tired to help a friend. He was always available, dry or rain.

We are united at this moment to pay a last tribute to our dear Max and to remind ourselves how he marked us by his friendship, his love, and his manner of being. Because this man not only was a good husband, a good father, a good brother, a good uncle, a good doctor, but he was the friend of everyone. Yes, he was good friend of everyone. Max was a hospitable and sincere man. And if I had to add, I would say, Max was a RICH man. And please, this wealth has got nothing to do in material properties, but rather with the fundamental values that he possessed, such as: Respect, Integrity, Character, and Honesty.

As we are saying goodbye to Max, we must remind ourselves his death how mankind is fragile and how our existence is the inevitable, only God is eternal. My friends, death does not have prejudice or discrimination. It does not warn us when, where, and how it will strike. However, all of us have a set day and time to meet death. The question to ask is: Are we ready? Are we ready?

Max preceded us in death, but as we are still on this earth, we must inspire of him notably of the way he made things, of encouraged others, this is the best method to continuing his work so that he will always be alive through us.

Grieving parents and friends please be comforted this morning, because I, who speak to you, have a feeling that our friend is still alive. The fair Judge will never miss to give him or I can say, reward him properly for his efforts and good deeds that he had done on earth.

Because we were all in the sky, God sent us on the earth and we must go back up to the sky. Therefore, do not cry! Do not cry! Max is not dead. Beyond the cloud, there is another life. This life is reserved for us good Christians. Let's remind ourselves that Max was indeed a good man, a good Christian. Finally, don't be trouble, one day you will see him such as he was.

May God bless you and may He keeps your life, because we are pilgrims and passengers. Allow me to say to you, one more time, Max is not dead.

*Buddy, the whole community is here. We are not saying goodbye
but see you later. We know that you will always be with us. Go
with peace, we will be there for Emmelyne. Oh! Buddy, don't you
be worried whenever there is a party in the community, I will eat
and drink for you. If I am not there, our Friend Michel will eat
and drink for you.*

"Buddy" I love you and I am going to miss you very much.

Jean Noel Tingue (Père Noël)

I describe that next person as follow: My uncle, my godfather,
and my adopted father (three in one); Jean Noel. He was born on
December 25 1926. Because of this date, his parents called him by
his middle name, Noël, and because of me everyone, including
his biological children, called him "Père Noël." Père Noël loved
me unconditionally from the time I was in my mom's womb. He
told my parents that he would want to be my godfather and if I
were to be a boy that he would want to adopt me. After he made
it clear to my folks, he began to take care of my mom while she
was carrying me. And after I was born, he continued to care for
me. I would spend most of my vacation times and weekends over
at his house until my parents moved us to Miragoâne. Père Noël
has seven biological children: Edith, Guilaine, Renel, Madone,
Mirèille, Nicole, and Ninon. You can see why he wanted to adopt
me. So God heard his prayer. It is very difficult for me not to
think or believe that Père Noël was not my biological dad.

My being redundant is only to make a point. While living
with the Tingués, I bought a hamburger and a glass of orange
juice one morning while on the job. I took a few bites of the
hamburger and decided that it had a bad taste. I stopped eating
it, and I drank the orange juice. On my way home, I felt worse.

I had a severe stomachache. At home, I went straight to bed,
but the pain was getting worse. Later on, I went to the hospital.
There I was treated and released. The diagnosis was food poison-
ing. Unfortunately, I went back and was admitted to the hospital.

One of the doctors suggested that my family contact a surgeon immediately. They did so. The matter got worse. I began to experience an excruciating abdominal pain. They took me right to the operating room. The surgery lasted eight hours. During my stay in the hospital, Père Noël pretty much spent most of his time there with me. He would not leave me, because he was afraid that I would die without him being there. I have already said enough about my Dad throughout the book; nevertheless, I can never really say too much about him. I am only implying that I do not want to repeat everything that I have already said about him. I know that the man loved me unconditionally and if there is one single person that really, really, really loved me throughout my whole life, that was Père Noël. I wish I had more time with him. If I did not call Dad for two weeks, he would be mad and wonder what was happening. I made sure that I called all the time and on time. During his last months, weeks, and days, I called more often, not only because I love him, but because he was running his last miles on earth, he was in the hospice, but more or so, because of guilt. When I know for sure if it were me in that condition, he would have spent a lot of time with me. I could not be there with him long enough and I could not even go back to see him alive one last time.

Early on December 25, I got a phone call from a cousin telling me that Dad was not well. In the afternoon, my brother in-law called to tell me that he was in a coma and that he was transferred to the hospital. I knew it was the time, but found it bizarre for him to die on his birthday. Usually, I would call to wish him "Happy Birthday," but didn't because of the time difference between Florida and California. I waited a little bit. I called my sister Nicole who lives there; I asked her to go to the hospital to find out what was happening. They, hospital personnel, would not talk with me over phone. At 11:00 p.m. (Florida Time) I got the phone call; Dad has passed, yes, on his birthday, December 25, 2008. He was eighty-two years old.

Be still, and know that I am God; I will be exalted among the nations, I will be exalted in the earth.

Psalm 46: 10 (New International Version)

CONCLUSION
God does not like to share his glory with anyone

Despite all that happened to me, each day that I find myself awake and alive, I thank God and try to enjoy the day to the fullest. I know that I have to continue to press on, nothing is given for free, and there is always a price attached to it. I also continue to talk to myself about where I came from and what I was. I mentioned through the book that there was a time that I did not have a pair of shoes, a good pair of pants, a good shirt, and sometimes not even a good meal to eat. As I am working on this book, I have enough pairs of shoes that even if I cease to buy shoes for the rest of my life, and let's say I have forty years to live, I would not need to buy another pair of shoes. Honestly, it is the same when it comes to clothing. I can say that for the time being,

I have every single thing that I need and so does my family. At home, we have a nickname for Kettline, "Mrs. Marcos," because she has hundreds of pairs of shoes. I am doing very well financially, and I am not about to settle for less. We bought a nice town home in July 2009. God is a great God. As I said in the beginning of the book, I was born in Haiti, from a middle class family, which lost everything when I was about ten years old. That was when I began to feel the pain and the taste of misery. I slept in a church that did not have any doors and practically, I can say that I slept outdoors. Because the church not only did not have doors, but all the windows were made out of blocks which contained a lot of holes for air passage. For five years, I did not have a bed, and I did not even have a sleeping bag. I slept on something called *"A tè méyor." Quelque chose mieux que rien posé sur le sol;* a thin floor mat made of banana trees' skins.

I have to tell you that I have never felt discouraged. I kept a positive attitude toward life. I always told everyone outside the family and the family, that one day I would be somebody. Remember, when I left Miragoâne to go to Port-au-Prince for my secondary studies, there again I faced some challenges, I have been ridiculed time after time, but I kept on pressing for what was ahead of me. When Mr. Herring called me all kind of names, and asked Mrs. Dalencour to fire me, I was very humiliated and trashed; there again, I kept pressing. I always put into my mind that someone else was in a worse position than I was in. At one point, I really felt that I was helpless, that was when I saw my Mom waiting for a bus to go to work under the snow. I wanted to die that day. I felt like I hit rock bottom. When I left Haiti, I had a brand new car, which my brother took over the payment, because I had it for only three months. There I was without a car to help Mom to go to work. The worst part was the fact that she was covered with snow. I firmly believe that was my worst moment ever, besides the event that took place in December 2003. I remembered telling one of my friends the story. He told me that no matter what happened, or what is happening in your life, *"Vous n'êtes pas le premier, et vous ne serez pas le dernier."* (You are not the first, nor will you be the last.) I lived and I continue to live with this thought in mind. I really try not to let anything destroy my spirit. You remember when I suffered the mighty depression after the birth of my first son, there again, I pressed on. The things that happened throughout my life helped me to be and remain strong. I would like to give credit to the late Pastor Globig for one of his sermons preached in the early 90s about people who are sympathetic to others' adversities, simply because they were sitting on that same chair. After listening to this particular sermon, I said to myself, *I am going to use the above statement everywhere and anywhere.* I used it in my job constantly, especially during conflict resolution and reprimanding fellow workers. I also said, "If I am to write a book, I will use this statement as the main focus of the book." The more I went through tough adversities and the more I am going through the dark clouds as we speak, I have no fear. God makes us a promise that He will be with us always. Always! *Quand je marche dans la vallée de l'ombre de la mort, je ne crains rien, aucun mal, car tu es avec moi. Psaume 23, verset 4.* "Even though, I walk through the valley of the shadow of death, I will fear no evil, for you are with me." The promise of the Lord can be found in the book of Deuteronomy 31:6: *"Be strong and courageous, do not be afraid or tremble at them, for the L*ord *your God is the one who goes with you. He will not fail you or forsake you."* Because I know that God is preparing me for something He has for me, I am getting ready to receive it and use it for His glory. One day, I will be telling others that are going through tough times, and enduring calamity, "Be strong and courageous. You are not alone, just trust Him and follow His path. I sat where you sit." Therefore, I feel compelled to use *I Sat Where You Sit* as the title of my book.

I love people genuinely; I treat them far better than how I would want to be treated. I always think that I can endure more than the next person around me. So, I always cede the better seat to next person. I am not kidding you; every time an occasion presents itself for me to give up my seat to someone who does not have one, I always get something better in return. One time, Kettline and I had an argument about how a guest room is supposed to be. Kettline thinks that a guest room needs to be cleaned and well decorated; not necessarily spacious, not the second best bedroom in a house. For example, if a house has four bedrooms, which includes the master bedroom and three full bathrooms, and occupied by a family of four, husband and wife and two children. That means Mom and Dad have the master bedroom that has its own bathroom, the oldest child has the second bedroom, which also has its own bathroom, and the other two rooms will share the third bathroom. Therefore, the second child will have the third and largest bedroom among the two. That left the fourth bedroom as "guest room." I think the bedroom that has its own bathroom is to be utilized as guest room. I feel that a guest should have the best room in the house. Because the Bible said that when you receive a guest in your house it is as if you receive Christ in your house. If Jesus were to be a guest in your household, how would you receive Him? I would like for guests that visited my house to feel that they were treated like a king or a queen. That was what I meant when I said that I treat people much better than how I would want to be treated.

I have taken time, in the last three years, to really analyze my thoughts, my feelings toward family, friends, and other people. I found that I unwillingly and unintentionally hurt people around me, people who really loved and respected me as much as I love and respect them. Why did I use "unwillingly and unintentionally?" Because that was what I kept hearing from them. Also, because of that behavior, family and friends are more or so getting tired of me. I don't think it is paranoia or a guilty feeling. In the last year, I have been told one way or another that I care for people so much that I forget to take of myself. One of my sisters, Nicole, has reminded me very often to "put the oxygen mask on your face first." Those same people who are around me are also getting mad at me for destroying my future. Some of them went so far as to say that I am losing my level of confidence, and that I am no longer as sharp as I used to be. I was so afraid that I began to believe what they were saying. I started to look at myself and what was happening to me; am I really losing it? Of course, if you are looking for dirt, you will find dirt. Well, I came up with the following issues: I was getting depressed, losing self-control, and self-confidence, I was very submissive, which is definitely not me, my twenty-nine year marriage was failing rapidly, and among a few other issues, my finance situation was increasingly getting worse. Don't tell me that was not enough to throw anyone out of bounds.

If it were not for my beloved brother in-law, Dr. Marvin Wells, and my beautiful sister Nicole, our life would be a total disaster. There is no other way to put it; God sent these angels to save my family. I will never be able to repay them, even if I would be the next Bill Gates of the world. My old pastor, Paul Beresford, always uses "in-love" instead of "in-law" when it comes to parent in-laws. I find it spiritually and materially correct to call Dr. Wells my "brother in-love." Marvin and Nicole provided for my family every necessity to live, not to survive. I thank God for them. I love them and they know it. I continue with my self-analysis after hearing so many negatives around me. I was living in a world that I could not call mine. I honestly was living like a zombie. I have prayed and I found strength to fight those demonic feelings. I was more convinced when my son, Joey, brought to my attention that I was not the same "strong-minded man" that I used to be. He realized that I was accepting, or more or so agreeing, with everything that was said to me. At that time I said to myself, "Joel, wake up, wake up, so you can tell others that, 'I Sat Where You Sit.'" I suddenly got an eye opener.

Do I really hurt people who love me the most? Let's look at it together. I care for people, not only those I know, but those I don't even know. I think the problem is: Someone who loves and respects me and would do everything and anything for me, should do the same for every other person he/she also calls friends. If I find out that this person, who loves and treats me nicely and respectfully, is treating someone else badly, whether the one who is mistreated is family, an acquaintance of ours, or a subordinate, I would get upset and I would bring it to my friend's attention. Not only that, I would demand that my friend give the person a "break" or depending of the situation I would even push for an apology. I firmly believe it is an effort to promote peace and respect. I like to be on the side of the less fortunate people. I like to be the voice for the unspoken. That was why, when I told my brother Jarman that I moved to human resources management, he quickly told me that branch was not the right branch for me. The reason he gave me was, I love people too much. I thought because I love people that was the best reason to join the human resource management. Never did I compromise my integrity deliberately, but I stepped on some friendly toes. I put my foot into my mouth sometimes. I am not going to deny that, but always in an effort to promote peace, human equality, and fairness. Almondo used to say, "Right is Right, you have to do what is right." Unfortunately, sometimes things may be legal but not right, so do you do the right thing?

The following instances may not exactly be about what is right or legal, but rather how people misinterpreted my thoughts or my actions because I love people too much. I developed a great relationship with an ex-boss of mine, whom I will call Frantz. Frantz was my manager and there was a group of seven of us. One day, Frantz called me and told that he could no longer work with one member of that team. That person at that point had been working for Frantz for nine consecutives years. Frantz told him that he would be reassigned to a new position and that he would not need to have an office. He was also told to clear and clean his office. Frantz did not have to, but he entrusted me with his feelings about that particular employee.

I found the situation harsh and uncomfortable; I went around finding him a desk and a chair. I had them placed in a corner of the department area, so he would not feel too devastated. My act, to me was not evil or bad, but in accordance with my boss, and other people, it was bad. Frantz reprimanded me for going above and beyond to make that person feel comfortable, while he was trying to "tick her off."

A married couple was working the second shift and wanted to attend evening Bible Study on Wednesdays, so they made arrangements with their supervisor so they could work on Wednesday morning to have the afternoon free. That was moving along well until other employees wanted the same favor for other personal reasons. When the situation became unmanageable, management put a stop to it. That particular couple was told that they were no longer authorized to work in the morning on Wednesdays. Unfortunately, which I am sorry to say, I used to go to the same Bible study. The couple announced that they were not going to be able to continue with the lessons because they were restricted from working a different shift. The pastor, who knew that I worked with them, asked me to see what I could do. The following day, I went to their boss's office and asked him why the couple was restricted from working in the morning so they could get the afternoon off. The boss said that the situation was getting out of hand. I said, "Okay, I did not know that." The supervisor went and told the folks that it was okay for them to resume their coming in the morning on Wednesdays. Next thing I know, Frantz called me in his office and asked me, "Who has died and left you boss?' I told him that I did not know what he was talking about. He told me that the couple's supervisor told him that I said to let them work in the morning so they could attend Bible study in the evening. There again, I did not mind my own business. Or should I say, "What was wrong to ask the supervisor what was happening?" *Sérieusement and honnêtement,* I did not tell the supervisor to let them continue their normal routine. And guess what? Frantz was the one who put the stop to it. There were few other examples where I would ask a friend for something he/she would give it to me and another person would ask the same friend for a similar thing, and would not get it. I would raise "hell" to my friend for not rendering the same service to the other person. If I am standing in a group of four friends, another friend comes and hands a $100.00 bill to me and walks away. I would be extremely embarrassed, because he did not give anything to the other guys and also did not ask that I share the money with them. In turn, I would automatically share the money with them. The worst part is, I would later tell my other friend that what he did was wrong instead of thanking him for giving me some cash. Before I put an end to this, I would like to use a Bible history to illustrate my personality. I hope you pay attention to it so you can better analyze my frustration. Why would I torture people who were and are helping me? I simply wish that they like other people as much as they like me and treat them with kindness even if they don't know them. Let's look in at the history of Moses. Who was Moses? He was an Israelite and Hebrew, born into the tribe of Levi. The Levites were one of the twelve tribes of Israel. In particular, they were the ones charged with priestly duties. Levites were God's spiritual leaders. Just prior to Moses's birth, the ruler Pharaoh had decreed that all Israelite male children should be drowned. Did Pharaoh know about the prophecies that said a Messiah would come from the nation of Israel and that He would come as a child? That's doubtful, but God used Pharaoh to accomplish His purposes all the same. Because the Hebrew nation was growing significantly in number, Pharaoh felt threatened by their ever-growing presence, so he issued the heartless decree. God had a plan, and after Moses was born, his mother and sister would act on his behalf.

Moses' mother and sister put Moses in a basket and placed him in the Nile River when he was a child. His sister noticed that Pharaoh's daughter found the child in the basket. She named him Moses, which in Hebrew means, "Drawn forth." Without revealing her relationship to the child, Moses' sister asked Pharaoh's daughter if she should go get one of the Hebrew women to nurse the baby for her. When Pharaoh's daughter, who had decided to adopt Moses as her own son, agreed to this, Moses's sister ran for her own mother. So Moses's mother was able to nurture him in secret, on behalf of Pharaoh's daughter. Moses grew up in the tradition of the Egyptians.

The parallel action:

"Moses was educated in all the wisdom of the Egyptians and was powerful in speech and action. When Moses was forty years old, he decided to visit his fellow Israelites. He saw one of them being mistreated by an Egyptian, so he went to his defense and avenged him by killing the Egyptian. Moses thought that his own people would realize that God was using him to rescue them, but they did not. The next day Moses came upon two Israelites who were fighting. He tried to reconcile them by saying, 'Men, you are brothers; why do you want to hurt each other?' But the man who was mistreating the other pushed Moses aside and said, "Who made you ruler and judge over us? Do you want to kill me as you killed the Egyptian yesterday?"

Acts 7:22–27 (New International Version)

I am certainly not comparing myself with Moses; I wanted to use this as an analogy to demonstrate that I do not ignore what others do for me, or how kind they are with me. I just want to show Moses acting angrily toward an Egyptian that was hurting an Israelite. Was it because he was ungrateful to the Egyptians or because he was taking sides with his countryman? What about stepping in between the two Israelites who were fighting? I'll let you be the judge.

I have suffered a great deal of disappointment during the quest of getting back in the corporate world. I repeat, if it were not for Marvin and Nicole I would be eating dirt. I had a job; I worked for my family, which at the same time gave me freedom to look for a higher paying job and more or so into my field, human resources, which I do not think I want to get back in anymore. I have people who I thought would help me to get a job where they were VPs, presidents, and CEOs, and they did not. Nicole told me once that God does not like to share His glory. She meant that sometimes, when God wants to help someone, especially someone like me who is calling everyone and begging for help, at the same time asking God to do something. He would not do it until the help seeker addresses Him and Him only. Nicole could not be more right. I would like to conclude this journey with a brilliant and optimistic illustration of how God has deliberately removed me from captivity and blessed me in a way that I have no one else to thank but Him. *Gloire a Dieu!* Glory to God! *Merci Seigneur!*

As I have repeated several times, I thought that because I know so many people, I would not have any problems finding employment. I have also explained several times that I did contact most of the folks that I thought were my friends and/ or acquaintances; none of them did anything to help me. To prove the point of my sister Nicole, about "God is a jealous God, He does not share his glory with anyone," I want to go back to the early months of the year 2009. I phoned an old friend of mine who I knew was working for a company in Tampa, Florida that is a similar manufacturer to the place I used to work for. I asked him if there is a way that he could talk to someone there about helping me out. I specifically asked him for the Metallurgical Laboratory Testing area. Please keep this in mind, because I am going someplace with it. My friend at that time told me that his whole corporation was sold to a much bigger corporation and that Arnold LeBlanc, whom I changed his real name for privacy of identity, is the CEO and Chairman of the big corporation. Furthermore, my friend told me that Mark Bellefleur, whose name I also changed, is the president of all aircraft component facilities, which includes his. I knew and worked for both of those gentlemen when they were General Managers and VPs. Arnold, at one point told me that I was one of the men that he trusts the most in the industry. That was a man that will call me back within a twenty-four hour time duration if I called and left him a message. This is even if he were halfway around the world. I can say the same thing for Mark. Both of them always answered my calls and responded to my e-mails. After my conversation with my Tampa friend, I was charged with hope knowing that both Arnold and Mark were no longer affiliated with the company that I worked for, that was my first class ticket to get back to the aircraft parts manufacturing or repairing industry. First I sent an e-mail to Arnold to congratulate him and ask him to help me get to one of his mega plants. He, as usual responded quickly. I have attached the actual e-mail that I received from him, of course, without his real name:

Joel,

I am in the early stage of fixing a large company … mid level management positions are months away … we are beginning the consolidation process which will result in a large work force reduction across the all the US locations.

I am currently in Asia visiting my sites in this area.

Anna will print off this email and file in my résumé file for future consideration, but frankly it could be a year from now before we have a possible slot.

Take care of yourself.

Arnold

There was a level of hope, but the timing was not ideal, so I proceeded to contact Mark. I did call him in his new office after 5:00 p.m., knowing that he always worked late. He knew the call was from me and he picked up. He was surprised to hear from me, because that was his second week on the job. I did not take too long to ask him for a job. He asked me what position I was looking for. Before I could answer his question, he interjected, "Joel, I thought you were doing a great job in the Metallurgical Lab. I think we need to look in this area." I said, "Yes sir, you are right, but I really need a job." Of course, he was new to the company, but he told me that he was going to visit his Tampa plant and there he would chat with his general manager about me. Two to three weeks passed and I did not hear from him;

I sent him an e-mail reminding him that I was still looking. I have done the same as for Arnold; I have attached his response as well:

> *Joel,*
>
> *Please provide me a copy of your current résumé - I will then distribute to the appropriate people in Tampa.*
>
> *We are not currently hiring, but you should be ready if the opportunity arises!*
>
> *Thx.*
>
> *Mark Bellefleur*

I did again as instructed and waited. A couple months went by, I did not get any news, and I sent an e-mail to Mark to get an update. Of course, I got a response, but it was not what I was expecting. Please read for yourself:

> *Joel,*
>
> *We will keep you in mind. Unfortunately, with the current state of the economy and our industry in particular, we are not looking for anyone with your background.*
>
> *Mark Bellefleur*

Per my interpretation, I concluded that I needed to move on. Then another player came on the scene. I'll call him Michael Charles. I worked with Michael in the early 80s right after his college graduation as a Metallurgical Engineer. I believe in late 2005 or early 2006, I found out that Michael was a general manager and vice president of a major company. I got his number and I placed a phone call to him. We talked briefly and as a custom, he asked me to forward my résumé to him. Shortly after, I called him to find out that he was no longer working for that particular company. Life goes on! That was between December 2005 and January of 2006. So, after my disappointment from Arnold and Mark, it came to my mind to look for Michael and find out where he worked and what would be the possibility of getting a job from him. I went on the Web and Googled him. To my biggest surprise, I found out that he is the president of a division in a major corporation. He is responsible for two plants. I did not waste any time, I called his office and left a message for him to call me back. He called right back, I was not able to get his call, so he left a message and his private phone number to call. We finally got to talk to each other. I cannot describe the emotion and the joy we shared during our long conversation. We reviewed almost the entire time that lapsed between 83/84 to 2009. Of course, I told him my working situation and how badly I needed a job. He did tell me that his companies were going through a tough time, but send him my résumé and he would take it from there. I had more faith in him than I had in Arnold and Mark. I definitely knew that was it. This guy was going to do the impossible to help me out. I sent the résumé to him right away. Please read his answer in the following attachment:

Joel,

It was great catching up with you. You sound like you are doing really well and this résumé is very impressive. You are a good friend. I will see what I can do, as I believe you would be a great asset to any company. These are difficult economic times, but we will recover from them. Please tell Keke I said hello and wish her a quick recovery

Your friend
Michael

Great! I had my hope back. Help was really on the way! I waited and prayed. Thank God for my brother in-love, he continued to support me by allowing me to keep my job, even though I was job hunting. After I did not hear anything from Michael, I sent him an e-mail requesting an update. He promptly responded to my request. I have attached his response:

Joel

Hello my friend. I hope Keke is feeling much better, please tell her hello from me.

I have not forgotten you. We are going through a significant reduction in force. I need to get through this, and then I will consider your position opportunities. I hope you understand, our business is going through a major downturn.

I recognize that you are man of integrity and a great talent. You have a wonderful résumé. I will not forget this, but please realize that this is not going to be easy (at least in the near term). But, please do not think that this is a NO, because if I couldn't do it, I would tell you. I am just not sure how I can make it work right now.

> *Thanks*
> *Michael*

You cannot get any better than that. I will continue to show these responses just to help you to see my point. Please be patient, you are going to see how God will show his power, and how I will forgive everyone I thought let me down. Michael is a great man, as much as the other gentlemen. Anyway, in the end, I would call and leave messages for Michael and he would not return my calls. How deceitful! I was very patient and calm. A couple months later, I knocked on Michael's door again, but at the time I told him about my working on this book. This how it went:

Hello Joel

Congratulations on the BOOK!! I am impressed. This is unbelievable to me!! I can't wait to read it. When will it be in print?

How is Keke feeling? Fully recovered?

We had our second round of layoffs at both plants. Not fun. It will get better—I hope.

It is getting hot here. How about there?

I am watching the Giro d'Italia as I write. Do you know what that is?

> *Michael*

After that correspondence, I believe we talked on the phone once or I got a last e-mail and since then, everything is dead. I let it go. By now, I was getting more depressed and discouraged for I saw no way back to manufacturing, no way of getting a decent paying job. I called a daughter of an old friend of mine, Nadia, who lives in Jacksonville, Florida. Knowing that Nadia is married to a gentleman from a well-known and influential family in Jacksonville, I asked her to help me find a higher paid job. I also told her that I would not have any problem relocating. She told me that she had a good contact, whom I call Adrian, in Tallahassee and asked me to forward a copy of my résumé to her as soon as possible. She took time to tell me about her contact, which I found out was extremely hopeful for the influence that he has in the region. I quickly updated the résumé and forwarded it to her, via e-mail. Nadia wasted no time sending the résumé to her contact, and also copied me. Great! In the next day, I got an e-mail from Adrian's office. The e-mail was written by his secretary concerning my résumé. It was a beautiful note explaining that the résumé was forwarded to the human resources manager of the organization, which was highly recommended per Adrian. As a follow-up, I had a very productive telephone conversation with Adrian's secretary, who gave me some instructions to follow. I did what I had to do and waited. Meanwhile, I got an email from Nadia about a lead. After reading it, my mouth dropped. She was just received an e-mail from a classmate at her law school asking her to find him a candidate rapidly to fill an HR position. The description of the job matches my résumé to a T. "This is it!" I said. I feel compelled to attach Nadia's e-mail and the follow up e-mail for you:

Nadia

Do you know anyone in Jacksonville looking for employment during these tough times? Hope everything is good with you and the family.

Client is seeking a recruiter in Jacksonville.

Salary $45k - $50k.

Let me know if you want me to put in a good word for someone friendly to the firm.

Regards, Mark

Nadia forwarded the e-mail:

Hey Joel,

Please see the attached job announcement and send your résumé ASAP to Attorney Mark. He is a friend I went to law school with. His email is below. Please copy me in the email.

Thank you,
Nadia

Continue:

8 September 2009
Mr. Mark, Esq.

Dear Mr. Mark,

Ms. Nadia has forwarded the Staffing Manager's position to me and asked that I forward my résumé for your review. Ms. Nadia is a longtime family friend. I am an experienced Human Resources Professional and I am very interested in the position. I would appreciate any considerations that you may give to my résumé. I look forward to an opportunity to further discuss my qualifications with you.

Respectfully,
Joel

Response:

Joel,
I will submit this today with a nice note saying how far back we go! I like your prompt responses.

Best, Mark

In the meanwhile, I continued sending résumés out. Another lead was about to sting me like a bee. In early August 2009, I received an e-mail from a human resources manager whom I call Tamara, of a major company in Colorado. In the e-mail, Ms. Tamara explained that she saw my résumé on <u>monster.com</u> and she wanted to know if I was still in the market. She attached the description of an open position at her company that she thought was parallel with my skills, for my review. She also gave me the Web site of the company, in case I was interested. I replied to her instantly letting her know that I was very interested. Oh! The job was in the HR field. A couple days later, to be precise, I had a brief phone conversation with Ms. Tamara about the position on July 31, 2009. She wanted to have a phone interview with me right on the spot. I told her that it was not a good day for it, so she set up a formal phone interview for August 3, 2009 at 8:00 a.m. my time and 6:00 a.m. her time. On Monday, right on time I was on the phone with her. The interview went well. She asked me how soon I could come and meet with her staff and her boss, the Vice President of HR. I told her sometime in the following week, because my sister Nicole's daughter Wendy was getting married on Saturday, August 8, 2009. Therefore my parents and all my siblings were going to be in town a few days before the wedding. I did not want to miss that opportunity. Especially since that was the first time we were, the entire family, going to be together in about forty years. She asked me if I could come on Tuesday, the next day. I told her that I could leave in the afternoon on Tuesday. She was very happy with my answer, and she said that she would call me back. In the next hour, I got a call from her. She said that someone was going to call me with an itinerary. On Tuesday, August 4, 2009, I was on a plane flying to Colorado. The company had arranged a two-night stay and car rental for three days for me. Meanwhile, the lead from Tallahassee was fading out the same way. Do you feel me? It sucks! On Wednesday, August 5, 2009, I was in the company at 9:00 a.m. sharp. I interviewed with Ms. Tamara and with two other managers. Everything went well. Then she brought a few more employees to meet and she introduced me to them as the new HR guy-to-be. They asked a few questions, which I answered to their satisfaction, I believe. I was told that I would be meeting and interviewing with the VP and another manager later. I had lunch with the whole HR group, minus the VP. Up to that point I really thought that I was in.

Deuxième séance, I sat with the VP and the other manager, both guys. The previous meeting was with ladies only. The séance began, right after a couple of usual questions, such as: "Why would you want to leave Florida to come to Denver? Where do you see yourself in the following five years?" The VP dropped the bombshell, just like that: "Joel, I am going to tell you why you would not take this job: You have an MBA, nine and a half years experience in HR; you were in a management position. Look at your shoes! Your sophisticated tailored suit! They are top notch. The job is not even non-exempt salary, you will be working under everyone here as an hourly employee, and you won't be able to bring anything on the table until after six months." After that long speech, he made reference to a captain of a giant ship who takes a job on a dock loading small ships. I laughed so hard that both of them looked at me asking, "What is funny?" I came pretty close to telling the VP that was the most disgusting comparison I have ever heard of in my entire working life. I did not, because I really wanted to maintain a Christian-like attitude. I cracked a couple jokes and found a way to close the interview kindly and professionally. Come on! Whose manager, in her or his right mind, would schedule an interview for a candidate from out of town, paying hotel, not only overnight, but two nights, and car rental for three days for an hourly position? Something went wrong somewhere. Awful! It is sad to say, but that hope was just like the others: Smoke, nothing but smoke! And believe it or not, the Tallahassee lead died just like the others. Sometimes, it is hard not to say, life sucks, isn't it? Looking for jobs is hard and torturous. Even when you are a good and faithful Christian, there are times you are tempted to lose it. I am not lying, there were days that I doubted and I asked myself if were being punished.

During that particular moment, I kept having mixed feelings. The following are the questions that crossed my mind: "What did I do wrong? Did my past employers put a black mark in my record? Did I step on a wrong toe?" So many questions and no answers! I temporarily lost my self-confidence. I found myself asking: Is it because I am black or because I speak with a course accent? Is it because I have an intimidated appearance? But, I would quickly get to reality. "*No! I have nothing wrong in me, my being black and speak with an accent were always a blessing to me, and no one gave bad references about me*", I said to myself.

As I stated before, I knew I had the tendency of being arrogant at times and because of that when I presented myself somewhere, people mistakenly portrayed me as being intimidating. Still, I managed to regain focus on the timing. It was not the right time. Our time is not God's time. God is always on time. I had no reasons, nor do I have any reasons, to blame God after everything that He has done for me. For instance, He brought me back to life after my colon surgery, lifted me up in front of friends that ridiculed me in Port-au-Prince, never left me alone when old friends abandoned me when I got technically fired at my job of twenty-five years and a half. God allowed me to live a much better life and continued to grant my wishes of living in a nice house and driving a newer BMW. Instead, I came to understand and believe in the statement that my sister made about God: "God is a jealous God; He does not like to share his glory with anyone." I was stopping myself from getting a job, because I was putting my trust in man. In accordance with Psalms 118:08, we need to put our trust in God, Jesus Christ, not in man. God still showed mercy on me and He loves me. I am appreciated by my family and friends, and most people will do a lot to help me. I could not be discouraged, because I knew, *"Après la pluie, c'est le beau temps."*

God is about to answer my entire request at once. I have asked you to keep in mind the following words and title: metallurgical, metallography, and Metallurgical Laboratory Technician. The first time the previous terms were mentioned I was at my highest point of hope to find a better paying job in the last eight months of the year, when Mr. Mark Bellefleur told me that if he could remember well, I was one of the best Metallurgical Laboratory Supervisor and the best Metallographer in the aircraft manufacturing parts industry. During that same time, my brother Jarman said it in a different way. He told me he thought it would be in my best advantage that I look to get back into the metallurgical laboratory, instead of seeking to stay in the human resources field. *Allons voir!* (Let go see!)

On September 4, 2009, my sister Nicole and I left Jacksonville, Florida, to visit Mom and Dad in St. Petersburg, Florida. We drove Nicole's car down there. I mentioned whose car we drove for a good reason. Please, be patient. Throughout the trip down, I kept thinking about my dilemma. I kind of felt bad, because I was trying so hard to get a better-paying job while I was working for Nicole and Marvin. They could have judged me as an inconsiderate man; they didn't. At the time, I knew they were a number of people who were out of job, plain and simple. I was so confused and somewhat embarrassed for the fact that not only Nicole provided a means for me to get a salary, but provided my lunch at work on a daily basis and filled my gas tank from time to time. If it were not to start trouble, I would say all the time. Still, I wanted to have another job. This is why I always use the term, "Better-paying job." Then, I thought about when we were kids, we always asked Mom and Dad to pray for us when we were hurt or when things did not go well. We did not know any better than that and we did not have the means to go see a doctor or to buy what we were lacking. There were a lot of things that my boys had at their fingertips that were not an option for us. Right then, I thought about asking for prayers. I have to tell you that during my previous trip down to St. Pete, I asked Mom and Dad to pray for me. I told them that I needed to kneel so they could put their hands over my head while praying. They did not get it. Instead they told that they pray for me every day. Therefore, it was not necessary to pray for me at that time. I left them alone. From time to time, Nicole and I have a conversation about the family or work. Suddenly, the family prayer warrior, Sister Ronese Confident, came into my mind. We call her "*Sœur Ronese*" informally at home and at church. Because of our Christian faith, we are constantly sought for prayers when things seem to go wrong. Soeur Ronese had prayed for me in the past, but I never asked her directly to pray for me, I knew that she had prayed to the Lord for some of my siblings and other friends and whatever their adversities or dilemma were, God got them out of it. Our belief is not in Soeur Ronese, but we believe that when she intercedes to the Lord for us, He hears her and grants her what she asks. I decided that upon my arrival to St. Pete, I would have one of my sisters to call Soeur Ronese for me so I could ask her to pray "*a special prayer*" for me for complete deliverance. After that thought, I told Nicole what I have been wrestling with. She told me that was a wonderful idea.

In St. Pete, I shared the thought with my sister Giscelaine, and she was very receptive of it. She offered to get Soeur Ronese's telephone number for me. By the way, Soeur Ronese lives in St. Pete also. I called her and asked if she could put some time aside to pray with and for me. I also told her that I needed a special prayer, which includes oil-blessed ointment. She was happy to hear from me and granted my request. She asked me to come over to her house on Monday, September 7, 2009 in the morning. I woke up early and I called Soeur Ronese; it was 9:00 a.m. She gave me directions to go over to her place and told me to drive safely. I said thanks and that I would. I woke up Nicole to let her know that I was going to Soeur Ronese's house. I grabbed her car keys and left. We spent the night at my sister Ruth's apartment. I got in the car and started moving backward. There was a drive thru that went around the apartments and speed limits were five mile per hour. I looked at both sides, I did not see any car coming, so I proceeded; next thing I know, I heard a funny noise, like a crash. There was a driver who was coming with a speed of I would say was twenty miles per hour. My first thought was, "I messed up Nicole's BMW." Then, "I hope neither car is damaged." I got out of the car and the driver of the other car was a female. She apologized and told me that she did not see my car and that she was speeding. I asked her if she was all right. She said yes and she asked me the same. "Yes, I am," I said. Then I took a look at my sister's car; the back bumper was slightly damaged. The other driver was not that lucky. Her car was badly damaged. Once again, no one got hurt, thank God. I telephoned my sister to tell her about the accident. At first she thought I was joking but later realized that it was not a joke. Then later on, I called Soeur Ronese and told her about the accident. She told me that was a devil act to sabotage the work of the Lord, so she will come over my sister's apartment, where she will pray with me and for me. Well, once again the devil was defeated. Within an hour or so, Soeur Ronese has arrived with her husband at the apartment and she led the prayer. What I am about to tell will require, somewhat, a degree of comprehension about faith and spirituality to understand the content. During the prayer session, Soeur Ronese revealed to me that the devil was out to destroy my family, everything that I worked for, and even to kill me. The devil has done a great deal of his mission, but God is going to stop him and God will restore my life professionally, financially, and restore my marriage as well. At the same time, she told me to continue to pray and uplift my priesthood role in the family. I suddenly felt like someone had taken a heavy burden off my head and I began to sob. She approached closer to me and held my head with both hands and started to speak in tongues. She spoke in a language that I did not understand, but I knew what was happening by being a Pentecostal pastor's kid; she was anointed by the Holy Spirit. She prophesied that I would find a good job very soon. Then, she continued with the following

instructions, "Brother Joel, you will need to tithe first and foremost; from your first paycheck, you take some money to give an
'Action de grace' (thanksgiving prayer) to thank God for his mercy
on you." She specifically asked that the thanksgiving services
occur in Miragoâne at our church there. Ordinarily, these types
of action de grace require that attendees have plenty to eat and
drink, of course, no alcoholic beverages. She also prophesied that
I might not be able to be at Mirâgoane during the thanksgiving
prayer. I would not have to worry about that, but I would need to
send adequate money to provide foods and drinks for the saints
(brothers and sisters.)

Furthermore, she instructed me to read five psalms, which
she numbered one by one, and asked that I read them on a daily
basis for a month. She added that I would have to pray throughout the entire house, room by room, hallways, porch, and if possible all around the house. Nicole and I were supposed to leave
for Jacksonville that Monday, but because of the accident and
our emotional state, we decided to leave on the following day. I
started my daily devotion in the morning of Tuesday, September
8, 2009 before we left and upon my arrival home, I did all that she
asked me to do, except praying around the house, because I live
in a townhouse, but I prayed in the front and the back. I did not
say a word to Kéké about the prayer that I received and the reason why I prayed all over the house that Tuesday. Nevertheless,
she did not ask any questions either. I continued with my nightly
ritual, job-hunting through the Web, and my morning devotion.
When time permitted, I also read my psalms during lunchtime
followed by a short prayer.

Eight days later, on Tuesday, September 15, 2009, while I was
searching for job openings in the Internet, I suddenly thought
about metallurgical testing and metallography of metals studies.
Automatically, I remembered of the suggestions from my brother
Jarman and the comment of Mark Bellefleur about getting back
in Metallurgical field. I went to my favorite Web page, www.
indeed.com, and typed Metallurgical Laboratory Technician and

Metallographer. There were three postings as such in the whole nation that particular night. One of the job descriptions was written as if they were looking for a candidate with my background, not only did it described everything that I did during my seventeen years of metallurgical testing experience, but also it required that the candidate be familiar with two major aircraft engines manufacturing companies, Pratt & Whitney and General Electric. I have dealt with representatives from both of them in the plant I used to work for and at their respective facilities. I could have applied for that position only, but I did not want to take the chance, I applied for all three.

On Wednesday, September 16, 2009 I got a phone call from an aviation-recruiting firm about one of the position I applied for. At first, I was hesitant because I did not know what position they were calling for. Guess what? You are absolutely right. They were calling about the position that I thought was a perfect fit for me. I had a brief conversation with the recruiter and set up an appointment for a more convenient time. I want to pause here a moment to remind you of where I am going with this. I need to take you back to the Scripture from the Bible: *"I am the one who is holy and true, and I have the keys that belonged to David. When I open a door, no one can close it. And when I close a door, no one can open it. Listen to what I say. I know everything you have done. And I have placed before you an open door that no one can close. You were not very strong, but you obeyed my message and did not deny that you are my followers." Revelation 3:7–8 (New International Version)*

Facts: I have seventeen plus years of materials control and metallography experience. I started on October 20, 1980, as a Metallurgical Laboratory Technician and on March 5, 1998, I was transferred to the Human Resources department as a HR Representative. Up to that time I was the supervisor of the laboratory. Now, we are in September of 2009. Do you feel me? The last time I performed a metallurgical testing and examination was eleven plus years ago.

"Revenons à nos moutons." (Let's get back to where we stopped.) On my formal phone interview with the recruiter, whom I call Mr. TG, he brought up that length of time that I have not been working in the field. I paused for a second. "I sold the tools, but I kept the profession," I replied. That was a Haitian Créole proverb, *"Moin vann zout'm, min moin pa vann métié ya."* Mr. TG laughed and I laughed with him. Then he said, "I understand, and besides, your résumé is outstanding." "Thank you, sir," I said. I continued, "I was transferred to another department, but within the same company. Meaning I was not too far from the lab." That was because I realized that he was serious about considering me for the position. I convinced him that I was the best qualified candidate for the job, he agreed. Mr. TG told me if I could present some certificates that qualified my skills, the job is mine. He told me that he was not interested in my academic degrees, but in the trade and technical institute's certificates proving my metallography techniques. By then, I felt comfortable to ask in what state the company was located. He said that it was a Saudi company. "But, in what state?" I asked. He said, "It is in Riyadh, The Kingdom of Saudi Arabia." "You must be kidding?" I replied. "Are you still interested?" he asked. "Yes, I am, but I did not know that was an international opportunity," I responded. We both laughed. I affirmed to him that I was interested. He asked that I e-mail or fax a Word Version of my résumé and the documents to him as soon as possible. I thanked him and I promised to forward the documents to him.

All the time I was talking with the gentleman, I knew I had some certificates from Metals Engineering Institute and Academy for Metals and Materials, but I did not have a clue where they were. I called my son Ricky in Ohio and asked him to turn the house upside down to look for any old certificates that he could find for me about metallurgical or metallographic training that I had. To God be the glory! Ricky called me back, he said, "Dad, I got good news and bad news." "Give me the good news," I replied. "I found some," he said. "What is the bad news?"

I asked Ricky. He told me the certificates he found were not the originals, but photocopies. I asked him to send them anyway. Unfortunately, because of the time constraint he had to fax them to me. Upon receiving them, I called TG and asked him if it would be a problem to send photocopies in lieu of the originals. He said to go ahead and forward them. I did just that. That was on Friday, September 18, 2009.

On Monday, September 21, 2009 at about 1:30 p.m., I got a job offer. That was without further interview and contacts. The offer was conveyed to me verbally. I asked the recruiter to send me an e-mail confirming the offer and the salary. The salary was acceptable. Within minutes, I got it in writing. TG, in the e-mail, mentioned to respond with an acceptance or counteroffer. Have I not been given a choice, I would gladly accept the offer. This is to say, I countered the offer by a large margin. I thanked God, but I did not pray before making the decision. I was in a hurry to think about it. Beside Soeur Ronese, there were two other folks praying for me, my sister-in law, Mirèille Espérance, Pastor Bob's wife, and a friend of my brother, Pastor Paul, Pastor Fortin. I received words of advice from both telling me that I need to be vigilant and think before making any decisions. They also told me that God had revealed to them that He was going to open doors for me and my life was going to be much better. Well, I was so excited that I forgot to take time to think. So, I opened a can of worms by countering the offer. The hiring company began to ask questions and seek documents that they did not ask for before. They needed an assessment of my résumé on a detailed cover letter, an updated résumé, and specific details of my knowledge on plasma spray coating samples preparation for metallographic evaluation and image analysis. I took time to prepare the documents, I prayed on them and I sent them to TG, who forwarded them to the hiring manager in Saudi. That was in Ramadan period. I impatiently waited for two weeks to get some answers, which were not what I had anticipated. I was told that they needed more time to process my information. A week later

I got a phone call directly from Saudi. I spoke with an American Technician in their shop, who told me bluntly I was overqualified for the position. I told him that my being overqualified is an advantage to his company and that I was still interested. The gentleman told me to give him some time, he will talk with the hiring manager and that someone will contact me. A week passed with no contact. Each week seemed like a month to me. Then, another American technician called, we discussed my documents and knowledge of their process and we came up with a better understanding. He told me that he would talk with the hiring manager and someone would call me tomorrow. That was more positive and hopeful than the previous interviewer. The following day, Wednesday, October 14, 2009, I got an e-mail from Mr. TG confirming an approval for hire for the Metallurgical Laboratory Instructor with a salary of an *X-amount* above the previous offer, contingency of pre-physical employment examination, criminal background, and obtaining an entry visa to the kingdom. *"Door that God opened, no man can close it."* The position was in Khamis Mushayt, Saudi Arabia instead of Riyadh. Thank you Jesus, glory to God, Praise the Lord. It would take another month to get the above condition met. The whole process was rocky and interesting at the same time.

I feel compelled to tell about, or should I say how, God works when he wants to make sure that He shares his glory with no man. During the negotiation process after I countered the offer, remember that no one helped me to get the previous offer for the job, but God Almighty, and He alone. I would attempt to call "man" for help. God will manifest His authority and prove that He shares His glory with no man. I had contacted a number of friends for help, especially when the recruiter talked about certificates confirming my ability to perform metallographic examination. Since I did know what would be the outcome, I thought I could get some old friends to vouch for me since I worked with them in the past.

I called my friend at the Chromalloy plant in Tampa, Florida; he was no longer working there. I started with him because I wanted to get some information from their metallurgical laboratory. Chromalloy is in repair and enhanced aircraft engine parts, so they would be helpful to me. Then, I called two friends, metallurgists that worked with me for many years, to ask for possible letters of recommendation on my behalf. They both turned me down telling me that it would take weeks to have a letter ready for me. Even though the Saudi people did not ask for letters of recommendations, I was nervous and I wanted to be ahead of the game. Again, I forgot that I should be still and let God. Lastly, I called a gentleman who taught me metallography and who is a pioneer in the industry. He has taught and written several articles about thermal barrier and plasma spray coating for years, which was the main focus of job. I had not seen or talked with him, whom I will call Altore, for over fifteen years. He was so happy to get my phone call. We talked about our meeting at Pratt Whitney and Mentor, Ohio; we talked about how we were doing and about our families. During our conversation, I found out that he was still teaching Plasma Coating applications. After a good fifteen minutes into our conversation, I told him about the possibility of getting back in metallography and that I had a lead abroad. Then I told him that the job would involve teaching how to prepare Plasma Spray Coating samples for metallographic examination. He gave me some tips, names and addresses of schools and people to call. I asked in the meanwhile, to write a note to "To Whom It May Concern:" on my behalf justifying my metallographic skills and my working relationships with Pratt Whitney. He bluntly told me because of his relationships with the school he has been working with he won't be able to write the letter. However, if I send a copy of the job description and my cover letter to him, he would be glad to take a look at them. On the same day, I e-mailed the job description to him and let him know that I was going to take time to write the letter at night. He responded positively and asked that I bring the letter with me to work and he will call early in the morning. He emphasized, "Make sure you have a copy of your résumé and the letter ready so we can discuss them." I did not know what happened, but I did not get any phone call from Altore. Though I told him about the urgency of the matter, he forgot completely about it. I was very disturbed by the fact that no one wanted to help me. Then it became clear to me that it was not their fault, God wanted to make it happen all by himself. And yes, He did! Glory to God, Almighty!

I am completing this chapter en route to the Kingdom of Saudi Arabia. Actually, I am the passenger in seat 32B on a Saudi Arabian 727 airplane, which is cruising at 640 mph with an altitude of 36000 feet. Oh, Glory to God! From time to time, I would take a peek through the window, over the passenger seating in 32A, and I would also take a peek at the business class that was not too far from where I sat. I thought about the many times I flown first or business class. Oh well! For the sake of the book, I said to myself, "I sat where they sit."

I have, as many of you, received a number of "motivational group e-mails" in the past years, but one in particular sticks in my mind. I would like to share it with you so you can share it with others. Its title was, "Test your Bible knowledge." I later checked on the Internet and found some information about it, but was not concrete. Therefore, I will use the information that I got from my e-mail. The whole thing has to do with Psalms 118:8. There are 1189 Chapters in the bible, and the Psalms 118:8 is the center verse. Please, enjoy:

Q. What is the shortest chapter in the Bible?
A. Psalms 117

Q. What is the longest chapter in the Bible?
A. Psalms 119

Q. Which chapter is in the center of the Bible?
A. Psalms 118

Facts: There are 594 chapters before Psalms 118;
there are 594 chapters after Psalms 118

Add these numbers up and you get 1188 (118:8)

Q. What is the center verse in the Bible?

A. Psalms 188:8

"It is better to trust in the LORD than to put confidence in man."
Psalms 118:8 (New King James Version)

Does this verse say something significant about God's perfect will for our lives?

The next time some of your friends say they would like to find God's perfect will for their lives and that they want to be in the center of His will, just tell them about the center verse in the Bible that is His word! Then, I urge you to pray this small prayer with them: *Father God, bless my friends in whatever it is that you know they may need today. May their life be full of your peace, prosperity, and power as they seek to have a closer relationship with you. Amen.*

IN MEMORY OF REVEREND JOSEPH JOEL ESPERANCE

Dad, beloved husband, father, grandfather, great-grandfather, brother, friend, evangelist and minister of the Gospel of God, went to be with the Lord on Tuesday, January 19, 2010.

Dad was born in Leogane, Haiti on January 21, 1913, son of the late Estelancieu Jean-Philippe and Zulie (Domingue) Espérance. He grew up in Petion-Ville, Haiti, where he met and married his wife, my mom, of 63 years. Dad was ordained minister in 1956 and later migrated to Miragoâne, in the southwest of Haiti to become the Pentecostal Church of God's 1st Superintendent of the southern region. Dad founded and pastored hundreds of churches, bringing countless souls to the Lord and Savior Jesus Christ. Dad recognized that the body needed to be fed in order for the soul to be nourished, so he opened a cantina that fed 100s of families daily. He didn't restrict himself to just building churches, he also opened many schools to afford children an education that they would otherwise not have been able to get. In the area of Haiti where Dad lived, medical care was scarce, so he took it upon himself to open up a clinic and, with limited medical knowledge; he provided first-aid and routine care to his community, thereby saving many lives. He received numerous awards and recognitions for his work during his lifetime, one of which is a school in Miragoâne named after him. Dad was a pillar of his community, and the enumerating his accomplishments and the many lives he's touched, the many people he's mentored, who've gone on to accomplish great things, would fill a novel. Even with such great success, Dad was a humble man, who considered himself a servant of the Lord first. He instilled the same value in his nine children, twenty-three grandchildren, and eighteen great-grandchildren, leaving behind eight active ordained ministers from his offspring.

French Version: Papa, mari bien-aimé, père, grand-père, arrière grand-père, frère, ami, évangéliste, et ministre de l'Evangile S'en est allé au Seigneur le mardi 19 janvier 2010, à l'age de 96 ans.

Papa a pris naissance à Léogane, en Haïti, le 21 janvier 1913. Il était le fils unique du défunt Estélancieu Jean-Philippe et la défunte Zulie Espérance, née Zulie Domingue. Cependant, c'est à Petion-Ville, une ville de la capitale Haïtienne qu'il a grandit. C'est aussi dans cette ville qu'il fit la connaissance de sa femme, son épouse pendant 63 ans, ma mère, Anne Espérance, née Anne Martineau. Papa était ministre ordonné en 1956 et peu plus tard il déménagea à Miragoâne, une ville située dans le Sud Quest d'Haïti, ou il devint le premier Superintendant de l'église de Dieu de la Pentecôte pour la région du Sud. Il fonda et dirigea de façon directe ou indirecte des centaines églises, amenat une multitude d'âmes à notre Seigneur et Sauveur JESUS-CHRIST. Son travail ne se limita pas à la fondation d'églises seulement car, il comprit une vérité essentielle à savoir que le corps doit être alimenté afin d'être mieux disposé à recevoir la nourriture de l'âme. De ce fait il a ouvert une cantine qui alimenta plus d'une centaine de familles par jour. Son ministère s'étendit encore plus loin. Il a ouvert plusieurs écoles afin de permettre aux enfants démunis d'accéder à une éducation scolaire, qu'ils n'auraient pas eu sans son aide. Dans la région, Mirâgoane, où papa vivat, le soin médical était rare, ainsi il a pris en charge d'ouvrir une clinique médicale, et avec une connaissance médicale très limitée ; il a fourni des soins de santé de base dans sa communauté, De ce fait, il a sauvé beaucoup de vies

Son grand ministère lui valut plusieurs récompenses et primes de reconnaissance, pour les travaux accomplis durant sa vie, et l'un d'eux est une école à Miragoâne qui porte son nom. Papa était un pilier dans sa communauté, et l'énumération de ses accomplissements et des nombreuses vies qu'il a touché, les nombreuses personnes qu'il a formé, peuvent remplir un livre. Cependant, malgré tout ce succès, Papa était un homme d'une humilité sans borne, qui se considérait juste un simple serviteur dans le travail du Seigneur. Papa a inculqué la même valeur à ses 9 enfants, 23 petits-enfants et 18 arrière petits-enfants. Il a laissé 8 actifs pasteurs ordonnés dans sa progéniture.